# The Definitive Guide to JSF in Java EE 8

## Building Web Applications with JavaServer Faces

Bauke Scholtz

Arjan Tijms

*The Definitive Guide to JSF in Java EE 8: Building Web Applications with JavaServer Faces*

Bauke Scholtz
Willemstad, Curaçao

Arjan Tijms
Amsterdam, Noord-Holland, The Netherlands

ISBN-13 (pbk): 978-1-4842-3386-3
https://doi.org/10.1007/978-1-4842-3387-0

ISBN-13 (electronic): 978-1-4842-3387-0

Library of Congress Control Number: 2018942178

Managing Director, Apress Media LLC: Welmoed Spahr
Acquisitions Editor: Steve Anglin
Development Editor: Matthew Moodie
Coordinating Editor: Mark Powers

Cover designed by eStudioCalamar

Cover image designed by Freepik (www.freepik.com)

Distributed to the book trade worldwide by Springer Science+Business Media New York, 233 Spring Street, 6th Floor, New York, NY 10013. Phone 1-800-SPRINGER, fax (201) 348-4505, e-mail orders-ny@springer-sbm.com, or visit www.springeronline.com. Apress Media, LLC is a California LLC and the sole member (owner) is Springer Science + Business Media Finance Inc (SSBM Finance Inc). SSBM Finance Inc is a **Delaware** corporation.

For information on translations, please e-mail editorial@apress.com; for reprint, paperback, or audio rights, please email bookpermissions@springernature.com.

Apress titles may be purchased in bulk for academic, corporate, or promotional use. eBook versions and licenses are also available for most titles. For more information, reference our Print and eBook Bulk Sales web page at http://www.apress.com/bulk-sales.

Any source code or other supplementary material referenced by the author in this book is available to readers on GitHub via the book's product page, located at www.apress.com/9781484233863. For more detailed information, please visit http://www.apress.com/source-code.

Printed on acid-free paper

*To caffeine and our (not so) patient wives.*

# Table of Contents

# About the Authors

**Bauke Scholtz** is an Oracle Java Champion, a member of the JSF 2.3 Expert Group, and the main creator of the JSF helper library OmniFaces. On the Internet, he is more commonly known as BalusC, who is among the top users and contributors on Stack Overflow. Bauke has integrated several OmniFaces solutions into JSF 2.3. He is a web application specialist and consults or has consulted for Mercury1 Limited, MyTutor, Nava Finance, LinkPizza, ZEEF, M4N/Zanox, ITCA, RDC, and more clients from fintech, affiliate marketing, social media, and more as part of his 17 years of experience. This book offers Bauke the opportunity to go into depth to answer most frequently asked questions and correctly solve most commonly encountered problems while using JSF.

**Arjan Tijms** works for Payara Services Ltd and is a JSF (JSR 372) and Security API (JSR 375) Expert Group member. He is the co-creator of the popular OmniFaces library for JSF, which was a 2015 Duke's Choice Award winner, and is the main creator of a set of tests for the Java EE authentication SPI (JASPIC) used by various Java EE vendors. Arjan holds an MSc degree in Computer Science from the University of Leiden, The Netherlands. Writing about this topic was a natural choice for Arjan; He has already written much about it on his blog and wanted to expand that by contributing to a book.

# About the Technical Reviewer

**Chád ("Shod") Darby** is an author, instructor, and speaker in the Java development world. As a recognized authority on Java applications and architectures, he has presented technical sessions at software development conferences worldwide (in the United States, UK, India, Russia, and Australia). In his 15 years as a professional software architect, he's had the opportunity to work for Blue Cross/Blue Shield, Merck, Boeing, Red Hat, and a handful of startup companies.

Chád is a contributing author to several Java books, including *Professional Java E-Commerce* (Wrox Press), *Beginning Java Networking* (Wrox Press), and *XML and Web Services Unleashed* (Sams Publishing). Chád has Java certifications from Sun Microsystems and IBM. He holds a BS in computer science from Carnegie Mellon University. You can visit Chád's blog at `www.luv2code.com` to view his free video tutorials on Java. You can also follow him on Twitter at @darbyluvs2code.

**CHAPTER 1**

# History

This chapter describes the history of JSF, starting from its early conception and ending where we are today at the moment of writing. We'll discuss how the JSF API (application programming interface) itself evolved, which important events took place during that evolution, and who some of the people were that were involved in all of this.

This is in no way a complete description of the history and the reader should take notice of the fact that many more events took place and many more people were involved than we were able to mention here.

## In the Beginning . . .

JSF goes back a long time. Its initial JSR, JSR 127, started in 2001. At that time the Struts web framework was wildly popular, although it wasn't that long ago that it was released itself (around 2000). Despite Struts' popularity, a large number of other web frameworks were in use in the Java space, and new ones were popping up all the time. JavaServer Faces (JSF) was conceived as an attempt to bring a standardized MVC (model-view-controller) web framework base into the overall Java EE platform.

Controversies are quite common in the web framework space, and JSF is no exception here. Right at the start of its inception there was a big controversy where Apache opposed the creation of JSF on the bases that Apache Struts already existed and a closed source alternative would have little value. Apache therefore voted against the creation of JSF with the following comment:

> *This JSR conflicts with the Apache open source project Struts. Considering Sun's current position that JSRs may not be independently implemented under an open source license, we see little value in recreating a technology in a closed environment that is already available in an open environment.*

1

B. Scholtz and A. Tijms, *The Definitive Guide to JSF in Java EE 8*, https://doi.org/10.1007/978-1-4842-3387-0_1

*To the extent that this JSR extends beyond Struts today, we would encourage the Sun developers proposing this JSR to join the Sun developers already leading Struts to create an open solution at Apache, something which when finished would be assured of being able to be implemented as open source.*

Eventually the conflict was resolved when after about a year into the process spec lead Amy Fowler (from Swing fame) was replaced by Craig McClanahan, the very father of the Struts project that JSF was said to be competing with. The open source restriction was lifted as well, and the open source JSF implementation, called MyFaces, was developed in parallel with the (then nameless) RI and hence the specification itself. MyFaces initially started as an LGPL licensed project at sourceforge.net in December 2002 and had an initial 0.1 release conforming to what was then called an "Early Access Specification" in January 2003.

Open source implementations are the most common implementations in Java EE 8, and there's barely any EE specification at the time of this writing (2018) that's still implemented as closed source. In 2001, however, this was not just uncommon; it was actually not allowed for new JSRs. Allowing for an open source implementation was therefore quite a change, and the honor fell to JSF to be the first of its kind for which this was allowed.

Despite the open source implementation being allowed, the actual development of the spec was still done in secret and behind closed doors. There was no public mailing list, and no tracker (e.g., a JIRA instance) for the public to create issues or express wishes. Occasionally interviews were being done, and in the fall of 2002 by then former spec lead Amy Fowler did reveal quite a few details about JSF, but largely the project was shrouded in mystery for the general public.

The team behind JSF was, however, hard at work. The first e-mail to the internal JSR-127 list was sent on August 17, 2001. As with most projects, the team spent the initial months on gathering requirements and looking at the existing competing products. A package name was chosen as well. The initial placeholder package, which was `javax.servlet.ui`, now `javax.faces`, was chosen as the package to use. The very first technical architecture to be considered was the component model. For a component-based MVC framework this is obviously one of the most important aspects. During the last month of 2001 and the first two months of 2002 the team looked at what is now known as the Managed Bean (called "Object Manager" then). Managed beans with their scopes, names, and dependency injection are clearly another cornerstone of the JSF framework. Events and the model behind it were being looked at as well during that time frame.

In the second quarter of 2002 two other cornerstones of JSF were discussed: the Expression Language (inspired by JSTL), which is instrumental for the so-called bindings of beans from a template to backing code, and the factory finder, which allowed key parts of JSF to be replaced and although perhaps not fully realized at the time may have contributed greatly to JSF still being relevant some 16 years later.

It was in this same quarter that Craig McClanahan took over as spec lead, father of Struts and architect of Tomcat's Servlet container, took over. Not long after the discussion about using JSP started, a discussion, perhaps unbeknownst to the team at the time, that would, unfortunately, have a rather negative impact on JSF later on. Around the end of the year 2002, Ed Burns, who like McClanahan had also worked on Tomcat before, joined the team as co-spec lead. Burns is the person who would eventually become the main spec lead of JSF for well over a decade.

While the team continued to work on things like the aforementioned managed beans and the so-called value binding, which is the Java representation of the also aforementioned expression language binding, the first dark cloud appeared when in the spring of 2003 team member Hans Bergsten realized that there were very real and major issues with using JSP as the templating language for JSF. He brought these concerns to the team, but ultimately they weren't addressed and instead the following months were spent, among other things, on a variant of the value binding; it later on became clear that the method binding and the state saving mechanism were another of JSF's less than ideal implementations.

JSF 1.0 and its still nameless RI were eventually released on March 11, 2004—coincidentally, a mere two weeks before the release of another framework that's still strong today, Spring 1.0. MyFaces released its 1.0.0 alpha version only days later, on March 19. It's perhaps an interesting observation that JSF went final with a full-fledged XML-based dependency injection (DI) framework just before Spring, which is largely known for its DI, went final.

JSF 1.0 was generally well received; despite a rather crowded market with competitors such as Tapestry, WebObjects, Velocity, and Cocoon operating, not less than three books from writers such as Horst Caymann and Hans Bergsten appeared in the months after, and the eXo platform (a Digital Collaboration Platform) started using JSF right away.

Hans Bergsten's earlier concerns, however, become painfully clear almost just as quickly; the JSP technology is based on processing a template from start to end, immediately writing to the response as tags are encountered. JSF, however, requires a phased approach where components need to be able to inspect and act on the component tree, which is built from the tags on the page, before starting to write anything to the response. This mismatch led to many strange issues, such as content disappearing or being rendered out of order.

Only three months after the introduction of JSF, Hans Bergsten made a strong case of dropping JSP in his legendary article "Improving JSF by Dumping JSP." There Bergsten explains how ill-suited JSP is for use a template language in JSF, but he also presents a glimmer of hope; because of JSF's great support for extendibility, it's relatively easy to introduce alternative templating simply by replacing the so-called view handler, something which JSF explicitly allows. It would, however, take five long years until JSF would indeed ship with a more suitable view templating language, and even though JSP had been essentially deprecated at that point it's still present in JSF at the time of writing.

# The Adolescent Years

Back in 2004 another first befell JSF; on June 28 Ed Burns announced that the source of the RI was released by Sun. This represented a major milestone as before that date most technology in active use by Sun was closed source. Initially the source was licensed under the somewhat exotic JRL, but later this would be changed to dual licenses, GPL with classpath exception and CDDL. At the same time as this announcement, the tradition was established that every new feature or bug fix should be accompanied by a test, and that all existing tests should be executed before committing the change. Some 14 years later there's a largely different set of people working on the RI source, and the project structure and code conventions have changed as well, but the test-driven tradition is still being uphold in its original form.

At that point Ed Burns decided to focus more on the specification aspects of JSF as the JSF 1.2 spec work had started right away, and Jayashri Visvanathan, one of the early team members, took on the lead role concerning the implementation aspects, with Ryan Lubke, working as the TCK (testing) engineer.

Still only a few months old, a variety of component libraries for JSF had already started to pop up, although all of them commercial. Among those was the one from Oracle, ADF Faces. ADF Faces was put on Oracle's roadmap well before JSF 1.0 went final, and the first early access release was presented on August 17, 2004. Its lead was Adam Winer, who represented Oracle in the team that created JSF 1.0. ADF Faces primarily contained a set of rich components, but also a dialog framework, and remarkably already featured partial page rendering (PPR), quite a bit ahead of the later crop of AJAX solutions. ADF Faces also contained a "for each" tag (`af:forEach`) that actually worked. Adam Winer explained in these early days that such tag is not quite trivial to build but promised that Oracle would contribute the knowledge back to JSF itself.

The ADF Faces components originated mostly from the earlier User Interface XML (UIX) framework, of which Adam Winer was the lead architect as well. Earlier versions of UIX used the names "Cabo," "Baja," and "Marlin." UIX was a rich client framework for use in the browser. With JSF sharing more than a few similarities to UIX, and with its lead, Adam Winer, being part of the original JSF team, it's perhaps not unreasonable to surmise that UIX influenced JSF. Such similarities include the concept of components with separate renderers, JSP tag handlers and declarative options to compose a page, and the ability to instantiate those same components programmatically in Java. There was even a conceptually similar data binding, although with a less elegant syntax. Instead of, say, `value="#{user.age}"`, UIX would use `data:value="age@user"` but also required a kind of producer to be defined on each page to declare where "user" comes from, and then nest the page's content within that declaration. By contrast, JSF and EL have always used global definitions and left it up to the user to avoid name clashes.

One of the first, if not the first open source component library in 2004 was Matthias Unverzagt's OurFaces. As JSF did not had its own resource API (application programming interface) at the time to serve up things like images, OurFaces required a Servlet to be added to `web.xml`, the so-called `SkinServlet` (`ourfaces.common.webapp.SkinServlet`). The significance of this is that it became a rather common thing for JSF libraries in those days to ask their users: add something manually to `web.xml` before the component library can be used.

Most of the last months of 2004 and early months of 2005 were spent by the JSF 1.2 expert group (EG) working on various JSP and EL issues, such as the JSTL `<c:forEach>` support and the generation of IDs in JSP, as well as on the dreaded "content interweaving" issue, which refers to the aforementioned content that appears at wrong places in the response when rendering.

While OurFaces may have been one of the first component libraries, it didn't last and few will remember it or have even heard about it today. This is not quite the same for another framework that has its roots in early 2005, namely, Alexander Smirnov's Telamon framework, later renamed Ajax4jsf. This framework was one of the first of its kind that combined JSF and the then new and fresh AJAX technology. The beauty of Ajax4Jsf was that it could add AJAX support to existing components, which weren't built with AJAX support in mind at all by enclosing them among others in the `<a4j:region>`

5

tag. This technology was incorporated in the Exadel Visual Component Platform, which was released in March 2006 and would later be renamed RichFaces, and would become one of the most memorable JSF component libraries.

At around the same time Alexander Smirnov started work on what eventually would become RichFaces, a company called ICEsoft started working on a JSF component library. ICEsoft had been in business for a couple of years and had been working on a product called ICEbrowser, a Java-based browser, and a product called ICEbrowser beans, which were "lightweight, configurable Javabean components that can be rapidly integrated into Java client applications." During JavaOne 2005 of that year, on 27 June, ICEsoft announced their its component library for JSF—ICEfaces. This was based on AJAX as well but incorporated AJAX directly into the components. ICEsoft called its specific technique "patent pending Direct-to-DOM™," which basically meant that changes coming from the server were directly injected into the DOM tree structure of a web page. A final version wasn't available right away though, but an early access release was provided. This was closed source but cost-free.

Meanwhile, JSF EG member Jacob Hookom, inspired by Hans Bergsten's concerns about the unsuitability of JSP, grabbed the bull by the horns and started working himself on that alternative templating language envisioned by Bergsten. In August 2005 this work had progressed into a usable initial version. The name of this templating language? Facelets! It immediately took the JSF world by storm. Kito Mann published the first part of a series of articles about it on JSFCentral the very first month, and Richard Hightower published the famous article "Facelets fits JSF like a glove" several months later.

Oracle had not been sitting still either in 2005, and after about 16(!) early access releases it announced in late 2005 at the JavaPolis conference in Antwerpen (nowadays called Devoxx) that ADF Faces would be donated to MyFaces and thus become open source.

In the first month of 2006, Jacob Hookom and Adam Winer contemplated the terrible implementation of JSF's state save mechanism. This worked by first creating a component tree from a template and then, near the end of the request, blindly serializing the entire tree with all data that may have been put there during the request. During a postback the tree is restored from this serialized form (hence the name of the phase "restore view"). This is a tremendous waste, as the majority of this information is already available in the template. Especially when doing AJAX requests with client-side state saving this poses a very big burden, but it is also a problem when storing this state on the server as it massively increases JSF's memory usage. One of the main reasons for doing state saving in such terrible way again has to do with that one decision: to support JSP. With JSF 1.2 about to go final, there was unfortunately no time left to fix this for version 1.2.

Even though it was clear at this point that Facelets was the future of JSF, when JSF 1.2 was eventually released in May 2006 it still contained only JSP. Not all was bad though. Thanks to a cooperation between the JSF and JSP EGs, a revision of JSP was released, JSP 2.1, which was much better aligned with the demands of JSF. On top of that, JSP's expression language and JSF's expression language were merged. The result was UEL (Unified Expression Language). A very practical advantage of UEL is that JSF components no longer have to convert Strings manually into expressions but directly receive a ValueExpression from the templating language. Both JSP 2.1 and JSF 1.2 became part of Java EE 5, which was released at the same time.

On June 13, 2006, the MyFaces community announced that the donated project would have its name changed to Trinidad. ADF Faces kept existing at Oracle, though, but was based on Trinidad with some extra features (such as support for Portals, JSR 227, etc.). Just two weeks prior to that, on May 31, 2006, ICEsoft announced its free, although still closed source, community edition. A few months later, on November 14, 2006, ICEsoft would fully open source ICEfaces under the MPL license. RichFaces, still closed source at that point and being sold by Exadel, would not stay behind for long though, and some four months later, on March 29, 2007, Exadel announced a partnership with Red Hat that made RichFaces available under an open source license and available and supported via its JBoss group.

# On to Maturity

On May 22, 2007, the specification work for JSF 2.0 began. The scope was hugely ambitious and promised not only to fix many of the issues that people had been complaining about but also to introduce quite a bunch of new features. Mentioned among the many goals in the JSR was a particularly interesting one when looking at the bigger picture—extracting the managed bean facility from JSF and making it available for the entire platform.

During the fall of 2007 the community was polled for a name for the JSF RI. Four names rose to the top, but as is often the case none of these names could be approved by Sun's legal department. Eventually Mojarra was proposed, and perhaps to the surprise of some this one did pass legal's scrutiny. Ryan Lubke, one of the main JSF committers then, made the official announcement on December 5, 2007.

A little under a year later, on October 29, 2008, Çağatay Çivici started a new library, PrimeFaces. The name derives from Çağatay's nickname, which is Optimus Prime, the courageous leader of the heroic autobots in the fictional Transformers universe. Çağatay had been involved with JSF development for a long time and had worked on the YUI4JSF JSF component library before. PrimeFaces was initially based on JSF 1.x, but with JSF 2.x looming and the project still young it would soon after switch to JSF 2.x.

On July 1, 2009, the long-awaited JSF 2.0 finally arrived. JSF 2.0 indeed fixed nearly every problem that the industry had with JSF; finally, Facelets was included as the default view templating language. JSP was effectively deprecated. The state saving concerns that Hookom and Winer brought forward more than three years earlier were addressed as well; from then on JSF only saved delta state (state changes), and in restore view the component tree was reloaded from the template, instead of actually restored.

Another big concern brought forward by the JSF community over the years, JSF's over-the-top emphasis on postbacks, was addressed too; GET requests became a first-class citizen in JSF 2.0. A well-known usability problem with JSF, sometimes called "The Trap," was that for a number of operations the data involved needed to be the same during both the original request and the postback. This is not entirely trivial to guarantee in JSF 1.x. JSF 2.0 introduced the so-called view scope for this, which elegantly solved the problem. The creation of custom components, yet another problem area of JSF 1.x, was made much simpler as well. JSF 2.0 also introduced core support for AJAX, modeled after the way Ajax4Jsf worked, a resource API, system events, and quite a few other things.

One of JSF 2.0's goals, making its managed bean facility usable outside JSF, was implicitly reached by the CDI spec, which was introduced together with JSF 2.0 in Java EE 6. The CDI spec itself has a long history too, but one of its defining characteristics is that CDI Beans are strongly based on JSF Managed Beans and are essentially a super set of those.

Altogether the impact of all those fixes and new features was such that it split the community essentially in two; those who had used JSF 1.x and never looked at it again and those who switched to JSF 2.x or, specifically, the ones who started using JSF with 2.0 and never saw 1.x. This often led to heated debates, with the 1.x side arguing that JSF is horrible, and the 2.x side not understanding at all why that would be the case. Even at the time of this writing, which is almost nine years after JSF 2.0 was released, and a longer period than JSF 1.x ever existed, these sentiments still remain to some degree.

Despite the many things that JSF 2.0 did right, there was one missed opportunity; even though CDI was now available and superseded JSF's Managed Beans, JSF chose not to deprecate its managed bean facility right away. Even worse, it introduced an annotation-based alternative to the XML-based system JSF 1.x used to define managed beans. With CDI already out there having annotations like `javax.enterprise.context.RequestScoped`, simultaneously introducing a `javax.faces.bean.RequestScoped` annotation that did exactly the same thing seems debatable as best. The EG seemed to be aware of this conflict, as a warning was put in place that these new annotations would possibly be superseded by platform functionality before long.

On December 23, Cay Horstmann raised his concerns about this very unwanted situation in an article titled "Is @javax.faces.bean.ManagedBean Dead on Arrival?" The response was quite clear; people, including Java EE book writer Antonio Goncalves, asked for this huge mistake that JSF 2.0 had made to be corrected as soon as possible and to deprecate javax.faces.bean.ManagedBean right away in the upcoming JSF 2.1 maintenance release which was called for, among other things, to rectify another mistake (namely, the problem JSF 2.0 introduced that in addition to a custom ResourceResolver it was also necessary to provide a custom ExternalContext, which was very unclear). Why javax.faces.bean.ManagedBean indeed wasn't deprecated in the JSF 2.1 MR remains a mystery to this day.

While applications written against the JSF 1.x APIs would mostly run unchanged on JSF 2.0, or only needed a few small changes, the component libraries had a much harder time. Specifically, the platform-provided AJAX support meant that the existing component libraries would have to forego their own AJAX implementations and rebase on the standard APIs. Clearly that was no small feat, and it took a long time for component libraries to migrate, with some never really making the switch at all.

Here PrimeFaces was clearly at an advantage. Being a relatively new library without much legacy, it made the switch relative easy. Be it a coincidence or not, PrimeFaces' ascension in popularity seemed to start right after JSF 2.0 was released, which was also the exact same time that both ICEfaces and RichFaces seemed to become less popular. Although it must be noted that hard statistics are difficult to obtain and contain many facets (downloads, deployments, book, questions asked, available jobs, taking different industries into account, etc.), somewhere around 2012 PrimeFaces had seemingly become the more popular JSF component library.

In the beginning of that same year, February 19, 2012, Arjan Tijms and Bauke Scholtz (by coincidence also the authors of this book) started the OmniFaces library for JSF. The goal of OmniFaces was to be a utility library for JSF, essentially what Apache Commons and Google Guava are to Java SE. Tijms and Scholtz had worked on a JSF-based web site together and found that they both had a collection of private JSF utilities that they reused for different projects, and also that a great number of similar utilities were essentially rewritten again and again for many JSF projects and were partially floating around in places like forum messages and blog posts. OmniFaces was set up in particular not to not compete component libraries like PrimeFaces but to work together with those. Hence, visual-oriented components were largely out of scope for OmniFaces.

In 2012 the specification process for JSF 2.2 was also in full swing. JSF 2.2 was eventually released on the May 21, the next year. JSF 2.2 specifically came up with a formal version of the alternative mode in which Facelets could operate; instead of putting component tags on a view, plain HTML was put on it, with a special ID linking the tag to a component. Such a mode is generally speaking somewhat less interesting to JSF developers but appeals specifically to web designers who can more easily use plain HTML tools for such views. JSF 2.2 also introduced a CDI compatible @ViewScoped annotation, which removed one of the last reasons to still use the JSF managed bean facility in JSF 2.1, namely, that in that version @ViewScoped only worked on those beans. JSF 2.2 also introduced two new big features, Faces Flow and Resource Contracts, but these seem to have seen little uptake in practice.

Just prior to the start of JSF 2.3, on July 20, 2014, RichFaces lead Brian Leathem announced on his blog that RichFaces 5, the next-generation version of RichFaces, would be canceled. Instead, RichFaces would "pursue a path of stability over innovation," which means that JBoss will make RichFaces 4.x compatible with JSF 2.2 and port back a few things that were in development for RichFaces 5. While the post was somewhat optimistic, it strongly looked like the writing was on the wall for RichFaces.

On August 26, 2014, the specification work for JSF 2.3 started. A new co-spec lead was introduced—Manfred Riem, who up to then had been working mostly on the implementation side of Mojarra, doing such things as migrating hundreds of the tests for which JSF is famous away from the ancient and retired Cactus framework to a more modern Maven-based one, and making sure the gazillions of open Mojarra issues were reduced to a manageable number. JSF 2.3 started off with a perhaps somewhat remarkable message that Oracle had only a few resources available. During the specification process those few resources dropped to a number that few would have expected—absolutely zero. Basically, after JavaOne 2015, nearly all of the spec leads just vanished and most specs as a result abruptly ground to a halt. Josh Juneau reported about this in his famous study, "Java EE 8, What Is the Current Status: Case Study for Completed Work Since Late 2015," which undeniable makes it clear by showing graphs of e-mails, commits, and issues resolved that Oracle had just walked away.

The openness of the JSF and its RI Mojarra were fortunately such that the specification work and implementation thereof in Mojarra can largely be carried on by the other EG members, which indeed happens.

Meanwhile on February 12, 2016, Red Hat announced that RichFaces would be end of lived (EOL) later that year, namely, in June 2016. One of the most popular JSF component libraries at some point, often named something like "One of the big three," effectively was no more. On June 20, 2016, the last real commit to the project was done, "RF-14279: update JSDoc." Two days later Red Hat released RichFaces 4.5.17 and the GitHub repos were put into archived (read only) mode. Brian Leathem, who is still a JSF 2.3 EG member, announced a few days later on February 18 that he would no longer be doing any JSF-related work.

# Rejuvenation

In late 2016 the JSF spec leads briefly returned, but with the message that the spec must be completed in only a few weeks, so the (somewhat) lengthy finalization process could start. On March 28, 2017, JSF 2.3 was then eventually released, bringing with it the start of replacing JSF native artifacts with CDI versions, and finally something which should have happened years ago: the deprecation of the JSF managed bean facility in favor of using CDI beans. Other features are support for WebSocket using the Java EE WebSocket APIs donated by OmniFaces, the introspection of available view resources in the system, and a search expression framework donated by PrimeFaces.

Following the somewhat turbulent development of the JSF 2.3 spec is the even more turbulent announcement by Oracle in 2017 that Java EE, thus including JSF, would be transferred to the Eclipse foundation. Oracle would stop leading the specs it owned before, which again includes JSF. This would mean that Mojarra would be re-licensed, and JSF would be evolved by a new process with likely different leads. At the time of writing, this transfer is in full swing.

# CHAPTER 2

# From Zero to Hello World

In this chapter you will learn how to set up a JSF (JavaServer Faces) development environment with the Eclipse IDE (integrated development environment), the Payara application server, and H2 database from scratch.

## Installing Java SE JDK

You probably already know that Java SE is available as JRE for end users and as JDK for software developers. Eclipse itself does not strictly require a JDK as it has its own compiler. JSF being a software library does not require a JDK to run either. Payara, however, does require a JDK to run, primarily in order to be able to compile JSP files, even though JSP has been deprecated as JSF view technology since JSF 2.0.

Therefore, you need to make sure that you already have a JDK installed as per Oracle's instructions. The current Java SE version is 9, but as Java EE 8 was designed for Java SE 8 which is currently more mature, JDK 8 is recommended: `https://docs.oracle.com/javase/8/docs/technotes/guides/install/install_overview.html`.

The most important parts are that the `PATH` environment variable covers the `/bin` folder containing the Java executables (e.g., `"/path/to/jdk/bin"`), and that the `JAVA_HOME` environment variable is set to the JDK root folder (e.g., `"/path/to/jdk"`). This is not strictly required by JSF, but Eclipse and Payara need this. Eclipse will need the `PATH` in order to find the Java executables. Payara will need the `JAVA_HOME` in order to find the JDK tools.

## What About Java EE?

Note that you do **not** need to download and install Java EE from Oracle.com even though JSF itself is part of Java EE. Java EE is basically an abstract specification of which the so-called application servers represent the concrete implementations. Examples of those application servers are Payara, WildFly, TomEE, GlassFish, and Liberty. It is exactly those application servers that actually provide among others JSF (JavaServer Faces),

13

B. Scholtz and A. Tijms, *The Definitive Guide to JSF in Java EE 8*, https://doi.org/10.1007/978-1-4842-3387-0_2

EL (Expression Language), CDI (Contexts and Dependency Injection), EJB (Enterprise JavaBeans), JPA (Java Persistence API), Servlet, WebSocket, and JSON-P (JavaScript Object Notation Processing), APIs (application programming interfaces) out of the box.

There also exist so-called servlet containers which provide basically only the Servlet, JASPIC (Java Authentication Service Provider Interface for Containers), JSP (JavaServer Pages), EL, and WebSocket APIs out of the box, such as Tomcat and Jetty. However, it would require some work to manually install and configure, among others, JSF, JSTL (JSP Standard Tag Library), CDI, EJB, and JPA on such a servlet container. It is not even trivial in the case of EJB as it requires modifying the servlet container's internals. That is, by the way, exactly why TomEE exists. It's a Java EE application server built on top of the barebones Tomcat servlet container engine.

Coming back to the Java EE download at Oracle.com, it would give you basically the GlassFish server, along with a bunch of documentation and optionally the Netbeans IDE. We do not need it as we are already using Payara as the Java EE application server, and are targeting Eclipse as IDE. Therefore, the Java SE JDK is sufficient.

# Installing Payara

Payara is an open source Java EE application server which is in 2014 forked from GlassFish. It is basically a response to Oracle's announcement to stop its commercial support for GlassFish, so companies previously using GlassFish commercially could effortlessly switch to Payara and continue enjoying commercial support. Thanks to commercial support for business customers previously using GlassFish, the Payara application server software can continuously be bug-fixed and improved.

The first Payara version with JSF 2.3 integrated is 5. You can download it from https:// payara.fish. Make sure you choose either the "Payara Server Full" or "Payara Server Web Profile" download and not, for example, the "Payara Micro" or "Payara Embedded," as they have other purposes. Installing is basically a matter of unzipping the downloaded file and putting it somewhere in your home folder. We'll leave it there until we have Eclipse up and running, so that we can then integrate Payara in Eclipse and let it manage the server.

# How About Other Servers?

The choice for Payara in this book is primarily because it is at time of this writing one of the very few available Java EE application servers with JSF 2.3 integrated. The other one is GlassFish, but we would rather not advocate it as it would basically offer no commercial support or bug fixes. GlassFish must be seen as a true reference implementation for other application server vendors so they can, if necessary, build their application server implementation by example.

WildFly, TomEE, and Liberty did not, at the time of writing, have a version available with JSF 2.3 integrated.

# Installing Eclipse

Eclipse is an open source IDE written in Java. It is basically like notepad but with thousands if not millions of extra features, such as automatically compiling class files, building a WAR file with them, and deploying it to an application server without the need to manually fiddle around with `javac` in a command console.

Eclipse is available in a lot of flavors. As we're going to develop with Java EE, we need the one saying "Eclipse IDE for Java EE developers." It's usually the top-ranked download link at `http://eclipse.org/downloads/eclipse-packages/`. Also here, installing is basically a matter of unzipping the downloaded file and putting it somewhere in your home folder.

In Windows and Linux you'll find the `eclipse.ini` configuration file in the unzipped folder. In Mac OS this configuration file is located in `Eclipse.app/Contents/Eclipse`. Open this file for editing. We want to increase the allocated memory for Eclipse. At the bottom of `eclipse.ini`, you'll find the following lines:

```
-Xms256m
-Xmx1024m
```

This sets, respectively, the initial and maximum memory size pool which Eclipse may use. This is a bit too low when you want to develop a bit of a decent Java EE application. Let's at least double both the values.

```
-Xms512m
-Xmx2g
```

Watch out that you don't declare more than the available physical memory. When the actual memory usage exceeds the available physical memory, it will continue into virtual memory, usually in a swap file on disk. This will greatly decrease performance and result in major hiccups and slowdowns.

Now you can start Eclipse by executing the `eclipse` executable in the unzipped folder. You will be asked to select a directory as workspace. This is the directory where Eclipse will save all workspace projects and metadata.

After that, Eclipse will show a welcome screen. This is not interesting for now. You can click the *Workbench* button on the right top to close the welcome screen. Untick if necessary "Always show Welcome at start up" on the bottom right. After that, you will enter the workbench. By default, it looks like the screenshot in Figure 2-1.

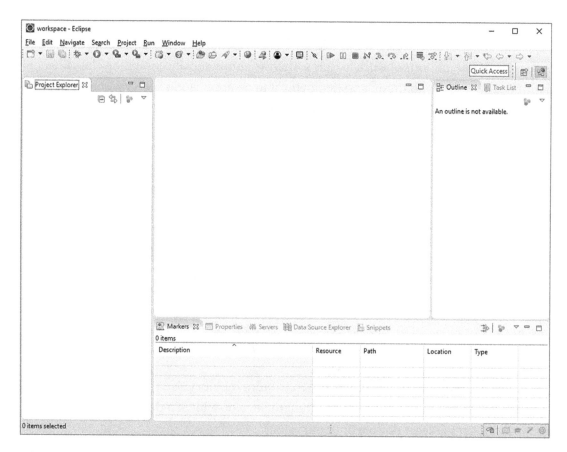

*Figure 2-1.*  *Eclipse workbench*

## Configuring Eclipse

Before we can start writing code, we would like to fine-tune Eclipse a bit so that we don't eventually end up in trouble or with annoyances. Eclipse has an enormous amount of settings, and some of its default values should not have been the default values. You can verify and configure the settings via *Window* ➤ *Preferences*.

- *General* ➤ *Workspace* ➤ *Text file encoding* must be set to **UTF-8**. Particularly in Windows this might otherwise default to the proprietary encoding CP-1252 which does not support any characters beyond the Latin range. When reading and saving Unicode files with CP-1252, you risk seeing unintelligible sequences of characters. This is also called "mojibake".[1]

- *General* ➤ *Workspace* ➤ *New text file line delimiter* must be set to **Unix**. It works just fine on Windows as well. This will particularly keep version control systems happy. Otherwise, developers pulling code on different operating systems might face confusing conflicts or diffs caused by different line endings.

- *General* ➤ *Editors* ➤ *Text editors* ➤ *Spelling* should preferably be **disabled**. This will save you from a potentially big annoyance, because it unnecessarily also spellchecks XML configuration files such as `faces-config.xml` and `web.xml`, causing confusing errors and warnings in those files.

- *Java* ➤ *Compiler* ➤ *Compiler compliance level* must be set to **1.8**. This is the minimum required Java version for Java EE 8.

- *Java* ➤ *Installed JREs* must be set to the **JDK**, not to the JRE. This setting will normally also be used to execute the integrated application server which usually requires the JDK.

## Installing JBoss Tools Plug-in

Standard Eclipse for Java EE in its current version does not support any CDI tools. It has no wizards to create CDI managed beans, or autocompletion and hyperlinking for CDI managed beans in JSF pages. The JBoss Tools plug-in is an extensive plug-in which offers among others the CDI tools.[2] This is very useful when developing a Java EE web application.

---

[1]`https://en.wikipedia.org/wiki/Mojibake`.
[2]`http://tools.jboss.org/features/cdi.html`.

In order to install it, go to *Help* ➤ *Eclipse Marketplace*. Enter in the search field "JBoss Tools" and click *Go*. Scroll a bit through the results until you see JBoss Tools Final and then click *Install* (see Figure 2-2).

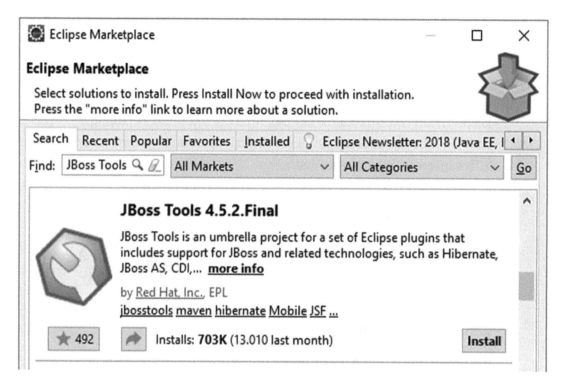

***Figure 2-2.*** *JBoss Tools in the Eclipse Marketplace*

In the next step, you'll see a fairly large list of all JBoss Tools' offerings. We don't need all of them. The list indeed also includes some JSF-related tools, but they are not terribly useful. The Visual Page Editor is not at all useful. Dragging and dropping together a JSF page doesn't make you a good JSF developer. That can only be achieved by just writing code yourself. Moreover, having too many unused features installed and even implicitly enabled may make Eclipse terribly slow. The fewer features you select, the less chance that you will be surprised about changes in the IDE behavior. So, untick the top check box and then tick only the check box which says "Context and Dependency Injection Tools" (see Figure 2-3).

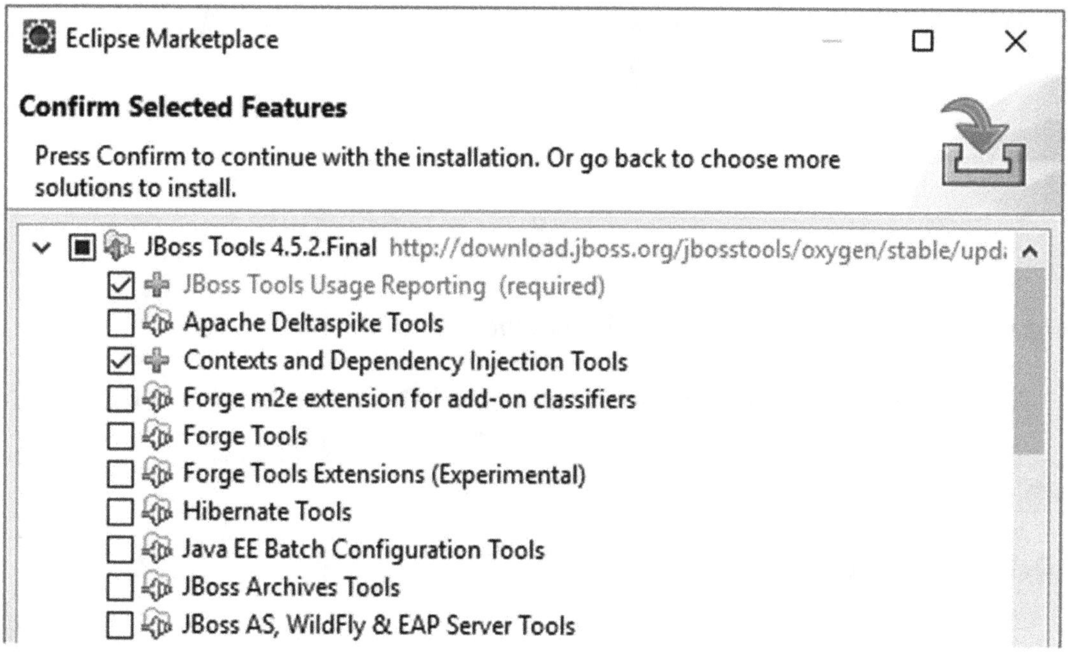

**Figure 2-3.**  *Select only the CDI tools for now*

Next, accept the terms of the license agreement and complete the wizard until Eclipse is restarted.

## Integrating New Server in Eclipse

We need to familarize Eclipse with any installed application servers so that Eclipse can seamlessly link its Java EE API libraries in the project's build path (read: the compile time classpath of the project). This is mandatory in order to be able to import classes from the Java EE API in your project. You know, the application server itself represents the concrete implementation of the abstract Java EE API.

In order to integrate a new application server in Eclipse, first check the bottom section of the workbench with several tabs representing several *Views* (you can add new ones via *Window* ➤ *Show View*). Click the *Servers* tab to open the servers view (see Figure 2-4). Click the link which says "No servers are available. Click this link to create a new server. . . ."

**Figure 2-4.** *Servers view of Eclipse Workbench*

From the list of available server tools, select *Oracle ➤ GlassFish Tools* (see Figure 2-5).

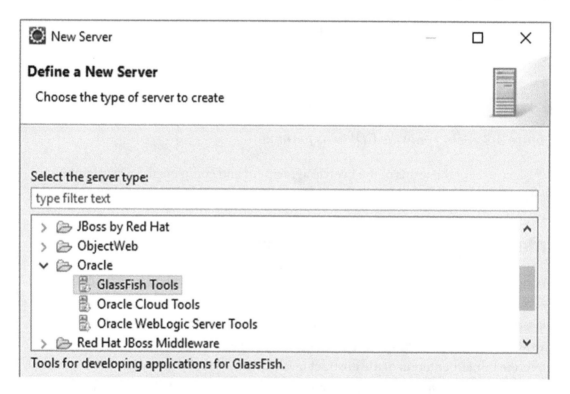

**Figure 2-5.** *Selecting GlassFish Tools in New Server wizard*

After clicking *Next* for the first time, it will download the plug-in in the background and request you to accept the license agreement before installing the plug-in. This plug-in is mandatory in order to manage any GlassFish-based server from inside the workbench—among others, adding and removing Eclipse projects to the deployments folder, starting and stopping the server, and running the server in debug mode. Once it's finished installing, it will request you to restart Eclipse. Take action accordingly.

Once returned into the workspace, click the same link in the *Servers* view again. You'll now see a *GlassFish* ➤ *GlassFish* option. Select this and set the *Server name* field to "Payara" (see Figure 2-6).

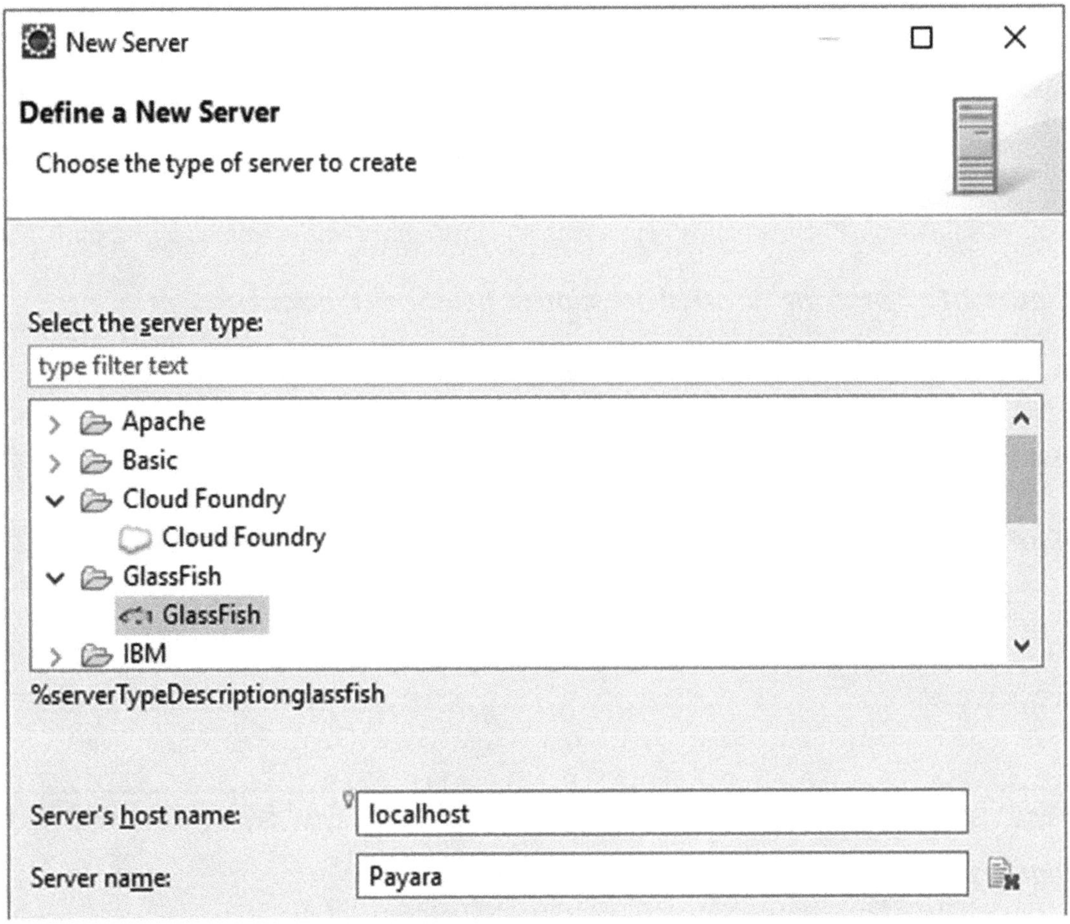

*Figure 2-6.* *Selecting GlassFish server in New Server wizard and naming it Payara*

Advance to the next step. Here, you should point the *GlassFish location* field to the glassfish subfolder of the Payara installation, there where you have unzipped it after downloading (see Figure 2-7).

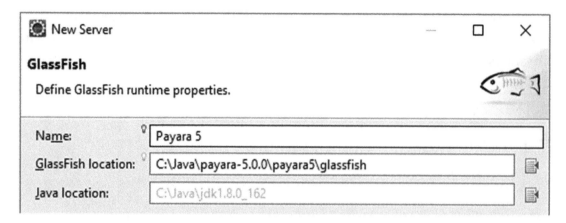

***Figure 2-7.*** *Specifying GlassFish location in New Server wizard*

Complete the remainder of the *New Server* wizard with default settings. You don't need to edit any other fields. The newly added server will now appear in the *Servers* view (see Figure 2-8).

***Figure 2-8.*** *The Payara server in Servers view*

# Creating New Project in Eclipse

We're now ready to create a new project for our JSF application in Eclipse. This can be done via the left section of the workbench which by default shows only one tab representing the *Project Explorer* view (also here, you can add new views via *Window* ➤ *Show View*). Right-click anywhere in this view and select *New* ➤ *Project*. It'll show the *New Project* wizard which may have a bit too many options.

Eclipse, being an IDE for many different project tasks, offers a bewildering amount of different project types from which to choose. For a Java EE-based application which is going to be deployed as a simple WAR file, there are basically two project types that we could choose from: *Web ➤ Dynamic Web Project* and *Maven ➤ Maven Project.*

The difference is that the first is an Eclipse native project that really only works on Eclipse, while the latter is a universal type of project that can be built by any IDE, as well as easily on the command line and by various CI servers such as Travis and Jenkins. For this reason, the Maven project type is really the only viable choice (see Figure 2-9).

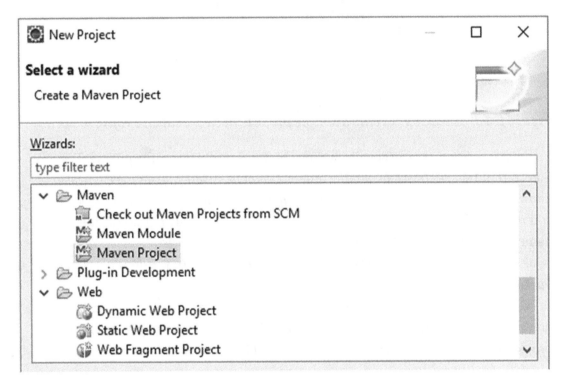

***Figure 2-9.*** *Selecting Maven Project in New Project wizard (note the Dynamic Web Project as another but non-viable option)*

In the next step, make sure that the option *Create a simple project (skip archetype selection)* is checked (see Figure 2-10). This will let us start with a really empty Maven project so that we can configure and populate it ourselves. Of course, you could also choose from an archetype, which is basically a template project with several already prepared files and configurations. But we don't need any for now.

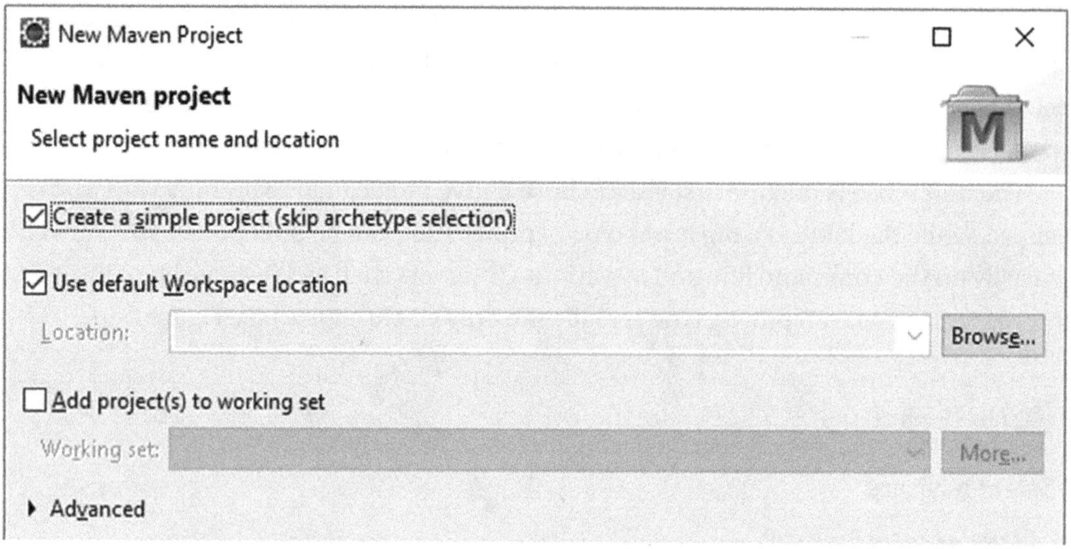

**Figure 2-10.** *Checking "Create a simple project" in New Maven Project wizard*

In the next step, we can specify our own Maven coordinates of the project. The Maven coordinates consist of, among others, *Group Id*, *Artifact Id,* and *Version*, also known as GAV in the Maven world. The *Group Id* usually matches the root package name you're going to use, such as com.example. The *Artifact Id* usually represents the project name you're going to use. For simplicity and in order to be consistent in the rest of the book, we'll use project. The *Version* can be kept default at 0.0.1-SNAPSHOT. Finally the *Packaging* should be set to war.

Complete the remainder of the *New Maven Project* wizard (see Figure 2-11). You don't need to edit any other fields. Once you've finished the wizard, you'll get to see the project structure in the *Project Explorer* view (see Figure 2-12).

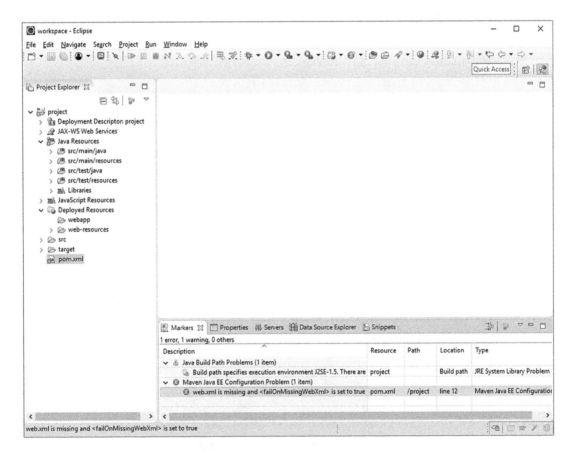

**Figure 2-11.**  *Filling out the Maven GAV in new Maven Project wizard*

**Figure 2-12.**  *The newly created Maven project in Eclipse*

Unfortunately, the Eclipse-generated pom.xml, which is the main indicator of the project being a Maven project and containing its configuration, is less than ideal. It's not current any more, even when generated by the latest Eclipse, the Oxygen 2 (December 2017). You can already see that by the pom.xml file which is marked with an alarming red cross and an error message in the *Markers* view. Any project that has at least one such red cross cannot be built and won't be deployable. The error message literally says "web.xml is missing and <failOnMissingWebXml> is set to true." In other words, Maven somehow thinks that it's still a pre-Java EE 6 project, when this was indeed disallowed.

In order to solve this problem and to catch up the Eclipse-generated pom.xml with the current standards, we need to open pom.xml for editing and adjust it as shown in the following code:

```xml
<project
    xmlns="http://maven.apache.org/POM/4.0.0"
    xmlns:xsi="http://www.w3.org/2001/XMLSchema-instance"
    xsi:schemaLocation="http://maven.apache.org/POM/4.0.0
        http://maven.apache.org/xsd/maven-4.0.0.xsd"
>
    <modelVersion>4.0.0</modelVersion>

    <groupId>com.example</groupId>
    <artifactId>project</artifactId>
    <version>0.0.1-SNAPSHOT</version>
    <packaging>war</packaging>

    <properties>
        <project.build.sourceEncoding>
            UTF-8
        </project.build.sourceEncoding>
        <project.reporting.outputEncoding>
            UTF-8
        </project.reporting.outputEncoding>
        <maven.compiler.source>1.8</maven.compiler.source>
        <maven.compiler.target>1.8</maven.compiler.target>
        <failOnMissingWebXml>false</failOnMissingWebXml>
    </properties>
```

```
    <dependencies>
        <dependency>
            <groupId>javax</groupId>
            <artifactId>javaee-api</artifactId>
            <version>8.0</version>
            <scope>provided</scope>
        </dependency>
    </dependencies>
</project>
```

Once you save this file, Eclipse will automatically sort it out by itself and clear out the alarming red cross. Now that looks much better. We'll briefly go through the most important settings here.

- Packaging **war**—indicates the project is a "web" project, and that the project's contents will be assembled into a web archive.

- Encoding **UTF-8**—sets the encoding that the source files are in and with which the (reporting) output files should be generated. This makes the build repeatable, as it otherwise would default to the system default encoding (again, a rather bad default).

- Compiler **1.8**—sets both the version of Java used in the .java source files as well as the byte code output in the .class files. Without setting this, Maven defaults to the oldest version possible, and sometimes even a lower version than that.

- failOnMissingWebXml **false**—older versions of Java EE required the /WEB-INF/web.xml to be present. Even though this has not been required any more since Java EE 6, which was released in 2009, Maven still checks for this file to be present. Setting this to false prevents this unnecessary check.

- Dependency **javax:javaee-api:8.0 provided**—this declares a dependency on the Java EE 8 API, and makes sure all the Java EE types like @Named are known to the compiler. This dependency is set to provided" since those types are already provided by the target runtime, which is in our case Payara. They will then only be used to compile the source code against and won't be included in the generated `.war`. You need to make absolutely sure that any compile time dependency which is already provided by the target runtime is set to `provided`; otherwise it will eventually end up in the generated `.war` and you may run into class loading trouble wherein duplicate different versioned libraries are conflicting with each other. In case you're actually not targeting a full-fledged Java EE server but a barebones servlet container, you would need to adjust the dependencies as instructed in the README of Mojarra,[3] one of the available JSF implementations and actually the one used under the cover of Payara.

Now, in Eclipse's *Markers* view, there's only one warning left which says "Build path specifies execution environment J2SE-1.5. There are no JREs installed in the workspace that are strictly compatible with this environment." Well, that basically means that Eclipse recognizes this Maven project as a Java 1.5-only project while we don't actually have Java SE 5 installed, and in spite of the compiler version in `pom.xml` being set to `1.8`.

In order to tell Eclipse that this is really a Java 1.8 project, we need to right-click the project in *Project Explorer* view and choose *Properties*. In the *Project Facets* section you should change the version of the *Java* facet from `1.5` to `1.8` (or 9 if you have JDK 9 installed) (see Figure 2-13). While at it, we also need to update the Servlet API version and add the CDI, JSF, and JPA facets. The Servlet API is represented by the "Dynamic Web Module" entry. This needs to be set to version `4.0`, which matches Java EE 8. Further the "CDI," "JavaServer Faces," and "JPA" entries need to be selected. The "CDI" facet is, by the way, only available after having installed the JBoss Tools as instructed in the section "Installing JBoss Tools Plug-in."

---

[3]https://github.com/javaserverfaces/mojarra/blob/master/README.md.

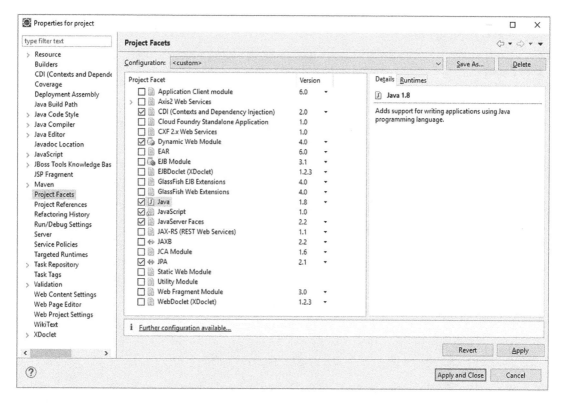

***Figure 2-13.*** *The Project Facets section of the project properties (note that the Servlet API version is represented by "Dynamic Web Module")*

Unfortunately, in the latest available Eclipse version, Oxygen 2 from December 2017, there isn't a JSF 2.3 or JPA 2.2 version available yet in the dropdown. The highest available versions are JSF 2.2 and JPA 2.1. This is not a big problem. Its only influence is on the available code generators and wizards. We can always adjust the Eclipse-generated `faces-config.xml` and `persistence.xml` files afterward to match the Java EE 8 compatible versions.

As you can see in the yellow warning bar, only Eclipse requires further configuration. This concerns the newly selected JSF and JPA facets. When clicking the link, we get to see the *Modify Faceted Project* wizard (see Figure 2-14).

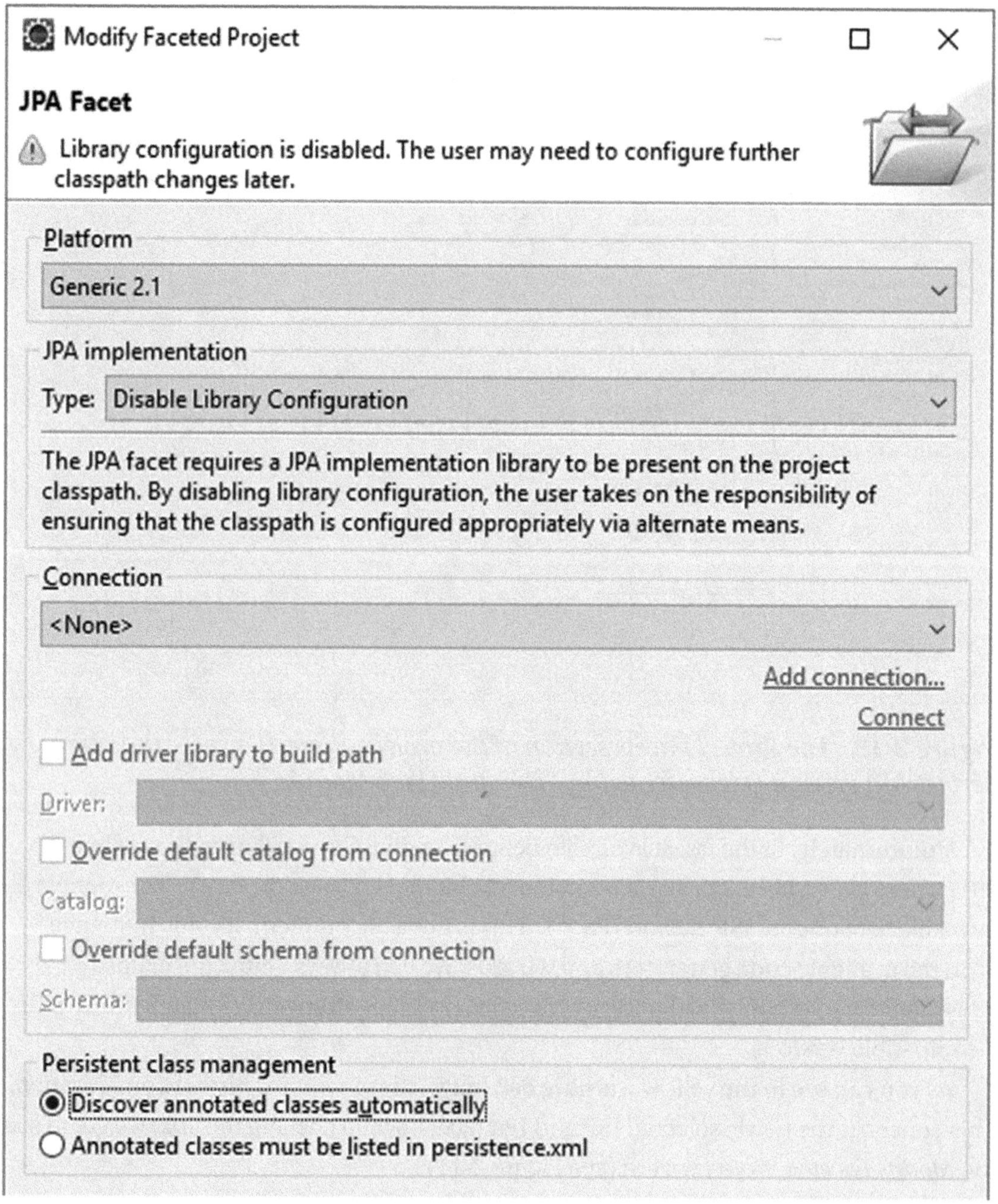

**Figure 2-14.** *The JPA Facet configuration*

The first step of the *Modify Faceted Project* wizard allows us to configure the JPA facet. We need to make sure that Eclipse is being instructed that the JPA implementation is already provided by the target runtime and thus Eclipse doesn't need to include any libraries. This can be achieved by choosing the "Disable Library Configuration" option in the *JPA implementation* field. As we're going to use the Payara-provided Hibernate as the actual JPA implementation, which automatically supports discovering of `@Entity` annotated classes, we'd like to instruct Eclipse to do the same; otherwise it would automatically add entities to the `persistence.xml` when going through the entity code generation wizard, or show warnings when we create one manually and don't add it to the `persistence.xml`.

Note that configuring a database connection is not necessary for now as we're going to use an embedded database.

In the next step of the *Modify Faceted Project* wizard, we can configure the JSF capabilities (see Figure 2-15). Also here, we need to make sure that Eclipse is being instructed that the JSF implementation is already provided by the target runtime and thus Eclipse doesn't need to include any libraries. This can be achieved by choosing the "Disable Library Configuration" option in the *JSF Implementation Library* field. Further, we need to rename the servlet name of the `FacesServlet` to match the fictive instance variable name: `facesServlet`. Last but not least, we need to change the URL mapping pattern from the Jurassic `/faces/*` to the modern `*.xhtml`.

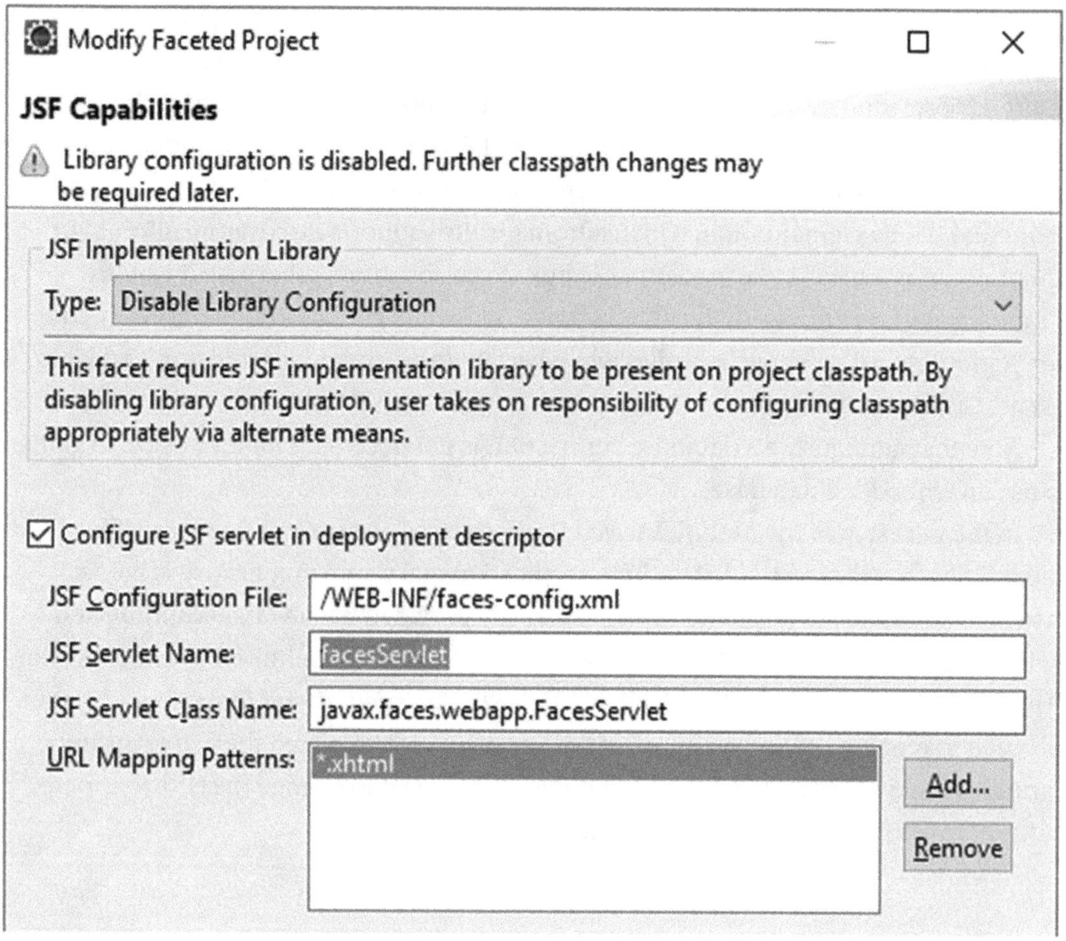

**Figure 2-15.** *The JSF Capabilities configuration*

Actually, the entire registration of the FacesServlet in web.xml is, since JSF 2.2, not strictly necessary any more; you could even uncheck the *Configure JSF servlet in deployment descriptor* option and rely on the default auto-registered mappings of /faces/*, *.faces, *.jsf and *.xhtml. However, as this allows end users and even search bots to open the very same JSF page by different URLs, and thus causes confusion among end users and duplicate content penalties among search bots, we'd better restrict to only one explicitly configured URL pattern.

Now, finish and apply all the wizards and dialogs. The JPA plug-in only puts the generated persistence.xml at the wrong place. You need to manually move it into src/main/resources/META-INF. Figure 2-16 shows us how the workbench looks now.

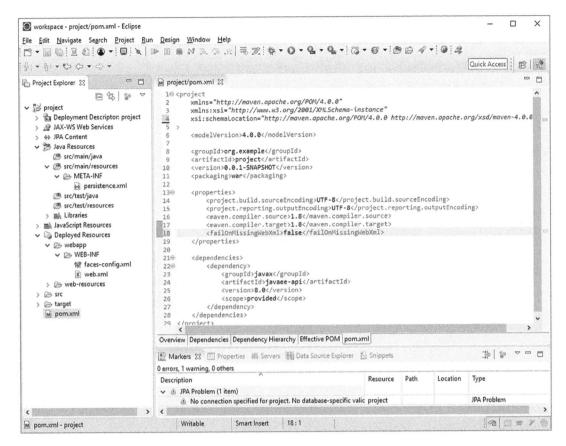

***Figure 2-16.*** *Correctly configured Java EE 8 Maven project in Eclipse*

We only need to adjust all the deployment descriptors to catch up to the actually used Servlet, JSF, JPA, and CDI versions. This is normally done by adjusting the root element of the deployment descriptor XML file to set the desired XML schemas and the version.

You can find all Java EE 8 schemas at http://xmlns.jcp.org/xml/ns/javaee, which is an actual web page which currently redirects to some landing page at Oracle.com. This may change in the future given that Java EE 8 is currently in the process of being transferred from Oracle to Eclipse. You can open the deployment descriptor XML file for editing by double-clicking it and then selecting the *Source* tab in the editor. The correct root element declarations for Java EE 8 compatible deployment descriptors are thus as follows:

src/main/webapp/WEB-INF/web.xml for Servlet 4.0:
```
<?xml version="1.0" encoding="UTF-8"?>
<web-app
    xmlns="http://xmlns.jcp.org/xml/ns/javaee"
```

```
    xmlns:xsi="http://www.w3.org/2001/XMLSchema-instance"
    xsi:schemaLocation="http://xmlns.jcp.org/xml/ns/javaee
        http://xmlns.jcp.org/xml/ns/javaee/web-app_4_0.xsd"
    version="4.0"
>
    <!-- Servlet configuration here. -->
</web-app>
```

src/main/webapp/WEB-INF/faces-config.xml for JSF 2.3:

```
<?xml version="1.0" encoding="UTF-8"?>
<faces-config
    xmlns="http://xmlns.jcp.org/xml/ns/javaee"
    xmlns:xsi="http://www.w3.org/2001/XMLSchema-instance"
    xsi:schemaLocation="http://xmlns.jcp.org/xml/ns/javaee
        http://xmlns.jcp.org/xml/ns/javaee/web-facesconfig_2_3.xsd"
    version="2.3"
>
    <!-- JSF configuration here. -->
</faces-config>
```

src/main/resources/META-INF/persistence.xml for JPA 2.2:

```
<?xml version="1.0" encoding="UTF-8"?>
<persistence
    xmlns="http://xmlns.jcp.org/xml/ns/persistence"
    xmlns:xsi="http://www.w3.org/2001/XMLSchema-instance"
    xsi:schemaLocation="http://xmlns.jcp.org/xml/ns/persistence
        http://xmlns.jcp.org/xml/ns/persistence/persistence_2_2.xsd"
    version="2.2"
>
    <!-- JPA configuration here. -->
</persistence>
```

Only the currently available JPA plug-in of Eclipse will show an error on this. You could ignore this by disabling the JPA validator in the project's properties, but you can also just step back to a JPA 2.1 compatible persistence.xml for the time being.

Finally, for sake of completeness we need to create one more deployment descriptor file, the one for CDI 2.0. This isn't automatically generated as it's not required. CDI is by default always enabled in any Java EE 8 compatible web application. It's even mandatory for the functioning of JSF. Among others the new <f:websocket> relies fully on CDI. Right-click the /WEB-INF folder of the project and choose *New* ➤ *beans.xml File*. The *New beans.xml File* wizard which appears now is part of the JBoss Tools plug-in. Just keep all options default and finish the wizard. It'll generate the file as follows:

```
src/main/webapp/WEB-INF/beans.xml for CDI 2.0:
<?xml version="1.0" encoding="UTF-8"?>
<beans
    xmlns="http://xmlns.jcp.org/xml/ns/javaee"
    xmlns:xsi="http://www.w3.org/2001/XMLSchema-instance"
    xsi:schemaLocation="http://xmlns.jcp.org/xml/ns/javaee
        http://xmlns.jcp.org/xml/ns/javaee/beans_2_0.xsd"
    version="2.0" bean-discovery-mode="annotated"
>
    <!-- CDI configuration here. -->
</beans>
```

## Creating the Backing Bean Class

With the project now correctly configured we can start with developing the actual MVC application. The Controller part of MVC is already configured as FacesServlet in web.xml. The Model part of MVC is what we're going to create now. It's basically just a simple Java class which is by JSF convention called a *Backing Bean* since it "backs" a View.

Right-click the src/main/java folder of the project and choose *New* ➤ *Bean*. The *New CDI Bean* wizard which appears now is also part of the JBoss Tools plug-in (see Figure 2-17). In this wizard, set the *Package* to com.example.project.view, set the *Name* to HelloWorld, tick the *Add @Named* chec kbox, and finally set the *Scope* to @RequestScoped. The rest of the fields can be kept default or empty.

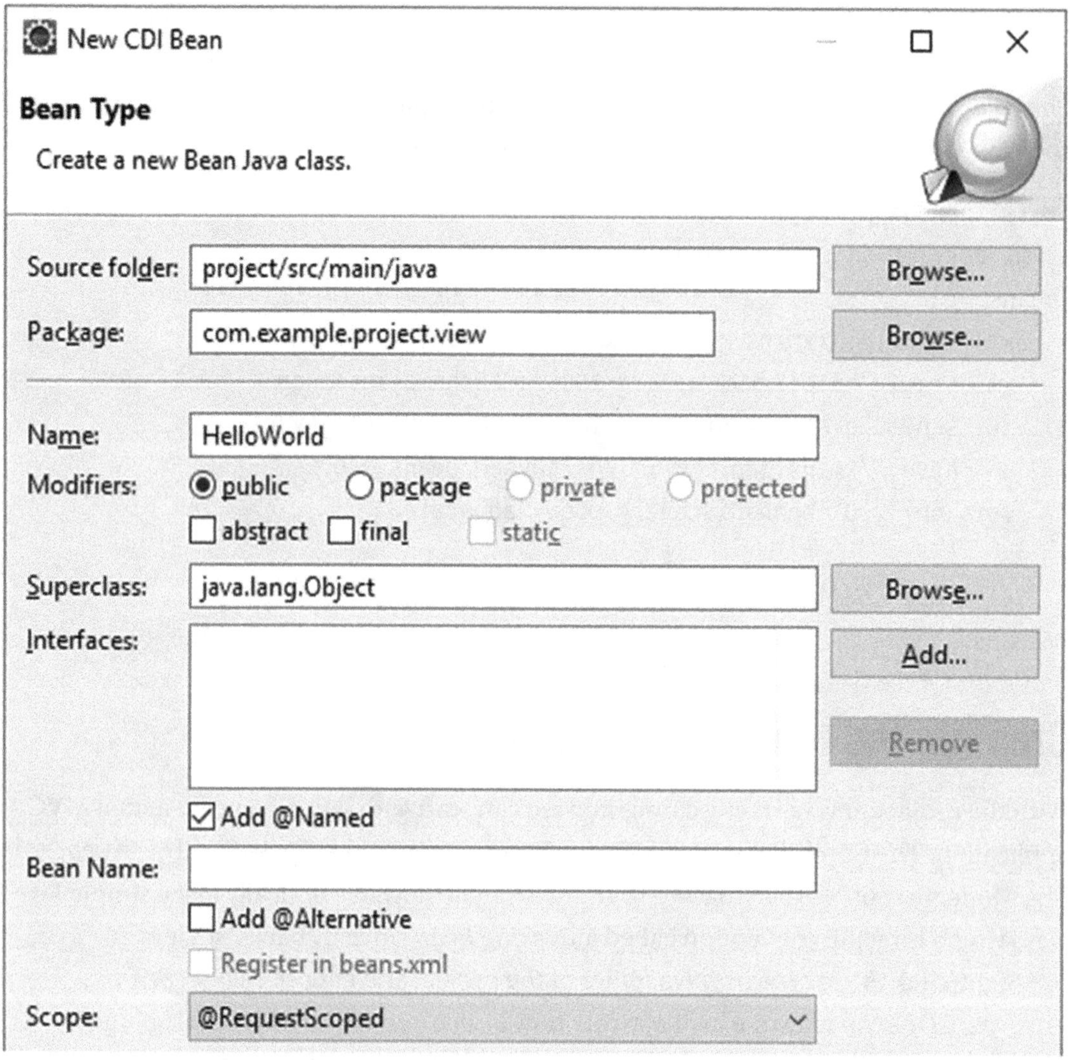

*Figure 2-17.* *The JBoss Tools-provided New CDI Bean wizard in Eclipse*

The class editor will now open with the newly created backing bean class. We'll modify it to get rid of the useless constructor; add two properties, input and output; and accompany the input property with a getter and setter pair, the output property with only a getter, and a submit() action method which prepares the output property based on the input property. As a hint, in Eclipse after entering the properties, you can right-click anywhere in the class editor and choose *Source ➤ Generate Getters and Setters* to have the IDE to generate them. In its entirety, the edited backing bean class should look as follows:

```java
package com.example.project.view;

import javax.enterprise.context.RequestScoped;
import javax.inject.Named;

@Named @RequestScoped
public class HelloWorld {

    private String input;
    private String output;

    public void submit() {
        output = "Hello World! You have typed: " + input;
    }

    public String getInput() {
        return input;
    }

    public void setInput(String input) {
        this.input = input;
    }

    public String getOutput() {
        return output;
    }
}
```

We'll briefly go through the annotations that are used here.

- **@Named**—gives the bean a name, which is primarily used to reference it via EL. Without any attributes this name defaults to the simple class name with the first letter in lowercase, thus "helloWorld" here. It will be available by #{helloWorld} in EL. This can be used in JSF pages.

- **@RequestScoped**—gives the bean a scope, which means the same instance of the bean is used within a given lifespan. In this case that lifespan is the duration of an HTTP request. When the scope ends, the bean is automatically destroyed. You can read more about scopes in Chapter 8.

## Creating the Facelets File

Next, we'll create the View part of MVC. It's basically just a XHTML file which is by JSF interpreted as a *Facelets file* or just *Facelet*. This Facelets file will ultimately generate the HTML markup that is sent to the browser in response to a request. With help of EL, it can reference a bean property and invoke a bean action.

Right-click the webapp folder of the project and choose *New* ➤ *XHTML Page* (see Figure 2-18). The *New XHTML Page* wizard which appears now is also part of the JBoss Tools plug-in. In this wizard, set the *File name* to hello.xhtml and finish the wizard.

**Figure 2-18.** *The JBoss Tools-provided New XHTML Page wizard in Eclipse*

The XHTML editor will now open with the newly created Facelets file. You'll also notice that the *Palette* view shows up in bottom box. This is essentially not useful for JSF-based web development. So let's close it. Coming back to the newly created Facelets file, it's initially empty. Fill it with the following content:

```
<!DOCTYPE html>
<html lang="en"
    xmlns="http://www.w3.org/1999/xhtml"
    xmlns:f="http://xmlns.jcp.org/jsf/core"
    xmlns:h="http://xmlns.jcp.org/jsf/html"
>
```

```
<h:head>
    <title>Hello World</title>
</h:head>
<h:body>
    <h1>Hello World</h1>
    <h:form>
        <h:outputLabel for="input" value="Input" />
        <h:inputText id="input" value="#{helloWorld.input}" />
        <h:commandButton value="Submit"
            action="#{helloWorld.submit}">
            <f:ajax execute="@form" render=":output" />
        </h:commandButton>
    </h:form>
    <h:outputText id="output" value="#{helloWorld.output}" />
</h:body>
</html>
```

We'll briefly go through the JSF-specific XHTML tags that are used here.

- **\<h:head\>**—generates the HTML \<head\>. It gives JSF the opportunity to automatically include any necessary JavaScript files, such as the one containing the necessary logic for \<f:ajax\>.

- **\<h:body\>**—generates the HTML \<body\>. You can also use a plain HTML \<body\> in this specific Facelet, but then it doesn't give any other JSF tag the opportunity to automatically include any necessary JavaScript in the end of the HTML \<body\>.

- **\<h:form\>**—generates the HTML \<form\>. JSF will automatically include the view state in a hidden input field.

- **\<h:outputLabel\>**—generates the HTML \<label\>. You can also use a plain HTML \<label\> in this specific Facelet, but then you'd have to manually take care of figuring out the actual ID of the target input element.

- **\<h:inputText\>**—generates the HTML \<input type="text"\>. JSF will automatically get and set the value in the bean property specified in the value attribute.

- **<h:commandButton>**—generates the HTML <input type="submit">. JSF will automatically invoke the bean method specified in the action attribute.

- **<f:ajax>**—generates the necessary JavaScript code for Ajax behavior. You can also do as well without it, but then the form submit won't be performed asynchronously. The execute attribute indicates that the entire <h:form> must be processed on submit and the render attribute indicates that the tag identified by id="output" must be updated on complete of the Ajax submit.

- **<h:outputText>**—generates the HTML <span>. This is the one being updated on completion of the Ajax submit. It will merely print the bean property specified in the value attribute.

Those JSF-specific XHTML tags are also called *JSF Components*. There will be more on Facelets files and JSF components in the upcoming chapters. Note that you can also perfectly embed plain vanilla HTML in a Facelets file. JSF components should only be used when the functionality requires so, or is easily achievable with them.

## Deploying the Project

In the *Servers* view, first start the Payara server. You can do so by selecting it and then clicking the green arrow icon whose tool tip says "Start the server." You can, of course, also use the bug icon whose tool tip says "Start the server in debug mode." The *Console* view will briefly show the server startup log. Wait until the server starts up and has, in the *Servers* view, gained the status *Started* (see Figure 2-19).

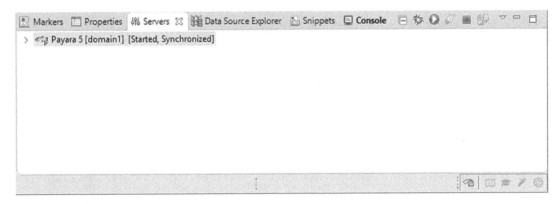

***Figure 2-19.*** *The Payara server in Servers view with the status Started (note that the Console view is highlighted as it has unread server logs)*

41

Now right-click the Payara server entry and choose *Add and Remove*. It will show the *Add and Remove* wizard (see Figure 2-20) which gives you the opportunity to add and remove WAR projects to the server. Do so for our newly created project and finish the wizard.

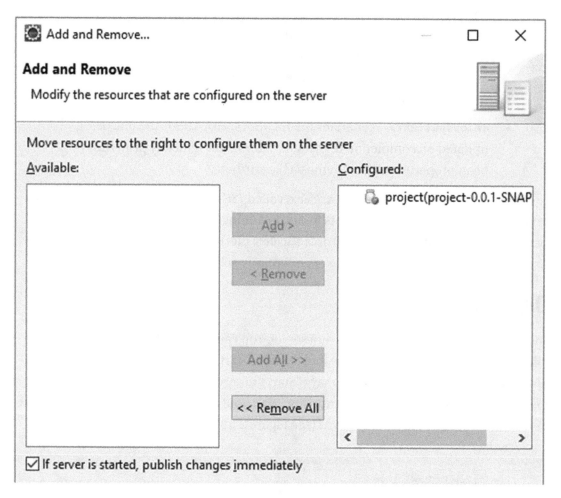

***Figure 2-20.*** *The Add and Remove wizard wherein the project has been deployed to the server by moving it to the right*

It must be explicitly mentioned that in case of Payara and GlassFish servers this is best to be done while the server is already started. When removing a project while the server is shut down, it may still linger around in the server's deployment folder. That's just GlassFish's own quirk. For example, in the case of WildFly and Tomcat servers, this is not necessary.

Now, open a tab in your favorite web browser (see Figure 2-21) and enter the address http://localhost:8080/project/hello.xhtml in order to open the newly created JSF page.

***Figure 2-21.*** *The Hello World page in Chrome browser wherein the input field is filled with the text "some message" and the submit button has been pressed*

Coming back to the URL, the "localhost:8080" part is by convention the default domain of any Java EE server which is running in development mode. The same address is also used by, among others, WildFly and TomEE. The "/project" part is by convention the name of the Eclipse project. This is in Servlet terms called the "context path" and obtainable by HttpServletRequest#getContextPath() and in JSF delegated by ExternalContext#getRequestContextPath().

The context path part can also be set to an empty string; the deployed web application will then end up in the domain root. In Eclipse, this can be set in the project's properties as well. First remove the project from the deployment using the *Add and Remove* wizard. Then right-click the project, choose *Properties*, and select *Web Project Settings*. Then set the *Context root* field to a forward slash "/" and close the properties. Finally, add the project back to the deployment using *Add and Remove* wizard. Now it will be deployed to the domain root and you can access the JSF page by `http://` `localhost:8080/hello.xhtml`. We can even get a step further by making `hello.xhtml` the default landing file so that this also doesn't need to be specified in the URL. This can be achieved by adding the following entry to the `web.xml`:

```
<welcome-file-list>
    <welcome-file>hello.xhtml</welcome-file>
</welcome-file-list>
```

Note that Payara can be configured to automatically publish changes to the deployment whenever a resource is changed in the project. Before saving the edited `web.xml`, double-click the Payara server in *Servers* view, unfold the *Publishing* section, and select *Automatically publish when resource change* along with a low interval of like 0 seconds (see Figure 2-22).

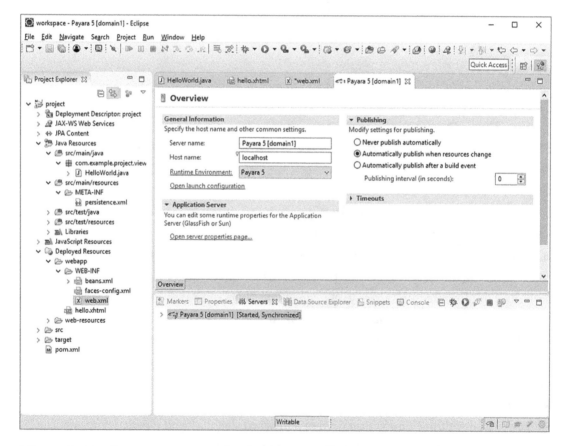

***Figure 2-22.*** *Payara server configuration in Eclipse with automatic publishing enabled and interval set to 0 seconds*

Now, save the web.xml and you'll notice that Eclipse will immediately trigger Payara to publish the changes while still running. Coming back to the web browser, you'll notice that the JSF page is now also accessible by just http://localhost:8080 (see Figure 2-23).

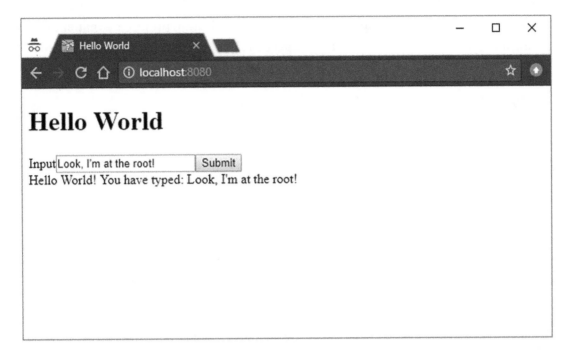

***Figure 2-23.***   *The Hello World page is now at the root*

# Installing H2

H2[4] is an in-memory SQL database. It's an embedded database useful for quickly modeling and testing JPA entities, certainly in combination with autogenerated SQL tables based on JPA entities. Adding H2 to your web application project is a matter of adding the following dependency to the `<dependencies>` section of the `pom.xml`:

```
<dependency>
    <groupId>com.h2database</groupId>
    <artifactId>h2</artifactId>
    <version>1.4.196</version>
</dependency>
```

That's basically it. The JDBC (Java Database Connectivity) driver is already built in.

# Configuring DataSource

In order to be able to interact with a SQL database, we need to configure a so-called data source in the web application project. This can be done by adding the following section to the `web.xml`:

```
<data-source>
    <name>java:global/DataSourceName</name>
    <class-name>org.h2.jdbcx.JdbcDataSource</class-name>
    <url>jdbc:h2:mem:test;DB_CLOSE_DELAY=-1</url>
</data-source>
```

The data source name represents the JNDI (Java Naming and Directory Interface) name. The class name represents the fully qualified name of the `javax.sql.DataSource` implementation of the JDBC driver being used. The URL represents the JDBC driver-specific URL format. The syntax is dependent on the JDBC driver being used. For an in-memory H2 database with a database name of "test," that's thus `jdbc:h2:mem:test`. The H2-specific `DB_CLOSE_DELAY=-1` path parameter basically instructs its JDBC driver not to automatically shut down the database when it hasn't been accessed for some time, even though the application server is still running.

---

[4]`http://www.h2database.com`.

A concrete instance of the DataSource can now be injected in any servlet container managed artifact such as a servlet or filter as follows:

```
@Resource
private DataSource dataSource;
```

You could get a SQL connection from it via DataSource#getConnection() for the plain old JDBC work. However, as we're going to use Java EE, it's better to use Java EE's own JPA for this instead.

# Configuring JPA

In order to familiarize JPA with the newly added data source, we need to add a new persistence unit to the persistence.xml which uses the data source as a JTA data source.

```
<persistence-unit name="PersistenceUnitName" transaction-type="JTA">
    <jta-data-source>java:global/DataSourceName</jta-data-source>

    <properties>
        <property
            name="javax.persistence.schema-generation.database.action"
            value="drop-and-create" />
    </properties>
</persistence-unit>
```

You see, the data source is identified by its JNDI name. You'll also notice a JPA-specific javax.persistence.schema-generation.database.action property with a value of "drop-and-create" which basically means that the web application should automatically drop and create all SQL tables based on JPA entities. This is, of course, only useful for prototyping purposes, as we're going to do with this project in the rest of the book. For real-world applications, you'd better pick either "create" or "none" (which is the default). The transaction type being set to "JTA" basically means that the application server should automatically manage database transactions. This way every method invocation on an EJB from its client (usually, a JSF backing bean) transparently starts a new transaction and when the EJB method returns to the client (usually, the calling backing bean), the transaction is automatically committed and flushed. And, any runtime exception from an EJB method automatically rolls back the transaction.

# Creating the JPA Entity

Now we're going to create a JPA entityc. Basically, it's a JavaBean class which represents a single record of a database table. Each bean property is mapped to a particular column of the database table. Normally, JPA entities are modeled against existing database tables. But, as you've read in the previous section, "Configuring JPA," about the `persistence.xml`, it's also possible to do it the other way round: database tables are generated based on JPA entities.

Right-click the `src/main/java` folder of the project and choose *New* ➤ *JPA Entity*. In the wizard, set the *Package* to `com.example.project.model` and set the *Name* to `Message`. The rest of the fields can be kept default or empty (see Figure 2-24).

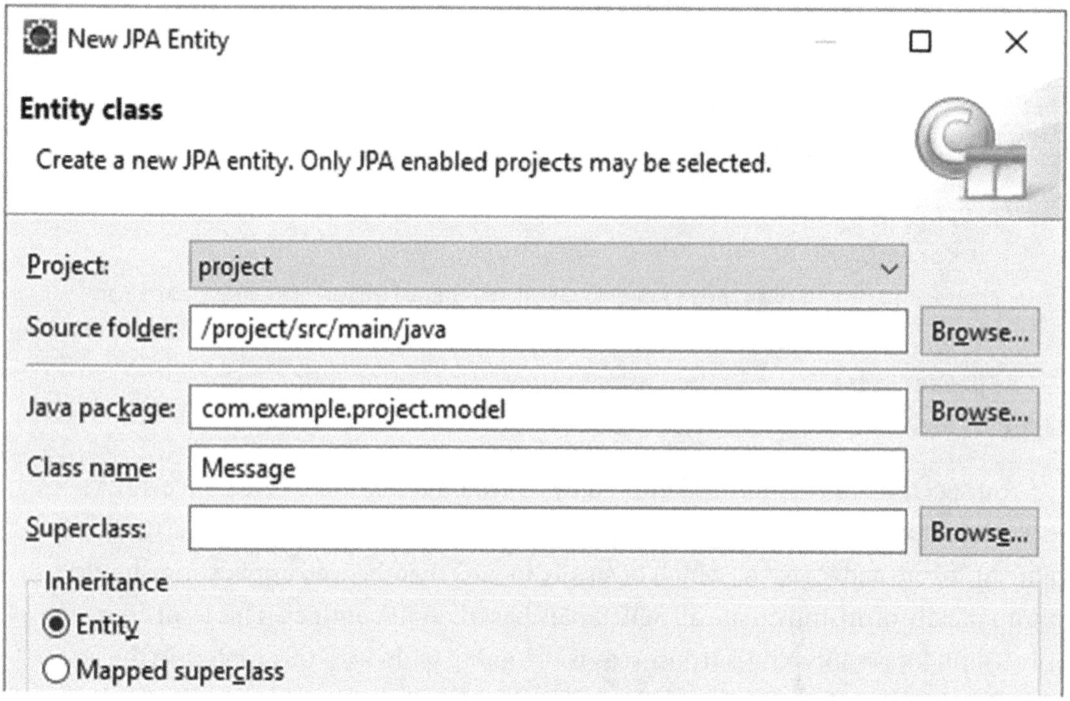

*Figure 2-24.* *The New JPA Entity wizard in Eclipse*

Modify the new entity class as follows:

```
package com.example.project.model;

import java.io.Serializable;
import javax.persistence.Column;
```

```java
import javax.persistence.Entity;
import javax.persistence.GeneratedValue;
import javax.persistence.GenerationType;
import javax.persistence.Id;
import javax.persistence.Lob;
import javax.validation.constraints.NotNull;

@Entity
public class Message implements Serializable {
    private static final long serialVersionUID = 1L;

    @Id @GeneratedValue(strategy=GenerationType.IDENTITY)
    private Long id;

    @Column(nullable = false) @Lob
    private @NotNull String text;

    // Add/generate getters and setters.
}
```

As a reminder, you can let Eclipse generate getters and setters by right-clicking anywhere in the class editor and choosing *Source ➤ Generate Getters and Setters*.

We'll briefly go through the annotations that are used here.

- **@Entity**—marks the bean as a JPA entity, so that the JPA implementation will automatically collect database-related metadata based on all its properties.

- **@Id @GeneratedValue(strategy=IDENTITY)**—marks a property to be mapped to a database column of SQL "IDENTITY" type. In MySQL terms, that's the equivalent of "AUTO_INCREMENT". In PostgreSQL terms, that's the equivalent of "BIGSERIAL".

- **@Column**—marks a property to be mapped to a regular database column. The actual database column type depends on the Java type being used. Without the additional @Lob annotation, that's a VARCHAR(255) whose length can be manipulated by @Column(length=n). With the @Lob annotation, however, the column type becomes TEXT.

- **@Lob**—marks a String property to be mapped to a database column of type TEXT instead of a limited VARCHAR.

- **@NotNull**—this is actually not part of JPA but of "Bean Validation."
  To the point, it ensures that the bean property is being validated
  never to be null when submitting a JSF form and when persisting the
  JPA entity. (See Chapter 5.) Also note that this basically replicates
  the @Column(nullable=false), but that's only because JPA doesn't
  consider any Bean Validation annotations as valid database metadata
  in order to generate appropriate SQL tables.

## Creating the EJB Service

Next, we need to create an EJB in order to be able to save an instance of the
aforementioned JPA entity in the database, and to obtain a list of JPA entities.

Right-click the src/main/java folder of the project and choose *New* ➤ *Class*. In
the wizard, set the *Package* to com.example.project.service and set the *Name* to
MessageService (see Figure 2-25). The rest of the fields can be kept default or empty.

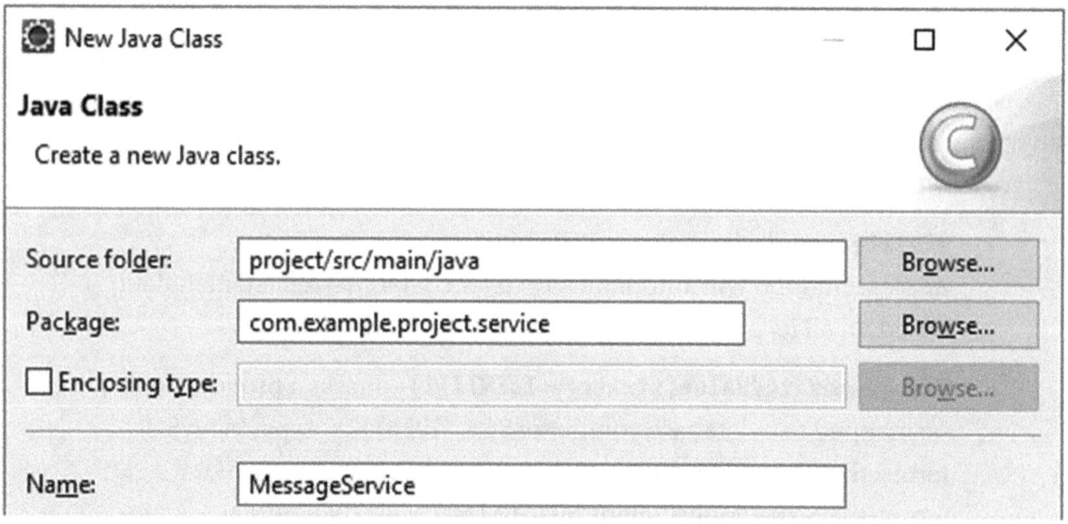

*Figure 2-25.*  *The New Java Class wizard in Eclipse*

Modify the new service class as follows:

```
package com.example.project.service;

import java.util.List;
```

```java
import javax.ejb.Stateless;
import javax.persistence.EntityManager;
import javax.persistence.PersistenceContext;

@Stateless
public class MessageService {

    @PersistenceContext
    private EntityManager entityManager;

    public void create(Message message) {
        entityManager.persist(message);
    }

    public List<Message> list() {
        return entityManager
            .createQuery("FROM Message m", Message.class)
            .getResultList();
    }
}
```

That's basically it. Let's briefly go through the annotations.

- **@Stateless**—marks the bean as a stateless EJB service, so that the application server knows whether it should pool them and when to start and stop database transactions. The alternative annotations are @Stateful and @Singleton. Note that a @Stateless does not mean that the container will make sure that the class itself is stateless. You as developer are still responsible to ensure that the class doesn't contain any shared and mutable instance variables. Otherwise, you'd better mark it as either @Stateful or @Singleton, depending on its purpose.

- **@PersistenceContext**—basically injects the JPA entity manager from the persistence unit as configured in the project's persistence. xml. The entity manager is, in turn, responsible for mapping all JPA entities against a SQL database. It will, under cover, do all the hard JDBC work.

# Adjusting the Hello World

Now we're going to adjust the earlier created HelloWorld backing bean in order to save the messages in the database and display all of them in a table.

```java
@Named @RequestScoped
public class HelloWorld {

    private Message message = new Message();
    private List<Message> messages;

    @Inject
    private MessageService messageService;

    @PostConstruct
    public void init() {
        messages = messageService.list();
    }

    public void submit() {
        messageService.create(message);
        messages.add(message);
    }

    public Message getMessage() {
        return message;
    }

    public List<Message> getMessages() {
        return messages;
    }
}
```

Note that you don't need setters for message and messages. We're going to use the getters and setters of the Message entity itself.

Finally, adjust the <h:body> of hello.xhtml as follows:

```
<h1>Hello World</h1>
<h:form>
    <h:outputLabel for="input" value="Input" />
    <h:inputText id="input" value="#{helloWorld.message.text}" />
    <h:commandButton value="Submit"
        action="#{helloWorld.submit}">
        <f:ajax execute="@form" render=":table" />
    </h:commandButton>
</h:form>
<h:dataTable id="table" value="#{helloWorld.messages}" var="message">
    <h:column>#{message.id}</h:column>
    <h:column>#{message.text}</h:column>
</h:dataTable>
```

Now reload the page in your favorite web browser and create some messages (see Figure 2-26).

***Figure 2-26.***  *The Hello World using JSF, CDI, EJB, and JPA*

# CHAPTER 3

# Components

JSF (JavaServer Faces) is a component-based MVC (Model-View-Controller) framework. In essence, JSF parses the view definition into a "component tree." The root of this tree is represented by the "view root" instance associated with the current instance of the faces context.

```
UIComponent tree = FacesContext.getCurrentInstance().getViewRoot();
```

The view is usually defined using XHTML+XML markup in a Facelets file. XML is a markup language which is very suitable for defining a tree hierarchy using a minimum of code. The component tree can also be created and manipulated using Java code in a Java class, but this generally ends up in very verbose code in order to declare value or method expressions and to correlate parents and children with each other. Frequently, developers who do so aren't aware of how tag handlers such as JSTL (JavaServer Pages Standard Tag Library) can be used to manipulate the component tree using just XML.

The component tree basically defines how JSF should consume the HTTP request in order to apply request values coming from input components, convert and validate them, update the managed bean model values, and invoke the managed bean action. It also defines how JSF should produce the HTTP response by generating the necessary HTML output using renderers tied to the components whose attributes can in turn reference managed bean properties. In other words, the component tree defines how the phases of the JSF life cycle should be processed. The diagram in Figure 3-1 shows how a HTTP postback request is usually being processed by JSF.

© Bauke Scholtz, Arjan Tijms 2018
B. Scholtz and A. Tijms, *The Definitive Guide to JSF in Java EE 8*, https://doi.org/10.1007/978-1-4842-3387-0_3

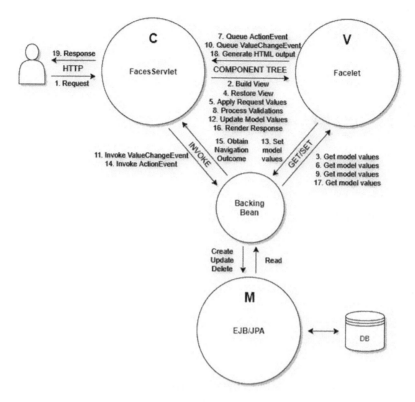

**Figure 3-1.**  *How JSF processes the HTTP postback request within the MVC architecture (the numbers represent the ordering)*

Following is a brief description of each step:

1. End user sends a HTTP request which matches the mapping of the FacesServlet and thus invokes it.

2. The FacesServlet will build the component tree based on the Facelet file identified by the HTTP request path.

3. The component tree will if necessary get the current model values from the backing bean during building the view. Any attribute of a Facelets template tag and a JSTL core tag and only the "id" and "binding" attributes of a JSF component will get executed.

4. The FacesServlet will restore the JSF view state on the component tree.

5. The `FacesServlet` will let the component tree apply the HTTP request parameters and input components will store them as "submitted value."

6. The input and command components will if necessary get the current model values from the backing bean during consulting the `"rendered"`, `"disabled"`, and `"readonly"` attributes in order to check whether they are allowed to apply the request parameters.

7. The command components will queue the `ActionEvent` when it detects, based on HTTP request parameters, that it was being invoked in the client side.

8. The `FacesServlet` will let the component tree process all registered converters and validators on the submitted values and input components will store the newly converted and validated value as "local value."

9. The input components will get the old model value from the backing bean and compare them with the new value.

10. If the new value is different from the old model value, then the input component will queue the `ValueChangeEvent`.

11. When all conversion and validation are finished, the `FacesServlet` will invoke the listener methods of any queued `ValueChangeEvent` on the backing bean.

12. The `FacesServlet` will let the component tree update all model values.

13. The input components will set the new model values in the backing bean.

14. The `FacesServlet` will invoke the listener methods of any queued `ActionEvent` on the backing bean.

15. The final action method of the backing bean will if necessary return a non-`null` `String` outcome referring the target view.

16. The `FacesServlet` will let the component tree render the response.

17. The component tree will if necessary get the current model values from the backing bean during generating the HTML output. Practically any attribute of a Facelet component and a JSF component which is involved in generating the HTML output will get executed.

18. The component tree will write the HTML output to the HTTP response.

19. The `FacesServlet` will return the HTTP response to the end user.

This is different from a request-based MVC framework wherein the developer needs to write more boilerplate code in the "controller" class associated with the view in order to define which request parameters need to be applied, and/or how they should be converted and validated before populating the entity. The developer also often needs to manually populate the entity by manually invoking a bunch of getters and setters before passing the entity to the service layer while invoking the action. This all is unnecessary in JSF.

It should be noted that the backing bean has a rather unique position in the MVC paradigm. It can act as a Model, a View, and the Controller, depending on the point of view. This is detailed in Chapter 8.

# Standard HTML Components

The default JSF implementation already provides an extensive set of components for authoring HTML pages with the help of Facelets view technology. Those HTML components are available under the `http://xmlns.jcp.org/jsf/html` XML namespace URI (Uniform Resource Identifier) which should be assigned to the "h" XML namespace prefix.

```
xmlns:h="http://xmlns.jcp.org/jsf/html"
```

The most important HTML components which should always be present in your JSF page are the `<h:head>` and `<h:body>`. Without them, JSF won't be able to auto-include any script or stylesheet resources associated with a particular component. For example, the `<h:commandButton>`, which generates a HTML submit button, requires for its Ajax functionality the `jsf.js` script file to be included in the HTML document.

- `<h:commandButton>`, generates a HTML submit button.

- `<h:commandButton>`, can optionally contain Ajax functionality.

- The Ajax functionality requires a jsf.js script file in the HTML document.

The renderer of that component will automatically take care of that, but that would only work if `<h:head>` is present. The `<h:body>` is slightly less important here, but there may exist components which need to add a script to the end of the HTML body, such as the `<f:websocket>`. In other words, the most minimal and HTML5-valid JSF page would look as follows:

```
<!DOCTYPE html>
<html lang="en"
    xmlns="http://www.w3.org/1999/xhtml"
    xmlns:h="http://xmlns.jcp.org/jsf/html"
>
    <h:head>
        <title>Title</title>
    </h:head>
    <h:body>
        ...
    </h:body>
</html>
```

The generated HTML response, as you can inspect by right- clicking *View page source* in the average web browser, should look as follows:

```
<!DOCTYPE html>
<html lang="en" xmlns="http://www.w3.org/1999/xhtml">
    <head>
        <title>Title</title>
    </head>
    <body>
        ...
    </body>
</html>
```

You see, JSF basically replaces all components in the page by their generated HTML output. As discussed previously, JSF provides an extensive set of standard HTML components. Table 3-1 provides an overview.

*Table 3-1.*  *Standard HTML Components Provided by JSF*

| Component tag | Component superclass | Value type | HTML output | Since |
|---|---|---|---|---|
| <h:body> | UIOutput | - | <body> | 2.0 |
| <h:button> | UIOutcomeTarget | String | <button onclick=window. location> | 2.0 |
| <h:column> | UIColumn | - | <td> (for h:dataTable) | 1.0 |
| <h:commandButton> | UICommand | String | <input type=submit> | 1.0 |
| <h:commandLink> | UICommand | String | <a onclick=form.submit()> | 1.0 |
| <h:commandScript> | UICommand | - | <script> (function to submit a form) | 2.3 |
| <h:dataTable> | UIData | Object[] | <table> (dynamic) | 1.0 |
| <h:doctype> | UIOutput | - | <!DOCTYPE> | 2.0 |
| <h:form> | UIForm | - | <form method=post> | 1.0 |
| <h:graphicImage> | UIGraphic | - | <img src> | 1.0 |
| <h:head> | UIOutput | - | <head> | 2.0 |
| <h:inputFile> | UIInput | Part | <input type=file> | 2.2 |
| <h:inputHidden> | UIInput | Object | <input type=hidden> | 1.0 |
| <h:inputSecret> | UIInput | Object | <input type=password> | 1.0 |
| <h:inputText> | UIInput | Object | <input type=text> | 1.0 |
| <h:inputTextarea> | UIInput | Object | <textarea> | 1.0 |
| <h:link> | UIOutcomeTarget | String | <a href> | 2.0 |
| <h:message> | UIMessage | - | <span> (if necessary) | 1.0 |
| <h:messages> | UIMessages | - | <ul> | 1.0 |
| <h:messages layout=table> | UIMessages | - | <table> | 1.0 |
| <h:outputFormat> | UIOutput | Object | <span> (if necessary) | 1.0 |
| <h:outputLabel> | UIOutput | String | <label> | 1.0 |
| <h:outputText> | UIOutput | Object | <span> (if necessary) | 1.0 |

(*continued*)

**Table 3-1.** (*continued*)

| Component tag | Component superclass | Value type | HTML output | Since |
|---|---|---|---|---|
| <h:outputScript> | UIOutput | - | <script> | 2.0 |
| <h:outputStylesheet> | UIOutput | - | <link rel=stylesheet> | 2.0 |
| <h:panelGrid> | UIPanel | - | <table> (static) | 1.0 |
| <h:panelGroup> | UIPanel | - | <span> | 1.0 |
| <h:panelGroup layout=block> | UIPanel | - | <div> | 1.2 |
| <h:selectBooleanCheckbox> | UIInput | Boolean | <input type=checkbox> | 1.0 |
| <h:selectManyCheckbox> | UIInput | Object[] | <table><input type=checkbox>* | 1.0 |
| <h:selectManyListbox> | UIInput | Object[] | <select multiple size=n><option>* | 1.0 |
| <h:selectManyMenu> | UIInput | Object[] | <select multiple size=1><option>* | 1.0 |
| <h:selectOneListbox> | UIInput | Object | <select size=n><option>* | 1.0 |
| <h:selectOneMenu> | UIInput | Object | <select size=1><option>* | 1.0 |
| <h:selectOneRadio> | UIInput | Object | <table><input type=radio>* | 1.0 |
| <h:selectOneRadio group> | UIInput | Object | <input type=radio name=group> | 2.3 |

The "Component superclass" column specifies the most important UIComponent superclass the component extends from. You must interpret the specified class to be from the javax.faces.component package.

The "Value type" column specifies the supported type of the model value behind the component's value attribute, if it has any. If the value type is String, it means that only the model value's toString() outcome will be used as value of the component, generally in components which would render it as some sort of label. If it's Object, it means that it supports any kind of value, generally in components which would render it as text or parse it as input value, if necessary with help of an implicit or explicit Converter. If the value type is Object[],it means that it requires an array or collection of objects as model value, generally in data and multi-selection input components, if necessary with an implicit or explicit `Converter`.

There are two specialized input components. The `<h:inputFile>` binds the uploaded file to a `javax.servlet.http.Part` property and doesn't support outputting it—for security reasons—and the `<h:selectBooleanCheckbox>` which binds the checked value to a `boolean` property. Those two input components don't support a `Converter` and therefore don't support any other model value type.

The "HTML output" column specifies the minimum generated HTML output. If the HTML output says "if necessary," then it means that the specified HTML element is only emitted when the component has any attribute specified that requires being outputted as a HTML element attribute, such as `id`, `styleClass`, `onclick`, etc. That is, a component can have attributes that don't end up in the generated HTML output at all, such as `binding`, `rendered`, `converter`, etc. If a component can have multiple HTML element representations, then that's usually controlled by the `layout` attribute as you can see with `<h:messages>` and `<h:panelGroup>`. If the HTML output contains "*" (an asterisk), then it means that the component may emit zero or more of the specified nested HTML elements.

The "Since" column indicates the first JSF version the HTML component was available in. At the time this book was written, the following JSF versions were available: 1.0 (March 2004), 1.1 (May 2004), 1.2 (May 2006), 2.0 (July 2009), 2.1 (November 2010), 2.2 (March 2013), and 2.3 (March 2017).

The individual HTML components are detailed in Chapters 4 and 6.

# Standard Core Tags

Next to the standard HTML components, JSF also provides a set of "core" tags. Those are essentially "helper" tags which allow you to declaratively configure one or more target HTML components by either nesting in them or wrapping around them. Those core tags are available under the `http://xmlns.jcp.org/jsf/core` XML namespace URI which should be assigned to the `"f"` XML namespace prefix.

```
xmlns:f="http://xmlns.jcp.org/jsf/core"
```

Technically, those tags are intended to be reusable on non-HTML components. JSF offers the possibility of attaching a different render kit to the component tree which doesn't generate HTML output but a different markup—hence the different XML namespace. Table 3-2 provides an overview.

*Table 3-2.* *Standard Core Tags Provided by JSF*

| Core tag | Creates/handles | Target component | Since |
|---|---|---|---|
| <f:actionListener> | javax.faces.event.ActionListener | ActionSource | 1.0 |
| <f:ajax> | javax.faces.component.behavior.AjaxBehavior | ClientBehaviorHolder(s) | 2.0 |
| <f:attribute> | UIComponent#getAttributes() | UIComponent | 1.0 |
| <f:attributes> | UIComponent#getAttributes() | UIComponent | 2.2 |
| <f:convertDateTime> | javax.faces.convert.DateTimeConverter | (Editable)ValueHolder | 1.0 |
| <f:convertNumber> | javax.faces.convert.NumberConverter | (Editable)ValueHolder | 1.0 |
| <f:converter> | javax.faces.convert.Converter | (Editable)ValueHolder | 1.0 |
| <f:event> | javax.faces.event.ComponentSystemEvent | UIComponent | 2.0 |
| <f:facet> | UIComponent#getFacets() | UIComponent | 1.0 |
| <f:importConstants> | javax.faces.component.UIImportConstants | UIViewRoot (metadata) | 2.3 |
| <f:loadBundle> | java.util.ResourceBundle | UIViewRoot | 1.0 |
| <f:metadata> | javax.faces.view.ViewMetadata | UIViewRoot | 2.0 |
| <f:param> | javax.faces.component.UIParameter | UIComponent | 1.0 |
| <f:passthroughAttribute> | UIComponent#getPassthroughAttributes() | UIComponent | 2.2 |
| <f:passthroughAttributes> | UIComponent#getPassthroughAttributes() | UIComponent | 2.2 |
| <f:phaseListener> | javax.faces.event.PhaseListener | UIViewRoot | 1.0 |
| <f:selectItem> | javax.faces.component.UISelectItem | UISelectOne/UISelectMany | 1.0 |
| <f:selectItems> | javax.faces.component.UISelectItems | UISelectOne/UISelectMany | 1.0 |

*(continued)*

*Table 3-2.* (*continued*)

| Core tag | Creates/handles | Target component | Since |
|---|---|---|---|
| <f:setPropertyActionListener> | javax.faces.event.ActionListener | ActionSource | 1.0 |
| <f:subview> | javax.faces.component.NamingContainer | UIComponents | 1.0 |
| <f:validateBean> | javax.faces.validator.BeanValidator | UIForm | 2.0 |
| <f:validateDoubleRange> | javax.faces.validator.DoubleRangeValidator | EditableValueHolder | 1.0 |
| <f:validateLength> | javax.faces.validator.LengthValidator | EditableValueHolder | 1.0 |
| <f:validateLongRange> | javax.faces.validator.LongRangeValidator | EditableValueHolder | 1.0 |
| <f:validateRegex> | javax.faces.validator.RegexValidator | EditableValueHolder | 2.0 |
| <f:validateRequired> | javax.faces.validator.RequiredValidator | EditableValueHolder | 2.0 |
| <f:validateWholeBean> | javax.faces.validator.BeanValidator | UIForm | 2.3 |
| <f:validator> | javax.faces.validator.Validator | EditableValueHolder | 1.0 |
| <f:valueChangeListener> | javax.faces.event.ValueChangeListener | EditableValueHolder | 1.0 |
| <f:view> | javax.faces.component.UIViewRoot | UIComponents | 1.0 |
| <f:viewAction> | javax.faces.component.UIViewAction | UIViewRoot (metadata) | 2.2 |
| <f:viewParam> | javax.faces.component.UIViewParameter | UIViewRoot (metadata) | 2.0 |
| <f:websocket> | javax.faces.component.UIWebsocket | UIViewRoot (body resource) | 2.3 |

Historically, there's one more, the `<f:verbatim>`, but this was targeted to the since JSF 2.0 deprecated JSP (Java Server Pages) view technology and is hence also deprecated since JSF 2.0.

The "Creates/handles" column specifies the thing which the core tag creates or handles on the specified target component.

The "Target component" column specifies the target component superclass or interface supported by the core tag. You must interpret the specified class or interface to be from the `javax.faces.component` package. If the target component is optionally pluralized as in `UIComponent(s)`, then it means that the core tag can either be nested in the target component or wrapped in one or more target components. If the target component is explicitly pluralized as in `UIComponents`, then it means that the core tag can only wrap one or more target components and thus not be nested.

As to target component interfaces, the `ActionSource` interface is implemented by `UICommand` components. The `ClientBehaviorHolder` interface is implemented by `UIForm`, `UIInput`, `UICommand`, `UIData`, `UIOutput`, `UIPanel`, and `UIOutcomeTarget` components. The `ValueHolder` interface is implemented by `UIOutput` and `UIInput` components. The `EditableValueHolder` interface is implemented by `UIInput` components. Based on Table 3-1 you should be able to derive the actual HTML components from them.

The "Since" column indicates the first JSF version the core tag was available in. At the time this book was written, the following JSF versions were available: 1.0 (March 2004), 1.1 (May 2004), 1.2 (May 2006), 2.0 (July 2009), 2.1 (November 2010), 2.2 (March 2013), and 2.3 (March 2017).

Most of the individual core tags are detailed in separate chapters.

# Life Cycle

JSF has a very well defined life cycle. It is broken down into six phases. Each of those phases runs the HTTP request through the component tree, performs operations on it, and fires component system events. A brief description was already given in the introduction of this chapter, along with a diagram (Figure 3-1). The following sections describe each of the phases of the life cycle.

# Restore View Phase (First Phase)

First create the UIViewRoot instance and set its properties such as locale from any <f:view> tag. The component tree is at that moment still empty. Only when the current request is a postback request, or when the view has a <f:metadata> with children, then build the full component tree based on the view definition. Basically, a specific UIComponent subclass will be instantiated based on the component tag defined in the view and populated with all attributes defined in the view and then UIComponent#setParent() will be invoked, passing the actual parent component.

The UIComponent#setParent() method will first check if there isn't already an existing parent, and if so, it will fire the PreRemoveFromViewEvent on the old parent. Then, when the new parent has been set, and thus the current component has become part of the component tree, it will fire the PostAddToViewEvent with the current component.

If the current request is a postback request, then it will restore the "view state" identified by the javax.faces.ViewState request parameter into the freshly built component tree. After that, the PostRestoreStateEvent is explicitly fired for each component in the tree, even when the component tree has actually not been built or restored. In other words, even when it's not a postback request, that event is fired. You'd better reinterpret that event as "PostRestoreViewPhase". In case, during the PostRestoreStateEvent, you're actually interested in whether it's a postback request, you should consult the FacesContext#isPostback() as well.

By the end of the phase, if the full component tree has actually not been built, then immediately advance to the render response phase (sixth phase), thereby skipping any phase in between.

# Apply Request Values Phase (Second Phase)

The UIComponent#processDecodes() will be invoked on UIViewRoot. The processDecodes() method will first invoke processDecodes() on each child and facet and then invoke UIComponent#decode() on itself. Finally, invoke UIViewRoot#broadCastEvents() to fire any FacesEvent queued for the current phase. The default JSF API (application programming interface) doesn't offer such events, but developers can create and queue their own.

The default implementation of the decode() method will delegate to the Renderer#decode() method. In the decode() method of either the component or the renderer, the implementation has the opportunity to extract the submitted value from the request parameter and set it as an internal property. From the standard HTML component set, the only components that do that are the HTML form-based components deriving from UIForm, UIInput, and UICommand. The UIForm component will invoke UIForm#setSubmitted() with true. The UIInput component will invoke UIInput#setSubmittedValue() with the request parameter value. The UICommand component will queue the ActionEvent for the invoke application phase (fifth phase).

## Process Validations Phase (Third Phase)

The UIComponent#processValidators() will be invoked on UIViewRoot. The processValidators() method will basically first fire PreValidateEvent for the current component, then invoke processValidators() on each child and facet, and then invoke PostValidateEvent for the current component. Finally, it will invoke UIViewRoot#broadCastEvents() to fire any FacesEvent queued for the current phase, which is usually an instance of ValueChangeEvent.

From the standard HTML component set, only UIInput components behave differently here. Right before calling processValidators() on each child and facet, they will first invoke UIInput#validate() on itself. If there's a submitted value set during the apply request values phase (second phase), then they will first invoke Converter#getAsObject() on any attached Converter. When it doesn't throw ConverterException, then they will invoke Validator#validate() on all attached Validator instances, regardless of whether any of them has thrown ValidatorException.

When no ConverterException or ValidatorException was thrown, then UIInput#setValue() will be invoked with the converted and validated value and the UIInput#isLocalValueSet() flag will return true and UIInput#setSubmittedValue() will be invoked with null.

When any ConverterException or ValidatorException was thrown, then UIInput#setValid() will be invoked with false and the message of the exception will be added to the faces context via FacesContext#addMessage(). Finally, when UIInput#isValid() returns false, then FacesContext#setValidationFailed() will be invoked with true.

By the end of the phase, when FacesContext#isValidationFailed() returns true, immediately advance to the render response phase (sixth phase), thereby skipping any phase in between.

# Update Model Values Phase (Fourth Phase)

UIComponent#processUpdates() will be invoked on UIViewRoot. The processUpdates() method will in turn invoke the processUpdates() method on each child and facet. Finally, it will invoke UIViewRoot#broadCastEvents() to fire any FacesEvent queued for the current phase. The default JSF API doesn't offer such events, but developers can create and queue their own.

Also during this phase, from the standard HTML component set, only UIInput components have a hook here. After calling processUpdates() on each child and facet, they will invoke UIInput#updateModel() on itself. When both the UIInput#isValid() and UIInput#isLocalValueSet() return true, they will invoke the setter method behind the value attribute with getLocalValue() as argument and immediately invoke UIInput#setValue() with null and clear out the UIInput#isLocalValueSet() flag.

When a RuntimeException is thrown here, usually caused by a bug in the setter method itself, it will invoke UIInput#setValid() with false and queue the UpdateModelException and immediately advance to the render response phase (sixth phase), thereby skipping any phase in between.

# Invoke Application Phase (Fifth Phase)

The UIViewRoot#processApplication() will be invoked. This method will in turn invoke the UIViewRoot#broadCastEvents() to fire any FacesEvent queued for the current phase, which is usually an instance of AjaxBehaviorEvent or ActionEvent. Note that the processApplication() method is only defined on the UIViewRoot class and does not traverse the component tree.

# Render Response Phase (Sixth Phase)

When the component tree is still empty, i.e., when the request is not a postback request, or when the view has no <f:metadata> with children, or when the developer has in the meanwhile explicitly invoked FacesContext#setViewRoot() with its own instance, then build the full component tree based on the view definition. When the component tree is present, first fire the PreRenderViewEvent for the UIViewRoot, then invoke UIComponent#encodeAll() on the UIViewRoot, and then invoke PostRenderViewEvent for the UIViewRoot.

The UIComponent#encodeAll() method will basically first invoke encodeBegin() on itself, then if UIComponent#getRendersChildren() returns true, it will invoke encodeChildren() on itself, or else invoke UIComponent#encodeAll() on each child, and then invoke encodeEnd() on itself. This all happens only if UIComponent#isRendered() returns true—that is, when the rendered attribute of the component tag doesn't evaluate to false.

The default implementation of the encodeBegin() method will first fire the PreRenderComponentEvent for the current component and then delegate to Renderer#encodeBegin(). The default implementation of the encodeChildren() method will delegate to Renderer#encodeChildren(). The default implementation of the encodeEnd() method will delegate to Renderer#encodeEnd(). If the component has no renderer attached, that is, when UIComponent#getRendererType() returns null, then no HTML output will be rendered to the response.

In the encodeBegin() method, the component or the renderer implementation has the opportunity to write the opening HTML element and all of its attributes to the response. In the encodeChildren() method the component or the renderer implementation has the opportunity to decorate or override the rendering of the children if necessary. In the encodeEnd() method the component or the renderer implementation has the opportunity to write the closing HTML tag. Writing to the response happens with the response writer as available by FacesContext#getResponseWriter().

For any mentioned XxxEvent class which has been fired in any phase, if any listener method throws javax.faces.event.AbortProcessingException,[1] then the currently running phase will be immediately aborted and the life cycle will immediately advance to the render response phase (sixth phase), thereby skipping any phase in between.

# Ajax Life Cycle

The life cycle is almost identical during Ajax requests. Only the second, third, fourth, and sixth phases are slightly different. The processDecodes(), processValidators(), and processUpdates() methods will only be invoked on the UIViewRoot itself and any component covered by the component search expression specified in <f:ajax execute>. And, the encodeAll() method will only be invoked on the UIViewRoot itself

---

[1]https://javaee.github.io/javaee-spec/javadocs/javax/faces/event/AbortProcessingException.html.

and any component covered by the component search expression specified in <f:ajax render>. Read more on search expressions in Chapter 12.

Note thus that there would be no difference in the Ajax life cycle when the component search expression contains the "@all" keyword. In other words, use "@all" with care. There are no sensible real-world use cases for <f:ajax execute="@all">. On the HTML side, it's not possible to submit multiple forms at once. Only the enclosing form is submitted. The biggest value is thus <f:ajax execute="@form">. However, there is one sensible real-world use case for <f:ajax render="@all">, namely, rendering a full error page in case an exception is thrown during an Ajax request. Even then, this can only be programmatically triggered via PartialViewContext#setRenderAll(). For more detail, see Chapter 9.

# View Build Time

The "view build time" is not tied to a particular phase of the JSF life cycle. The view build time is that moment when the physical UIViewRoot instance is populated with all of its children based on the view definition.

When JSF is about to create an UIComponent instance based on the view definition, it will first check whether the binding attribute of the component representation returns a concrete UIComponent instance and, if so, then continue using it instead, or else create the UIComponent instance based on the "component type" associated with it and then invoke the setter behind the binding attribute, if any, with it. If the id attribute of the component representation in the view definition is specified, then UIComponent#setId() will be invoked with it. Finally, UIComponent#setParent() will be invoked with the parent component and then the component instance becomes physically part of the component tree. This tree will exist until the end of the render response phase (sixth phase). Then it becomes eligible for the garbage collector, along with the released faces context instance.

Effectively, UIComponent instances are thus request scoped. The binding attribute can refer a managed bean property, but as UIComponent instances are inherently request scoped, the target managed bean must be request scoped and may not be in a broader scope. This won't be checked by the JSF API, so you as the developer should make absolutely sure that you don't reference a broader scoped managed bean in the binding attribute of any component.

However, when the binding attribute references a managed bean in a broader scope than the request scope, then you're not only basically saving the entire component tree in the HTTP session in case the bean is view or session scoped, but you're also essentially sharing the entire component tree across multiple HTTP requests which are concurrently accessing the very same managed bean instance—very inefficient and thus dangerous.

The view build time can technically happen during any JSF life cycle phase. Generally, that's the restore view phase (first phase), particularly during a postback request, or when the view has `<f:metadata>` with children. It can also happen during the render response phase (sixth phase), particularly during a GET request when the view has no `<f:metadata>` with children, or when a non-redirect navigation has taken place during a postback. It will also happen when the developer programmatically invokes `Vi ewDeclarationLanguage#buildView()`, which can be implicitly done via, among others, `ViewHandler#createView()` as shown in the following action method code example which forces us to fully rebuild the current view from scratch:

```
public void rebuildCurrentView() {
    FacesContext context = FacesContext.getCurrentInstance();
    UIViewRoot currentView = context.getViewRoot();
    String viewId = currentView.getViewId();
    ViewHandler viewHandler = context.getApplication.getViewHandler();
    UIViewRoot newView = viewHandler.createView(context, viewId);
    context.setViewRoot(newView);
}
```

Do note that the view state is not per definition during the view build time restored into the component tree. The view state is only restored into the component tree during the restore view phase (first phase), and that happens after it has executed the view build time by itself. In other words, the above shown `rebuildCurrentView()` method does not restore the current view state into the newly created component tree. Programmatically restoring the view state is generally not recommended when programmatically rebuilding the view as above, as in a real-world JSF application the sole reason to rebuild the current view is usually to get rid of any changes caused by the persistent view state, and/or to re-execute any JSTL tags based on the freshly changed values in the managed bean.

# View Render Time

The "view render time" is also not tied to a particular phase of the JSF life cycle. The view render time is that moment when `UIComponent#encodeAll()` of a particular component is invoked.

True, it's by default always executed on the UIViewRoot during the render response phase (sixth phase), but this doesn't stop you from programmatically invoking it during a different phase, such as the invoke application phase (fifth phase), for example, in order to obtain the generated HTML output of an arbitrary component as a String variable.

# View State

As explained in the section "View Build Time," the UIComponent instances resembling the component tree are inherently request scoped. They are created during the view build time and they are destroyed right after the render response phase (sixth phase). Any changes to properties of the UIComponent instances, which are not referenced by an EL (Expression Language) expression, and are different from the default values, will be saved as "view state." In other words, the "view state" is very definitely not the same as the "component tree." Moreover, if the entire component tree itself would be saved in the view state, then this would result in not only an unnecessarily bloated view state but also bad application behavior as UIComponent instances are inherently not thread safe and may therefore absolutely not be shared across multiple HTTP requests.

Saving the view state happens during the view render time. Therein JSF will write out the view state to a javax.faces.ViewState hidden input field of the generated HTML representation of every JSF form. When the JSF state saving method has the default setting "server," then the hidden input value represents a unique identifier referring the serialized view state object which is stored in the HTTP session. When the JSF state saving method is explicitly set to "client" using the following web.xml context parameter, then the hidden input value itself represents the encrypted form of the serialized view state object.

```
<context-param>
    <param-name>javax.faces.STATE_SAVING_METHOD</param-name>
    <param-value>client</param-value>
</context-param>
<env-entry>
    <env-entry-name>jsf/ClientSideSecretKey</env-entry-name>
    <env-entry-type>java.lang.String</env-entry-type>
    <env-entry-value>[AES key in Base64 format]</env-entry-value>
</env-entry>
```

Note that explicitly specifying the `jsf/ClientSideSecretKey` environment entry with a fixed AES (Advanced Encryption Standard) key is mandatory in case you're running the JSF application on a cluster of servers ("cloud"), or when you'd like the view state still to be valid after a server restart. You can generate a Base64-encoded AES key yourself using the following plain Java snippet:

```
KeyGenerator keyGen = KeyGenerator.getInstance("AES");
keyGen.init(256); // Or 128 in case you don't have JCE.
byte[] rawKey = keyGen.generateKey().getEncoded();
String key = Base64.getEncoder().encodeToString(rawKey);
System.out.println(key); // Prints AES key in Base64 format.
```

The standard JSF form, as represented by `<h:form>`, submits by default using the POST method to the very same requested URI as where the JSF page containing the form is being requested. In other words, when you request a JSF page by `http://example.com/project/page.xhtml`, then it will submit to the very same `http://example.com/project/page.xhtml` URI. This is in web development terms known as "postback." When JSF needs to process an incoming postback request, then the restore view phase (first phase) will, after the view build time, extract the view state from the `javax.faces.ViewState` parameter and restore all changed properties into the newly created `UIComponent` instances of the current request so that the component tree ultimately reflects exactly the same state as it had during the view render time of the previous request.

On an average JSF web application, the majority of the saved view state is represented by internal properties of `UIComponent` instances implementing the `javax.faces.component.EditableValueHolder` interface,[2] which covers all `UIInput` components such as `<h:inputText>`. When submitting a JSF form fails with a conversion or validation error, then all changed "is valid?" states and "local value" states, which can be either the submitted string value or the already converted and validated value, will for all involved `UIInput` components be saved in the view state. This has the major advantage that that the developer doesn't need to worry about manually keeping track of them in order to re-present the submitted form with all valid and invalid values preserved to the web site user while keeping the model (the managed bean properties) completely free of those values. This is a major usability advantage for both the JSF developer and the web site user.

---

[2]`https://javaee.github.io/javaee-spec/javadocs/javax/faces/component/EditableValueHolder.html`.

The minority of the saved view state is represented by programmatic changes to the component tree hierarchy, or to component attributes. Among others, any programmatic changes to readonly, disabled, and rendered attributes are tracked in the view state so that a hacker doesn't have any chance to spoof the request in such way that those attributes flip to the wrong side so that the hacker could do potentially hazardous things. This is a major security advantage.

# View Scope

The Servlet API, which JSF, among others, is built on top of, offers three well-defined scopes: the request scope, the session scope, and the application scope. Basically, the request scope is established by storing the object of interest as an attribute of the HttpServletRequest. Equivalently, the session scope is established by storing the object of interest as an attribute of the HttpSession and the application scope is established by storing the object of interest as an attribute of the ServletContext.

JSF adds one more scope to this, the view scope. This must not be confused with the component tree itself. The component tree (the physical UIViewRoot instance) is created and destroyed during the very same HTTP request and is therefore clearly request scoped. This must also not be confused with the view state, although they are closely related.

When the end user fires a postback request on a JSF form, and the application doesn't perform any kind of navigation (i.e., the action method returns null or void), then the view state identifier will stay the same and the view scope will be prolonged to the next postback request, until the application performs an explicit navigation, or when the HTTP session expires. You can establish the view scope by storing the object of interest as an entry of UIViewRoot#getViewMap(). This is exactly where JSF stores its @ViewScoped managed beans. No, this map is not in turn stored in the view state, not even when the JSF state saving method is explicitly set to "client." The view scope is stored in the HTTP session, separate from the view state. Only the view scope identifier is stored in the view state. Only the changed attributes of the UIViewRoot instance are stored in the view state.

# Phase Events

The `javax.faces.event.PhaseListener` interface[3] can be used to listen on any phase of the JSF life cycle. This interface defines three methods: `getPhaseId()`, which should return the phase you're interested in; `beforePhase()`, which will be invoked right before the specified phase is executed; and `afterPhase()`, which will be invoked right after the specified phase is executed. In the `beforePhase()` and `afterPhase()` methods you thus have the opportunity to run some code before or after the phase specified by `getPhaseId()`.

The `javax.faces.event.PhaseId` class[4] defines a set of public constants. It still dates from JSF 1.0 which was released only a few months before Java 1.5 and hence was too late in the game in order to become a real enum. The constants are listed below with their ordinal values.

- `PhaseId.ANY_PHASE` (0)

- `PhaseId.RESTORE_VIEW` (1)

- `PhaseId.APPLY_REQUEST_VALUES` (2)

- `PhaseId.PROCESS_VALIDATIONS` (3)

- `PhaseId.UPDATE_MODEL_VALUES` (4)

- `PhaseId.INVOKE_APPLICATION` (5)

- `PhaseId.RENDER_RESPONSE` (6)

Phase listener instances can be registered in various ways. Declaratively, they can be registered application-wide via `faces-config.xml`.

```
<lifecycle>
    <phase-listener>com.example.project.YourListener</phase-listener>
</lifecycle>
```

---

[3]https://javaee.github.io/javaee-spec/javadocs/javax/faces/event/PhaseListener.html.

[4]https://javaee.github.io/javaee-spec/javadocs/javax/faces/event/PhaseId.html.

Or view-wide via `<f:phaseListener>` tag enclosed in `<f:view>`.

```
<f:view>
    <f:phaseListener type="com.example.project.YourListener" />
    ...
</f:view>
```

Programmatically, they can be added and removed application-wide via the `addPhaseListener()` and `removePhaseListener()` methods of `javax.faces.lifecycle.Lifecycle` instance.[5] However, obtaining the current `Lifecycle` instance is slightly convoluted as there's no direct getter method for that in the public JSF API (yet).

```
FacesContext context = FacesContext.getCurrentInstance();
String lifecycleId = context.getExternalContext()
    .getInitParameter(FacesServlet.LIFECYCLE_ID_ATTR);
if (lifecycleId == null) {
    lifecycleId = LifecycleFactory.DEFAULT_LIFECYCLE;
}
LifecycleFactory lifecycleFactory = (LifecycleFactory)
    FactoryFinder.getFactory(FactoryFinder.LIFECYCLE_FACTORY);
Lifecycle lifecycle = lifecycleFactory.getLifecycle(lifecycleId);
```

And they can be added and removed view-wide via the `addPhaseListener()` and `removePhaseListener()` methods of `UIViewRoot`. A concrete example of a `PhaseListener` is given in the section "Custom Component System Events."

# Component System Events

As noted in the section "Life Cycle," a bunch of component system events are fired during the life cycle. They extend from the `javax.faces.event.ComponentSystemEvent` abstract class.[6] In summary, those are

---

[5]https://javaee.github.io/javaee-spec/javadocs/javax/faces/lifecycle/Lifecycle.html.

[6]https://javaee.github.io/javaee-spec/javadocs/javax/faces/event/ComponentSystemEvent.html.

- `PreRemoveFromViewEvent`: fired when a component is about to be removed from the component tree.

- `PostAddToViewEvent`: fired when a component has been added to the component tree.

- `PostRestoreStateEvent` (read: "`PostRestoreViewEvent`"): fired for each component when the restore view phase ends. Note that this event is only fired for `UIViewRoot` when the view build time hasn't yet taken place during this phase. If the view build time has taken place during this phase, then this event is fired for any component in the tree.

- `PreValidateEvent`: fired when a component is about to process its converter and validators, and also when there are actually none.

- `PostValidateEvent`: fired when a component is finished processing its converter and validators, and also when there are actually none.

- `PreRenderViewEvent`: fired when the `UIViewRoot` is about to write HTML output to the HTTP response. Note that this is the latest possible safe moment to change the destination of the HTTP response, or to programmatically manipulate the component tree. When doing so after this moment, there's no guarantee that any programmatic changes to the response or the component tree will take place as intended, because by then the response may already be committed, or the view state may already be saved.

- `PreRenderComponentEvent`: fired when a component is about to write its HTML output to the HTTP response.

- `PostRenderViewEvent`: fired when the `UIViewRoot` is finished writing the HTML output to the HTTP response. Note that this event is new since JSF 2.3. All others are from JSF 2.0.

There are two more component system events that were left unmentioned in the section "Life Cycle."

- `PostConstructViewMapEvent`: fired when the `UIViewRoot` has just started the view scope.

- `PreDestroyViewMapEvent`: fired when the `UIViewRoot` is about to destroy the view scope.

These two are not strictly tied to the six-phase component-based life cycle and can happen basically any time during the life cycle. The PostConstructViewMapEvent is fired when the application invokes UIViewRoot#getViewMap() for the first time. By default, this happens only when the first @ViewScoped managed bean of the current view state has been created. The PreDestroyViewMapEvent is fired when the application invokes Map#clear() on the UIViewRoot#getViewMap(), which usually only happens when FacesContext#setViewRoot() is invoked while there is already an existing instance set. This will end the view scope and destroy any active @ViewScoped managed bean. Normally, this happens only when the action method has returned a non-null navigation outcome.

You can listen on any of those component system events using the javax.faces.event.ComponentSystemEventListener interface.[7] In the JSF API, the UIComponent class itself already implements ComponentSystemEventListener. This interface provides a processEvent() method with a ComponentSystemEvent argument which in turn has among others a getComponent() method returning the concrete UIComponent instance the event was fired on. The default implementation of UIComponent#processEvent() basically checks if the current event is an instance of PostRestoreStateEvent and if the binding attribute is specified, and if so, then invokes the setter method with the component instance itself as argument.

There are three ways to subscribe listeners to those component system events. The first is to declaratively use the <f:event> tag in the view. This can be attached to any component tag. One example you'll see in relatively a lot of JSF 2.0/2.1 targeted resources is the following:

```
<f:metadata>
    <f:viewParam name="id" value="#{bean.id}" />
    <f:event type="preRenderView" listener="#{bean.onload()}" />
</f:metadata>
```

where in the onload() method is often implemented as follows:

```
public void onload() {
    FacesContext context = FacesContext.getCurrentInstance();
    if (!context.isPostback() && !context.isValidationFailed()) {
        // ...
    }
}
```

---

[7]https://javaee.github.io/javaee-spec/javadocs/javax/faces/event/ComponentSystemEventListener.html.

Note that the `<f:event listener="#{bean.onload}">` by default expects a method with `ComponentSystemEvent` argument, but if you don't need it, it can be omitted for brevity and the method expression should be parenthesized, although the EL implementation may be forgiving in this.

The `<f:event type="preRenderView">` is in essence a work-around in order to be able to perform the invoke application phase upon a GET request based on model values set by the `<f:viewParam>`. This was needed because the `@PostConstruct` was unsuitable as it was invoked directly after bean's construction but far before the model values were updated. Since JSF 2.2 with its new `<f:viewAction>`, this `<f:event>` trick is not needed any more:

```
<f:metadata>
    <f:viewParam name="id" value="#{bean.id}" />
    <f:viewAction action="#{bean.onload}" />
</f:metadata>
```

where in the `onload()` method is just implemented as follows:

```
public void onload() {
    // ...
}
```

Another real-world example of `<f:event>` is to have a `@PostConstruct`-like behavior in the backing component of a composite component wherein you can safely perform any necessary initialization based on its attributes.

```
<cc:interface componentType="someComposite">
    ...
</cc:interface>
<cc:implementation>
    <f:event type="postAddToView" listener="#{cc.init()}" />
    ...
    #{cc.someInitializedValue}
</cc:implementation>
```

and wherein the init() method of the SomeComposite class looks as follows:

```
private Object someInitializedValue; // +getter

public void init() {
    Map<String, Object> attributes = getAttributes();
    someInitializedValue = initializeItBasedOn(attributes);
}
```

The second way is to programmatically use UIComponent#subscribeToEvent() in Java code. This allows you to conditionally subscribe a component system event listener on an existing component. It is important to keep in mind that a component system event listener is saved in the view state. In other words, it's restored in the component instance during the restore view phase of the subsequent postback request. Keep this in mind when using UIComponent#ubscribeToEvent(); otherwise you may end up subscribing the very same listener multiple times. The JSF implementation Mojarra has an internal guard against it, provided that the equals() method of the listener implementation is correctly implemented, but MyFaces doesn't have a guard here because the JSF specification doesn't say so (yet).

This all makes it a little complicated to correctly register a component system event listener programmatically for a specific component. If it's an existing component, you'd better use <f:event> instead, or if it's a custom component, you'd better use @ListenerFor annotation, which is actually the third way. Below is a kickoff example of correctly registering a component system event listener programmatically, provided that YourListener class has its equals() and hashCode() methods correctly implemented, and that it implements Serializable or Externalizable or javax.faces.component. StateHolder so that it can be saved correctly in view state.

```
Class<PreRenderViewEvent> event = PreRenderViewEvent.class;
ComponentSystemEventListener listener = new YourListener();

List<SystemEventListener> existingListeners =
    component.getListenersForEventClass(event);

if (existingListeners != null && !existingListeners.contains(listener)) {
    component.subscribeToEvent(event, listener);
}
```

Yes, that `null` check is necessary. The `UIComponent#getListenersForEventClass()` isn't specified to return an empty list instead. All in all, this is clearly not a carefully thought out API. You'd better use `<f:event>` or `@ListenerFor` instead to avoid dirty code and confusion.

As previously stated, the third way is declaratively to use the `@ListenerFor` annotation. You can put this annotation only on a `UIComponent` or `Renderer` class. You can't put this annotation on a backing bean class. For that, you should use `<f:event>` instead. The `@ListenerFor` annotation takes the target event(s) as value. The concrete `ComponentSystemEventListener` instance is the `UIComponent` instance itself. If the annotation is declared on a `Renderer` class, then the target component is the `UIComponent` instance whose `UIComponent#getRendererType()` refers the particular `Renderer` class. The following example shows it for a custom component `YourComponent`:

```
@FacesComponent("project.YourComponent")
@ListenerFor(systemEventClass=PostAddToViewEvent.class)
public class YourComponent extends UIComponentBase {

    @Override
    public void processEvent(ComponentSystemEvent event) {
        if (event instanceof PostAddToViewEvent) {
            // ...
        }
        else {
            super.processEvent(event);
        }
    }

    // ...
}
```

Yes, that `instanceof` check is necessary. As noted in the section "Life Cycle," the `PostRestoreStateEvent` is by default explicitly fired for any component in the tree. The `super.processEvent(event)` call is necessary in case this component has the `binding` attribute specified; that is, the default `UIComponent#processEvent()` implementation calls during `PostRestoreStateEvent` the setter method behind the binding attribute.

# Custom Component System Events

You can create your own ComponentSystemEvent types. Basically all you need to do is to extend from the ComponentSystemEvent abstract class and declare the @NamedEvent annotation on it and finally invoke Application#publishEvent() at the desired moment.

Imagine that you want to create a custom component system event which is fired before the invoke application phase (fifth phase), a PreInvokeApplicationEvent. The custom event looks as follows:

```
@NamedEvent(shortName="preInvokeApplication")
public class PreInvokeApplicationEvent extends ComponentSystemEvent {
    public PreInvokeApplicationEvent(UIComponent component) {
        super(component);
    }
}
```

And here's how you can use a PhaseListener to publish it.

```
public class PreInvokeApplicationListener implements PhaseListener {

    @Override
    public PhaseId getPhaseId() {
        return PhaseId.INVOKE_APPLICATION;
    }

    @Override
    public void beforePhase(PhaseEvent event) {
        FacesContext context = FacesContext.getCurrentInstance();
        context.getApplication().publishEvent(context,
            PreInvokeApplicationEvent.class, context.getViewRoot());
    }

    @Override
    public void afterPhase(PhaseEvent event) {
        // NOOP.
    }
}
```

After registering this phase listener in `faces-config.xml`, you can use `<f:event>` or `@ListenerFor` to listen on this event. One real-world example would be nested in the `<f:view>` or a master template, or in a particular `<h:form>`, so that you don't need to copy/paste the very same `<f:actionListener>` over multiple `UICommand` components in template clients or forms.

```
<f:event type="preInvokeApplication"
         listener="#{bean.prepareInvokeApplication}" />
```

# JSTL Core Tags

If you have ever developed with JSP, then you'll most likely have stumbled upon JSTL tags. In Facelets, however, only a limited subset of JSTL tags is reincarnated. They are `<c:if>`, `<c:choose><c:when><c:otherwise>`, `<c:forEach>`, `<c:set>`, and `<c:catch>`. Essentially, the XML namespace and tag names are identical to those from JSP, but they are completely rewritten for Facelets.

This group of tags is formally called "JSTL core Facelets tag library" instead of "JSTL core JSP tag library" and is also documented separately from JSP.[8] Those JSTL tags are available under the `http://xmlns.jcp.org/jsp/jstl/core` XML namespace URI which should be assigned to the `"c"` XML namespace prefix.

```
xmlns:c="http://xmlns.jcp.org/jsp/jstl/core"
```

Yes, astonishingly with `"/jsp"` path in the URI. Historically, the predecessor of Facelets in JSF 2.0 had those JSTL tags also implemented, but it didn't use the namespace URI as in the more recent JSTL 1.1 specification. Instead, it used the namespace URI as in the JSTL 1.0 specification: `http://java.sun.com/jstl/core`. However, this was "rectified" for Facelets in JSF 2.0. In my humble opinion, this is outright confusing as the JSTL 1.1 XML namespace URI suggests that those are actually JSP tags and not Facelets tags. But it is what it is.

The technical reason behind the original change of the JSTL namespace URI is the migration of EL from JSTL to JSP. It was introduced in JSTL 1.0 and worked only in JSTL tags and thus not outside JSTL tags. JSP 2.0 wanted to make use of the potential of EL as well and so it was migrated from JSTL to JSP. JSTL 1.1 thus shipped without EL

---

[8]https://javaserverfaces.github.io/docs/2.3/vdldocs/facelets/c/tld-summary.html.

and wasn't backward- compatible with JSTL 1.0 any more—hence the namespace URI change to distinguish this.

JSTL tags have a different life cycle than JSF's standard HTML components. JSTL tags already run directly during the view build time while JSF is busy building the component tree based on the view definition. JSTL tags don't end up in the JSF component tree. In other words, you can use JSTL tags to control the flow of building of the JSF component tree.

Note that using JSTL to control the component tree building isn't as easily possible as using JSF on JSP instead of Facelets. That is, JSTL tags for JSP can only recognize JSP-specific ${} expressions and not JSF-specific #{} expressions. This means that JSTL tags in JSP can't recognize JSF managed beans if they aren't yet created by JSF at that moment, and that JSF components can't access the var attribute of a <c:forEach>. In Facelets, the JSTL tags are thus retrofitted so that they support the #{} expressions. This makes them very powerful.

When developing JSF pages with JSTL tags the most important thing that you need to keep in mind is that they run during the view build time and that they don't participate in the JSF life cycle. Below I have demonstrated the most important differences between a JSTL tag and its JSF/Facelets counterpart.

### <c:forEach> versus <ui:repeat>

Following is a <c:forEach> example iterating over a List<Item> with three instances of an example Item entity having id and value properties:

```
<c:forEach items="#{bean.items}" var="item">
    <h:outputText id="item_#{item.id}" value="#{item.value}" />
</c:forEach>
```

During the view build time, this creates three separate <h:outputText> components in the component tree, roughly represented as follows:

```
<h:outputText id="item_1" value="#{bean.items[0].value}" />
<h:outputText id="item_2" value="#{bean.items[1].value}" />
<h:outputText id="item_3" value="#{bean.items[2].value}" />
```

In turn, they individually generate their HTML output during view render time, as follows:

```
<span id="item_1">one</span>
<span id="item_2">two</span>
<span id="item_3">three</span>
```

Do note that the `id` attribute of a JSF component is also evaluated during the view build time and thus you need to manually ensure the uniqueness of the resulting component ID. Otherwise JSF will throw an `IllegalStateException` with a message which goes like this: "Duplicate component ID found in view." The only other JSF component attribute which is also evaluated during the view build time is the `binding` attribute. If you absolutely need to bind a JSTL-generated component to a backing bean property, which is rare, then you should be specifying a unique array index, collection index, or map key. Following is an example provided that `#{bean.components}` refers an already prepared `UIComponent[]`, `List<UIComponent>`, or `Map<Long, UIComponent>` property.

```
<c:forEach items="#{bean.items}" var="item">
    <h:outputText binding="#{bean.components[item.id]}"
        id="item_#{item.id}" value="#{item.value}" />
</c:forEach>
```

The Facelets counterpart of the `<c:forEach>` is the `<ui:repeat>`. This is in essence a `UIComponent` which doesn't generate any HTML output by itself. In other words, the `<ui:repeat>` itself also ends up in the JSF component tree during the view build time, and only runs during the view render time. It basically re-renders its children during every iteration round against the currently iterated item as `var` attribute.

```
<ui:repeat id="items" value="#{bean.items}" var="item">
    <h:outputText id="item" value="#{item.value}" />
</ui:repeat>
```

During the view build time the above ends up exactly as is in the JSF component tree: a single `UIRepeat` instance with one nested `HtmlOutputText` instance whereas the `<c:forEach>` creates here three `HtmlOutputText` instances. Then, during the view render time, the very same `<h:outputText>` component is being reused to generate its HTML output based on current iteration round.

```
<span id="items:0:item">one</span>
<span id="items:1:item">two</span>
<span id="items:2:item">three</span>
```

Do note that the `<ui:repeat>` as a `NamingContainer` component already ensured the uniqueness of the client ID based on the iteration index. It's technically also not possible to reference its `var` attribute in the `id` attribute of any child component as the `var` attribute is only set during view render time while the `id` attribute is already set during view build time.

### `<c:if>/<c:choose>` versus `rendered`

Imagine that we have a custom tag file which can be used as follows:

```
<t:input type="email" id="email" label="Email" value="#{bean.email}" />
```

And the `input.xhtml` tag file contains the following Facelets markup conditionally adding different tags using a `<c:choose>` (you can also use `<c:if>` for this):

```
<c:choose>
    <c:when test="#{type eq 'password'}">
        <h:inputSecret id="#{id}" label="#{label}" value="#{value}" />
    </c:when>
    <c:when test="#{type eq 'textarea'}">
        <h:inputTextarea id="#{id}" label="#{label}" value="#{value}" />
    </c:when>
    <c:otherwise>
        <h:inputText id="#{id}" label="#{label}" value="#{value}"
            a:type="#{type}">
        </h:inputText>
    </c:otherwise>
</c:choose>
```

Note that a more elaborate example can be found in the section "Tag Files" in Chapter 7. This construct will then only create the `<h:inputText>` component in the component tree, roughly represented as follows:

```
<h:inputText id="email" label="Email" value="#{bean.email}"
    a:type="email">
</h:inputText>
```

and when using the `rendered` attribute instead of `<c:choose>` as follows:

```
<h:inputSecret id="#{id}_password" rendered="#{type eq 'password'}"
    label="#{label}" value="#{value}">
</h:inputSecret>
```

```
<h:inputTextarea id="#{id}_textarea" rendered="#{type eq 'textarea'}"
    label="#{label}" value="#{value}">
</h:inputTextarea>
<h:inputText id="#{id}_text"
    rendered="#{type ne 'password' and type ne 'textarea'}"
    label="#{label}" value="#{value}">
</h:inputText>
```

Then they will all end up in the component tree roughly as follows:

```
<h:inputSecret id="email_password" rendered="#{type eq 'password'}"
    label="Email" value="#{bean.email}">
</h:inputSecret>
<h:inputTextarea id="email_textarea" rendered="#{type eq 'textarea'}"
    label="Email" value="#{bean.email}">
</h:inputTextarea>
<h:inputText id="email_text"
    rendered="#{type ne 'password' and type ne 'textarea'}"
    label="Email" value="#{bean.email}">
</h:inputText>
```

You see, this will thus end up in an unnecessarily bloated component tree with a lot of unused components when you have many of them, particularly when the type attribute is actually static (i.e., it does not ever change, at least during the view scope). Also note that the id attribute of each component has a static suffix so that you don't end up with "Duplicate component ID found in view" exceptions.

### <c:set> versus <ui:param>

They are not interchangeable. The <c:set> sets a variable in the EL scope, which is accessible only after the tag location during the view build time, but anywhere else in the view during the view render time. The <ui:param> should only be nested in <ui:include>, <ui:decorate template>, or <ui:composition template> and sets a variable in the EL scope of the Facelets template, which is accessible only in the template itself. Older JSF versions had bugs whereby the <ui:param> variable was also available outside the Facelets template in question. This should never be relied upon.

The `<c:set>` without a `scope` attribute will behave like an alias. It does not cache the result of the EL expression in any scope. Its primary purpose is to be able to have a shortcut to a relatively long EL expression which is repeated several times in the same Facelets file. It can thus be used perfectly well inside, for example, iterating JSF components.

```
<ui:repeat value="#{bean.products}" var="product">
    <c:set var="price" value="#{product.price}" />
    #{price}
</ui:repeat>
```

It's only not suitable, for example, for calculating the sum in a loop. The following construct will never work:

```
<c:set var="total" value="#{0}" />
<ui:repeat value="#{bean.products}" var="product">
    <c:set var="total" value="#{total = total + product.price}" />
    #{product.price}
</ui:repeat>
Total price: #{total}
```

For that, use EL 3.0 stream API instead.

```
<ui:repeat value="#{bean.products}" var="product">
    #{product.price}
</ui:repeat>
Total price: #{bean.products.stream().map(product->product.price).sum()}
```

However, when you set the `scope` attribute with one of allowable values `request`, `view`, `session`, or `application`, then it will be evaluated immediately during the view build time and stored in the specified scope.

```
<c:set var="DEV"
    value="#{facesContext.application.projectStage eq 'Development'}"
    scope="application" />
```

This will be evaluated only once during the first time this view is being built and available as an EL variable #{DEV} throughout the entire application. You'd best declare such `<c:set>` in the master template file which is used by every single Facelets file in the entire application. Note that the EL variable is capitalized to conform to Java naming conventions for constants.

---

**CAVEATS**

Using JSTL tags will only lead to unexpected results when a JSTL tag attribute references an EL variable which is not available during view build time. Examples of such EL variables are those defined by `var` attribute of iterating components such as `<h:dataTable>` and `<ui:repeat>`, and those set in model by `<f:viewParam>`, `<f:viewAction>`, and `<f:event type="preRenderView">`.

In a nutshell, use JSTL tags only to control flow of JSF component tree building and use JSF UI components only to control flow of HTML output generation. In JSTL tags, do not rely on EL variables which are not available during view build time.

---

# Manipulating the Component Tree

This can be done declaratively using JSTL tags as well as programmatically using Java code. The JSTL approach has already been elaborated in the previous section. It's also possible to use Java code instead. As a precaution, this generally ends up in very verbose and hard-to-maintain code. Tree-based hierarchies in code are best readable and maintainable when using a hierarchical markup language such as XML. Facelets itself is already XML based. JSTL is also XML based and therefore seamlessly integrates in a Facelets file. JSTL is therefore the recommended approach to dynamically manipulate the component tree, rather than Java code.

The Javadoc of `javax.faces.component.UIComponent`[9] specifies when you could safely manipulate the component tree:

*Dynamically modifying the component tree can happen at any time, during and after restoring the view, but not during state saving and needs to function properly with respect to rendering and state saving.*

---

[9]https://javaee.github.io/javaee-spec/javadocs/javax/faces/component/UIComponent.
html.

In other words, the earliest moment when you can guarantee safely modifying the component tree is during the `PostAddToViewEvent` and the latest moment when you can guarantee safely modifying the component tree is during the `PreRenderViewEvent`. Any moment in between is thus also possible. Before the `PostAddToViewEvent` there's not necessarily a means of a concrete `UIViewRoot` instance. After the `PreRenderViewEvent` there's a risk that the state is already saved and you'd rather not get trapped here. In other words, manipulating the component tree during the render response phase (sixth phase) is a bad idea.

When you intend to manipulate the component tree by means of adding new components based on a Java model which is at least view scoped, then listen on the `PostAddToViewEvent` of the parent component of interest. When you intend to manipulate the component tree based on the fully built component tree by means of adding/moving/removing components, then listen on the `PreRenderViewEvent` of the `UIViewRoot`.

The following example programmatically populates a dynamic form based on a Java model during the `PostAddToViewEvent`:

```
<h:form id="dynamicFormId">
    <f:event type="postAddToView" listener="#{dynamicForm.populate}" />
</h:form>
```

wherein the #{dynamicForm} looks something like the following:

```
@Named @RequestScoped
public class DynamicForm {

    private transient UIForm form;
    private Map<String, Object> values = new HashMap<>();

    @Inject
    private FieldService fieldService;

    public void populate(ComponentSystemEvent event) {
        form = (UIForm) event.getComponent();
        List<Field> fields = fieldService.list(form.getId());
        fields.forEach(field -> field.populate(this));
    }
```

```java
public void createOutputLabel(Field field) {
    HtmlOutputLabel label = new HtmlOutputLabel();
    label.setId(field.getName() + "_l");
    label.setFor(field.getName());
    label.setValue(field.getLabel());
    form.getChildren().add(label);
}

public void createInputText(Field field) {
    HtmlInputText text = new HtmlInputText();
    text.setId(field.getName()); // Explicit ID is required!
    text.setLabel(field.getLabel());
    text.setValueExpression("value", createValueExpression(field));
    form.getChildren().add(text);
}

public void createMessage(Field field) {
    HtmlMessage message = new HtmlMessage();
    message.setId(field.getName() + "_m");
    message.setFor(field.getName());
    form.getChildren().add(message);
}

public static ValueExpression createValueExpression(Field field) {
    String el = "#{dynamicForm.values['" + field.getName() + "']}"
    FacesContext context = FacesContext.getCurrentInstance();
    ELContext elContext = context.getELContext();
    return context.getApplication().getExpressionFactory()
        .createValueExpression(elContext, el, Object.class);
}

public Map<String, Object> getValues() {
    return values;
}
}
```

and wherein the abstract class Field represents your custom model of a form field with at least type, name, and label properties and the concrete implementation of a TextField#populate() looks something like the following:

```
public void populate(DynamicFormBean form) {
    form.createOutputLabel(this);
    form.createInputText(this);
    form.createMessage(this);
}
```

Note the naming pattern of concrete UIComponent classes. For HTML components they follow exactly the convention "Html[TagName]". For the <h:inputText> that's thus HtmlInputText, and so on. The above Java example will basically create the following XML representation:

```
<h:outputLabel id="name_l" for="name" value="Label" />
<h:inputText id="name" value="#{dynamicForm.values['name']}" />
<h:message id="name_m" for="name" />
```

It only does that quite verbosely. Essentially, you're here reinventing the job of Facelets. There's really nothing which is impossible using XML and only possible in Java. As long as you understand how you can use JSTL for this:

```
<h:form id="dynamicFormId">
    <c:forEach items="#{dynamicForm.fields}" var="field">
        <t:field type="#{field.type}"
            id="#{field.name}" label="#{field.label}"
            value="#{dynamicForm.values[field.name]}">
        </t:field>
    </c:forEach>
</h:form>
```

wherein the #{dynamicForm} instead looks something like the following:

```
@Named @RequestScoped
public class DynamicForm {

    private List<Field> fields;
    private Map<String, Object> values = new HashMap<>();
```

```
@Inject
public FieldService fieldService;

public List<Field> getFields() {
    if (fields = null) {
        FacesContext context = FacesContext.getCurrentInstance();
        UIComponent form = UIComponent.getCurrentComponent(context);
        fields = fieldService.list(form.getId());
    }
    return fields;
}

public Map<String, Object> getValues() {
    return values;
}
}
```

You see, there is no need to mess with manually creating and populating UIComponent instances. Facelets does that all for you based on simple XML. The <t:field> can be found in the section "Tag Files" in Chapter 7.

# CHAPTER 4

# Form Components

These are the most important components of the standard JSF (JavaServer Faces) component set. Without them, JSF wouldn't have been very useful in the first place. When using plain HTML elements instead of JSF components, you'd end up polluting the controller with code to manually apply, convert, and validate submitted values; to update the model with those values; and to figure out the action method to be invoked. That's exactly the hard work JSF should take off your hands as being a component-based MVC (Model-View-Controller) framework for HTML form-based web applications.

## Input, Select, and Command Components

All input components extend from the UIInput superclass. All selection components extend from a subclass thereof, which can be UISelectBoolean, UISelectOne, or UISelectMany. (See Chapter 3, Table 3-1, for a comprehensive list of standard JSF components.) All input and select components implement the EditableValueHolder interface which allows attaching a Converter, Validator, and ValueChangeListener. All command components extend from the UICommand superclass and implement the ActionSource interface which allows defining one or more managed bean methods which should be invoked during the invoke application phase (fifth phase). They can have only one "action" method and multiple "action listener" methods.

HTML requires all input, select, and command elements to be nested in a form element. The standard JSF component set offers only one such component, the <h:form>, which is from the UIForm superclass. You could also use a plain HTML <form> element, but that wouldn't automatically include the mandatory javax. faces.ViewState hidden input field in the form which represents the JSF view state. The renderer of the <h:form> is the one responsible for automatically including it in every generated HTML representation of the JSF form. Without it, JSF won't recognize the request as a valid postback request. In other words, the FacesContext.

95

© Bauke Scholtz, Arjan Tijms 2018
B. Scholtz and A. Tijms, *The Definitive Guide to JSF in Java EE 8*, https://doi.org/10.1007/978-1-4842-3387-0_4

getCurrentInstance().isPostback() would return false and then JSF wouldn't even process the submitted values, let alone invoke the action method. A plain HTML <form> element in a JSF page is only useful for GET requests in combination with <f:viewParam> tags which should take care of processing the submitted input values. This will be detailed later in the section "GET Forms."

All command components have an action attribute which can be bound to a managed bean method. This method will be invoked during the invoke application phase (fifth phase), as long as there's no conversion or validation error. Conversion and validation are covered in Chapter 5, so we'll skip detailing this step here.

# Text-Based Input Components

All text-based input components have a value attribute which can be bound to a managed bean property. The getter of this property will, during the view render time, be consulted to retrieve and display any preset value. And, the setter of this property will, during the update model values phase (fourth phase) of the postback request, be invoked with the submitted and already converted and validated value, if applicable. Following is a basic usage example which demonstrates all text-based input components.

Facelets file /test.xhtml:

```
<h:form>
    <h:inputText value="#{bean.text}" />
    <h:inputSecret value="#{bean.password}" />
    <h:inputTextarea value="#{bean.message}" />
    <h:inputHidden value="#{bean.hidden}" />
    <h:commandButton value="Submit" action="#{bean.submit}" />
</h:form>
```

Backing bean class com.example.project.view.Bean:

```
@Named @RequestScoped
public class Bean {

    private String text;
    private String password;
    private String message;
    private String hidden;
```

```
    public void submit() {
        System.out.println("Form has been submitted!");
        System.out.println("text: " + text);
        System.out.println("password: " + password);
        System.out.println("message: " + message);
        System.out.println("hidden: " + hidden);
    }

    // Add/generate getters and setters for every property here.
}
```

Generated HTML output:

```
<form id="j_idt4" name="j_idt4" method="post"
    action="/project/test.xhtml"
    enctype="application/x-www-form-urlencoded">
    <input type="hidden" name="j_idt4" value="j_idt4" />
    <input type="text" name="j_idt4:j_idt5" />
    <input type="password" name="j_idt4:j_idt6" />
    <textarea name="j_idt4:j_idt7"></textarea>
    <input type="hidden" name="j_idt4:j_idt8" />
    <input type="submit" name="j_idt4:j_idt9" value="Submit" />
    <input type="hidden" name="javax.faces.ViewState"
        id="j_id1:javax.faces.ViewState:0"
        value="-4091383829147627416:3884402765892734278"
        autocomplete="off" />
</form>
```

Rendering in Chrome browser (with newlines added):

```
some text
```

```
........
```

```
some message
with a newline
```

```
Submit
```

97

You'll notice several things in the generated HTML output. Undoubtedly the first thing noticeable is that JSF has also automatically generated id and name attributes of the HTML elements, all with a j_id prefix which is defined by the public API (application programming interface) constant UIViewRoot.UNIQUE_ID_PREFIX. The "t" basically stands for "tree" and the number basically represents the position of the component in the component tree. This is thus prone to be changed whenever you add, remove, or move around components in the Facelets file. This is thus also subject to headaches when QA (quality assurance) needs to write integration tests for the web application wherein more than often the HTML element IDs need to be used.

JSF will use an autogenerated ID when it's mandatory for the functionality in order to have an id and/or a name attribute in the generated HTML output. The id attribute is mandatory in order to be able to find the HTML element by any JavaScript code which can also be autogenerated by JSF, such as functions responsible for the Ajax works. As this makes the generated HTML code rather hard to read and, frankly, ugly, we'd like to just explicitly specify the id attribute of any JSF form, input, select, and command component. This way JSF will just use it for the id and name attributes of the HTML elements instead of autogenerating one. Now, let's rewrite the Facelets file /test. xhtml for that. A good practice is to let the ID attribute of the input component match exactly the bean property name, and the ID attribute of the command component match exactly the bean method name. This would end up in more self-documenting code and generated HTML output.

```
<h:form id="form">
    <h:inputText id="text" value="#{bean.text}" />
    <h:inputSecret id="password" value="#{bean.password}" />
    <h:inputTextarea id="message" value="#{bean.message}" />
    <h:inputHidden id="hidden" value="#{bean.hidden}" />
    <h:commandButton id="submit" value="Submit"
        action="#{bean.submit}" />
</h:form>
```

Now, the generated HTML output looks as follows:

```
<form id="form" name="form" method="post" action="/project/test.xhtml"
    enctype="application/x-www-form-urlencoded">
    <input type="hidden" name="form" value="form" />
    <input id="form:text" type="text" name="form:text" />
```

```
<input id="form:password" type="password" name="form:password" />
<textarea id="form:message" name="form:message"></textarea>
<input id="form:hidden" type="hidden" name="form:hidden" />
<input id="form:submit" type="submit" name="form:submit"
    value="Submit" />
<input type="hidden" name="javax.faces.ViewState"
    id="j_id1:javax.faces.ViewState:0"
    value="-7192066430460949081:-3987350607752016894"
    autocomplete="off" />
</form>
```

That's already clearer. Note that when you explicitly set a component ID, it will always end up in the generated HTML output. The generated HTML element ID, then, represents the "client ID" which may be different from the component ID, depending on its parents. If the component has any parent which is an instance of NamingContainer interface, then the ID of the NamingContainer parent will be prepended to the client ID of the component. From the standard JSF HTML component set, only the <h:form> and <h:dataTable> are instances of NamingContainer. Others are <ui:repeat> and <f:subview>.

If you look closer at the generated HTML output, there's only one generated ID left. It's the one of the view state hidden input field, which is always j_id1. It represents the ID of the UIViewRoot instance, which by default cannot be set from a Facelets file on. When using JSF in Portlet-based web applications instead of Servlet-based web applications, it is overridable and would represent the unique name of the Portlet. In a Portlet-based web application it is possible to have multiple Portlet views in a single JSF page. In other words, a single JSF page in a Portlet-based web application can have multiple UIViewRoot instances.

Coming back to the generated HTML output, the name attribute of the HTML input element is mandatory for HTML in order to be able to send the submitted values as request parameters via HTTP. It will become the request parameter name. In any decent web browser you can inspect the request parameters in the "Network" section of the web developer's toolset, which is accessible by pressing F12 in the web browser. Figure 4-1 shows how Chrome presents the postback request after submitting the form with some values filled out, as you can see in the "Form Data" section of the figure.

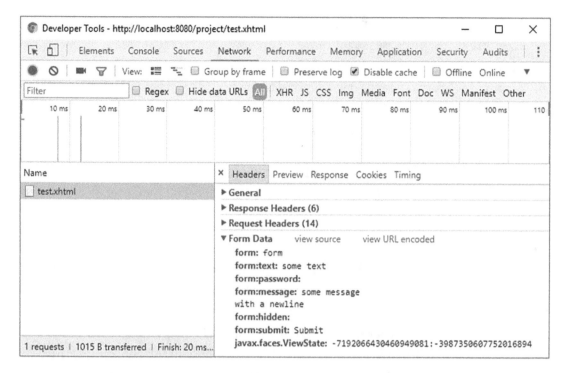

***Figure 4-1.*** *Chrome Developer Tools—Network—Headers—Form Data*

The hidden input field with the name representing the ID of the `<h:form>` will signal JSF which form exactly was submitted during the postback request. That is, a single HTML document can have multiple form elements. This way JSF can, during the apply request values phase (second phase), determine whether the current form component was actually submitted. It will cause the `UIForm#isSubmitted()` of the form component to return true. The hidden input field with the name `javax.faces.ViewState` represents the unique identifier referring the serialized view state object which is stored in the session. Both hidden input fields are automatically included by the renderer associated with the `UIForm` component. The `autocomplete="off"` on the view state hidden input field is, by the way, not a technical requirement but just a work-around against some browsers overriding it with the last known value when the back button is pressed, which may not be the correct value per se.

Our example hidden input field has an empty value. It's effectively useless in this form. Such a hidden input field is generally only useful when its value is being set by some JavaScript code which you'd like to capture in the managed bean. There's generally no point to "transferring" managed bean properties from one to the next request using hidden input fields. Instead, such properties should be assigned to a managed bean which is declared to be in a broader scope than the request scope, such as the view, flow, or session scope. This saves the effort of hassling with hidden input fields. The bean scopes will be detailed in Chapter 8.

The other request parameters should speak for themselves if you're familiar with basic HTML. They represent the name/value pairs of the involved input elements. You should be able to determine which values were actually entered in the form prior to submitting. JSF will also be able to do the same. It will traverse the component tree and use the "client ID" of the component as request parameter name to obtain the value from the request parameter map. Basically, the following code will under the hood be executed for each input component during apply request values phase (second phase). This happens in the UIInput#decode() method.

```
FacesContext context = FacesContext.getCurrentInstance();
ExternalContext externalContext = context.getExternalContext();
Map<String, String> formData = externalContext.getRequestParameterMap();

String clientId = component.getClientId(context);
String submittedValue = formData.get(clientId);
component.setSubmittedValue(submittedValue);
```

And, during the same phase, the following code is basically executed for each command component in the decode method of the renderer associated with the component:

```
if (formData.get(clientId) != null) {
    component.queueEvent(new ActionEvent(context, component));
}
```

During the process validations phase (third phase), JSF will set the submitted value of every involved input component as "local value" after performing the necessary conversion and validation if any converter or validator is registered on the component or associated bean property and has executed without errors. This happens in the UIInput#validate() method whose core logic is shown in the following code in a (very!) simplified form:

```
String submittedValue = component.getSubmittedValue();
try {
    Converter converter = component.getConverter();
    Object newValue = component.getConvertedValue(submittedValue);
    for (Validator validator : component.getValidators()) {
```

```
        validator.validate(context, component, newValue);
    }
    component.setValue(newValue);
    component.setSubmittedValue(null);
}
catch (ConverterException | ValidatorException e) {
    context.addMessage(clientId, e.getFacesMessage());
    context.validationFailed(); // Skips phases 4 and 5.
    component.setValid(false);
}
```

When there are no validation errors and the FacesContext#isValidationFailed() thus returns false, then JSF will advance to the update model values phase (fourth phase). During this phase, the "local value" of the input components will ultimately be set as managed bean properties associated with the value attribute of the input components. This will happen in the UIInput#updateModel() method which is simplified as follows:

```
ValueExpression el = component.getValueExpression("value");
if (el != null) {
    el.setValue(context.getELContext(), component.getValue());
    component.setValue(null);
}
```

The el variable basically represents the Expression Language (EL) statement as defined in the value attribute, which is, in case of our <h:inputText> example, thus #{bean.text}. The ValueExpression#setValue() will basically trigger the setter method behind this expression with the component's value. So, effectively it will execute bean.setText(component.getValue()).

Once all model values have been updated, JSF will advance to the invoke application phase (fifth phase). Any ActionEvent which is, during the apply request values phase (second phase), queued in a command component will be broadcasted. It will ultimately invoke all methods associated with the command component. In the case of our <h:commandButton> example, which has #{bean.submit} defined as an action attribute, it will invoke the Bean#submit() method. Finally, JSF will advance to the last phase, the render response phase (sixth phase), generating the HTML output and thereby invoking the getter methods in order to obtain the model values to be embedded in the HTML output.

# File-Based Input Component

Yes, there is only one file-based input component. That's the `<h:inputFile>`. It has only one additional requirement on the `<h:form>` it is being placed in, its enctype attribute has to be explicitly set to `multipart/form-data` to conform the HTML specification. This has no effect on other input components; they will continue to work just fine. It's just that the default form encoding `application/x-www-form-urlencoded` doesn't support embedding binary data. The `multipart/form-data` encoding supports this, but it is only slightly more verbose. Every request parameter value is preceded by a boundary line, a Content-Disposition header with the request parameter name, a Content Type header with the content type of the value, and two newlines. It is very inefficient compared to the default encoding wherein the URL-encoded request parameter name/value pairs are just concatenated by the & character, but it's actually the only reliable way to be able to embed files in a HTTP POST request without inducing ambiguity, particularly when uploading text files whose content coincidentally resembles name/value pairs.

The value attribute of the `<h:inputFile>` should be bound to a bean property of the `javax.servlet.http.Part` interface.

Facelets file `/test.xhtml`:

```
<h:form id="form" enctype="multipart/form-data">
    <h:inputFile id="file" value="#{bean.file}" />
    <h:commandButton id="submit" value="Submit"
        action="#{bean.submit}" />
</h:form>
```

Backing bean class `com.example.project.view.Bean`:

```
@Named @RequestScoped
public class Bean {

    private Part file;

    public void submit() throws IOException {
        System.out.println("Form has been submitted!");
        System.out.println("file: " + file);
        if (file != null) {
            System.out.println("name: " + file.getSubmittedFileName());
            System.out.println("type: " + file.getContentType());
```

```
            System.out.println("size: " + file.getSize());
            InputStream content = file.getInputStream();
            // Write content to disk or DB.
        }
    }

    // Add/generate getters and setters for every property here.
}
```

Generated HTML output:

```
<form id="form" name="form" method="post" action="/project/test.xhtml"
    enctype="multipart/form-data">
    <input type="hidden" name="form" value="form" />
    <input id="form:file" type="file" name="form:file" />
    <input id="form:submit" type="submit" name="form:submit"
        value="Submit" />
    <input type="hidden" name="javax.faces.ViewState"
        id="j_id1:javax.faces.ViewState:0"
        value="6034213708100805615:8835868421785849982"
        autocomplete="off" />
</form>
```

Rendering in Chrome browser (with newlines added):

Choose File   No file chosen

Submit

The request processing life cycle is the same as for text-based input components, except for the apply request values phase (second phase). Instead of extracting the submitted file as a request parameter in the UIInput#decode() method, the submitted file is being extracted as a request part in the renderer associated with the file input component. The default implementation basically looks as follows:

```
FacesContext context = FacesContext.getCurrentInstance();
ExternalContext ec = context.getExternalContext();
HttpServletRequest request = (HttpServletRequest) ec.getRequest();
```

```
String clientId = component.getClientId(context);
Part submittedValue = request.getPart(clientId);
component.setSubmittedValue(submittedValue);
```

# Selection Components

JSF offers a bunch of selection components of the UISelectBoolean, UISelectOne, and UISelectMany component families which all extend from UIInput. Except for the UISelectBoolean, they all expect the available items for selection to be provided via <f:selectItems> or <f:selectItem> tags nested in the selection component. The value attribute of a UISelectBoolean component can only be bound to a bean property of boolean or Boolean type and doesn't support a converter, while others support a converter. The value attribute of a UISelectOne component has to be bound to a single-value property such as String, and the value attribute of a UISelectMany component can only be bound to a multi-value property such as Collection<String> or String[].

In real-world HTML-based web applications, the <h:selectOneListbox> (single-select list box) and <h:selectManyMenu> (multi-select drop-down) aren't terribly useful. Generally the <h:selectOneMenu> (single-select drop-down) and <h:selectManyListBox> (multi-select list box) are preferred as they are more user friendly. Following is a basic usage example which demonstrates all selection components except for the aforementioned least useful ones. In case you want to use them anyway, just follow the demonstrated approach with a different tag name.

Facelets file /test.xhtml:

```
<h:form id="form">
    <h:selectBooleanCheckbox id="checked" value="#{bean.checked}" />
    <h:selectOneMenu id="oneMenu" value="#{bean.oneMenu}">
        <f:selectItems value="#{bean.availableItems}" />
    </h:selectOneMenu>
    <h:selectOneRadio id="oneRadio" value="#{bean.oneRadio}">
        <f:selectItems value="#{bean.availableItems}" />
    </h:selectOneRadio>
    <h:selectManyListbox id="manyListbox" value="#{bean.manyListbox}">
        <f:selectItems value="#{bean.availableItems}" />
    </h:selectManyListbox>
    <h:selectManyCheckbox id="manyCheckbox" value="#{bean.manyCheckbox}">
```

```
        <f:selectItems value="#{bean.availableItems}" />
    </h:selectManyCheckbox>
    <h:commandButton id="submit" value="Submit"
        action="#{bean.submit}" />
</h:form>
```

Backing bean class com.example.project.view.Bean:

```java
@Named @RequestScoped
public class Bean {

    private boolean checked;
    private String oneMenu;
    private String oneRadio;
    private List<String> manyListbox;
    private List<String> manyCheckbox;
    private List<String> availableItems;

    @PostConstruct
    public void init() {
        availableItems = Arrays.asList("one", "two", "three");
    }

    public void submit() {
        System.out.println("Form has been submitted!");
        System.out.println("checked: " + checked);
        System.out.println("oneMenu: " + oneMenu);
        System.out.println("oneRadio: " + oneRadio);
        System.out.println("manyListbox: " + manyListbox);
        System.out.println("manyCheckbox: " + manyCheckbox);
    }

    // Add/generate getters and setters for every property here.
    // Note that availableItems property doesn't need a setter.
}
```

Generated HTML output:

```
<form id="form" name="form" method="post" action="/project/test.xhtml"
    enctype="application/x-www-form-urlencoded">
    <input type="hidden" name="form" value="form" />
    <input id="form:checked" type="checkbox" name="form:checked" />
    <select id="form:oneMenu" name="form:oneMenu" size="1">
        <option value="one">one</option>
        <option value="two">two</option>
        <option value="three">three</option>
    </select>
    <table id="form:oneRadio">
        <tr>
            <td>
                <input id="form:oneRadio:0" type="radio"
                    name="form:oneRadio" value="one" />
                <label for="form:oneRadio:0"> one</label>
            </td>
            <td>
                <input id="form:oneRadio:1" type="radio"
                    name="form:oneRadio" value="two" />
                <label for="form:oneRadio:1"> two</label>
            </td>
            <td>
                <input id="form:oneRadio:2" type="radio"
                    name="form:oneRadio" value="three" />
                <label for="form:oneRadio:2"> three</label>
            </td>
        </tr>
    </table>
    <select id="form:manyListbox" name="form:manyListbox"
        multiple="multiple" size="3">
        <option value="one">one</option>
        <option value="two">two</option>
        <option value="three">three</option>
    </select>
```

```
<table id="form:manyCheckbox">
    <tr>
        <td>
            <input id="form:manyCheckbox:0" type="checkbox"
                name="form:manyCheckbox" value="one" />
            <label for="form:manyCheckbox:0"> one</label>
        </td>
        <td>
            <input id="form:manyCheckbox:1" type="checkbox"
                name="form:manyCheckbox" value="two" />
            <label for="form:manyCheckbox:1"> two</label>
        </td>
        <td>
            <input id="form:manyCheckbox:2" type="checkbox"
                name="form:manyCheckbox" value="three" />
            <label for="form:manyCheckbox:2"> three</label>
        </td>
    </tr>
</table>
<input id="form:submit" type="submit" name="form:submit"
    value="Submit" />
<input type="hidden" name="javax.faces.ViewState"
    id="j_id1:javax.faces.ViewState:0"
    value="403461711995663039:117935361680169981"
    autocomplete="off" />
</form>
```

Rendering in Chrome browser (with newlines added):

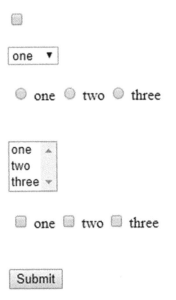

Submit

In the generated HTML output, you'll immediately notice that `<h:selectOneRadio>` and `<h:selectManyCheckbox>` generate an HTML table around the inputs. Such a markup is indeed frowned upon since Web 2.0. This is somewhat a leftover of JSF 1.0, when Web 2.0 didn't exist yet. For the `<h:selectManyCheckbox>` this could easily be worked around by using a bunch of `<h:selectBooleanCheckbox>` components in the desired HTML markup which are bound against a slightly adjusted model.

Facelets file `/test.xhtml`:

```
<h:form id="form">
    <ul>
        <ui:repeat id="many" value="#{bean.availableItems}" var="item">
            <li>
                <h:selectBooleanCheckbox id="checkbox"
                    value="#{bean.manyCheckboxMap[item]}" />
                <h:outputLabel for="checkbox" value="#{item}" />
            </li>
        </ui:repeat>
    </ul>
```

```
    <h:commandButton id="submit" value="Submit"
        actionListener="#{bean.collectCheckedValues}"
        action="#{bean.submit}" />
</h:form>
```

Backing bean class com.example.project.view.Bean:

```
@Named @RequestScoped
public class Bean {

    private List<String> manyCheckbox;
    private List<String> availableItems;
    private Map<String, Boolean> manyCheckboxMap = new LinkedHashMap<>();

    @PostConstruct
    public void init() {
        availableItems = Arrays.asList("one", "two", "three");
    }

    public void collectCheckedValues() {
        manyCheckbox = manyCheckboxMap.entrySet().stream()
            .filter(e -> e.getValue())
            .map(Map.Entry::getKey)
            .collect(Collectors.toList());
    }

    public void submit() {
        System.out.println("Form has been submitted!");
        System.out.println("manyCheckbox: " + manyCheckbox);
    }

    // Add/generate getters for availableItems and manyCheckboxMap.
    // Note that setters are not necessary for them.
}
```

Generated HTML output:

```
<form id="form" name="form" method="post" action="/project/test.xhtml"
    enctype="application/x-www-form-urlencoded">
    <input type="hidden" name="form" value="form" />
```

```
<ul>
    <li>
        <input id="form:many:0:checkbox" type="checkbox"
            name="form:many:0:checkbox" />
        <label for="form:many:0:checkbox">one</label>
    </li>
    <li>
        <input id="form:many:1:checkbox" type="checkbox"
            name="form:many:1:checkbox" />
        <label for="form:many:1:checkbox">two</label>
    </li>
    <li>
        <input id="form:many:2:checkbox" type="checkbox"
            name="form:many:2:checkbox" />
        <label for="form:many:2:checkbox">three</label>
    </li>
</ul>
<input id="form:submit" type="submit" name="form:submit"
    value="Submit" />
<input type="hidden" name="javax.faces.ViewState"
    id="j_id1:javax.faces.ViewState:0"
    value="-2278907496447873737:-4769857814543424434"
    autocomplete="off" />
</form>
```

Rendering in Chrome browser:

- ☐ one
- ☐ two
- ☐ three

Submit

That's already more Web 2.0 friendly. The bullets of the <ul> can of course be hidden by setting the CSS (Cascading Style Sheets) list-style-type property to none. Note that the actionListener attribute of the <h:commandButton> always runs before the action attribute. The same approach was not possible for <h:selectOneRadio> for a long time.

There's no such component as <h:radioButton> or anything like that. Solutions were sought in third-party component libraries such as PrimeFaces. Since JSF 2.2 this could be tricked with the new "pass-through elements" and "pass-through attributes" feature on plain HTML <input type="radio"> elements.[1] Only since JSF 2.3 has it been natively possible with help of the new group attribute which basically represents the same as the name attribute of the plain HTML <input type="radio"> element.

Facelets file /test.xhtml:

```
<h:form id="form">
    <ul>
        <ui:repeat id="one" value="#{bean.availableItems}" var="item">
            <li>
                <h:selectOneRadio id="radio" group="groupName"
                    value="#{bean.oneRadio}">
                    <f:selectItem itemValue="#{item}" />
                </h:selectOneRadio>
                <h:outputLabel for="radio" value="#{item}" />
            </li>
        </ui:repeat>
    </ul>
    <h:commandButton id="submit" value="Submit"
        action="#{bean.submit}" />
</h:form>
```

Backing bean class com.example.project.view.Bean:

```
@Named @RequestScoped
public class Bean {

    private String oneRadio;
    private List<String> availableItems;

    @PostConstruct
    public void init() {
        availableItems = Arrays.asList("one", "two", "three");
    }
```

---

[1]http://balusc.omnifaces.org/2015/10/custom-layout-with-hselectoneradio-in.html.

```
    public void submit() {
        System.out.println("Form has been submitted!");
        System.out.println("oneRadio: " + oneRadio);
    }

    // Add/generate getters and setters for every property here.
    // Note that availableItems property doesn't need a setter.
}
```

Generated HTML output:

```
<form id="form" name="form" method="post" action="/project/test.xhtml"
    enctype="application/x-www-form-urlencoded">
    <input type="hidden" name="form" value="form" />
    <ul>
        <li>
            <input type="radio" id="form:one:0:radio"
                name="form:groupName" value="form:one:0:radio:one" />
            <label for="form:one:0:radio">one</label>
        </li>
        <li>
            <input type="radio" id="form:one:1:radio"
                name="form:groupName" value="form:one:1:radio:two" />
            <label for="form:one:1:radio">two</label>
        </li>
        <li>
            <input type="radio" id="form:one:2:radio"
                name="form:groupName" value="form:one:2:radio:three" />
            <label for="form:one:2:radio">three</label>
        </li>
    </ul>
    <input id="form:submit" type="submit" name="form:submit"
        value="Submit" />
    <input type="hidden" name="javax.faces.ViewState"
        id="j_id1:javax.faces.ViewState:0"
        value="3336433674711048358:164229014603307903"
        autocomplete="off" />
</form>
```

113

Rendering in Chrome browser:

- ⚪ one
- ⚪ two
- ⚪ three

Submit

Technically, the <h:selectManyCheckbox> could support the group attribute too, but this hasn't yet been implemented. Perhaps it will be in JSF.next.

# SelectItem Tags

Providing available items for UISelectOne and UISelectMany components can be done in several ways. As demonstrated in the previous section, you can use the <f:selectItems> and <f:selectItem> tags nested in the selection component for this. You can use the <f:selectItem> tag to define the available items entirely on the view side. Following is an example using <h:selectOneMenu>, but you can use it the same way in any other UISelectOne and UISelectMany component:

```
<h:selectOneMenu id="selectedItem" value="#{bean.selectedItem}">
    <f:selectItem itemValue="#{null}" itemLabel="-- select one --" />
    <f:selectItem itemValue="one" itemLabel="First item" />
    <f:selectItem itemValue="two" itemLabel="Second item" />
    <f:selectItem itemValue="three" itemLabel="Third item" />
</h:selectOneMenu>
```

Note that a select item with value of #{null} can be used to present the default selection in case the bean property associated with selection component's value attribute is null. If you have consulted the tag documentation of <f:selectItem>, then you'll perhaps have noticed the noSelectionOption attribute and have thought that it was intended to represent a "no selection option." Actually, this isn't true. Many starters indeed think so, as you can see in many forums, Q&A sites, and poor-quality tutorials on the Internet. In spite of the misleading attribute name, it does not represent a "no selection option." A better attribute name would have been

hideWhenOtherOptionIsSelected, and even then it works only when the parent
selection component has explicitly a hideNoSelectionOption="true" attribute set like
the one that follows:

```
<h:selectOneMenu id="selectedItem" value="#{bean.selectedItem}"
    hideNoSelectionOption="true">
    <f:selectItem itemValue="#{null}" itemLabel="-- select one --"
        noSelectionOption="true" />
    <f:selectItem itemValue="one" itemLabel="First item" />
    <f:selectItem itemValue="two" itemLabel="Second item" />
    <f:selectItem itemValue="three" itemLabel="Third item" />
</h:selectOneMenu>
```

So, hideWhenOtherOptionIsSelectedAndHideNoSelectionOptionIsTrue would
ultimately have been the most self-explanatory attribute name. Unfortunately, this
wasn't very well thought out when the noSelectionOption was implemented in JSF 1.2.
Requiring two attributes for this attribute to function shouldn't have been necessary. The
primary purpose of this attribute pair is to prevent the web site user from being able to
re-select the "no selection option" when the component has already a non-null value—
for example, by having it prepared in a @PostConstruct method, or by re-rendering the
component after a form submit with a non-null value.

That said, the itemValue attribute of the <f:selectItem> represents the value
that will be set as bean property when the form is submitted, and the value that will be
preselected from any non-null bean property when the HTML output is to be generated.
The itemLabel attribute represents the label that will be displayed to the web site user.
When the itemLabel attribute is absent, JSF will default to itemValue. Note that the label
is in no way submitted back to the server. That is, in the generated HTML output, the
<option> label is not part of the <option> value.

You can use the <f:selectItems> tag to reference a Collection, Map, or array of
available items in the backing bean. You can even mix this with <f:selectItem> tags.

```
<h:selectOneMenu id="selectedItem" value="#{bean.selectedItem}">
    <f:selectItem itemValue="#{null}" itemLabel="-- select one --" />
    <f:selectItems value="#{bean.availableItems}" />
</h:selectOneMenu>
```

They will be rendered in the same order as they are declared in the view. Only when you use an unordered Map implementation as value, such as HashMap, the order of items provided by <f:selectItems> will be undefined. It's therefore better to use an ordered Map implementation, such as TreeMap or LinkedHashMap. When populating the available items as a Map, keep in mind that the map key represents the item label and the map value represents the item value. You'd perhaps intuitively expect it to be the other way around, but this was a technical limitation. That is, on the Java side, the map key enforces uniqueness while the map value doesn't. And on the HTML side, the option label is supposed to be unique while the option value doesn't need to be. Following is how you can populate such a map:

```
private Map<String, String> availableItems;

@PostConstruct
public void init() {
    availableItems = new LinkedHashMap<>();
    availableItems.put("First item", "one");
    availableItems.put("Second item", "two");
    availableItems.put("Third item", "three");
}

// Add/generate getter. Note that a setter is unnecessary.
```

As said, you can also use a TreeMap or HashMap, but then the item labels will become, respectively, sorted or unsorted, regardless of the insertion order.

In case you'd really like to swap the map keys and values around on the view side, you can always do so by manually assigning the map entry value as an item label and the map entry key as an item value. You can do that with help of the var attribute of the <f:selectItems> by which you can declare the EL variable name of the currently iterated item. This can, in turn, be accessed in the itemValue and itemLabel attributes of the same tag. When you pass Map#entrySet() to the value attribute of the <f:selectItems>, then each iterated item will represent a Map.Entry instance. This has, in turn, getKey() and getValue() methods which are thus perfectly usable as EL properties.

```
<f:selectItems value="#{bean.availableItems.entrySet()}" var="entry"
    itemValue="#{entry.key}" itemLabel="#{entry.value}">
</f:selectItems>
```

This also works when using a `Collection` or array as available items. You don't explicitly need to first convert it to a `Set` (more specifically, `Iterable`), as demonstrated above. This is particularly useful when you have a `Collection` or an array of complex objects as available items, such as model entities.

Model entity representing a "country":

```
public class Country {

    private Long id;
    private String code;
    private String name;

    // Add/generate getters and setters.
}
```

Backing bean:

```
@Named @RequestScoped
public class Bean {

    private String countryCode;
    private List<Country> availableCountries;

    @Inject
    private CountryService countryService;

    @PostConstruct
    public void init() {
        availableCountries = countryService.getAll();
    }

    // Add/generate getters and setters.
    // Note that a setter is unnecessary for availableCountries.
}
```

View:

```
<h:selectOneMenu id="countryCode" value="#{bean.countryCode}">
    <f:selectItem itemValue="#{null}" itemLabel="-- select one --" />
    <f:selectItems value="#{bean.availableCountries}" var="country">
```

```
        itemValue="#{country.code}" itemLabel="#{country.name}"
    </f:selectItems>
</h:selectOneMenu>
```

Note that any persistence framework-specific annotations, such as JPA's @Entity and @Id, and the actual implementation of CountryService, are omitted for clarity. Those are irrelevant to any front-end framework, such as JSF.

With the above construct, the value as obtained from Country#getCode() will end up as value of the generated HTML <option> element. Now, when the form is submitted, it will become the submitted value of the selection component, which will in turn invoke the setter method behind the #{bean.countryCode} property with exactly that value. Of course, you can also use the whole Country object as the property value of the selection component, but that would require a converter which can convert between the complex object and a unique string suitable to be embedded in HTML output and sent as an HTTP request parameter. You can read more in Chapter 5.

# SelectItemGroup

In case you'd like to group a bunch of options under a common label, you can use the javax.faces.model.SelectItemGroup, which you in turn reference in the value attribute of the <f:selectItems>. Unfortunately, this cannot be done declaratively in the Facelets file on a custom nested model. You really have to map your model into the JSF-provided javax.faces.model.SelectItem for this. Following is a kickoff example:

```
private List<SelectItem> availableItems;

@PostConstruct
public void init() {
    SelectItemGroup group1 = new SelectItemGroup("Group 1");
    group1.setSelectItems(new SelectItem[] {
        new SelectItem("Group 1 Value 1", "Group 1 Label 1"),
        new SelectItem("Group 1 Value 2", "Group 1 Label 2"),
        new SelectItem("Group 1 Value 3", "Group 1 Label 3")
    });
```

```
SelectItemGroup group2 = new SelectItemGroup("Group 2");
group2.setSelectItems(new SelectItem[] {
    new SelectItem("Group 2 Value 1", "Group 2 Label 1"),
    new SelectItem("Group 2 Value 2", "Group 2 Label 2"),
    new SelectItem("Group 2 Value 3", "Group 2 Label 3")
});
availableItems = Arrays.asList(group1, group2);

// Add/generate getter for availableItems.
// Note that a setter is unnecessary.
}
```

Noted that both model APIs have basically not changed since JSF 1.0 (2004) and that's why you still see a SelectItemGroup#setSelectItems() method taking a SelectItem[] array instead of a SelectItem... varargs argument. This will certainly be worked on for JSF.next. When referencing it as <f:selectItems value="#{bean.availableItems}" /> in any selection component, below is how it would look for each of them.

The <h:selectOneMenu> will render each group as HTML <optgroup>:

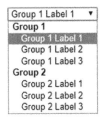

The <h:selectOneRadio layout="pageDirection"> will render it as a nested table:

Group 1

- ◯ Group 1 Label 1
- ◯ Group 1 Label 2
- ◯ Group 1 Label 3

Group 2

- ◯ Group 2 Label 1
- ◯ Group 2 Label 2
- ◯ Group 2 Label 3

The `<h:selectManyListbox>` will render each group as HTML `<optgroup>`:

The `<h:selectManyCheckbox layout="pageDirection">` will render it as a nested table:

Group 1

- ☐ Group 1 Label 1
- ☐ Group 1 Label 2
- ☐ Group 1 Label 3

Group 2

- ☐ Group 2 Label 1
- ☐ Group 2 Label 2
- ☐ Group 2 Label 3

Note the importance of the `layout="pageDirection"` attribute in `<h:selectOneRadio>` and `<h:selectManyCheckbox>`. This will look much better than the default of `layout="lineDirection"` which would render everything in a big single table row.

## Label and Message Components

In an average well-designed form, input elements are usually accompanied with a label element and a message element targeting the input field. In HTML, labels are represented by the `<label>` element. In JSF, you can use the `<h:outputLabel>` component to generate an HTML `<label>` element. HTML does not have a dedicated element to represent a message. In JSF, the `<h:message>` component generates a HTML `<span>` element and the `<h:messages>` component generates either a `<ul>` element or a `<table>` element, depending on the value of the `layout` attribute.

The label element has various SEO (search engine optimization) and usability advantages. It tells in text about the associated input element. Screen readers, like those used by people with visual disabilities, will find the label and tell its contents by sound. Search bots will find the label and index the associated input element as such. And, the label will focus and activate the associated input element when being clicked itself.

120

Text-based input elements will then show the text cursor. Check box and radio input elements will then be toggled. List box and drop-down input elements will then be focused. File input elements will then open the browse dialog. Submit buttons will then be invoked.

The message element is usually to be used to display conversion and validation error messages coming from the server side. This way, the end user is informed about the state of the form and can act accordingly, usually by correcting the input values. You can also use it to display warning or informal messages.

In JSF, the <h:outputLabel>, <h:message> and <h:messages> components have a for attribute wherein you normally define the ID of the associated UIInput component. Following is an example in the flavor of a login form:

```
<h:form id="login">
    <fieldset>
        <legend>Login</legend>
        <section>
            <h:outputLabel for="email" value="Email address" />
            <h:inputText id="email" value="#{login.email}"
                required="true" />
            <h:message id="m_email" for="email" />
        </section>
        <section>
            <h:outputLabel for="password" value="Password" />
            <h:inputSecret id="password" value="#{login.password}"
                required="true" />
            <h:message id="m_password" for="password" />
        </section>
        <footer>
            <h:commandButton id="submit" value="Login"
                action="#{login.submit}" />
        </footer>
    </fieldset>
</h:form>
```

You can actually use any arbitrary component search expression in the for attribute. For the <h:outputLabel> component, this doesn't make much sense. For the <h:message> and <h:messages> components, referring the ID of a non-UIInput component would only make sense when you want to programmatically add a faces message from the managed bean on. But you would then need to know the client ID of the target component.

```
<h:form id="login">

    ...

            <h:commandButton id="submit" value="Login"
                action="#{login.submit}" />
            <h:message id="m_submit" for="submit" />

    ...
</h:form>
```

The above `<h:commandButton>` will generate a client ID of "login:submit" in the HTML output. You can then programmatically add a faces message as follows:

```
public String submit() {
    try {
        yourAuthenticator.authenticate(email, password);
        return "/user/home.xhtml?faces-redirect=true";
    }
    catch (YourAuthenticationException e) {
        FacesContext context = FacesContext.getCurrentInstance();
        FacesMessage message = new FacesMessage("Authentication failed");
        context.addMessage("login:submit", message);
        return null;
    }
}
```

A better practice, however, is to add the faces message as a global message by passing `null` as the client ID.

```
        context.addMessage(null, message);
```

Such a message will then only end up in a `<h:messages globalOnly="true">`.

```
            <h:commandButton id="submit" value="Login"
                action="#{login.submit}" />
            <h:messages id="messages" globalOnly="true"
                rendered="#{component.namingContainer.submitted}" />
```

Note the logic in the rendered attribute of the messages component. It will thus only be rendered when the submitted property of the NamingContainer parent evaluates to true. In this specific case, it's consulting the UIForm#isSubmitted(). This is very useful in case you have multiple non-Ajax forms each with its own global messages component and/or a "catch-all" <h:messages redisplay="false"> component somewhere near the bottom of the JSF page, which is then using CSS fixed positioned on top. Otherwise the global message would unintentionally show up over there as well.

This message-rendering logic is not necessary in Ajax forms as you could just fine-tune the message rendering by simply explicitly specifying the message(s) component(s) in the render attribute of <f:ajax>. Moreover, the UIForm#isSubmitted() would unexpectedly return false when the execute attribute of the <f:ajax> does not explicitly target the form as in execute="@form".

# Command Components

You'll have noticed examples of the <h:commandButton> in the previous sections about input and select components. This thus generates an HTML <input type="submit"> element, which is the HTML way to send all input values of the <form> element it is sitting in to the server. On the server side, this component is also capable of invoking one or more Java methods, which are usually defined in the action or actionListener attribute, or via a <f:actionListener> tag nested in the command component. You'll also have read that the action listener method always runs before the method associated with the action attribute.

You can use the <f:actionListener> tag to register one or more additional action listeners on the very same command component. All those action listeners are invoked in the same order as they're declared in the view and attached to the component. The target method can be declared in three ways on the <f:actionListener> tag. One way is via the type attribute and the other two ways are via the binding attribute.

```
<h:commandButton ...>
    <f:actionListener type="com.example.project.SomeActionListener" />
    <f:actionListener binding="#{beanImplementingActionListener}" />
    <f:actionListener binding="#{bean.someActionListenerMethod()}" />
<h:commandButton>
```

The type attribute in the first way must basically represent the fully qualified name of the class implementing the ActionListener interface.

```
package com.example.project;

import javax.faces.event.ActionListener;
import javax.faces.event.ActionEvent;

public class SomeActionListener implements ActionListener {

    @Override
    public void processAction(ActionEvent event) {
        // ...
    }
}
```

The binding attribute in the second way must basically reference a managed bean instance implementing the ActionListener interface.

```
@Named @RequestScoped
public class BeanImplementingActionListener implements ActionListener {

    @Override
    public void processAction(ActionEvent event) {
        // ...
    }
}
```

And the binding attribute in the third way can basically reference any arbitrary managed bean method which is declared void.

```
@Named @RequestScoped
public class Bean {

    public void someActionListenerMethod() {
        // ...
    }
}
```

Note that the third way is more or less undocumented. It has only been possible since the introduction of EL 2.2 (2009), wherein developers could start explicitly declaring method expressions by simply adding the parenthesis, if necessary with arguments. Coincidentally, the `binding` attribute of the `<f:actionListener>` could deal with them. Under the hood of the `binding` attribute is treated as a `ValueExpression` and the logic expected to obtain a managed bean instance implementing the `ActionListener` interface when invoking `ValueExpression#getValue()`. However, instead of a getter, a void method was invoked and returned nothing which is interpreted as `null`. So, the logic continued silently as if there were simply no bean instance available.

The action listeners have an additional feature on top of the `action` attribute. When a `javax.faces.event.AbortProcessingException` is explicitly thrown from an action listener, then JSF will swallow the exception and abort processing the invoke application phase (fifth phase) and immediately advance to the render response phase (sixth phase). All remaining action listeners and the action method, if any, will be skipped. The swallowed exception won't end up in any error response. Given this fact, and the fact that action listeners are always invoked before the action method, you could (ab)use it to perform some conversion and validation based on already updated model values before the action method is invoked.

```
public void someActionListenerMethod() {
    try {
        convertOrValidate(this);
    } catch (SomeConversionOrValidationException e) {
        FacesContext context = FacesContext.getCurrentInstance()
        context.addMessage(null, new FacesMessage(e.getMessage()));
        throw new AbortProcessingException(e);
    }
}

public void someActionMethod() {
    // Won't be invoked when AbortProcessingException is thrown.
}
```

I'm saying "(ab)use" because it is essentially the responsibility of a normal `Converter` or `Validator` implementation to perform such task, so that the model values are not polluted with invalid values. However, for a long time in JSF it was not possible to perform conversion or validation based on multiple fields. Hence developers started using the action (listener) methods, which is essentially a violation of the JSF life cycle.

Only in JSF 2.3 was a new <f:validateWholeBean> tag introduced to perform validation on multiple fields. You can read more about this in Chapter 5. So this leaves only one reasonable real-world use case open for action listener methods: performing conversion based on one or more model values. One example has already been demonstrated in the section "Selection Components" (the case of using multiple <h:selectBooleanCheckbox> in <ui:repeat> to work around the fact that the <h:selectManyCheckbox> generates an HTML table). Another example would be invoking an external web service with the supplied model values and obtaining its result as a "converted" value. The action method should then still be used to execute business service logic. When the action method throws an exception, the request will end up as an HTTP 500 error response. You can find more about this in Chapter 9.

Apart from the <h:commandButton>, JSF offers two more command components: the <h:commandLink> and the <h:commandScript>. The <h:commandLink> has basically an identical life cycle as the <h:commandButton>, except that it generates an HTML <a> element which submits the enclosed form with the help of JavaScript. Everywhere where you use <h:commandButton>, it could be substituted with <h:commandLink>.

```
<h:form id="form">
    ...
    <h:commandLink id="submit" value="Submit" action="#{bean.submit}" />
</h:form>
```

Whereby the generated HTML output looks as follows:

```
<form id="form" name="form" method="post" action="/project/test.xhtml"
    enctype="application/x-www-form-urlencoded">
    <input type="hidden" name="form" value="form" />
    ...
    <script type="text/javascript"
        src="/project/javax.faces.resource/jsf.js.xhtml?ln=javax.faces">
    </script>
    <a id="form:submit" href="#" onclick="
        mojarra.jsfcljs(
            document.getElementById('form'),
            {'form:submit':'form:submit'},
            ''
        ); return false;">Submit</a>
```

```
<input type="hidden" name="javax.faces.ViewState"
    id="j_id1:javax.faces.ViewState:0"
    value="-69367918978966630173:-5064219023156239099"
    autocomplete="off" />
</form>
```

And the rendering in Chrome browser:

## Submit

In the generated HTML output, you'll notice that it auto-includes the jsf.js
JavaScript file. This contains, among other things, the jsf object and the JSF
implementation-specific helper functions which are in case of the Mojarra
implementation put in the mojarra object. In plain HTML, there's no way to submit a
<form> using an <a> element. Hence, some JavaScript has to be thrown into the game.

In Mojarra's specific case, the mojarra.jsfcljs() function will be invoked with
the parent form as the first argument, the command component's client ID as a
request parameter name and value as the second argument, and the target attribute
of the <h:commandLink> as the third argument, if any. Under the hood of the mojarra.
jsfcljs() function will create <input type="hidden"> elements for each name/value
pair in the second argument and add them to the form provided as the first argument,
making sure that those parameters end up a postback request. Then it will create a
temporary <input type="submit"> button, add it to the form, and invoke the click()
function on it, as if you would be using a regular submit button. Finally, it will remove all
of those dynamically created elements from the form.

This function is actually also used by the <h:commandButton>, but only when you
need to pass additional request parameters via one or more <f:param> tags nested in the
command component.

```
<h:form id="form">
    ...

    <h:commandButton id="submit" value="Submit" action="#{bean.submit}">
        <f:param name="id" value="#{otherBean.id}" />
    </h:commandButton>
</h:form>
```

Generated HTML output:

```
<form id="form" name="form" method="post" action="/project/test.xhtml"
    enctype="application/x-www-form-urlencoded">
    <input type="hidden" name="form" value="form" />
    <script type="text/javascript"
        src="/project/javax.faces.resource/jsf.js.xhtml?ln=javax.faces">
    </script>
    <input id="form:submit" type="submit" name="form:submit"
        value="Submit" onclick="mojarra.jsfcljs(
            document.getElementById('form'),
            {'form:submit':'form:submit','id':'42'},
            '');return false" />
    <input type="hidden" name="javax.faces.ViewState"
        id="j_id1:javax.faces.ViewState:0"
        value="886811437739939021:6102567809374231851"
        autocomplete="off" />
</form>
```

Rendering in Chrome browser:

Submit

You can obtain them in the managed bean via @Inject @ManagedProperty.

```
@Inject @ManagedProperty("#{param.id}")
private Integer id;

public void submit() {
    System.out.println("Submitted ID: " + id);
}
```

Make sure that you import the @ManagedProperty from the right package. JSF offers two, one from the javax.faces.bean package which is deprecated since JSF 2.3 and another one from javax.faces.annotation package which you should be using for CDI. You also need to make sure that you explicitly activate the JSF 2.3-specific feature of CDI-aware EL resolvers by having at least one managed bean in the web application explicitly annotated with @FacesConfig; otherwise the CDI-aware

@ManagedProperty would fail to find the current instance of FacesContext via CDI. Also here, <h:commandButton> is substitutable with <h:commandLink>.

There's another way of passing parameters around via command components—that is, by simply passing them as an action method argument.

```
<h:form id="form">
    ...
    <h:commandButton id="submit" value="Submit"
        action="#{bean.submit(otherBean.id)}">
    </h:commandButton>
</h:form>
```

Whereby the modified action method looks as follows:

```
public void submit(Integer id) {
    System.out.println("Submitted ID: " + id);
}
```

In case of the <h:commandButton>, this won't generate any JavaScript and it thus looks identical as when you aren't using any action method arguments. This thus also means that the #{otherBean.id} value isn't passed via HTML source code back to the server as a request parameter. This in turn means that it's only evaluated during the postback request when JSF is about to invoke the action method. This in turn means that the #{otherBean.id} must at least be @ViewScoped in order to be still available in the postback request. In other words, this argument passing approach is definitely not exchangeable with the <f:param> tag approach whereby both beans can be just @RequestScoped.

The last command component offered by the standard JSF component set is <h:commandScript>. This is new since JSF 2.3. It allows you to invoke a managed bean action method by just calling a named JavaScript function from your own script. The postback request will always be performed via Ajax.

```
<h:form id="form">
    <h:commandScript id="submit" name="invokeBeanSubmit"
        action="#{bean.submit}">
    </h:commandScript>
</h:form>
```

Generated HTML output:

```
<form id="form" name="form" method="post" action="/project/test.xhtml"
    enctype="application/x-www-form-urlencoded">
    <input type="hidden" name="form" value="form" />
    <script type="text/javascript"
        src="/project/javax.faces.resource/jsf.js.xhtml?ln=javax.faces">
    </script>
    <span id="form:submit">
        <script type="text/javascript">
            var invokeBeanSubmit = function(o) {
                var o = (typeof o==='object') && o ? o : {};
                mojarra.ab('form:submit',null,'action',0,0,{'params':o});
            }
        </script>
    </span>
    <input type="hidden" name="javax.faces.ViewState"
        id="j_id1:javax.faces.ViewState:0"
        value="3568384626727188032:3956762118801488231"
        autocomplete="off" />
</form>
```

It has no visible HTML rendering in web browsers. In the generated script, you'll see that it has generated a function variable with the same name as specified in the name attribute. In this example, it's indeed in the global scope. As this is considered poor practice in the JavaScript context ("global namespace pollution"), you'd better provide a namespaced function name. This only pre-requires that you've already declared your own namespace somewhere before in the HTML document, usually via a JavaScript file in the <head> element. The following example simplifies it with an inline script:

```
<h:head>
    ...
    <script>var mynamespace = mynamespace || {};</script>
</h:head>
<h:body>
    <h:form id="form">
        <h:commandScript id="submit" name="mynamespace.invokeBeanSubmit"
```

```
        action="#{bean.submit}">
      </h:commandScript>
    </h:form>
</h:body>
```

Coming back to the generated function variable, you'll also see that it accepts an object argument and passes it through as "`params`" property of the last object argument of the Mojarra-specific `mojarra.ab()` function. That helper function will, under the hood of the `mojarra.ab()` function, prepare and invoke the `jsf.ajax.request()` function of the standard JSF JavaScript API. In other words, you can pass JavaScript variables to a managed bean action method this way. They are injectable via `@ManagedProperty` the same way as if you were using `<f:param>`. The following example demonstrates the JavaScript call with hard-coded variables in a JavaScript object, but you can of course obtain those variables from anywhere else in JavaScript context:

```
var params = {
    id: 42,
    name: "John Doe",
    email: "john.doe@example.com"
};
invokeBeanSubmit(params);
```

Backing bean class:

```
@Inject @ManagedProperty("#{param.id}")
private Integer id;

@Inject @ManagedProperty("#{param.name}")
private String name;

@Inject @ManagedProperty("#{param.email}")
private String email;

public void submit() {
    System.out.println("Submitted ID: " + id);
    System.out.println("Submitted name: " + name);
    System.out.println("Submitted email: " + email);
}
```

The `<h:commandScript>` can also be used to defer the partial rendering of an HTML document to the window `load` event. To achieve this, simply set the `autorun` attribute to `true` and specify the client ID of the target component in the `render` attribute. The following example loads and renders a data table only when the page has finished loading in the client side:

```
<h:panelGroup layout="block" id="lazyPersonsPanel">
    <h:dataTable rendered="#{not empty bean.lazyPersons}"
        value="#{bean.lazyPersons}" var="person">
        <h:column>#{person.id}</h:column>
        <h:column>#{person.name}</h:column>
        <h:column>#{person.email}</h:column>
    </h:dataTable>
</h:panelGroup>
<h:form id="form">
    <h:commandScript id="loadLazyPersons" name="loadLazyPersons"
        autorun="true" action="#{bean.loadLazyPersons}"
        render=":lazyPersonsPanel">
    </h:commandScript>
</h:form>
```

Whereby the backing bean looks as follows:

```
@Named @RequestScoped
public class Bean {

    private List<Person> lazyPersons;

    @Inject
    private PersonService personService;

    public void loadLazyPersons() {
        lazyPersons = personService.getAll();
    }

    public List<Person> getLazyPersons() {
        return lazyPersons;
    }
}
```

And the `Person` entity looks as follows:

```
public class Person {

    private Long id;
    private String name;
    private String email;

    // Add/generate getters and setters.
}
```

Note that any persistence framework-specific annotations, such as JPA's `@Entity` and `@Id`, and the actual implementation of `PersonService`, are omitted for clarity. Those are, namely, irrelevant to any front-end framework, such as JSF.

Coming back to the available command components, it may speak for itself that `<h:commandScript>` is only useful in order to be able to invoke a JSF managed bean action method using native JavaScript, generally during a specific HTML DOM (Document Object Model) event. However, both `<h:commandLink>` and `<h:commandButton>` seem to do exactly the same thing; only the visual presentation is different. One renders a link and the other renders a button. The user experience (UX) consensus is that a button must be used to submit a form, and a link must be used to navigate to another page or jump to an anchor. Using a link to submit a form is therefore not always considered the best practice. It's only useful when you'd like to submit an HTML form using an icon or image. For all other cases, use a normal button. The following example shows how a command link can be used on a Font Awesome icon:

```
<h:commandLink id="delete" action="#{bean.delete}">
    <i class="fa fa-trash" />
</h:commandLink>
```

# Navigation

Sometimes, you'd like to navigate to a different JSF page when a certain form has been successfully submitted—for example, from the login page to the user home page, as demonstrated in the section "Label and Message Components," or from the detail page back to the master page.

Historically, navigation targets must be defined separately in `<navigation-rule>` entries in the `faces-config.xml` which then does the job based on the `String` return value from the action method of `UICommand` components. This approach turns out to be quite cumbersome in the long term, and not terribly useful for HTML-based web applications. This idea was more or less derived from desktop-oriented applications. Hence, JSF 2.0 introduced the "Implicit navigation" feature, which allows you to define the navigation target directly in the `String` return value itself. In other words, instead of the following action method:

```
public String someActionMethod() {
    // ...
    return "someOutcome";
}
```

And the following `faces-config.xml` entry:

```
<navigation-rule>
    <navigation-case>
        <from-outcome>someOutcome</from-outcome>
        <to-view-id>/otherview.xhtml</to-view-id>
    </navigation-case>
</navigation-rule>
```

you could just do as follows in the action method:

```
public String someActionMethod() {
    // ...
    return "/otherview.xhtml";
}
```

You could even leave out the default suffix of the view technology you're using.

```
public String someActionMethod() {
    // ...
    return "/otherview";
}
```

You can force a redirect by appending a faces-redirect=true query parameter.

```
public String someActionMethod() {
    // ...
    return "/otherview?faces-redirect=true";
}
```

Returning null would return to the very same view from where the form was submitted. In other words, the end user would stay in the same page. It is cleaner, however, to declare the action method as void.

```
public void someActionMethod() {
    // ...
}
```

Coming back to the redirect approach, this is also known as "Post-Redirect-Get" pattern[2] and makes a major difference with regard to bookmarkability and avoiding double submits. Without a redirect after a POST request on a JSF form, the URL (uniform resource locator) in the web browser's address bar wouldn't change to the URL of the target page but would just stay the same. That's caused by the nature of the "postback": submitting the form back to the very same URL from which the page with the form was served. When JSF is instructed to navigate to a different view without a redirect, then it will basically build and render the target page directly to the response of the current postback request.

This approach has disadvantages. One is that refreshing the page in the web browser would cause the POST request to be re-executed, and thus perform a so-called double submit. This would potentially pollute the data store in the back end with duplicate entries, particularly if the involved relational table doesn't have proper unique constraints defined. Another disadvantage is that the target page isn't bookmarkable. The URL currently in the browser's address bar basically represents the previous page. You won't get the target page back by bookmarking, copy/pasting, and/or sharing the URL and then opening it in a new browser window.

When JSF is instead instructed to navigate to a different view with a redirect, then it will basically return a very small HTTP response with a status of 302 and a Location header with the URL of the target page therein. When the web browser retrieves such

---

[2]https://en.wikipedia.org/wiki/Post/Redirect/Get.

a response, it will immediately fire a brand-new GET request on the URL specified in the Location header. This URL is reflected in the web browser's address bar and is thus bookmarkable. Also, refreshing the page would only refresh the GET request and therefore not cause a double submit.

# Ajaxifying Components

As you have noticed in <h:commandScript> in the section "Command Components," JSF is capable of firing Ajax requests and performing partial rendering as well. This capability was introduced in JSF 2.0 for the first time with the <f:ajax> tag. This tag can be nested in any component implementing ClientBehaviorHolder interface, or it can be wrapped around a group of components implementing this interface. In the standard JSF component set, almost all HTML components implement ClientBehaviorHolder as well. If you consult the ClientBehaviorHolder Javadoc,[3] then you'll find the following list:

**All Known Implementing Classes:**

HtmlBody, HtmlCommandButton, HtmlCommandLink, HtmlDataTable, HtmlForm, HtmlGraphicImage, HtmlInputFile, HtmlInputSecret, HtmlInputText, HtmlInputTextarea, HtmlOutcomeTargetButton, HtmlOutcomeTargetLink, HtmlOutputLabel, HtmlOutputLink, HtmlPanelGrid, HtmlPanelGroup, HtmlSelectBooleanCheckbox, HtmlSelectManyCheckbox, HtmlSelectManyListbox, HtmlSelectManyMenu, HtmlSelectOneListbox, HtmlSelectOneMenu, HtmlSelectOneRadio, UIWebsocket

That are thus the <h:body>, <h:commandButton>, <h:commandLink>, <h:dataTable>, <h:form>, <h:graphicImage>, <h:inputFile>, <h:inputSecret>, <h:inputText>, <h:inputTextarea>, <h:button>, <h:link>, <h:outputLabel>, <h:outputLink>, <h:panelGrid>, <h:panelGroup>, <h:selectBooleanCheckbox>, <h:selectManyCheckbox>, <h:selectManyListbox>, <h:selectManyMenu>, <h:selectOneListbox>, <h:selectOneMenu>, <h:selectOneRadio> and <f:websocket>.

You'll see that all visible input, select, and command components are covered as well.

---

[3]https://javaee.github.io/javaee-spec/javadocs/javax/faces/component/behavior/ ClientBehaviorHolder.html.

A requirement of the <f:ajax> is that the ClientBehaviorHolder component is nested in <h:form>, and that <h:head> is being used in the template. The <h:form> basically enables JavaScript to perform a postback request with the right JSF view state associated. The <h:head> basically enables <f:ajax> to automatically include the necessary jsf.js JavaScript file which contains, among others, the mandatory jsf. ajax.request() function.

```
<h:head id="head">
    <title>f:ajax demo</title>
</h:head>
<h:body>
    <h:form id="form">
        <h:inputText id="text" value="#{bean.text}">
            <f:ajax />
        </h:inputText>
        <h:commandButton id="submit" value="Submit"
            action="#{bean.submit}">
            <f:ajax execute="@form" />
        </h:commandButton>
    </h:form>
</h:body>
```

Generated HTML output:

```
<head id="head">
    <title>f:ajax demo</title>
    <script type="text/javascript"
        src="/project/javax.faces.resource/jsf.js.xhtml?ln=javax.faces">
    </script>
</head>
<body>
    <form id="form" name="form" method="post"
        action="/project/test.xhtml"
        enctype="application/x-www-form-urlencoded">
        <input type="hidden" name="form" value="form" />
        <input id="form:text" type="text" name="form:text"
            onchange="mojarra.ab(this,event,'valueChange',0,0)" />
```

```
        <input id="form:submit" type="submit" name="form:submit"
            value="Submit" onclick="mojarra.ab(
                this,event,'action','@form',0);return false;" />
        <input type="hidden" name="javax.faces.ViewState"
            id="j_id1:javax.faces.ViewState:0"
            value="6345708413515990903:-8460061657159853996"
            autocomplete="off" />
    </form>
</body>
```

Rendering in Chrome browser (with newlines added) is identical as without Ajax:

Submit

In the generated HTML output, you'll see that the `jsf.js` JavaScript file containing the necessary JSF Ajax API is auto-included in the HTML head. You'll also notice that `<f:ajax>` in `<h:inputText>` has generated an additional onchange attribute, and in `<h:commandButton>` an additional onclick attribute, both defining some JSF implementation-specific JavaScript code responsible for performing the Ajax request.

JSF specifies two internal Ajax event types: `valueChange` and `action`. Those are the default event types in case `<f:ajax>` doesn't have the event attribute specified. When `<f:ajax>` is attached to a component implementing the `EditableValueHolder` interface, then the default event type becomes `valueChange`. For components implementing the `ActionSource` interface, this is `action`. For all other `ClientBehaviorHolder` components, the default event is `click`. The actual generated HTML DOM event type for those internal event types depends on the component and the associated renderer.

In case of text-based input components and drop-down- and list box-based selection components, the default HTML DOM event type for `<f:ajax>` is `"change"`. In case of radio- and check box-based selection components and command components, this is `"click"`. You can see this in the generated HTML output, which can be overridden by explicitly specifying the event attribute on the `<f:ajax>` tag.

```
<h:inputText ...>
    <f:ajax event="blur" />
</h:inputText>
```

The above example will generate the JavaScript code in the `onblur` attribute instead of the `onclick` attribute. The supported values for the `event` attribute depend on the target `ClientBehaviorHolder` component. They can be found in the VDL documentation of the component of interest. All `on[event]` attributes are defined over there. When you remove the "on" prefix on them, then you have a list of supported event types. For example, the VDL documentation of `<h:inputText>`[4] indicates that the following event types are supported:

> `blur`, `change`, `click`, `dblclick`, `focus`, `keydown`, `keypress`, `keyup`, `mousedown`, `mousemove`, `mouseout`, `mouseover`, `mouseup`, `select`

When the desired DOM event type occurs on the client side and triggers the associated JSF implementation-specific JavaScript code defined in the `on[event]` attribute, then ultimately the `jsf.ajax.request()` function of the standard JSF JavaScript API will be invoked. It will prepare a bunch of predefined postback parameters of which `javax.faces.source` and `javax.faces.behavior.event` are the most important ones. The former specifies the client ID of the source component, essentially the value of `this.id` in JavaScript context. The latter specifies the event type, essentially the value of `event.type` in JavaScript context. You'll have guessed that they are derived from the first two arguments passed to the Mojarra-specific `mojarra.ab()` function as visible in the generated HTML output.

Once fired, the Ajax request will run through the JSF life cycle almost the same way as a non-Ajax request. The restore view phase (first phase), process validations phase (third phase), update model values phase (fourth phase), and invoke application phase (fifth phase) are identical. The apply request values phase (second phase) is slightly different. It will only decode the components that are covered by the `execute` attribute of the `<f:ajax>` tag, which defaults to `@this` ("the current component"). The render response phase (sixth phase) is completely different. Instead of generating a whole HTML document, it generates a special XML document which contains only the generated HTML output of components which are covered by the render attribute of the `<f:ajax>` tag, which defaults to `@none` ("no one component").

The execute and render attributes accept a space-separated collection of component search expressions. This can represent a client ID relative to the closest `NamingContainer` parent, or an absolute client ID which is always relative to the `UIViewRoot`, or standard or custom search keywords, or chained combinations thereof. See Chapter 12 for an

---

[4] https://javaserverfaces.github.io/docs/2.3/vdldocs/facelets/h/inputText.html.

in-depth explanation of them. For now, we only need to know about the standard search keywords @this, @form, and @none. As its name suggests, the @form keyword refers to the closest parent component of the UIForm type, such as <h:form>.

During the apply request values phase (second phase) of the Ajax request, JSF will, for each component covered by the execute attribute of the <f:ajax> tag in addition to the default decode process, also check if the javax.faces.source request parameter equals the current component's client ID. If so, then JSF will queue the AjaxBehaviorEvent for the invoke application phase (fifth phase). Under the hood of queueing the AjaxBehaviorEvent, it boils down to the following logic:

```
FacesContext context = FacesContext.getCurrentInstance();
ExternalContext externalContext = context.getExternalContext();
Map<String, String> formData = externalContext.getRequestParameterMap();

String clientId = component.getClientId(context);
String source = formData.get("javax.faces.source");
String event = formData.get("javax.faces.behavior.event");

if (clientId.equals(source)) {
    component.getClientBehaviors().get(event)
        .forEach(behavior -> component.queueEvent(
            new AjaxBehaviorEvent(context, component, behavior)));
}
```

Here, the ClientBehavior basically represents the definition of the <f:ajax> tag. Based on this logic, you will conclude that you can have multiple <f:ajax> tags attached in the very same component, even on same event types. The advantage is that you can, if necessary, register multiple Ajax behavior listeners on the very same event type.

```
<h:inputText id="foo" ...>
    <f:ajax listener="#{bean.onchangeFoo}" />
    <f:ajax listener="#{otherBean.onchangeFoo}" />
</h:inputText>
```

Those Ajax behavior listener methods will thus be invoked during the invoke application phase (fifth phase); of course, only when there's no conversion or validation error during the process validations phase (third phase). In case of command components, those Ajax behavior listener methods will always be invoked before the action listener methods and the action method. Regardless of the target component, the Ajax behavior listener method must be a `public void` method which can optionally take the `AjaxBehaviorEvent` argument.

```
public void onchangeFoo(AjaxBehaviorEvent event) {
    // ...
}
```

This gives you, in input and select components, the opportunity to perform some business task on a specific Ajax event. Most occurring real-world examples involve preparing another bean property which in turn gets rendered in another component. Think of cascading drop-down menus wherein the available items of the child drop-down menu depend on the selected item of the parent drop-down. In action components, `<f:ajax listener>` isn't terribly useful. You already have the possibility to perform the business task in action listener and/or action method. You can just continue using them even when having `<f:ajax>` attached.

During the render response phase (sixth phase) of the Ajax request, JSF will for each component covered by the `render` attribute of the `<f:ajax>` tag generate a XML `<update>` element which contains the generated HTML output of only the particular component and all of its children, if any. The `jsf.ajax.response()` function of the standard JSF JavaScript API, which is by the `jsf.ajax.request()` registered as Ajax callback function, will extract the `id` attribute of the `<update>` element, which represents the client ID of the target component, and obtain via JavaScript's `document.getElementById()` on the client ID the concrete HTML element and replace it in the HTML DOM tree with the contents of the `<update>` element.

Following is an example of a form with one required input field having a message attached, and a command button which explicitly targets the message component:

```
<h:form id="form">
    <h:inputText id="text" value="#{bean.text}" required="true" />
    <h:message id="m_text" for="text" />
    <br />
    <h:commandButton id="submit" value="Submit" action="#{bean.submit}">
        <f:ajax execute="@form" render="m_text" />
    </h:commandButton>
</h:form>
```

Figure 4-2 shows how Chrome presents the Ajax response after submitting the form with the input field not filled out. It's a big one-liner, so it's scrolled a bit so it starts at the `<update>` element of interest. It contains the generated HTML output of the `<h:message id="m_text">` component.

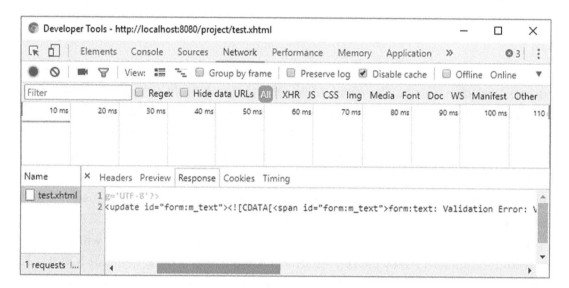

***Figure 4-2.***  *Chrome Developer Tools—Network—Response*

If you scroll further in the XML response, then you'll also notice an `<update id="j_id1:javax.faces.ViewState:0">` element containing the value of the `javax.faces.ViewState` hidden input element. This is important for JSF in order to maintain the view state across Ajax requests. When the `render` attribute happens to cover a `UIForm` component, then the `javax.faces.ViewState` hidden input element currently in the HTML document will basically be completely wiped out during the replacement of the element in the HTML DOM tree with contents of the `<update>` element of the Ajax response.

The missing `javax.faces.ViewState` hidden input element will eventually be appended to every `<form method="post">` of the current `UIViewRoot`. This approach is actually by design for two reasons: (1) because the view state value could change across Ajax requests and therefore the existing forms currently in the HTML document have to be updated to catch up this change, just in case those forms are not covered by the `render` attribute; and (2) because the value of the `javax.faces.ViewState` hidden input field can get quite large when the JSF state saving method is explicitly set to "client" and thus otherwise render an inefficient Ajax response when the `render` attribute happens to cover multiple forms.

# Navigation in Ajax

In UICommand components with a properly defined action method, it's not different. However, sometimes you'd like to perform navigation in an Ajax listener attached to n UIInput component. There are reasonable real-world use cases for this. However, the UIInput class doesn't support defining an action method and <f:ajax listener> doesn't support returning a navigation outcome. Therefore, your only option is to perform the navigation programmatically. This can be done in two ways. The first way is to use the javax.faces.application.NavigationHandler.[5]

```
public void ajaxListener(AjaxBehaviorEvent event) {
    // ...

    String outcome = "/otherview?faces-redirect=true";
    FacesContext context = FacesContext.getCurrentInstance();
    Application application = context.getApplication();
    NavigationHandler handler = application.getNavigationHandler();
    handler.handleNavigation(context, null, outcome);
}
```

The second way is to use the javax.faces.context.ExternalContext#redirect().[6]

```
public void ajaxListener(AjaxBehaviorEvent event) throws IOException {
    // ...

    String path = "/otherview.xhtml";
    FacesContext context = FacesContext.getCurrentInstance();
    ExternalContext externalContext = context.getExternalContext();
    String uri = externalContext.getRequestContextPath() + path;
    externalContext.redirect(uri);
}
```

There are several differences. Most important, the NavigationHandler can deal with implicit navigation outcome values, but ExternalContext#redirect() can only

---

[5]https://javaee.github.io/javaee-spec/javadocs/javax/faces/application/
NavigationHandler.html.

[6]https://javaee.github.io/javaee-spec/javadocs/javax/faces/context/ExternalContext.
html#redirect-java.lang.String-.

deal with actual paths and requires manual prefixing of the request context path when it concerns a web application resource. However, it can take basically any URI, such as an external URL as in `externalContext.redirect("http://example.com")`, whereas the `NavigationHandler` can't deal with them.

# GET forms

JSF has no concept of "GET forms," but you can just use plain HTML for this. JSF supports processing GET request parameters and invoking managed bean actions on GET requests. For this, `<f:viewParam>` and `<f:viewAction>` can be used. They must be placed in `<f:metadata>` which in turn can only be declared in the top-level page. So, when using templating, it must be declared in the template client and you can't declare it in the master template. In other words, `<f:metadata>` cannot be shared across template clients.

Technically, the location of `<f:metadata>` in the view doesn't matter, as long as it's in the top-level page. Most self-documenting would be to put it in the very top of the view, directly after the root tag.

```
<!DOCTYPE html>
<html lang="en"
    xmlns="http://www.w3.org/1999/xhtml"
    xmlns:f="http://xmlns.jcp.org/jsf/core"
    xmlns:h="http://xmlns.jcp.org/jsf/html"
>
    <f:metadata>
        ...
    </f:metadata>

    <h:head>
        ...
    </h:head>

    <h:body>
        ...
    </h:body>
</html>
```

When using templating, give it its own template definition.

```
<ui:composition template="/WEB-INF/templates/layout.xhtml"
    xmlns="http://www.w3.org/1999/xhtml"
    xmlns:f="http://xmlns.jcp.org/jsf/core "
    xmlns:h="http://xmlns.jcp.org/jsf/html"
>
    <ui:define name="metadata">
        <f:metadata>
            ...
        </f:metadata>
    </ui:define>

    <ui:define name="content">
        ...
    </ui:define>
</ui:composition>
```

No, you can't put `<f:metadata>` in the master template and keep `<f:viewParam>` and `<f:viewAction>` in the template client. This is a technical limitation. The best you can do is to create a custom `<f:event>` type which runs after the invoke application phase (fifth phase) and then declare it in the master template. An example is given in the section "Create Custom Component Event" in Chapter 3.

The `<f:viewParam>` tag is backed by the `UIViewParameter` component which in turn extends from `UIInput` superclass. This means that it behaves almost exactly like `<h:inputText>`, but then for GET parameters. The subtle differences are found in the process validations phase (third phase). By default, an empty parameter would skip any custom validators and bean validation. For example, the `@NotNull` bean validation annotation will only work when the context parameter `javax.faces.INTERPRET_EMPTY_STRING_SUBMITTED_VALUES_AS_NULL` is explicitly set to `true` in `web.xml`. The other difference is in the render response phase (sixth phase). Basically, it renders absolutely nothing.

The `<f:viewAction>` tag is backed by the `UIViewAction` component which in turn implements the `ActionSource` interface. This means that it behaves almost exactly like `<h:commandButton>`, but then for GET requests. Of course, you could also use a `@PostConstruct` annotated method on a `@ViewScoped` managed bean for performing logic on GET requests, but the problem is that it would run directly after the managed bean instance is created, when `<f:viewParam>` hasn't even had a chance to run.

`<f:viewAction>` will be invoked during the invoke application phase (fifth phase), after the model values are updated. It even supports returning a `String` representing a navigation outcome, which will then behave as a redirect.

Following is an example of a search form:

Facelets file `/search.xhtml`:

```
<f:metadata>
    <f:viewParam id="query" name="query" value="#{search.query}" />
    <f:viewAction action="#{search.onload}" />
</f:metadata>

<h:body>
    <form>
        <label for="query">Query</label>
        <input type="text" name="query"
            value="#{empty search.query ? param.query : search.query}">
        </input>
        <input type="submit" value="Search" />
        <h:message for="query" />
    </form>
    <h:dataTable id="results" rendered="#{not empty search.results}"
        value="#{search.results}" var="result">
        <h:column>#{result.name}</h:column>
        <h:column>#{result.description}</h:column>
    </h:dataTable>
</h:body>
```

Backing bean class `com.example.project.view.Search`:

```
@Named @RequestScoped
public class Search {

    private String query;
    private List<Result> results;

    @Inject
    private SearchService searchService;

    public void onload() {
```

```
        results = searchService.getResults(query);
    }

    // Add/generate getters and setters here.
    // Note that results doesn't need a setter.
}
```

In the Facelets file there are a couple of things to notice apart from the plain HTML form approach. The `value` attribute of the text input displays `#{param.query}` when `#{search.query}` is empty, because the submitted value would otherwise not show up at all when there's a conversion or validation error on `<f:viewParam>`. `#{param}` is actually an implicit EL object referring the request parameter map. `#{param.query}` basically prints the value of the request parameter with the name "query". Please note that this construct of the `value` attribute is invalid for JSF input components. It would throw a `javax.el.Pro pertyNotWritableException` during the update model values phase (fourth phase), and, moreover, it is already doing the very same logic under the hood of the `<f:viewParam>`.

`<h:message>` can be attached to `<f:viewParam>`. In this specific construct, however, it's not really used. Only when you add a converter or validator to `<f:viewParam>`, for example, by `<f:viewParam ... required="true">` would you see the error message in `<h:message>`, and then `<f:viewAction>` won't be invoked.

Now, when you open the page and submit the form, the submitted value will appear as a query string in the URL as in `/search.xhtml?query=jsf`. This is bookmarkable and re-executable every time you open the URL.

# Stateless Forms

State saving is particularly helpful in dynamically manipulated forms which use Ajax to conditionally render parts of the form, such as cascading drop-down menus and secondary input fields. JSF remembers the state of the form across Ajax postbacks on the same view. Generally, it is those forms where you absolutely need a view-scoped managed bean instead of a request-scoped managed bean.

When your web site has "public" and "private" sections, you'd like to postpone the HTTP session creation as much as possible until the end user has actually logged in. This way robots won't trigger the unnecessary creation of the HTTP session. However, if you have a standard JSF login form in the public section, the HTTP session would already be created by just accessing that page. This is an unnecessary cost in terms of server memory if the form has basically no dynamic state of its own and is tied to a request-scoped managed bean. You could consider using client-side state saving instead, but this will affect the entire web site and it has a cost in terms of network bandwidth and CPU (central procession unit) power. True, the cost is negligible if you have state-of-the-art hardware, but it's not negligible if you have a lot of visitors and/or relatively poor hardware.

In case of static forms tied to a request-scoped bean, such as a simple two-field login form which can theoretically safely be entirely cleared out on every postback, then the view state doesn't necessarily need to be saved. This can be achieved by setting the transient attribute of <f:view> to true.

```
<f:view transient="true">
    <h:form id="login">
        ...
    </h:form>
</f:view>
```

This way JSF won't create any view state and the javax.faces.ViewState hidden input field will receive a fixed value of "stateless". Note that this affects the entire view and there's no way to toggle this for only a specific form. JSF currently does not support configuring the state saving method on a per-form basis. Also, statelessness has an additional disadvantage in that it's theoretically easier to perform a CSRF (cross site request forgery) attack if there's an open XSS hole. (See also the section "Cross Site Request Forgery Protection" in Chapter 13.) Fortunately, with JSF it's already very hard to accidentally introduce a XSS hole. The only way to get a XSS hole is to use <h:outputText escape="false"> to redisplay user-controlled data.

# CHAPTER 5

# Conversion and Validation

At its core, JSF (JavaServer Faces) as an HTML form-based MVC (Model-View-Controller) framework basically needs to convert between Java objects (entities, beans, value objects, data transfer objects, and what not) and character sequences (strings) all the time. The HTTP request is basically broken down into plain vanilla strings representing headers and parameters, not as Java objects. The HTTP response is basically written as one big sequence of characters representing HTML or XML, not as some sort of serialized form of a Java object. However, the average Java model behind a JSF page doesn't necessarily contain String properties everywhere. That would defeat the strong typed nature of Java. This is where Converters come into the picture: converting between objects in model and strings in view.

Before updating the model values with freshly submitted and, if necessary, converted values, you would of course like to validate whether they conform to the business rules of the web application and, if necessary, present end users an informative error message so that they can fix any errors themselves. Usually, the business rules are already very well defined in the data store, such as a relational database management system. A decently designed database table already has strict constraints on the data type, maximum size, nullability, and uniqueness. You as a front-end developer should make absolutely sure that the submitted and converted values can be inserted in the database without errors.

If, for example, the e-mail address column is constrained as a unique and non-nullable column with a maximum size of 254 characters, then you should make sure that the submitted value is validated as such before inserting it in the database. Otherwise, the database insert would throw some exception which is generally cumbersome to break down into detailed information in order to tell the end user about the exact mistake. This is where Validators come into the picture: validating submitted (and converted) values before updating the model.

© Bauke Scholtz, Arjan Tijms 2018
B. Scholtz and A. Tijms, *The Definitive Guide to JSF in Java EE 8*, https://doi.org/10.1007/978-1-4842-3387-0_5

# Standard Converters

JSF has, from the beginning, provided a bunch of standard converters out the box. Most of them even do their job fully transparently based on the Java type of the model property. They are all available in the `javax.faces.convert` package[1] and they all implement the `Converter<T>` interface. Table 5-1 provides an overview of them.

***Table 5-1.*** *Standard Converters Provided by JSF*

| Converter class | Converter ID | Converter tag | Value type | Since |
|---|---|---|---|---|
| BigDecimalConverter | javax.faces. BigDecimal | n/a | java.math.BigDecimal | 1.0 |
| BigIntegerConverter | javax.faces. BigInteger | n/a | java.math.BigInteger | 1.0 |
| BooleanConverter | javax.faces.Boolean | n/a | boolean/java.lang. Boolean | 1.0 |
| ByteConverter | javax.faces.Byte | n/a | byte/java.lang.Byte | 1.0 |
| CharacterConverter | javax.faces. Character | n/a | char/java.lang.Character | 1.0 |
| DateTimeConverter | javax.faces.DateTime | <f:convertDateTime> | java.util.Date | 1.0 |
| | | | java.time.LocalDate | 2.3 |
| | | | java.time.LocalTime | 2.3 |
| | | | java.time.OffsetTime | 2.3 |
| | | | java.time.LocalDateTime | 2.3 |
| | | | java.time. OffsetDateTime | 2.3 |
| | | | java.time. ZonedDateTime | 2.3 |
| DoubleConverter | javax.faces.Double | n/a | double/java.lang.Double | 1.0 |

*(continued)*

---

[1]https://javaee.github.io/javaee-spec/javadocs/javax/faces/convert/package-summary. html.

***Table 5-1.*** (*continued*)

| Converter class | Converter ID | Converter tag | Value type | Since |
|---|---|---|---|---|
| EnumConverter | javax.faces.Enum | n/a | enum/java.lang.Enum | 1.0 |
| FloatConverter | javax.faces.Float | n/a | float/java.lang.Float | 1.0 |
| IntegerConverter | javax.faces.Integer | n/a | int/java.lang.Integer | 1.0 |
| LongConverter | javax.faces.Long | n/a | long/java.lang.Long | 1.0 |
| NumberConverter | javax.faces.Number | <f:convertNumber> | java.lang.Number | 1.0 |
| ShortConverter | javax.faces.Short | n/a | short/java.lang.Short | 1.0 |

The "Converter ID" column basically specifies the converter identifier as you could specify in the converter attribute of any ValueHolder component, or the converterId attribute of any nested <f:converter> tag in order to activate the specific converter. All UIOutput and UIInput components implement the ValueHolder interface. The converters which say "n/a" in the "Converter tag" column are implicit converters. In other words, you can just bind any bean property of type BigDecimal, BigInteger, boolean/Boolean, byte/Byte, char/Character, double/Double, enum/Enum, float/Float, int/Integer, long/Long, and short/Short to the value attribute of any ValueHolder component and have JSF to automatically convert it without any additional configuration. Only <f:convertDateTime> and <f:convertNumber> require explicit registration, because the desired conversion algorithm isn't necessarily obvious from the model value alone.

In all ValueHolder components, the converter will be invoked during the render response phase (sixth phase), converting the non-String-based model value to a String suitable for embedding in HTML. And in EditableValueHolder components, the converter will also be invoked during the process validations phase (third phase), converting the submitted String request parameter to the non-String-based model value. The EditableValueHolder interface extends the ValueHolder interface and is implemented by all UIInput components.

However, this implicit conversion doesn't work on bean properties where those types are parameterized. Imagine that you have a `List<Integer>` in the model and you'd like to be able to edit it as follows:

```
<ui:repeat value="#{bean.integers}" varStatus="loop">
    <h:inputText value="#{bean.integers[loop.index]}" />
</ui:repeat>
```

Then, after submitting, you would end up with unconverted `String` values in the list and get baffled by class cast exceptions when attempting to iterate over the list. The reason is that the EL (Expression Language) API (application programming interface), which is responsible for processing those #{...} things that are, behind the scenes, represented by `javax.el.ValueExpression` instances, is in its current version not capable of detecting the parameterized type of a generic collection and just returns `Object.class` on `ValueExpression#getType()`. JSF can't do much about that limitation of EL. All you can do is explicitly specify the desired converter on the input component.

```
<ui:repeat value="#{bean.integers}" varStatus="loop">
    <h:inputText value="#{bean.integers[loop.index]}"
        converter="javax.faces.Integer">
    </h:inputText>
</ui:repeat>
```

An alternative is to replace the `List<Integer>` by `Integer[]` or even `int[]`. EL will then be able to recognize the value expression as an integer type and hence JSF will be able to locate the desired converter for it. However, plain arrays instead of collections in the model are a "no-no" these days.

Coming back to the explicit standard converters `<f:convertNumber>` and `<f:convertDateTime>`, those can also be nested in any `ValueHolder` component. The difference between `<f:convertNumber>` and the implicit number-based converters is that the tags allow more fine-grained setting of conversion options, such as the number type or pattern, the amount of integer and/or fraction digits, whether grouping is used, and the locale.

# <f:convertNumber>

`<f:convertNumber>`[2] uses under the hood `java.text.NumberFormat`.[3] The `type` attribute specifies which instance will be obtained and defaults to `number`. Other allowable values are `currency` and `percent`. In other words, the following tags,

```
<f:convertNumber type="number" />
<f:convertNumber type="currency" />
<f:convertNumber type="percent" />
```

will under the hood obtain the `NumberFormat` instance as follows:

```
NumberFormat numberFormat = NumberFormat.getNumberInstance(locale);
NumberFormat currencyFormat = NumberFormat.getCurrencyInstance(locale);
NumberFormat percentFormat = NumberFormat.getPercentInstance(locale);
```

where the `locale` argument can be specified by the `locale` attribute of the `<f:convertNumber>` tag and defaults to `UIViewRoot#getLocale()` which in turn can be specified by the `locale` attribute of `<f:view>`. In other words, those instances will automatically apply the standard number format pattern based on the number type and the specified locale. The following example,

```
<f:view locale="pt_BR">
    ...
    <h:outputText value="#{product.price}">
        <f:convertNumber type="currency" locale="en_US" />
    </h:outputText>
</f:view>
```

will not format the price (a `BigDecimal` property) as R$ 12,34 (Brazilian real), but instead as $12.34 (US dollar). Note that the `locale` attribute of the `<f:convertNumber>` tag does not necessarily need to be specified as supported locale in `faces-config.xml`. Also noted should be that the `value` attribute doesn't necessarily need to refer a `BigDecimal`; any other `java.lang.Number` type is also supported, but for prices we'd of

---

[2]`https://javaserverfaces.github.io/docs/2.3/vldoc/f/convertNumber.html`.
[3]`https://docs.oracle.com/javase/8/docs/api/java/text/NumberFormat.html`.

course like to store the value in a BigDecimal instead of, for example, a Double or Float to avoid arithmetic errors due to the floating nature of floating point numbers.[4]

In case you need to change the standard number format pattern for some reason—for example, because you're working on a banking application which stores financial data with five fractions—and you'd like to present the full value in some back-end admin screen so that humans can if necessary verify them, then you can use the pattern attribute of the <f:convertNumber> tag to override the standard number format pattern conform the rules of java.text.DecimalFormat.[5]

```
<f:convertNumber pattern="¤ #,##0.00000" locale="pt_BR" />
```

Note that when the pattern attribute is specified, the type attribute is ignored. The "currency sign" pattern character "¤" specifies where the actual currency symbol must be inserted. The actual currency symbol depends on the specified locale. The "comma" pattern character "," specifies when the grouping separator must be inserted, which is relative to the decimal separator or the end of the value. The actual inserted grouping separator symbol is coincidentally also a comma in US dollar format but is a period in Brazilian real format. The "period" pattern character "." specifies the location of the decimal separator. The actual inserted decimal separator symbol is coincidentally also a period in US dollar format but is a comma in Brazilian real format. The "optional digit" pattern character "#" is in this pattern merely used to indicate when the grouping separator symbol should be inserted and won't show anything when the actual digit is absent. The "required digit" pattern character "0" specifies the minimum format which will show zero when the actual digit is absent. Following is an exercise code which should give insight into how <f:convertNumber> works under the hood:

```
Locale locale = new Locale("pt", "BR");
DecimalFormatSymbols symbols = new DecimalFormatSymbols(locale);

System.out.println("Currency symbol: " + symbols.getCurrencySymbol());
System.out.println("Grouping symbol: " + symbols.getGroupingSeparator());
System.out.println("Decimal symbol: " + symbols.getDecimalSeparator());

DecimalFormat formatter = new DecimalFormat("¤ #,##0.00000", symbols);
```

---

[4]http://floating-point-gui.de.

[5]https://docs.oracle.com/javase/8/docs/api/java/text/DecimalFormat.html.

```
System.out.println(formatter.format(new BigDecimal("12.34")));
System.out.println(formatter.format(new BigDecimal(".1234")));
System.out.println(formatter.format(new BigDecimal("1234")));
System.out.println(formatter.format(new BigDecimal("1234567.1234567")));
```

The output should look as follows:

```
Currency symbol: R$
Grouping symbol: .
Decimal symbol: ,
R$ 12,34000
R$ 0,12340
R$ 1.234,00000
R$ 1.234.567,12346
```

`<f:convertNumber>` will also render exactly those values. Apart from the `pattern` attribute, you can also fine-grain the `type` attribute with additional attributes such as `currencySymbol`, `integerOnly`, `groupingUsed`, `minIntegerDigits`, `maxIntegerDigits`, `minFractionDigits`, and `maxFractionDigits`. You can basically achieve the same formatting pattern "¤ #,##0.00000" as follows:

```
<f:convertNumber type="currency" locale="pt_BR"
    minFractionDigits="5" maxFractionDigits="5" />
```

This is actually more readable and more convenient in case you have a hard time getting out the currency sign placeholder from your keyboard. The `pattern` attribute is rarely more useful than fine-graining the `type` attribute with additional attributes.

In case you're using `<f:convertNumber>` in a UIInput component and thus require the end user to enter the value, you should keep in mind that currency and percent types explicitly require the end user to enter the currency or percent symbol as well. For the currency input, you can easily disable this by specifying an empty string as a currency symbol so that you can put it outside the input component.

```
<span class="currency">
    <span class="symbol">$</span>
    <h:inputText ...>
        <f:convertNumber type="currency" currencySymbol="" />
    </h:inputText>
</span>
```

For the percent type this is, unfortunately, not possible.

# <f:convertDateTime>

<f:convertDateTime>[6] uses under the hood java.text.DateFormat,[7] and, since
JSF 2.3, also java.time.formatter.DateTimeFormatter.[8] In other words, you can use
basically any kind of date for this. Also, this tag has a type attribute which must actually
correspond to the actual type of the model value. Historically, it was not possible to
programmatically detect the desired type based on a java.util.Date instance. This has
changed since the new java.time API which offers distinct classes for each date time
type. However, in order to be able to reuse the existing <f:convertDateTime> API for the
new java.time API, new types had to be added. Table 5-2 provides an overview.

***Table 5-2.*** *<f:convertDateTime type> Supported Values*

| Tag attribute | Value type | Actual formatter | Since |
|---|---|---|---|
| date (default) | java.util.Date (with zero time) | DateFormat#getDateInstance() | 1.0 |
| time | java.util.Date (with zero date) | DateFormat#getTimeInstance() | 1.0 |
| both | java.util.Date | DateFormat#getDateTimeInstance() | 1.0 |
| localDate | java.time.LocalDate | DateTimeFormatter#ofLocalizedDate() | 2.3 |
| localTime | java.time.LocalTime | DateTimeFormatter#ofLocalizedTime() | 2.3 |
| localDateTime | java.time.LocalDateTime | DateTimeFormatter#ofLocalizedDateTime() | 2.3 |
| offsetTime | java.time.OffsetTime | DateTimeFormatter#ISO_OFFSET_TIME | 2.3 |
| offsetDateTime | java.time.OffsetDateTime | DateTimeFormatter#ISO_OFFSET_DATE_TIME | 2.3 |
| zonedDateTime | java.time.ZonedDateTime | DateTimeFormatter#ISO_ZONED_DATE_TIME | 2.3 |

---

[6]https://javaserverfaces.github.io/docs/2.3/vdldoc/f/convertDateTime.html.
[7]https://docs.oracle.com/javase/8/docs/api/java/text/DateFormat.html.
[8]https://docs.oracle.com/javase/8/docs/api/java/time/format/DateTimeFormatter.html.

Along with the type attribute, you should preferably also specify the pattern attribute, particularly when requesting the end user to enter a java.util.Date or java.time.LocalXxx value via a UIInput component, because the actual pattern may vary in a not so self-documenting way across various locales. java.time.OffSetXxx and ZonedDateTime don't have that problem because they default to the universal ISO 8601 format.[9]

The pattern attribute of <f:convertDateTime> follows, for java.util.Date, the same rules as specified in the java.text.SimpleDateFormat Javadoc,[10] and for the java.time API, the same rules as specified in java.time.format.DateTimeFormatter Javadoc.[11] They are for the most part the same, but the java.time format supports more patterns. For both APIs, the "day of month" pattern character is "d", the "month of year" pattern character is "M", the "year" pattern character is "y", the "24h hour" pattern character is "H", the "minute" pattern is "m" , and the "second" pattern is "s". The ISO 8601 date format is "yyyy-MM-dd" and the ISO 8601 time format is "HH:mm:ss". The offset and zoned times require an additional offset after the time part, which is represented by the ISO 8601 time zone pattern character "X". Examples of valid values are "+01:00" for CET (Central European Time), "-03:00" for BRT (Brasilia Time), and "+5:30" for IST (Indian Standard Time). As before, the offset and zoned date and time need to be separated by the "T" character instead of a space. Following is an overview of all possible <f:convertDateTime> types whereby the localized ones have an explicitly specified pattern:

```
<h:form id="form">
    <h:inputText id="date" value="#{bean.date}">
        <f:convertDateTime type="date" pattern="yyyy-MM-dd" />
    </h:inputText>
    <h:inputText id="time" value="#{bean.time}">
        <f:convertDateTime type="time" pattern="HH:mm:ss" />
    </h:inputText>
    <h:inputText id="both" value="#{bean.both}">
        <f:convertDateTime type="both" pattern="yyyy-MM-dd HH:mm:ss" />
    </h:inputText>
```

---

[9]https://en.wikipedia.org/wiki/ISO_8601.

[10]https://docs.oracle.com/javase/8/docs/api/java/text/SimpleDateFormat.html.

[11]https://docs.oracle.com/javase/8/docs/api/java/time/format/DateTimeFormatter.html.

```
<h:inputText id="localDate" value="#{bean.localDate}">
    <f:convertDateTime type="localDate" pattern="yyyy-MM-dd" />
</h:inputText>
<h:inputText id="localTime" value="#{bean.localTime}">
    <f:convertDateTime type="localTime" pattern="HH:mm:ss" />
</h:inputText>
<h:inputText id="localDateTime" value="#{bean.localDateTime}">
    <f:convertDateTime type="localDateTime"
        pattern="yyyy-MM-dd HH:mm:ss">
    </f:convertDateTime>
</h:inputText>
<h:inputText id="offsetTime" value="#{bean.offsetTime}">
    <f:convertDateTime type="offsetTime" />
</h:inputText>
<h:inputText id="offsetDateTime" value="#{bean.offsetDateTime}">
    <f:convertDateTime type="offsetDateTime" />
</h:inputText>
<h:inputText id="zonedDateTime" value="#{bean.zonedDateTime}">
    <f:convertDateTime type="zonedDateTime" />
</h:inputText>
<h:commandButton value="submit" action="#{bean.submit}" />
<h:messages showSummary="false" showDetail="true"/>
</h:form>
```

Note that `<h:messages>` is here reconfigured to show the detail instead of just
the summary, because the detail message of a date time conversion error includes
in standard JSF an example value which is more useful for the end user in order to
understand the required format. Following is what the associated backing bean looks like:

```
@Named @RequestScoped
public class Bean {

    private Date date;
    private Date time;
    private Date both;
    private LocalDate localDate;
    private LocalTime localTime;
```

```
    private LocalDateTime localDateTime;
    private OffsetTime offsetTime;
    private OffsetDateTime offsetDateTime;
    private ZonedDateTime zonedDateTime;

    public void submit() {
        System.out.println("date: " + date);
        System.out.println("time: " + time);
        System.out.println("both: " + both);
        System.out.println("localDate: " + localDate);
        System.out.println("localTime: " + localTime);
        System.out.println("localDateTime: " + localDateTime);
        System.out.println("offsetTime: " + offsetTime);
        System.out.println("offsetDateTime: " + offsetDateTime);
        System.out.println("zonedDateTime: " + zonedDateTime);
    }

    // Add/generate getters and setters.
}
```

Now that HTML5 has been out for some time and more and more browsers support the new HTML5 date and time inputs,[12] you'd better activate it by default, because it comes with a very useful built-in date picker. The web browser may show the date pattern in the date picker in a localized format, but it will always submit the value in ISO 8601 format. This is thus very useful. The HTML5 date and time inputs can be activated by setting the type attribute of the input text field to "date",[13] "time",[14] or "datetime-local"[15] (and thus not "datetime" because it has been dropped). With the JSF <h:inputText>, you'd need to set it as a pass-through attribute. Following are some examples:

```
<h:form id="form">
    <h:inputText id="localDate" a:type="date" value="#{bean.localDate}">
        <f:convertDateTime type="localDate" pattern="yyyy-MM-dd" />
    </h:inputText>
```

---

[12]https://developer.mozilla.org/en-US/docs/Web/HTML/Element/input/date.

[13]https://developer.mozilla.org/en-US/docs/Web/HTML/Element/input/date.

[14]https://developer.mozilla.org/en-US/docs/Web/HTML/Element/input/time.

[15]https://developer.mozilla.org/en-US/docs/Web/HTML/Element/input/datetime-local.

```
<h:inputText id="localTime" a:type="time" value="#{bean.localTime}">
    <f:convertDateTime type="localTime" pattern="HH:mm" />
</h:inputText>
<h:inputText id="localDateTime" a:type="datetime-local"
    value="#{bean.localDateTime}">
    <f:convertDateTime type="localDateTime"
        pattern="yyyy-MM-dd'T'HH:mm">
    </f:convertDateTime>
</h:inputText>
<h:commandButton value="submit" action="#{bean.submit}" />
<h:messages showSummary="false" showDetail="true"/>
</h:form>
```

Following is how they're rendered in Chrome browser (with newlines added):

## Standard Validators

When the submitted value is successfully converted during the process validations phase (third phase), then JSF will immediately advance to perform validation on the converted value. JSF already provides a handful of standard validators out of the box. They are all available in the javax.faces.validator package[16] and they all implement the Validator<T> interface. Table 5-3 provides an overview of them.

---

[16]https://javaee.github.io/javaee-spec/javadocs/javax/faces/validator/package-summary.html

*Table 5-3.  Standard Validators Provided by JSF*

| Validator class | Validator ID | Validator tag | Value type | Since |
|---|---|---|---|---|
| LongRangeValidator | javax.faces.LongRange | <f:validateLongRange> | java.lang.Number | 1.0 |
| DoubleRangeValidator | javax.faces.DoubleRange | <f:validateDoubleRange> | java.lang.Number | 1.0 |
| LengthValidator | javax.faces.Length | <f:validateLength> | java.lang.Object | 1.0 |
| RegexValidator | javax.faces.RegularExpression | <f:validateRegex> | java.lang.String | 2.0 |
| RequiredValidator | javax.faces.Required | <f:validateRequired> | java.lang.Object | 2.0 |
| BeanValidator | javax.faces.Bean | <f:validateBean> | java.lang.Object | 2.0 |
| n/a | n/a | <f:validateWholeBean> | java.lang.Object | 2.3 |

The "Validator ID" column basically specifies the validator identifier as you could specify in the `validator` attribute of any `EditableValueHolder` component, or the `validatorId` attribute of any nested `<f:validator>` tag in order to activate the specific validator. Contrary to the converter, a single `EditableValueHolder` component can have multiple validators attached. They will all be executed regardless of each other's outcome.

# `<f:validateLongRange>`/`<f:validateDoubleRange>`

These validators allow you to specify a minimum and/or maximum allowed number value for an input component tied to a `java.lang.Number`-based property. Those can be specified with the `minimum` and `maximum` attributes.

```
<h:inputText value="#{bean.quantity}">
    <f:validateLongRange minimum="1" maximum="10" />
</h:inputText>
```

This is, via pass-through attributes, also combinable with the HTML5 input types "number" (spinner) and "range" (slider), which in turn require `min`, `max`, and optionally `step` as pass-through attributes. In this example, `#{bean.quantity}` is just an `Integer` and `#{bean.volume}` is a `BigDecimal`.

```
<h:inputText value="#{bean.quantity}"
    a:type="number" a:min="1" a:max="10">
    <f:validateLongRange minimum="1" maximum="10" />
</h:inputText>
<h:inputText value="#{bean.volume}"
    a:type="range" a:min="1" a:max="10" a:step="0.1">
    <f:validateLongRange minimum="1" maximum="10" />
</h:inputText>
```

Do note that you can just use `<f:validateLongRange>` on a `BigDecimal` property. It doesn't care about the actual `java.lang.Number` type of the property being a `Long` or not, but only the specified `minimum` and `maximum` attributes being a `Long`. In case you want to specify a fractional-based number as minimum and/or maximum, then use `<f:validateDoubleRange>` instead.

```
<h:inputText value="#{bean.volume}"
    a:type="range" a:min="0.1" a:max="10.0" a:step="0.1">
    <f:validateDoubleRange minimum="0.1" maximum="10.0" />
</h:inputText>
```

# <f:validateLength>/<f:validateRegex>

These validators are primarily designed for java.lang.String-based properties.
<f:validateLength> will first convert the submitted value to string by calling
Object#toString() on it and then validate the String#length() result based on the
specified minimum and/or maximum attributes. <f:validateRegex> will cast the submitted
value to String and then check if String#matches() returns true for the specified
pattern attribute. In other words, it doesn't accept any other property type than
java.lang.String. Imagine that you want to validate a value to be always three digits;
thus there are three possible ways:

```
<h:inputText value="#{bean.someStringOrInteger}" maxlength="3">
    <f:validateLength minimum="3" maximum="3" />
</h:inputText>
```

```
<h:inputText value="#{bean.someString}" maxlength="3">
    <f:validateRegex pattern="[0-9]{3}" />
</h:inputText>
```

```
<h:inputText value="#{bean.someInteger}" maxlength="3">
    <f:validateLongRange minimum="100" maximum="999" />
</h:inputText>
```

The maxlength="3" attribute is just there so that the end user can't enter more
than three characters on the client side anyway. Storing numbers as strings is plain
nonsense, so the second way is scratched. That leaves us with the first or third way.
Technically it does not really matter which one you pick. The first way is arguably more
self-documenting because you actually want to validate the length, not the range.

Coming back to <f:validateRegex>, the pattern attribute follows exactly the same
regular expression rules as specified in java.util.regex.Pattern.[17]

---

[17]https://docs.oracle.com/javase/8/docs/api/java/util/regex/Pattern.html.

However, there's one potential caveat: the necessary amount of escape backslashes depends on the currently used EL implementation. In Oracle's EL implementation (`com.sun.el.*`), you need two backslashes, exactly as in a regular Java String, but in Apache's EL implementation (`org.apache.el.*`), you must use one backslash, otherwise it will error out or it won't match as you'd expect. As of now, Payara, WildFly, Liberty, and WebLogic use Oracle's EL implementation, and TomEE and Tomcat use Apache's EL implementation. In other words, the following example will work on servers using Oracle EL but won't work on servers using Apache EL.

```
<h:inputText value="#{bean.someString}" maxlength="3">
    <f:validateRegex pattern="\\d{3}" />
</h:inputText>
```

When using Apache EL, you need `pattern="\d{3}"` instead. On the other hand, the regular expression pattern \d actually means "any digit" and thus matches not only the Latin digits but also the Hebrew, Cyrillic, Arabic, Chinese, etc. If that was not your intent, you'd better use the [0-9] pattern.

# <f:validateRequired>

This is a slightly odd beast. That is, all `UIInput` components already have a `required` attribute offering exactly the desired functionality. Why would you then use a whole `<f:validateRequired>` tag instead? It was added in JSF 2.0 specifically for "Composite Components" (more on this later, in Chapter 7). More to the point, in some composite component compositions the template client is given the opportunity to attach converters and validators to a specific `EditableValueHolder` interface exposed by the composite component, which in turn references one or more `UIInput` components enclosed in the composite component implementation. Following is an example of such a composite component:

```
<cc:interface>
    ...
    <cc:editableValueHolder
        name="inputs" targets="input1 input3">
    </cc:editableValueHolder>
</cc:interface>
```

```
<cc:implementation>

    ...
    <h:inputText id="input1" ... />
    <h:inputText id="input2" ... />
    <h:inputText id="input3" ... />

    ...
</cc:implementation>
```

And following is an example of the template client:

```
<my:compositeComponent ...>
    <f:validateRequired for="inputs" />
</my:compositeComponent>
```

As you might have guessed, the `for` attribute must exactly match the `name` attribute of exposed `<cc:editableValueHolder>` and this validator will basically target the enclosed input components identified by `input1` and `input3` (and thus not `input2`) and thus effectively make them `required="true"`. This `for` attribute is, by the way, also present on all other converter and validator tags.

# `<f:validateBean>/<f:validateWholeBean>`

When used, these tags have a required dependency on the Bean Validation API (application programming interface), previously more commonly known as "JSR 303." Like JSF, Bean Validation is part of the Java EE API, already included in any Java EE application server. In Tomcat and other servlet containers, you'd need to install it separately. In Java code, Bean Validation is represented by annotations and interfaces of the `javax.validation.*` package, such as `@NotNull`, `@Size`, `@Pattern`, `ConstraintValidator`, etc. Currently the most popular implementation is Hibernate Validator.[18]

JSF automatically detects the presence of Bean Validation and will in such a case transparently process all Bean Validation constraints during the end of the process validations phase (third phase), regardless of the outcome of JSF's own validators. If desired, this can be disabled application-wide with the following context parameter in `web.xml`:

---

[18]`http://hibernate.org/validator/`

165

```
<context-param>
    <param-name>
        javax.faces.validator.DISABLE_DEFAULT_BEAN_VALIDATOR
    </param-name>
    <param-value>true</param-value>
</context-param>
```

Or, if this is a little too rough, you can fine-grain it with help of the `<f:validateBean>` tag wrapping a group of `UIInput` components, or nested in them. When the `disabled` attribute of the `<f:validateBean>` tag is set to `true`, then any Bean Validation will be disabled on the target `UIInput` components. The following code will disable any Bean Validation only on the parent `UIInput` component.

```
<h:inputText ...>
    <f:validateBean disabled="true" />
</h:inputText>
```

And the following code will disable any Bean Validation only on `UIInput` components identified by input3, input4, and input5:

```
<h:inputText id="input1" ... />
<h:inputText id="input2" ... />
<f:validateBean disabled="true">
    <h:inputText id="input3" ... />
    <h:inputText id="input4" ... />
    <h:inputText id="input5" ... />
<f:validateBean>
```

It is important to keep in mind is that this will only disable JSF-managed Bean Validation and thus not, for example, JPA-managed Bean Validation. So, if you happen to use JPA (Java Persistence API) to persist your entities which are filled out by JSF components with Bean Validation disabled, then JPA would still perform Bean Validation on its behalf, fully independently from JSF. In case you want to disable Bean Validation on

the JPA side as well, you need to set the property javax.persistence.validation.mode to
NONE in persistence.xml (see also the javax.persistence.ValidationMode Javadoc).[19]

```
<property name="javax.persistence.validation.mode">NONE</property>
```

With the validationGroups attribute of the <f:validateBean> tag you can
if necessary declare one or more validation groups. In such a case, only the Bean
Validation constraints which are registered on the same group will be processed.
Imagine the following model:

```
@NotNull
private String value1;

@NotNull(groups=NotNull.class)
private String value2;

@NotNull(groups={NotNull.class, Default.class})
private String value3;
```

Note that the groups attribute of any Bean Validation constraint must reference an
interface, but it may be any one you want. For simplicity, in the above example we're just
reusing the javax.validation.constraints.NotNull interface as a group identifier. The
common practice is, however, to create your own marker interface for the desired group.

Also not unimportant is that the @NotNull would only work when you've configured
JSF to interpret empty string submitted values as null; otherwise it would pollute the
model with empty strings instead of nulls and cause the @NotNull not to be able to do its
job because an empty string is not null. As a reminder, the web.xml context parameter of
interest is as follows:

```
<context-param>
    <param-name>
        javax.faces.INTERPRET_EMPTY_STRING_SUBMITTED_VALUES_AS_NULL
    </param-name>
    <param-value>true</param-value>
</context-param>
```

---

[19]https://javaee.github.io/javaee-spec/javadocs/javax/persistence/ValidationMode.html.

Now, when submitting an empty form while having those model properties referenced in the following input components, without any `<f:validateBean>` on them:

```
<h:inputText value="#{bean.value1}" />
<h:inputText value="#{bean.value2}" />
<h:inputText value="#{bean.value3}" />
```

you will receive a validation error on Bean Validation constraints belonging to the `javax.validation.groups.Default` group, which are thus the groupless `value1` and the explicitly grouped `value3`. The `value2` won't be Bean-Validated as it doesn't have the default group explicitly declared.

And, when submitting an empty form while having `<f:validateBean>` with `validationGroups` set to `NotNull.class`:

```
<f:validateBean validationGroups="javax.validation.constraints.NotNull">
    <h:inputText value="#{bean.value1}" />
    <h:inputText value="#{bean.value2}" />
    <h:inputText value="#{bean.value3}" />
</f:validateBean>
```

you will receive a validation error on Bean Validation constraints belonging to the `javax.validation.constraints.NotNull` group, which are thus the `value2` and `value3`, which explicitly have this group declared. The groupless `value1` won't be Bean-Validated as it only implies the default group.

Finally, when submitting an empty form while having a `<f:validateBean>` with both groups specified in `validationGroups` attribute as a comma separated string:

```
<f:validateBean validationGroups="javax.validation.groups.Default,
                                   javax.validation.constraints.NotNull">
    <h:inputText value="#{bean.value1}" />
    <h:inputText value="#{bean.value2}" />
    <h:inputText value="#{bean.value3}" />
</f:validateBean>
```

you will receive a validation error on all inputs, because they all match at least one of the specified groups. In real-world applications, however, this grouping feature has very little use. It's only really useful when the grouped fields can be validated at the same time by the same validator. With Bean Validation, the only way to achieve that is to put a custom `Constraint` annotation on the bean class itself, get an instance of that bean with the values populated, and then pass it to the custom `ConstraintValidator` associated with the custom `Constraint` annotation. Imagine a "period" entity having a "start date" property which should always be before the "end date" property. It would look something like the following:

```
@PeriodConstraint
public class Period implements Serializable {

    @NotNull
    private LocalDate startDate;

    @NotNull
    private LocalDate endDate;

    // Add/generate getters and setters.
}
```

With the following custom constraint annotation:

```
@Constraint(validatedBy=PeriodValidator.class)
@Target(TYPE)
@Retention(RUNTIME)
public @interface PeriodConstraint {
    String message() default "Start date must be before end date";
    Class<?>[] groups() default {};
    Class<?>[] payload() default {};
}
```

And the following custom constraint validator:

```
public class PeriodValidator
    implements ConstraintValidator<PeriodConstraint, Period>
{
    @Override
    public boolean isValid
        (Period period, ConstraintValidatorContext context)
    {
        return period.getStartDate().isBefore(period.getEndDate());
    }
}
```

You see, Bean Validation expects that the model values are present when performing the validation. In the JSF perspective, this means that the model values must be updated before processing the validations. However, this doesn't fit into the JSF life cycle wherein the model values are only updated after the validations are successfully processed. Essentially, JSF would need to clone the bean instance, populate it with the desired model values, invoke Bean Validation on it, collect any validation errors, and then discard the cloned bean instance.

This is exactly what the `<f:validateWholeBean>` tag, introduced with JSF 2.3, is doing under the hood. Following is an example form wherein this code is being used:

```
<h:form>
    <h:inputText a:type="date" value="#{booking.period.startDate}">
        <f:convertDateTime type="localDate" pattern="yyyy-MM-dd" />
    </h:inputText>
    <h:inputText a:type="date" value="#{booking.period.endDate}">
        <f:convertDateTime type="localDate" pattern="yyyy-MM-dd" />
    </h:inputText>
    <h:commandButton value="Submit" />
    <h:messages />
    <f:validateWholeBean value="#{booking.period}" />
</h:form>
```

With this backing bean:

```
@Named @ViewScoped
public class Booking implements Serializable {

    private Period period = new Period();


    // Add/generate getter.
}
```

Do note that `<f:validateWholeBean>` is explicitly placed as the last child of the parent `<h:form>`, which ensures that the validation is performed as the last thing after all individual input components in the same form. This is as per the specification; the JSF implementation may throw a runtime exception when the tag is misplaced.

# Immediate Attribute

The EditableValueHolder, ActionSource, and AjaxBehavior interfaces also specify an immediate property which basically maps to the immediate attribute of all UIInput and UICommand components and the <f:ajax> tag. When set to true on an EditableValueHolder component, then anything that normally takes place during the process validations phase (third phase) as well as the update model values phase (fourth phase) will be performed during the apply request values phase (second phase). When conversion or validation fails on them, then the life cycle will also skip the process validations phase (third phase). When set to true on an ActionSource component or AjaxBehavior tag, then anything that normally takes place during the invoke application phase (fifth phase) will be performed during the apply request values phase (second phase) and then only if conversion and validation haven't failed.

Historically, this attribute was mainly used to be able to perform an "inner" action on the form, usually to load a child input component depending on the submitted value of the parent input component, without being blocked by conversion or validation errors coming from other input components in the same form. A common use case was populating a child drop-down on the change of a parent drop-down.

```
<h:selectOneMenu value="#{bean.country}" required="true" immediate="true"
    onchange="submit()" valueChangeListener="#{bean.loadCities}">
    <f:selectItems value="#{bean.countries}" />
</h:selectOneMenu>
<h:selectOneMenu value="#{bean.city}" required="true">
    <f:selectItems value="#{bean.cities}" />
</h:selectOneMenu>
```

This approach obviously predates the Web 2.0 era wherein you'd just use Ajax for this. Understand that the immediate attribute has essentially become useless for this purpose since the introduction of <f:ajax> in JSF 2.0. Exactly the same use case can be achieved in a much cleaner way as follows:

```
<h:selectOneMenu value="#{bean.country}" required="true">
    <f:selectItems value="#{bean.countries}" />
    <f:ajax listener="#{bean.loadCities}" render="city" />
</h:selectOneMenu>
```

171

```
<h:selectOneMenu id="city" value="#{bean.city}" required="true">
    <f:selectItems value="#{bean.cities}" />
</h:selectOneMenu>
```

As you learned in Chapter 4, the execute attribute of <f:ajax> already defaults to @this, so it's just omitted. This also means that all other EditableValueHolder components in the same form won't be processed and thus won't cause #{bean. loadCities} ever to be blocked by conversion or validation errors coming from other inputs.

These days, with Ajax magic and all, the immediate attribute has thus lost its main use case. JSF could do as well without it. Due to its historic use case, many starters may mistake its primary purpose to be "skip all validation." This is, however, not true. For that, you'd need to fine-tune the execute attribute of <f:ajax> so that it only covers the input components that really need to be validated. In case you want to actually "skip all validation" while submitting the entire form, you'd best use Bean Validation constraints instead (the @NotNull and friends) and simply have <f:validateBean disabled="true"> wrapping the entire form.

# Custom Converters

From the beginning JSF has supported custom converters. The main use case is to be able to convert a non-standard model value, such as a persistence entity specific to the web application. The less common use case is to extend an existing standard converter and set some commonly used defaults in its constructor so that you can get away with less code in order to declare the desired standard converter configuration in the view.

Imagine that you want to be able to create master-detail pages on your persistence entities wherein you'd like to pass the ID of the entity around as a request parameter from the master page to the detail page. Following is an example data table in the master page /products/list.xhtml based on a fictive Product entity:

```
<h:dataTable value="#{listProducts.products}" var="product">
    <h:column>#{product.id}</h:column>
    <h:column>#{product.name}</h:column>
    <h:column>#{product.description}</h:column>
```

```
    <h:column>
        <h:link value="Edit" outcome="edit">
            <f:param name="id" value="#{product.id}" />
        </h:link>
    </h:column>
</h:dataTable>
```

Note the last column of the table. It generates a link to the detail page /products/edit.xhtml whereby the ID of the entity is passed as a GET request parameter as in /product.xhtml?id=42. In the detail page, you can use <f:viewParam> to set the GET request parameter in the backing bean.

```
<f:metadata>
    <f:viewParam name="id" value="#{editProduct.product}"
        required="true" requiredMessage="Bad request">
    </f:viewParam>
</f:metadata>
...
<h:form>
    <h1>Edit product #{editProduct.product.id}</h1>
    <h:inputText value="#{editProduct.product.name}" />
    <h:inputText value="#{editProduct.product.description}" />
    ...
</h:form>
```

However, there's one small problem: the GET request parameter is in Java perspective basically a String representing the product ID while the product property of the EditProduct backing bean actually expects a whole Product entity identified by the passed-in ID.

```
@Named @ViewScoped
public class EditProduct implements Serializable {

    private Product product;

    // Getter+setter.
}
```

For exactly this conversion step, a custom converter has to be created which is capable of converting between a String representing the product ID and an Object representing the Product entity. JSF offers the javax.faces.convert.Converter interface[20] to get started. Following is a concrete example of such a ProductConverter:

```
@FacesConverter(forClass=Product.class, managed=true)
public class ProductConverter implements Converter<Product> {

    @Inject
    private ProductService productService;

    @Override
    public String getAsString
        (FacesContext context, UIComponent component, Product product)
    {
        if (product == null) {
            return "";
        }

        if (product.getId() != null) {
            return product.getId().toString();
        }
        else {
            throw new ConverterException(
                new FacesMessage("Invalid product ID"), e);
        }
    }

    @Override
    public Product getAsObject
        (FacesContext context, UIComponent component, String id)
    {
        if (id == null || id.isEmpty()) {
            return null;
        }
```

---

[20]https://javaee.github.io/javaee-spec/javadocs/javax/faces/convert/Converter.html.

```
    try {
        return productService.getById(Long.valueOf(id));
    }
    catch (NumberFormatException e) {
        throw new ConverterException(
            new FacesMessage("Invalid product ID"), e);
    }
  }
}
```

There are several important things to note here in the @FacesConverter annotation. First, the forClass attribute basically specifies the target entity type for which this converter should automatically run during the process validations phase (third phase) and the render response phase (sixth phase). This way you don't need to explicitly register the converter in the view. In case you wanted to do so, you'd replace the forClass attribute by the value attribute specifying the unique identifier of the converter, for example:

```
@FacesConverter(value="project.ProductConverter", managed=true)
```

Then you can specify exactly that converter ID in the converter attribute of any ValueHolder component, or the converterId attribute of any nested <f:converter> tag.

```
<f:viewParam name="id" value="#{editProduct.product}"
    converter="project.ProductConverter"
    required="true" requiredMessage="Bad request">
</f:viewParam>
```

But this is not necessary when you just keep using the forClass attribute. Note that you can't specify both. It's one or the other where the value attribute takes precedence over the forClass. So, if you specify both, the forClass attribute is essentially ignored. We don't want to have that as it's much more powerful for this particular purpose of transparently converting whole entities.

The second thing to note in the annotation is the managed attribute. This is new since JSF 2.3. Essentially, this manages the converter instance in the CDI context. Setting the managed attribute to true is mandatory in order to get dependency injection to work in the converter. Previously, this was worked around by making the converter itself a managed bean.[21]

If you have worked with JSF converters before, you'll also notice the interface now finally being parameterized. The interface predates Java 1.5 and was hence not parameterized from the beginning. With a `Converter<T>`, the `getAsObject()` now returns a `T` instead of `Object` and the `getAsString()` now takes a `T` as value argument instead of `Object`. This saves unnecessary `instanceof` checks and/or casts.

Note that JSF's own standard converters which predate JSF 2.3 (currently, basically all of them thus) are frozen in time and cannot take advantage of this as they would otherwise no longer be backward compatible. In other words, they are still raw types. That is, there's a small but not unavoidable chance that someone is programmatically using JSF converters in plain Java code instead of letting JSF deal with them. That plain Java code would no longer compile if the standard converters were parameterized. It's essentially the same reason that the `Map#get()` explicitly takes `Object` instead of `K` as argument. Further there's a yet smaller but still not unavoidable chance that someone has created a custom converter which extends a standard converter, but also explicitly redeclares the interface. Something like the following:

```
public class ExtendedNumberConverter
    extends NumberConverter implements Converter
{
    // ...
}
```

Such an obscure converter would no longer compile if `NumberConverter` was parameterized in some way. Even if we parameterize `NumberConverter` as a `Converter<Object>`, the compiler would error on `ExtendedNumberConverter` as follows and hence break backward compatibility:

> *The interface Converter cannot be implemented more than once with different arguments: Converter<Object> and Converter*

---

[21]https://stackoverflow.com/q/7665673/157882.

Coming back to our `ProductConverter` implementation, in the `getAsString()` you'll notice that the converter explicitly returns an empty string when the model value is `null`. This is as per the Javadoc.[22] The technical reason is that JSF won't render the associated HTML attribute when the evaluated value is `null`. In general, this is not a big problem. The fewer unused attributes in the generated HTML output, the better it is. Only, this won't work as expected for the `<option>` of a `<select>` element. If the custom converter would return `null` instead of an empty string, then the `<option>` element would be rendered without any `value` attribute and thus fall back to submitting its text content instead. Awkward indeed, but this is literally specified in the HTML specification.[23] In other words, if you have a converter that incorrectly returns `null` instead of an empty string, and you have a drop-down list with the associated entities along with a default option as follows:

```
<h:selectOneMenu value="#{bean.product}">
    <f:selectItem itemValue="#{null}" itemLabel="Please select ..." />
    <f:selectItems value="#{bean.products}"
        var="product" itemLabel="#{product.name}">
    </f:selectItems>
</h:selectOneMenu>
```

then the web browser would, during submitting the default option, send the literal string "Please select ..." to the server instead of an empty string. This would cause a `NumberFormatException` in `ProductConverter#getAsObject()` while we intend to return `null` here. The correct solution is thus to let the `getAsString()` return an empty string in case the model value is `null`.

In case you have more persistence entities for which you need a JSF converter, and want to avoid repeating essentially the same `ProductConverter` logic for all other persistence entities, you can create a generic JSF converter for them. This works only if all your persistence entities extend from the same base class wherein the `getId()` is defined.

```
@MappedSuperClass
public abstract class BaseEntity implements Serializable {

    @Id @GeneratedValue(strategy=IDENTITY)
    private Long id;
```

---

[22]https://javaee.github.io/javaee-spec/javadocs/javax/faces/convert/Converter.html.
[23]https://html.spec.whatwg.org/multipage/form-elements.html#attr-option-value.

```
    public Long getId() {
        return id;
    }
}
```

And if you have a base entity service for all of them:

```
@Stateless
public class BaseEntityService {

    @PersistenceContext
    private EntityManager entityManager;

    @TransactionAttribute(SUPPORTS)
    public <E extends BaseEntity> E getById(Class<E> type, Long id) {
        return entityManager.find(type, id);
    }
}
```

the generic converter can then look as follows:

```
@FacesConverter(forClass=BaseEntity.class, managed=true)
public class BaseEntityConverter implements Converter<BaseEntity> {

    @Inject
    private BaseEntityService baseEntityService;

    @Override
    public String getAsString
        (FacesContext context, UIComponent component, BaseEntity entity)
    {
        if (entity == null) {
            return "";
        }

        if (entity.getId() != null) {
            return entity.getId().toString();
        }
```

```
    else {
        throw new ConverterException(
            new FacesMessage("Invalid entity ID"), e);
    }
}

@Override
public BaseEntity getAsObject
    (FacesContext context, UIComponent component, String id)
{
    if (id == null || id.isEmpty()) {
        return null;
    }

    ValueExpression value = component.getValueExpression("value");
    Class<? extends BaseEntity> type = (Class<? extends BaseEntity>)
        value.getType(context.getELContext());

    try {
        return baseEntityService.getById(type, Long.valueOf(id));
    }
    catch (NumberFormatException e) {
        throw new ConverterException(
            new FacesMessage("Invalid entity ID"), e);
    }
}
}
```

The key here is thus the ValueExpression#getType() call. This returns the actual type of the property behind the EL expression associated with the component's value attribute. In case of <f:viewParam value="#{editProduct.product}"> this would thus return Product.class, which fits Class<? extends BaseEntity>.

Coming back to the less common use case of a custom converter, extending a standard converter, imagine that you have a <f:convertDateTime> configuration which is repeated everywhere in your web application:

```
<f:convertDateTime type="localDate" pattern="yyyy-MM-dd" />
```

And you'd like to replace it with something like the following:

```
<t:convertLocalDate />
```

Then one way is to just extend it, set the defaults in the constructor, register it in the `*.taglib.xml` file, and that's it. Following is what such a `LocalDateConverter` can look like:

```
@FacesConverter("project.ConvertLocalDate")
public class LocalDateConverter extends DateTimeConverter {

    public LocalDateConverter() {
        setType("localDate");
        setPattern("yyyy-MM-dd");
    }
}
```

And here's the `/WEB-INF/example.taglib.xml` entry.

```
<tag>
    <tag-name>convertLocalDate</tag-name>
    <converter>
        <converter-id>project.ConvertLocalDate</converter-id>
    </converter>
</tag>
```

Alternatively, you can also make it an implicit converter by getting rid of the converter ID and making it a `forClass` converter.

```
@FacesConverter(forClass=LocalDate.class)
```

This way you don't even need any `<t:convertLocalDate>` tag. Don't forget to remove the `<tag>` entry in `example.taglib.xml`. They cannot be used simultaneously. If you need such case, for example, because you want to able to change the `LocalDate` pattern, create another subclass.

You can even have a `forClass` converter for `java.lang.String` typed properties. This is very useful when you want have an automatic application-wide string-trimming strategy which should prevent the model from being polluted with leading or trailing whitespace on user-submitted values. Following is what such a converter can look like:

```
@FacesConverter(forClass=String.class)
public class TrimConverter implements Converter<String> {

    @Override
    public String getAsString
        (FacesContext context, UIComponent component, String modelValue)
    {
        return modelValue == null ? "" : modelValue;
    }

    @Override
    public String getAsObject(FacesContext context,
        UIComponent component, String submittedValue)
    {
        if (submittedValue == null || submittedValue.isEmpty()) {
            return null;
        }

        String trimmed = submittedValue.trim();
        return trimmed.isEmpty() ? null : trimmed;
    }
}
```

Last but not least, when you need to provide whole entities as SelectItem values of a selection component as below (see also Chapter 4), along with a custom converter for Country.class:

```
<h:selectOneMenu value="#{bean.country}">
    <f:selectItem itemValue="#{null}" itemLabel="-- select one --" />
    <f:selectItems value="#{bean.availableCountries}" var="country">
        itemValue="#{country}" itemLabel="#{country.name}"
    </f:selectItems>
</h:selectOneMenu>
```

where the associated backing bean properties are declared as follows:

```
private Country country;
private List<Country> availableCountries;
```

then you need to keep in mind that the entity has its equals() and hashCode() properly implemented. Otherwise JSF may throw a confusing validation error when submitting the form.

*Validation Error: Value is not valid*

This may happen when the bean is request scoped instead of view scoped and thus recreates the list of available countries during every postback. As part of safeguard against tampered requests, JSF will reiterate over the available options in order to validate if the selected option is indeed among them. JSF will use the Object#equals() method to test the selected option against each available option. If this hasn't returned true for any of the available options, then the above-mentioned validation error will be thrown.

Continuing with the BaseEntity example, here's how you'd best implement its equals() and hashCode() methods.

```
@Override
public boolean equals(Object other) {
    if (getId() != null
        && getClass().isInstance(other)
        && other.getClass().isInstance(this))
    {
        return getId().equals((((BaseEntity) other).getId());
    }
    else {
        return (other == this);
    }
}

@Override
public int hashCode() {
    if (getId() != null) {
        return Objects.hash(getId());
    }
```

```
    else {
        return super.hashCode();
    }
}
```

Note the bidirectional `Class#isInstance()` test in the `equals()` method. This is done instead of `getClass() == other.getClass()`, because that would return `false` when your persistence framework uses proxies, such as Hibernate.

# Custom Validators

Also, validators can be customized in JSF from the beginning. As almost every every basic use case is already covered by standard JSF validators and even Bean Validation constraints, such as length, range, and pattern validation, the most common use case left to a custom JSF validator is validating the data integrity by testing the submitted value against database-based constraints. Generally, those concern unique constraints.

A good real-world example is validating during e-mail-based signup or while changing the e-mail address in the user account management page when the specified e-mail address is not already in use. Particularly, the change event can't be tested with a Bean Validation constraint in a simple way, because Bean Validation doesn't offer the opportunity to compare the old value with the new value without re-obtaining the entity from the database. To start, just implement the `javax.faces.validator.Validator` interface[24] accordingly.

```
@FacesValidator(value="project.UniqueEmailValidator", managed=true)
public class UniqueEmailValidator implements Validator<String> {

    @Inject
    private UserService userService;

    @Override
    public void validate
        (FacesContext context, UIComponent component, String email)
            throws ValidatorException
```

---

[24]https://javaee.github.io/javaee-spec/javadocs/javax/faces/validator/Validator.html.

```
    {
        if (email == null || email.isEmpty()) {
            return; // Let @NotNull or required=true handle this.
        }

        String oldEmail = (String) ((UIInput) component).getValue();

        if (!email.equals(oldEmail) && userService.exist(email)) {
            throw new ValidatorException(
                new FacesMessage("Email already in use"));
        }
    }
}
```

In order to get it to run, just specify exactly the declared validator ID in the validator attribute of any EditableValueHolder component, or the validatorId attribute of any nested <f:validator> tag.

```
<h:inputText value="#{signup.user.email}"
    validator="project.UniqueEmailValidator">
</h:inputText>
```

When looking at the UniqueEmailValidator class, you'll notice that the annotation and the interface also got the same JSF 2.3 changes as the converter. Like the @FacesConverter, the @FacesValidator annotation, since JSF 2.3, also got a new managed attribute which should enable dependency injection in the validator implementation. And, like the Converter<T>, the Validator<T> also got parameterized whereby the validate() method now takes a T instead of Object as a value argument.

You also need to make sure that your validators are implemented so that they skip validation when the value argument is null or empty. Historically, in JSF 1.x, the validate() method would always be skipped when the value argument is null. However, this has changed since the integration of Bean Validation in JSF 2.0, thereby breaking backward compatibility on existing JSF 1.x-based custom validators. This breaking change could be turned off by explicitly setting the following web.xml context parameter:

```
<context-param>
    <param-name>javax.faces.VALIDATE_EMPTY_FIELDS</param-name>
    <param-value>false</param-value>
</context-param>
```

The disadvantage of this is that the `@NotNull` of Bean Validation won't be triggered by JSF and you'd basically need to repeat this constraint for all JSF input components by explicitly setting their `required` attribute to `true`. You'd better not do this and just keep performing the `null` and empty check in your custom validator. Having validation constraints at a single place in the model with help of Bean Validation is more Don't Repeat Yourself (DRY) than repeating the validation constraints across different layers using the very same model.

Finally, the old value can simply be obtained from `UIInput#getValue()` which basically returns the current `value` attribute of the `UIInput` component.

Coming back to the use case of validating the uniqueness of the submitted value, of course you could also skip this and insert the data anyway and catch any constraint violation exception coming from the persistence layer and display a faces message accordingly. However, this doesn't go well with the current trend of immediate feedback directly after changing the input field in the user interface.

In this specific use case of validating a unique e-mail address during signup, however, there may be another reason not to give away too much detail about the uniqueness of the specified e-mail address: security. In such a case, you'd best let the signup complete exactly the same way as if it was successful whereby you tell the user to check the mailbox, but behind the scenes actually send a different e-mail to the target recipient, rather than an activation e-mail, preferably not more than once daily. The e-mail would be similar to the following:

*Dear user,*

*It looks like you or someone else tried to sign up on <u>our web site</u> using your email address foo@example.com while it is already associated with an existing account. Perhaps you actually wanted to <u>log in</u> or to <u>reset your password</u>? If it actually wasn't you, please let us know by replying to this email and we'll investigate this.*

*Sincerely, Example Company*

Finally, you might also want to consider invalidating or deduplicating e-mails that contain the "+" character in the username part, followed by a sequence of characters, representing an e-mail alias. For a lot of e-mail providers, notably Gmail, e-mail addresses `foo@gmail.com` and `foo+bar@gmail.com` refer to exactly the same e-mail account, thereby basically allowing the end user to create a nearly unlimited amount of accounts.

# Custom Constraints

While not part of the JSF, for the sake of completeness we'd like to show another example of a custom Bean Validation constraint. An earlier example was already given in the section about <f:validateWholeBean>. The Bean Validation API already offers a lot of existing constraints out of the box which you can find in the javax.validation. constraints package.[25] A lot of new constraints have been added in Bean Validation 2.0, also part of Java EE 8 like JSF 2.3, such as @Email.

Most common use cases for a custom Bean Validation constraint are related to localized patterns. Think of phone numbers, zip codes, bank account numbers, and passwords. Of course, most of those could be done with just a @Pattern, but this may end up in less self-documenting code, particularly if the desired pattern is relatively complex.

Following is an example of a custom @Phone constraint which should match as many as possible internationally known phone numbers:

```
@Constraint(validatedBy=PhoneValidator.class)
@Target(FIELD)
@Retention(RUNTIME)
public @interface Phone {
    String message() default "Invalid phone number";
    Class<?>[] groups() default {};
    Class<?>[] payload() default {};
}
```

And here's the associated PhoneValidator:

```
public class PhoneValidator
    implements ConstraintValidator<Phone, String>
{
    private static final Pattern SPECIAL_CHARS =
        Pattern.compile("[\\s().+-]|ext", Pattern.CASE_INSENSITIVE);
    private static final Pattern DIGITS =
        Pattern.compile("[0-9]{7,15}");
```

---

[25]https://javaee.github.io/javaee-spec/javadocs/javax/validation/constraints/
package-summary.html.

```
@Override
public boolean isValid
    (String phone, ConstraintValidatorContext context)
{
    if (phone == null || phone.isEmpty()) {
        return true; // Let @NotNull/@NotEmpty handle this.
    }

    return isValid(phone);
}

public static boolean isValid(String phone) {
    String digits = SPECIAL_CHARS.matcher(phone).replaceAll("");
    return DIGITS.matcher(digits).matches();
}
}
```

In order to activate it, simply annotate the associated entity property.

```
@Phone
private String phone;
```

This will be triggered on both the JSF and JPA sides: in JSF, during the process validations phase (third phase); in JPA during the persist and merge. As noted in the `<f:validateBean>`/`<f:validateWholeBean>` section, it can be disabled on both sides.

# Custom Messages

Conversion and validation error messages coming from JSF as well as Bean Validation are fully customizable. Application-wide, they can be customized by supplying a properties file which specifies the desired message as the value of a predefined key. You can find predefined keys for JSF conversion and validation messages in Chapter 2.5.2.4, "Localized Application Messages," of the JSF 2.3 specification.[26] You can find predefined keys for Bean Validation messages in Appendix B, "Standard ResourceBundle Messages," of the Bean Validation 2.0 specification.[27] For JSF, the fully qualified name of the

---

[26]http://download.oracle.com/otn-pub/jcp/jsf-2_3-final-eval-spec/JSF_2.3.pdf.
[27]http://beanvalidation.org/2.0/spec/#standard-resolver-messages.

properties file must be registered as `<message-bundle>` in `faces-config.xml`. For Bean Validation, the exact fully qualified name of the properties file is `ValidationMessages`.

As an example, we're going to modify the default message of the JSF `required="true"` validation and the Bean Validation `@NotNull` constraint.

```
main/java/resources/com/example/project/i18n/messages.properties
javax.faces.component.UIInput.REQUIRED = {0} is required.
javax.faces.validator.BeanValidator.MESSAGE = {1} {0}
main/java/resources/ValidationMessages.properties
javax.validation.constraints.NotNull.message = is required.
```

Note the absence of the label placeholder in the Bean Validation message. Instead, the {1} of the `javax.faces.validator.BeanValidator.MESSAGE` represents the label associated with the JSF component and {0} represents the Bean Validation message. The custom Bean Validation message bundle file is already automatically picked up. The custom JSF message bundle file needs to be explicitly registered in the `faces-config.xml` first.

```
<application>
    <message-bundle>com.example.project.i18n.messages</message-bundle>
</application>
```

With those properties files in place, the following input components will thus show exactly the same validation error message:

```
<h:inputText id="field" label="First input"
    value="#{bean.field}" required="true">
</h:inputText>
<h:message for="field" />

<h:inputText id="notNullField" label="Second input"
    value="#{bean.notNullField}">
</h:inputText>
<h:message for="notNullField" />
```

In case you want to fine-grain the message on a per-component basis, you can use the converterMessage, validatorMessage, and/or requiredMessage attribute of the UIInput component. The converterMessage will be displayed on any conversion error.

```
<h:inputText value="#{bean.localDate}"
    converterMessage="Please enter date in pattern YYYY-MM-DD.">
    <f:convertLocalDate type="localDate" pattern="yyyy-MM-dd" />
</h:inputText>
```

The validatorMessage will be displayed on any validation error, as well as those triggered by Bean Validation.

```
<h:inputText value="#{bean.dutchZipCode}" required="true"
    validatorMessage="Please enter zip code in pattern 1234AB.">
    <f:validateRegex pattern="[0-9]{4}[A-Z]{2}" />
</h:inputText>
```

Note that this won't be shown when required="true" isn't satisfied. For that, you need to use requiredMessage instead.

```
<h:inputText value="#{bean.dutchZipCode}" required="true"
    requiredMessage="Please enter zip code."
    validatorMessage="Please enter zip code in pattern 1234AB.">
    <f:validateRegex pattern="[0-9]{4}[A-Z]{2}" />
</h:inputText>
```

Note that this won't be shown for any Bean Validation @NotNull. You should then use validatorMessage instead.

# CHAPTER 6

# Output Components

Technically, the input components as described in Chapter 4 are also output components. They are not only capable of processing any submitted input values but also capable of outputting the model value during the render response phase (sixth phase). This is also visible in the JSF (JavaServer Faces) API (application programming interface): the UIInput superclass extends from the UIOutput superclass.

There are also a bunch of components that merely output their model value or even just an HTML element. Those are the pure output components. They don't participate in all phases of the JSF life cycle. Sometimes they participate during the restore view phase (first phase), in case they are dynamically created or manipulated, but the majority of their job is executed during the render response phase (sixth phase), while generating the HTML output. During the other phases, they don't do many additional tasks.

## Document-Based Output Components

These components are <h:doctype>, <h:head>, and <h:body>. Note that there's no such component as <h:html>.  <h:doctype> is arguably the least used HTML component of the entire standard JSF HTML component set. You could get away with just a plain <!DOCTYPE html> element. <h:doctype> is only useful when you want to have a pure XML representation of the <!DOCTYPE> element, which is generally only the case when you need to store entire JSF views as part of another XML structure of some higher-level abstract layer around JSF.

<h:head> and <h:body> are, since JSF 2.0, the most important tags after <f:view> became optional in Facelets. Historically, <f:view> was mandatory in JSP in order to declare the JSP page being a JSF view. While generating the <head> and <body> elements of the HTML document doesn't require any special logic, and <h:head> and <h:body>

© Bauke Scholtz, Arjan Tijms 2018
B. Scholtz and A. Tijms, *The Definitive Guide to JSF in Java EE 8*, https://doi.org/10.1007/978-1-4842-3387-0_6

aren't mandatory for a Facelets page in order to be recognized as a JSF view, those tags are mandatory for the proper automatic handling of JavaScript and CSS (Cascading Style Sheets) resource dependencies, also introduced in JSF 2.0.

`<h:head>` and `<h:body>` allow JSF to automatically relocate JavaScript and CSS resource dependencies to the right places in the component tree so that they ultimately end up in the right place in the generated HTML output. From the standard JSF component set only `<h:commandLink>`, `<h:commandScript>`, `<f:ajax>`, and `<f:websocket>` utilize this facility. They all require the `jsf.js` JavaScript file being included in the final HTML document. During the view build time, they will basically use `UIViewRoot#addComponentResource()`[1] to register the component resource dependency at the specified target component, which can be either `<h:head>` or `<h:body>`. During the view render time, the renderer associated with the `<h:head>` and `<h:body>` component will obtain all so far registered component resource dependencies by `UIViewRoot#getComponentResources()`[2] and generate the appropriate `<link rel="stylesheet">` and `<script>` elements with a URL (uniform resource locator) referring the associated resource dependency.

As shown in the section "Standard HTML Components" in Chapter 3, the following code is what the most minimal and HTML5-valid JSF page looks like:

```
<!DOCTYPE html>
<html lang="en"
    xmlns="http://www.w3.org/1999/xhtml"
    xmlns:h="http://xmlns.jcp.org/jsf/html"
>
    <h:head>
        <title>Title</title>
    </h:head>
    <h:body>
        ...
    </h:body>
</html>
```

---

[1]https://javaee.github.io/javaee-spec/javadocs/javax/faces/component/UIViewRoot.html#addComponentResource-javax.faces.context.FacesContext-javax.faces.component.UIComponent-java.lang.String-.

[2]https://javaee.github.io/javaee-spec/javadocs/javax/faces/component/UIViewRoot.html#getComponentResources-javax.faces.context.FacesContext-java.lang.String-.

# Text-Based Output Components

These components are `<h:outputText>`, `<h:outputFormat>`, `<h:outputLabel>`, and `<h:outputLink>`. They all extend from the `UIOutput` superclass and have a `value` attribute which can be bound to a managed bean property. During the view render time, the getter will be consulted to retrieve and display any preset value. These components will never invoke the setter method and therefore it could be safely left out of the managed bean class in order to reduce unused code.

Historically, in JSF 1.x on JSP (Java Server Pages), `<h:outputText>` was mandatory in order to output a bean property as text. JSP didn't support JSF-style EL (Expression Language) #{...} in template text. Facelets supported JSF-style EL #{...} in template text and hence bean properties could be outputted directly in Facelets without the need for a whole JSF component. In other words, the following codes are equivalent in JSF on Facelets, `<h:outputText>`:

```
<p>Welcome, <h:outputText value="#{user.name}" />!</p>
```

And EL in template text:

```
<p>Welcome, #{user.name}!</p>
```

It doesn't need explanation that the latter code snippet is more terse and readable. `<h:outputText>` has, however, not become useless in Facelets. It's still useful for the following purposes:

- Disabling implicit HTML escaping.

- Attaching an explicit converter.

- Referencing in `<f:ajax render>`.

JSF has implicit HTML escaping everywhere. Anything outputted to the HTML response is checked on the HTML special characters "<", ">", "&", and optionally also """ when outputted within an attribute of an HTML element. Those HTML special characters will be replaced by "&lt;", "&gt;", "&amp;", and "&quot;", respectively. The web browser will then not interpret those characters as part of the generated HTML output but as plain text and, ultimately, will present them as literal characters to the end user.

Imagine that a user chooses `<script>alert('xss')</script>` as a username, and it's emitted via `#{user.name}` through either one of the above shown code snippets; then JSF will render it as follows in the generated HTML output:

```
<p>Welcome, <script>alert('xss')</script>!</p>
```

And the web browser will display it literally as "Welcome, <script>alert('xss')</script>!" instead of only "Welcome, !" along with a JavaScript alert with the text "xss" whereby the user-controlled JavaScript is unintentionally actually executed. The end user being able to execute arbitrary JavaScript code is dangerous. It would allow the malicious user to execute specific code which transfers information about session cookies to an external host when someone else logs in and views a page wherein the username of the malicious user is being rendered. (See also the section "Cross-Site Scripting Protection" in Chapter 13.)

On the other hand, there may also be cases whereby you'd like to embed safe HTML code in the generated HTML output. Most common use cases are related to posting messages for other users on a web site, whereby a limited subset of formatting is allowed, such as bold, italics, links, lists, headings, etc. Generally, those are to be entered in a text area element using a predefined human-friendly markup format, such as Markdown, or the lesser known Wikicode, or the ancient BBCode. They are all capable of parsing the raw text with the markup and converting it to safe HTML code whereby any malicious HTML code is already escaped or stripped out.

```
<h:inputTextarea value="#{message.text}" />
```

The raw text is at least always saved in the database for the record, and the resulting safe HTML code, along with the version of the parser used, can also be saved in the database for performance, so that the parser doesn't need to be unnecessarily re-executed for the same piece of raw text. Given that we're going to use Markdown with CommonMark[3] and having the following `Markdown` interface,

```java
private interface Markdown {
    public String getText();
    public void setHtml(String html);
    public String getVersion();
    public void setVersion(String version);
}
```

---

[3]https://github.com/atlassian/commonmark-java.

And the following MarkdownListener entity listener,

```java
public class MarkdownListener {

    private static final Parser PARSER = Parser.builder().build();
    private static final HtmlRenderer RENDERER =
        HtmlRenderer.builder().escapeHtml(true).build();
    private static final String VERSION = getCommonMarkVersion();

    @PrePersist
    public void parseMarkdown(Markdown markdown) {
        String html = RENDERER.render(PARSER.parse(markdown.getText()));
        markdown.setHtml(html);
        markdown.setVersion(VERSION);
    }

    @PreUpdate
    public void parseMarkdownIfNecessary(Markdown markdown) {
        if (markdown.getVersion() == null) {
            parseMarkdown(markdown);
        }
    }

    @PostLoad
    public void updateMarkdownIfNecessary(Markdown markdown) {
        if (!VERSION.equals(markdown.getVersion())) {
            parseMarkdown(markdown);
        }
    }

    private static String getCommonMarkVersion() {
        try {
            Properties properties = new Properties();
            properties.load(Parser.class.getResourceAsStream(
                "/META-INF/maven/com.atlassian.commonmark"
                    + "/commonmark/pom.properties"));
            return properties.getProperty("version");
        }
```

```
        catch (IOException e) {
            throw new UncheckedIOException(e);
        }
    }
}
```

then the Message entity implementing the Markdown interface and registered with the MarkdownListener entity listener can look as follows:

```
@Entity @EntityListeners(MarkdownListener.class)
public class Message implements Markdown, Serializable {

    @Id @GeneratedValue(strategy=IDENTITY)
    private Long id;

    @Column(nullable = false) @Lob
    private @NotNull String text;

    @Column(nullable = false) @Lob
    private String html;

    @Column(nullable = false, length = 8)
    private String version;

    @Override
    public void setText(String text) {
        if (!text.equals(this.text)) {
            this.text = text;
            setVersion(null); // Trigger for MarkdownListener @PreUpdate.
        }
    }

    // Add/generate remaining getters and setters.
}
```

Finally, in order to present the safe HTML code to the end user, you can use <h:outputText> with the escape attribute set to false, whereby you thus instruct JSF that it doesn't need to implicitly HTML-escape the value.

```
<h:outputText value="#{message.html}" escape="false" />
```

Next to implicit HTML escaping, JSF also supports implicit conversion. For any property type which is emitted via <h:outputText> or even EL in template text, JSF will look up the converter by class, invoke its Converter#getAsString() method, and render the result. In case you want to explicitly use a specific or a different converter, you have to replace any EL in template text by <h:outputText> and explicitly register the converter on it. Generally, it is those kinds of number- or datetime-related properties that need to be formatted in a locale-specific pattern.

```
<h:outputText value="#{product.price}">
    <f:convertNumber type="currency" locale="en_US" />
</h:outputText>
```

The last purpose of <h:outputText> is being able to reference a piece of inline text in <f:ajax render>. By default, <h:outputText> doesn't generate any HTML code. But if it has at least an attribute specified which must end up in the generated HTML output, such as id or styleClass, then it will generate an HTML <span> element. This is referenceable via JavaScript and thus useful for Ajax-updating specific parts of text. Of course, you could also opt for Ajax-updating some common container component, but this is far less efficient than Ajax-updating only specific parts which really need to be updated.

<h:outputFormat> is an extension of <h:outputText> which parses the value using java.text.MessageFormat API[4] beforehand. This is particularly useful in combination with localized resource bundles. An example can be found in the section "Parameterized Resource Bundle Values" in Chapter 14.

<h:outputLabel> basically generates the HTML <label> element, which is an essential part of HTML forms. This was already described in the section "Label and Message Components" in Chapter 4. It is important to note that <h:outputLabel> and <h:outputText> are, in HTML perspective, absolutely not interchangeable. In a relatively recent burst of low-quality programming tutorial sites on the Internet which basically show code snippets without any technical explanation for the sake of advertisement incomes, <h:outputLabel> is often incorrectly being used to output a piece of text in a Hello World JSF page. Such tutorial sites can better be ignored entirely.

<h:outputLink> generates an HTML <a> element. It's somewhat a leftover of JSF 1.x and isn't terribly useful since the introduction of the much more useful <h:link> in JSF 2.0. When you don't need to reference a JSF view with a link, for which you'd

---

[4]https://docs.oracle.com/javase/8/docs/api/java/text/MessageFormat.html.

use <h:link> instead, you could as well just use a plain HTML <a> element instead of <h:outputLink>. The following tags generate exactly the same HTML.

```
<h:outputLink value="http://google.com">Google</h:outputLink>
<a href="http://google.com">Google</a>
```

The plain HTML equivalent is terser.

# Navigation-Based Output Components

These components are <h:link> and <h:button>, both extending from the UIOutcomeTarget superclass. They have an outcome attribute which accepts a logical path to a JSF view. The path will actually be validated if it's a valid JSF view; otherwise, the link or button will be rendered as disabled. In other words, they don't accept a path to a non-JSF resource, let alone an external URL. For this, you'd need <h:outputLink> or plain HTML instead.

<h:link> will generate an HTML <a> element with the URL of the target JSF view specified as an href attribute. <h:button> will generate an HTML <input type="button"> element with an onclick attribute which assigns, with help of JavaScript, the URL of the target JSF view to window.location.href property. This is indeed somewhat awkward, but that's just a limitation of HTML. Neither <input type="button"> nor <button> supports an href-like attribute.

Given the following folder structure in a Maven WAR project in Eclipse,

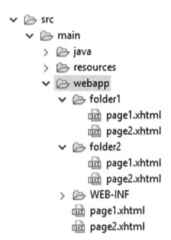

The following <h:link> and <a> pairs enclosed in /folder1/page1.xhtml will all generate exactly the same links.

```
<h:link outcome="page2" value="link1" />
<a href="#{request.contextPath}/folder1/page2.xhtml">link1</a>

<h:link outcome="/folder2/page1" value="link2" />
<a href="#{request.contextPath}/folder2/page1.xhtml">link2</a>

<h:link outcome="/folder2/page2" value="link3" />
<a href="#{request.contextPath}/folder2/page2.xhtml">link3</a>

<h:link outcome="/page1" value="link4" />
<a href="#{request.contextPath}/page1.xhtml">link4</a>

<h:link outcome="/page2" value="link5" />
<a href="#{request.contextPath}/page2.xhtml">link5</a>
```

Note thus that <h:link> already automatically prepends any context path of the web application project and appends the currently active URL pattern of the FacesServlet mapping. Also note that without the leading slash, the outcome is interpreted relative to the current folder, and with a leading slash, the outcome is interpreted relative to the context path.

# Panel-Based Output Components

These components are <h:panelGroup> and <h:panelGrid>, both extending from the UIPanel superclass. <h:panelGroup> has multiple responsibilities. It can generate an HTML <span>, or <div>, or even <td>, depending on the layout attribute and whether it's enclosed in a <h:panelGrid>.

By default, <h:panelGroup> generates just an HTML <span> element, like <h:outputText>. The main difference is that <h:panelGroup> doesn't have a value attribute. Instead, the content is represented by its children. It also doesn't support disabling HTML escaping or attaching a converter. That's up to any <h:outputText> child. In this context, it's not terribly useful. <h:panelGroup> is only more useful than <h:outputText> when you need to be able to reference using <f:ajax render> an inline element which in turn groups a bunch of closely related inline elements. Something like the following represents the "user profile," which should be Ajax-updatable from within some sort of user profile edit page.

```
<p>
    Welcome,
    <h:panelGroup id="userProfile">
        <img src="#{user.imageUrl}" />
        #{user.name}
    </h:panelGroup>
</p>
...
<h:form>
    ...
    <f:ajax ... render=":userProfile" />
    ...
</h:form>
```

When setting the layout attribute of <h:panelGroup> to block, then it will generate an HTML <div> element. In standard HTML, "inline elements"[5] don't start at a new line by default and don't allow block element children. And, "block-level elements"[6] always start at a new line by default and allow inline as well as block elements as children. Hence the supported values of the layout attribute of <h:panelGroup> are "inline" and "block". Historically, the layout attribute was only added in JSF 1.2 after complaints from JSF developers about a missing JSF component to represent an HTML <div> element. (See also Chapter 7.) This could be used to wrap larger sections which need to be Ajax-updatable; otherwise a plain HTML <div> is also sufficient.

```
<h:panelGroup layout="block" id="userProfile">
    <p>
        Welcome,
        <img src="#{user.imageUrl}" />
        #{user.name}
    </p>
</h:panelGroup>
```

Note that it's illegal in HTML to have a block element nested in an inline element. The <p> is a block element and hence the layout="block" is absolutely mandatory in

---

[5]https://developer.mozilla.org/en-US/docs/Web/HTML/Inline_elements.
[6]https://developer.mozilla.org/en-US/docs/Web/HTML/Block-level_elements.

the above construct. If you don't specify this attribute and thus effectively let JSF render an HTML <span> element, then the web browser behavior is unspecified. The average web browser will render the block element children outside the inline element and even possibly error out when this construct is manipulated by JavaScript, such as during a JSF Ajax update action.

Also keep in mind that in the above construct, the <p> tags and the "Welcome" text are also updated during any JSF Ajax update action on the <h:panelGroup>. This is essentially a waste of hardware resources, on both the server side and the client side, as those are static and never subject to changes. When Ajax-updating things, you should preferably ensure that <f:ajax render> only references components that absolutely need to be Ajax-updated and thus not an unnecessarily large section.

When <h:panelGroup> is being nested in a <h:panelGrid> component, which generates an HTML <table> element, then the layout attribute of <h:panelGroup> is ignored and the component will basically act as a container of components which should ultimately end up in the very same cell of the table. That is, the renderer of <h:panelGrid> considers every direct child component as an individual table cell.

Given the following two-column <h:panelGrid>, which should generate a two-column HTML table, what would you guess the actual generated HTML output should look like?

```
<h:panelGrid columns="2">
    one
    <h:outputText value="two" />
    three
    four
    <h:panelGroup>five</h:panelGroup>
    six
    seven
    <h:panelGroup>
        eight
        nine
    </h:panelGroup>
</h:panelGrid>
```

---

**Hint**   Each section of template text between two JSF components is internally considered a single JSF component. In Mojarra, it's represented by the internal `UIInstructions` component. The actual component tree hierarchy is thus roughly represented as below.

---

```
<h:panelGrid columns="2">
    <ui:instructions>one</ui:instructions>
    <h:outputText value="two" />
    <ui:instructions>
        three
        four
    </ui:instructions>
    <h:panelGroup>five</h:panelGroup>
    <ui:instructions>
        six
        seven
    </ui:instructions>
    <h:panelGroup>
        eight
        nine
    </h:panelGroup>
</h:panelGrid>
```

Note again that there's no such component as `<ui:instructions>` in Facelets. The above markup is purely for visualization so that your brain can better process it. This `<h:panelGrid>` has thus effectively six direct children which will each end up in their own table cell. With two columns, this will thus effectively generate three rows. Here's the actual generated HTML output (reformatted for readability).

```
<table>
    <tbody>
        <tr>
            <td>one</td>
            <td>two</td>
        </tr>
```

```
    <tr>
        <td>three four</td>
        <td>five</td>
    </tr>
    <tr>
        <td>six seven</td>
        <td>eight nine</td>
    </tr>
    </tbody>
</table>
```

Rendering in Chrome browser:

one         two
three four five
six seven  eight nine

You see, `<h:panelGroup>` makes sure that "five" and "eight nine" don't end up in the very same table cell as "six seven." Also note that it's unnecessary to wrap any JSF component in `<h:panelGroup>` if it should represent a single cell already. Therefore, `<h:outputText>` behind "two" doesn't need to be wrapped in `<h:panelGroup>`. You can, of course, do so for better source code readability, but this is technically unnecessary.

If you happen to have a dynamic amount of cells based on a view-scoped model, then you can nest a JSTL (JSP Standard Tag Library) `<c:forEach>` in `<h:panelGrid>` to have it generate them as a data grid with a fixed amount of columns.

```
<h:panelGrid columns="3">
    <c:forEach items="#{viewProducts.products}" var="product">
        <h:panelGroup>
            <h3>#{product.name}</h3>
            <p>#{product.description}</p>
        </h:panelGroup>
    </c:forEach>
</h:panelGrid>
```

Note thus that `<ui:repeat>` is unsuitable here as compared to `<c:forEach>`, as explained in the section "JSTL Core Tags" in Chapter 3. It will technically work just fine, but the renderer of `<h:panelGrid>` will interpret it as a single table cell.

Also note that it's very important for the model to be view scoped, particularly if you have JSF form components inside `<h:panelGrid>`. The technical reason is that during processing the postback request, JSF expects the model item behind the iteration index to be exactly the same as it was when the page was presented to the end user. In other words, when JSF is about to process a form submit, and an item has been added or removed or even reordered in the meanwhile, causing the iteration index to be changed, the submitted values and/or the invoked action would possibly be performed against the wrong item currently at the initially known index. This is dangerous for the integrity of the model. If you don't have any JSF form components inside `<h:panelGrid>`, or if the model isn't subject to changes during the view scope, e.g., because it's only created or updated during application startup, then the backing bean behind `#{viewProducts}` can safely be request scoped.

# Data Iteration Component

Yes, there's only one, `<h:dataTable>`, which extends from the `UIData` superclass and generates an HTML `<table>` based on an iterable data model whereby each item is represented as a single row. The other data iteration component available in JSF, the Facelets `<ui:repeat>`, doesn't extend from the `UIData` superclass and doesn't emit any HTML output and therefore doesn't technically count as an "output component." Also, in the standard JSF component set no such component generates an HTML `<ul>`, `<ol>`, or `<dl>`, but this can relatively easily be created as a custom component extending from `UIData`. (See also the section "Creating New Component and Renderer" in Chapter 11.)

The `value` attribute of `UIData` supports `java.lang.Iterable`. In other words, you can supply any Java collection as a model value. As index-based access is most used in `UIData`, most efficient is the `java.util.ArrayList` as it offers O(1) access by index. The renderer of the `<h:dataTable>` component supports only `<h:column>` as a direct child component. Anything else is ignored. As its name hints, `<h:column>` represents a single column. Each iteration round over the `value` of `<h:dataTable>` will basically re-render all columns against the currently iterated item. As with `<c:forEach>` and `<ui:repeat>`, the currently iterated item is exposed in EL scope by the `var` attribute. Following is a basic example which iterates over a `List<String>`.

```
<h:dataTable id="strings" value="#{bean.strings}" var="string">
    <h:column>#{string}</h:column>
</h:dataTable>
```

Backing bean class com.example.project.view.Bean:

```
@Named @RequestScoped
public class Bean {

    private List<String> strings;

    @PostConstruct
    public void init() {
        strings = Arrays.asList("one", "two", "three");
    }

    public List<String> getStrings() {
        return strings;
    }
}
```

Generated HTML output:

```
<table>
    <tbody>
        <tr><td>one</td></tr>
        <tr><td>two</td></tr>
        <tr><td>three</td></tr>
    </tbody>
</table>
```

Rendering in Chrome browser:

one
two
three

It is important to note that the variable name as specified by the var attribute shouldn't clash with existing managed bean names or even with implicit EL objects. Implicit EL objects have higher precedence in EL resolving. One example of an implicit EL object is #{header} which refers to ExternalContext#getRequestHeaderMap().[7] So when you happen to have

---

[7]https://javaee.github.io/javaee-spec/javadocs/javax/faces/context/ExternalContext.
html#getRequestHeaderMap--.

#{bean.headers} and you'd like to present it in an iterating component, then you can't use var="header" and you'd better think of a different name, such as var="head".

Following is a more elaborate example which shows a list of products. A similar table was shown earlier in Chapter 5.

```
<h:dataTable id="products" value="#{products.list}" var="product">
    <h:column>
        <f:facet name="header">ID</f:facet>
        #{product.id}
    </h:column>
    <h:column>
        <f:facet name="header">Name</f:facet>
        #{product.name}
    </h:column>
    <h:column>
        <f:facet name="header">Description</f:facet>
        #{product.description}
    </h:column>
</h:dataTable>
```

Backing bean class com.example.project.view.Products:

```
@Named @RequestScoped
public class Products {

    private List<Product> list;

    @Inject
    private ProductService productService;

    @PostConstruct
    public void init() {
        list = productService.list();
    }

    public List<Product> getList() {
        return list;
    }
}
```

Product entity: com.example.project.model.Product:

```
@Entity
public class Product {

    @Id @GeneratedValue(strategy=IDENTITY)
    private Long id;

    @Column(nullable = false)
    private @NotNull String name;

    @Column(nullable = false)
    private @NotNull String description;

    // Add/generate getters+setters.
}
```

Product service: com.example.project.service.ProductService:

```
@Stateless
public class ProductService {

    @PersistenceContext
    private EntityManager entityManager;

    @TransactionAttribute(SUPPORTS)
    public List<Product> list() {
        return entityManager
            .createQuery("FROM Product ORDER BY id DESC", Product.class)
            .getResultList();
    }
}
```

Generated HTML output:

```
<table>
    <thead>
        <tr>
            <th scope="col">ID</th>
```

```
            <th scope="col">Name</th>
            <th scope="col">Description</th>
        </tr>
    </thead>
    <tbody>
        <tr>
            <td>3</td>
            <td>Three</td>
            <td>The third product</td>
        </tr>
        <tr>
            <td>2</td>
            <td>Two</td>
            <td>The second product</td>
        </tr>
        <tr>
            <td>1</td>
            <td>One</td>
            <td>The first product</td>
        </tr>
    </tbody>
</table>
```

Rendering in Chrome browser:

3 Three  The third product
2 Two    The second product
1 One    The first product

It is important to note that the model behind the `value` attribute of `<h:dataTable>` must refer a bean property which is already prepared beforehand in a one-time life cycle event, such as `@PostConstruct` or `<f:viewAction>`. This doesn't apply specifically to `UIData` components but to basically every JSF component. That is, the getter method may be invoked multiple times during the JSF life cycle, especially when referenced in the `value` attribute of an iteration component or in the `rendered` attribute of any JSF component.

The technical reason is that any EL value expression is, behind the scenes, created as a javax.el.ValueExpression instance which internally basically just holds the literal EL string such as #{products.list} and any ValueExpression#getValue() call on it would simply re-evaluate the expression against the provided EL context. This is normally a very cheap operation, done in nanoseconds, but it may slow down drastically when the getter method in turn performs a relatively expensive database query which may take tens or even hundreds of milliseconds.

Iteration components may invoke the getter method during every phase of the JSF life cycle when the iteration component happens to have form components nested. When you prepare the model by obtaining a list from the database in the getter method, this would cause the database to be queried on every single getter method call, which is plainly inefficient. Moreover, the same problems with regard to resolving the iterated item of interest based on the iteration index may occur as described in the last paragraph of the previous section about <h:panelGrid> with <c:forEach>.

Another thing to note is <f:facet name="header">. This generates basically <thead> with the content in <th>. <h:dataTable> also supports <f:facet name="footer"> which will then generate the <tfoot> with the content in <td>. You can usually find all supported <f:facet> names in the tag documentation, as well as in the <h:dataTable> tag documentation.[8]

Basically, you can put anything inside <h:column> to represent the cell content. Even form components or a nested <h:dataTable> or <ui:repeat>. Following is a small example which shows a fictive Set<Tag> tags property of Product entity in a nested <ui:repeat>.

```
<h:dataTable id="products" value="#{products.list}" var="product">
    ...
    <h:column>
        <ui:repeat value="#{product.tags}" var="tag">
            #{tag.name}<br/>
        </ui:repeat>
    </h:column>
</h:dataTable>
```

---

[8]https://javaserverfaces.github.io/docs/2.3/vdldocs/facelets/h/dataTable.html.

# Editable <h:dataTable>

As to form components nested inside <h:column>, you can substitute EL in template text with input components as follows:

```
<h:form id="list">
    <h:dataTable id="products" value="#{products.list}" var="product">
        <h:column>
            <f:facet name="header">ID</f:facet>
            #{product.id}
        </h:column>
        <h:column>
            <f:facet name="header">Name</f:facet>
            <h:inputText id="name" value="#{product.name}" />
            <h:message for="name" />
        </h:column>
        <h:column>
            <f:facet name="header">Description</f:facet>
            <h:inputTextarea id="description"
                value="#{product.description}">
            </h:inputTextarea>
            <h:message for="description" />
        </h:column>
    </h:dataTable>
    <h:commandButton id="save" value="Save" action="#{products.save}">
        <f:ajax execute="@form" render="@form" />
    </h:commandButton>
</h:form>
```

Whereby the save() method of the backing bean class basically looks as follows, after having changed the backing bean class to be a @ViewScoped one instead of a @RequestScoped one:

```
public void save() {
    productService.update(products);
}
```

And the update() method of the service class in turn looks as follows:

```
@TransactionAttribute(REQUIRED)
public void update(Iterable<Product> products) {
    products.forEach(entityManager::merge);
}
```

Note that you don't need to worry at all about collecting the submitted values. JSF has already done that task for you. Also note that you don't need to worry about uniqueness of the component IDs within <h:dataTable>, as that component already implements the NamingContainer interface and prepends its own client ID and the iteration index to the client ID of the child components, as you can see in the following generated HTML output:

```
<table id="list:products">
    <thead>
        <tr>
            <th scope="col">ID</th>
            <th scope="col">Name</th>
            <th scope="col">Description</th>
        </tr>
    </thead>
    <tbody>
        <tr>
            <td>3</td>
            <td>
                <input id="list:products:0:name" type="text"
                    name="list:products:0:name" value="Three">
                </input>
            </td>
            <td>
                <textarea id="list:products:0:description"
                    name="list:products:0:description"
                >The third product</textarea>
            </td>
        </tr>
```

```
            <tr>
                <td>2</td>
                <td>
                    <input id="list:products:1:name" type="text"
                        name="list:products:1:name" value="Two">
                    </input>
                </td>
                <td>
                    <textarea id="list:products:1:description"
                        name="list:products:1:description"
                    >The second product</textarea>
                </td>
            </tr>
            <tr>
                <td>1</td>
                <td>
                    <input id="list:products:2:name" type="text"
                        name="list:products:2:name" value="One">
                    </input>
                </td>
                <td>
                    <textarea id="list:products:2:description"
                        name="list:products:2:description"
                    >The first product</textarea>
                </td>
            </tr>
        </tbody>
</table>
```

It must be said that having an editable table like this is not terribly efficient, certainly not when the table contains a lot of columns and rows. JSF can handle it pretty well; only the average web browser will have a hard time handling it, certainly when the number of rows exceeds a few thousand. And then I'm not speaking about the end user potentially going crazy from scrolling through the whole page all the time and basically having no clear overview. There are several solutions to this: first and foremost is pagination; second is filtering; third is row-based inline editing and updating; and fourth is external editing in a dialog or detail page.

All the mentioned table-specific performance and usability solutions are not offered by the standard `<h:dataTable>` and therefore require quite an amount of custom code. It's strongly recommended that you look for an existing JSF component library supporting these features in order to make your JSF life easier without the need to reinvent the wheel. Currently the most widely used one is PrimeFaces with its `<p:dataTable>`.[9] This can even be further simplified with `<op:dataTable>` of OptimusFaces,[10] which is in turn based on `<p:dataTable>`. Editing in a detail page is only doable with standard JSF, and it's demonstrated in the "Custom Converters" section of Chapter 5.

It should be said that in the specific case of the previously shown `List<String>` example, turning the column from output to input isn't as easily done as with the `List<Product>` example. In other words, the following example won't work at all.

```
<h:form>
    <h:dataTable value="#{bean.strings}" var="string">
        <h:column>
            <h:inputText value="#{string}" />
        </h:column>
    </h:dataTable>
    <h:commandButton value="Save" action="#{bean.save}">
        <f:ajax execute="@form" />
    </h:commandButton>
</h:form>
```

The technical problem is that `java.lang.String` is immutable and doesn't have a public setter method for its internal value. True, it indeed also doesn't have a getter, but EL already defaults to `Object#toString()` which in case of `String` just returns the very string itself. This can be solved by referencing the model value by an index as follows:

```
<h:form>
    <h:dataTable binding="#{table}" value="#{bean.strings}" var="string">
        <h:column>
            <h:inputText value="#{bean.strings[table.rowIndex]}" />
        </h:column>
    </h:dataTable>
```

---

[9]https://www.primefaces.org/showcase/ui/data/datatable/basic.xhtml.
[10]https://github.com/omnifaces/optimusfaces.

213

```
    <h:commandButton value="Save" action="#{bean.save}">
        <f:ajax execute="@form" />
    </h:commandButton>
</h:form>
```

Note the `binding` attribute. Basically, during the view build time, this sets the current `UIComponent` instance as an EL variable identified by the given name. In this particular snippet, it will thus make the `#{table}` variable to reference the concrete `HtmlDataTable` instance behind the `<h:dataTable>` tag. The `#{table}` variable is, then during the view build time, referenceable only after the tag location in the view and during the view render time anywhere in the view. In this way, you can access its properties as if it were a bean. `#{table.rowIndex}` basically thus refers to the `UIData#getRowIndex()` method,[11] which returns the current iteration index. And, finally, this is used to reference the item of interest in the list. During the update model values phase (fourth phase) JSF will simply replace the item at the specified index.

Also for the `binding` attribute it's very important that the variable name shouldn't clash with existing managed bean names or implicit EL objects and for sure not with other components in the same view. You can alternatively let the `binding` attribute reference a backing bean property as follows:

```
<h:dataTable binding="#{bean.table}" ...>
```

With:

```
private UIData table; // +getter +setter
```

But this is fairly useless if it isn't used anywhere else in the backing bean. Moreover, this is dangerous when the managed bean scope is wider than request (see also the section "View Build Time" in Chapter 3. It is better not to bind component instances to a backing bean at all; it might indicate a poor practice. The only reasonable real-world use case in JSF 2.x is binding composite component children to a backing component (see also the section "Composite Components" in Chapter 7).

In case you're using `<ui:repeat>` or `<c:forEach>` instead of `<h:dataTable>` on something like a `List<String>`, then you can obtain the iteration index in a much simpler way, via the `varStatus` attribute.

---

[11]https://javaee.github.io/javaee-spec/javadocs/javax/faces/component/UIData.
  html#getRowIndex--.

```
<h:form>
    <ui:repeat value="#{bean.strings}" var="string" varStatus="loop">
        <h:inputText value="#{bean.strings[loop.index]}" /><br/>
    </ui:repeat>
    <h:commandButton value="Save" action="#{bean.save}">
        <f:ajax execute="@form" />
    </h:commandButton>
</h:form>
```

## Add/Remove Rows in <h:dataTable>

Coming back to the <h:dataTable> with List<Product>, there may be cases in which you'd like to be able to add or remove items while staying in the same view, usually in some sort of an admin page. In order to add a new Product, we need to prepare a new instance in the managed bean, fill it in a separate form, persist it, and then refresh the table.

```
<h:form id="list">
    <h:dataTable id="products" value="#{products.list}" ...>
        ...
    </h:dataTable>
</h:form>
<h:form id="add">
    <h:outputLabel for="name" value="Name" />
    <h:inputText id="name" value="#{products.product.name}" />
    <h:message for="name" />

    <h:outputLabel for="description" value="Description" />
    <h:inputTextarea id="description"
        value="#{products.product.description}">
    </h:inputTextarea>
    <h:message for="description" />

    <h:commandButton id="add" value="Add" action="#{products.add}">
        <f:ajax execute="@form" render="@form :list:products" />
    </h:commandButton>
</h:form>
```

Whereby the relevant backing bean code looks as follows:

```
private List<Product> list; // +getter
private Product product = new Product(); // +getter

@PostConstruct
public void init() {
    list = productService.list();
}

public void add() {
    productService.create(product);
    list.add(0, product);
    product = new Product();
}
```

With this create() method in service class:

```
@TransactionAttribute(REQUIRED);
public Long create(Product product) {
    entityManager.persist(product);
    return product.getId();
}
```

Removing could be done in several ways. In any case, you may need an additional column to hold the submit buttons or radio buttons or check boxes. The easiest way is a column with a command button which deletes the currently iterated item and then refreshes the table.

```
<h:form id="list">
    <h:dataTable id="products" value="#{products.list}" var="product">
        ...
        <h:column>
            <h:commandButton id="delete" value="Delete"
                action="#{products.delete(product)}">
                <f:ajax render="@namingcontainer" />
```

```
            </h:commandButton>
        </h:column>
    </h:dataTable>
</h:form>
```

With this delete(Product) method in a @ViewScoped backing bean class:

```
public void delete(Product product) {
    productService.delete(product);
    list.remove(product);
}
```

And this delete() method in service class:

```
@TransactionAttribute(REQUIRED)
public void delete(Product product) {
    if (entityManager.contains(product)) {
        entityManager.remove(product);
    }
    else {
        Product managedProduct = getById(product.getId());

        if (managedProduct != null) {
            entityManager.remove(managedProduct);
        }
    }
}
```

Note the render attribute of <f:ajax>. It specifies @namingcontainer, which basically references the closest parent NamingContainer component. From the standard JSF HTML component set, only <h:form> and <h:dataTable> are instances of NamingContainer. In this specific construct, @namingcontainer thus references the <h:dataTable>. You could also have used <f:ajax render=":list:products"> instead; it's only slightly verbose. The <f:ajax render="products"> wouldn't work, because it will try to find it within the context of the currently iterated row, which is basically within all <h:column> components.

# Select Rows in <h:dataTable>

Having a radio button column in a <h:dataTable> is natively possible since JSF 2.3 thanks to the new group attribute of the <h:selectOneRadio> (see also the section "Selection Components" in Chapter 4).

```
<h:form id="list">
    <h:dataTable id="products" value="#{products.list}" var="product">
        <h:column>
            <h:selectOneRadio id="selected" group="selected"
                value="#{products.selected}">
                <f:selectItem itemValue="#{product}" />
            </h:selectOneRadio>
        </h:column>
        ...
    </h:dataTable>
    <h:commandButton id="deleteSelected" value="Delete selected product"
        action="#{products.deleteSelected}">
        <f:ajax execute="@form" render="products" />
    </h:commandButton>
</h:form>
```

With this deleteSelected() method in a @ViewScoped backing bean class:

```
private Product selected; // +getter +setter

public void deleteSelected() {
    productService.delete(selected);
    list.remove(selected);
}
```

Note that you need a ProductConverter or BaseEntityConverter here as well. Those are elaborated in the section "Custom Converters" in Chapter 5.

The check box selection is a little more convoluted. You'd intuitively grab <h:selectManyCheckbox>, but this doesn't yet support the group attribute as <h:selectOneRadio> does. You'd need to fall back to <h:selectBooleanCheckbox> with a Map<Product, Boolean> whereby the map key represents the currently iterated product and the map value represents the check box value.

```
<h:form id="list">
    <h:dataTable id="products" value="#{products.list}" var="product">
        <h:column>
            <h:selectBooleanCheckbox id="selection"
                value="#{products.selection[product]}">
            </h:selectBooleanCheckbox>
        </h:column>

        ...

    </h:dataTable>
    <h:commandButton id="deleteSelected" value="Delete selected products"
        action="#{products.deleteSelected}">
        <f:ajax execute="@form" render="products" />
    </h:commandButton>
</h:form>
```

The modified deleteSelected() method in the @ViewScoped backing bean looks as follows:

```
private Map<Product, Boolean> selection = new HashMap<>(); // +getter

public void deleteSelected() {
    List<Product> selected = selection.entrySet().stream()
        .filter(Entry::getValue)
        .map(Entry::getKey)
        .collect(Collectors.toList());
    productService.delete(selected);
    selected.forEach(list::remove);
    selection.clear();
}
```

The overloaded ProductService#delete(Iterable) method looks as follows:

```
@TransactionAttribute(REQUIRED)
public void delete(Iterable<Product> products) {
    products.forEach(this::delete);
}
```

# Dynamic Columns in <h:dataTable>

With <h:dataTable>, with the help of JSTL <c:forEach>, it is also possible to dynamically create multiple <h:column> instances based on a Java model which is at least view scoped. A request-scoped model can also, but this doesn't guarantee that during a postback request it is exactly the same as it was during the preceding request, and therefore there is a risk of the dynamic <h:column> composition being off.

The value of the <c:forEach> should reference a collection including at least the entity property names or even map keys. You can then use the brace notation in EL as in #{entity[propertyName]} or #{map[key]} to reference the actual value. This works for both UIOutput and UIInput components. The following example illustrates how you could achieve this for a List<Product>.

Backing bean:

```
@Named @RequestScoped
public class Products {

    private List<Product> list;
    private List<String> properties;

    @Inject
    private ProductService productService;

    @PostConstruct
    public void init() {
        list = productService.list();
        properties = Arrays.asList("id", "name", "description");
    }

    // Add/generate getters (setters not needed here).
}
```

Facelets file:

```
<h:dataTable value="#{products.list}" var="product">
    <c:forEach items="#{products.properties}" var="property">
        <h:column>#{product[property]}</h:column>
    </c:forEach>
</h:dataTable>
```

You could even generalize this further for other entities of a common superclass, such as BaseEntity, whereby you obtain the relevant property names from the entity service.

# Resource Components

JSF offers three resource components, <h:graphicImage>, <h:outputScript>, and <h:outputStylesheet>, for image resources, JavaScript resources, and CSS resources, respectively. They can reference physical resource files as well as dynamic resource files. The physical resource files themselves must be placed in the /resources subfolder of the main web folder. The dynamic resource files can be handled with a custom ResourceHandler which intercepts on a specific library name and/or resource name. Given the following folder structure in a Maven WAR project in Eclipse,

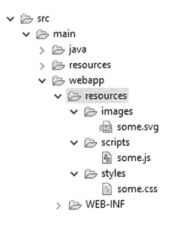

the resources are referenceable as follows:

```
<h:graphicImage name="images/some.svg" />
<h:outputScript name="scripts/some.js" />
<h:outputStylesheet name="styles/some.css" />
```

The generated HTML output looks as follows, provided that /project is the context path of the web application:

```
<img src="/project/javax.faces.resource/images/some.svg.xhtml" />
<script type="text/javascript"
    src="/project/javax.faces.resource/scripts/some.js.xhtml"></script>
<link type="text/css" rel="stylesheet"
    href="/project/javax.faces.resource/styles/some.css.xhtml" />
```

You'll see that it's prefixed with `/javax.faces.resource` path and suffixed with the currently active URL pattern of the `FacesServlet`. The `/javax.faces.resource` is represented by the constant `ResourceHandler#RESOURCE_IDENTIFIER`.[12] That the resource URL matches the URL pattern of the `FacesServlet` ensures that it will actually invoke the `FacesServlet` which in turn knows how to handle the resource. It will first invoke `ResourceHandler#isResourceRequest()`, which by default determines if the URL prefix starts with the known `RESOURCE_IDENTIFIER` constant, and if so then delegates to `ResourceHandler#handleResourceRequest()` instead of going through the JSF life cycle.

Also note that the web resources are not placed in the `src/main/resources` folder but in the `src/main/webapp/resources` folder. The `src/main/resources` folder is only for non-class resources which must end up in the classpath, such as resource bundle files. These classpath resources are then obtainable by `ClassLoader#getResource()`.[13] `src/main/webapp/resources` doesn't end up in the classpath; instead, it ends up in the web content. These web resources are then obtainable by `ExternalContext#getResource()`,[14] which delegates under the hood to `ServletContext#getResource()`.[15]

The `name` attribute thus basically represents the path to the resource relative to the `src/main/webapp/resources` folder. These components also support a `library` attribute. The `library` attribute must represent the unique resource library name of a JSF library. For standard JSF, the resource library name is "`javax.faces`", for PrimeFaces,[16] the resource library name is "`primefaces`", for OmniFaces,[17] the resource library name is "`omnifaces`", for BootsFaces,[18] the resource library name is "`bsf`", and so on. Normally, these library-specific resources are already automatically included by the JSF library in question, usually declaratively via the `@ResourceDependency` annotation on the

---

[12]https://javaee.github.io/javaee-spec/javadocs/javax/faces/application/
ResourceHandler.html#RESOURCE_IDENTIFIER.

[13]https://docs.oracle.com/javase/8/docs/api/java/lang/ClassLoader.html#getResource-
java.lang.String-.

[14]https://javaee.github.io/javaee-spec/javadocs/javax/faces/context/
ExternalContext.html#getResource-java.lang.String-.

[15]https://javaee.github.io/javaee-spec/javadocs/javax/servlet/ServletContext.
html#getResource-java.lang.String-.

[16]http://www.primefaces.org.

[17]http://omnifaces.org.

[18]http://bootsfaces.net.

UIComponent or Renderer class, and sometimes programmatically via UIViewRoot#add ComponentResource(). This is elaborated in the section "Resource Dependencies" in Chapter 11. Those resources can if necessary be referenced using a resource component whereby you thus explicitly specify the library attribute.

The following example explicitly includes the standard JSF jsf.js file:

```
<h:head>
    ...
    <h:outputScript library="javax.faces" name="jsf.js" />
</h:head>
```

This is usually unnecessary as the JSF components depending on this script, such as <h:commandLink>, <f:ajax>, and <f:websocket> already automatically include it. Here's another example which explicitly includes the jquery.js file from PrimeFaces library — this works of course only if you have PrimeFaces installed.

```
<h:head>
    ...
    <h:outputScript library="primefaces" name="jquery/jquery.js" />
</h:head>
```

This can be useful when you'd like to reuse the PrimeFaces-provided jQuery library on a page that doesn't necessarily contain PrimeFaces components. That is, this script won't be automatically included when the page doesn't contain any PrimeFaces component, but you might happen to have some web project-specific scripts which in turn depend on jQuery. JSF resource management will already make sure that both automatically included and explicitly included JavaScript and CSS resources don't get duplicated in the generated HTML output. In other words, the above line which explicitly includes jQuery can safely be used on a page that does contain a PrimeFaces component.

Note that there are currently a relatively large number of poor-quality JSF tutorials on the Internet which don't correctly use the library attribute. Instead, those tutorials incorrectly demonstrate the library attribute to represent the subfolder within the src/ main/webapp/resources folder—something like the following:

```
<h:graphicImage library="images" name="some.svg" />
<h:outputScript library="scripts" name="some.js" />
<h:outputStylesheet library="styles" name="some.css" />
```

This is outright wrong. It doesn't offer any custom resource handler to distinguish library-specific resources from each other. In the above example, you'd basically need to check three different resource libraries even though all those resources belong to the very same library—the web project itself.

Talking about custom resource handlers, imagine that you want to compel the web browser to forcibly reload the image, JavaScript, and/or CSS resource when it has changed in the server side instead. This can be achieved by adding a query string parameter to the resource URL whose value represents the version of the resource. This is also called "cache busting." In JSF, this can be achieved with a custom ResourceHandler which decorates the Resource to return its last modified timestamp as a query string parameter.

```
public class VersionResourceHandler extends ResourceHandlerWrapper {

    public VersionResourceHandler(ResourceHandler wrapped) {
        super(wrapped);
    }

    @Override
    public Resource createResource(String name, String library) {
        Resource resource = super.createResource(name, library);

        if (resource == null || library != null) {
            return resource;
        }

        return new ResourceWrapper(resource) {
            @Override
            public String getRequestPath() {
                String url = super.getRequestPath();
                return url
                    + (url.contains("?") ? "&" : "?")
                    + "v=" + getLastModified();
            }

            private long getLastModified() {
                try {
                    return getWrapped().getURL()
```

```
                 .openConnection().getLastModified();
         }
         catch (IOException ignore) {
             return 0;
         }
     }
   };
  }
}
```

In order to activate it, register it in the `faces-config.xml` as follows:

```
<application>
    <resource-handler>
        com.example.project.resourcehandler.VersionResourceHandler
    </resource-handler>
</application>
```

Note that the `createResource()` method returns the created resource unmodified when it's `null` or when the `library` is not `null`. The resource itself is `null` when the name is unknown. The `library` is null when it's unspecified and thus specific to the web project. You could of course also apply this logic to all resources of other libraries, but they usually already have their own version of a resource handler.

Coming back to the resource components, you can place `<h:graphicImage>` only inside the body, which can be both the plain HTML `<body>` or the JSF `<h:body>`. Obviously, in an HTML document, you can have an `<img>` element only inside the document body. You can place `<h:outputScript>` and `<h:outputStylesheet>` basically anywhere in the JSF page. The `<h:outputScript>` will by default generate the HTML `<script>` element at exactly the declared location, regardless of being in the head or the body of the document. `<h:outputStylesheet>`, however, will by default be moved to the end of `<h:head>` when declared inside `<h:body>`. That is, in HTML it's illegal to have a `<link rel="stylesheet">` outside `<head>`. The `<h:outputScript>` can also be automatically moved to end of document head when declared inside `<h:body>`

with the target attribute set to head. When the target attribute of <h:outputScript> is set to body, then it will be automatically moved to end of the document body. <h:outputStylesheet> doesn't support it. In other words, the following test Facelet,

```
<h:head>
    <title>Resource component relocation demo.</title>
    <h:outputStylesheet name="style1.css" />
    <h:outputScript name="script1.js" />
    <h:outputScript name="script2.js" target="head" />
    <h:outputScript name="script3.js" target="body" />
</h:head>
<h:body>
    <p>Paragraph 1</p>
    <h:outputStylesheet name="style2.css" />
    <h:outputScript name="script4.js" />
    <h:outputScript name="script5.js" target="head" />
    <h:outputScript name="script6.js" target="body" />
    <p>Paragraph 2</p>
</h:body>
```

will basically generate the following HTML output (URLs simplified for brevity).

```
<head>
    <title>Resource component relocation demo.</title>
    <script type="text/javascript" src="script1.js"></script>
    <link type="text/css" rel="stylesheet" href="style1.css" />
    <script type="text/javascript" src="script2.js"></script>
    <link type="text/css" rel="stylesheet" href="style2.css" />
    <script type="text/javascript" src="script5.js"></script>
</head>
<body>
    <p>Paragraph 1</p>
    <script type="text/javascript" src="script4.js"></script>
    <p>Paragraph 2</p>
    <script type="text/javascript" src="script3.js"></script>
    <script type="text/javascript" src="script6.js"></script>
</body>
```

In other words, the resource rendering order in the document head is:

1.  `<h:outputScript>` from `<h:head>` without `target`.

2.  `<h:outputStylesheet>` from `<h:head>`.

3.  `<h:outputScript>` from `<h:head>` with `target="head"`.

4.  `<h:outputStylesheet>` from `<h:body>`.

5.  `<h:outputScript>` from `<h:body>` with `target="head"`.

Note that `<h:outputStylesheet>` implicitly infers `target="head"` and is therefore rendered *after* `<h:outputScript>` without any target. All JavaScript and CSS resources which are automatically included via the `@ResourceDependency` annotation of components will end up between the resources declared in `<h:head>` and those declared in `<h:body>`. So if you happen to use a JSF library which automatically includes a bunch of CSS resources, and you'd like to override some of them, you'd best put such `<h:outputStylesheet>` in `<h:body>` so that you can guarantee that it's loaded *after* the library's.

Beware though, some JSF libraries will automatically override the default renderer of `<h:head>` which may mess up the default resource ordering. In such a case, you'd best consult the documentation of the JSF library in question for new ordering rules, or to restore the default renderer of `<h:head>` via the web project's `faces-config.xml`.

```
<render-kit>
    <renderer>
        <component-family>javax.faces.Output</component-family>
        <renderer-type>javax.faces.Head</renderer-type>
        <renderer-class>
            com.sun.faces.renderkit.html_basic.HeadRenderer
        </renderer-class>
    </renderer>
</render-kit>
```

In case you're using MyFaces instead of Mojarra as JSF implementation, use `org.apache.myfaces.renderkit.html.HtmlHeadRenderer` instead as the renderer class.

In case you intend to develop such a JSF library which automatically includes specific resources, keep in mind to use `@ResourceDependency` or `UIViewRoot#addComponentResource()` instead of replacing the default renderer of `<h:head>` for the purpose.

As annotations don't allow specifying dynamic values, any dynamic resources can best be added during the PostAddToView event of <h:head>. This can be achieved application-wide with a SystemEventListener as follows assuming that the JSF library's resource library name is "foo":

```
public class DynamicResourceListener implements SystemEventListener {

    private static final String LIBRARY = "foo";

    @Override
    public boolean isListenerForSource(Object source) {
        UIOutput output = (UIOutput) source;
        return "javax.faces.Head".equals(output.getRendererType());
    }

    @Override
    public void processEvent(SystemEvent event) {
        FacesContext context = event.getFacesContext();

        String scriptName = "foo.js"; // Can be dynamic.
        addResource(context, scriptName);

        String stylesheetName = "foo.css"; // Can be dynamic.
        addResource(context, stylesheetName);
    }

    private void addResource(FacesContext context, String name) {
        UIComponent resource = new UIOutput();
        resource.getAttributes().put("library", LIBRARY);
        resource.getAttributes().put("name", name);
        resource.setRendererType(context.getApplication()
            .getResourceHandler().getRendererTypeForResourceName(name));
        context.getViewRoot()
            .addComponentResource(context, resource, "head");
    }
}
```

which is registered in `faces-config.xml` as follows:

```
<system-event-listener>
    <system-event-listener-class>
        com.example.project.listener.DynamicResourceListener
    </system-event-listener-class>
    <system-event-class>
        javax.faces.event.PostAddToViewEvent
    </system-event-class>
    <source-class>javax.faces.component.UIOutput</source-class>
</system-event-listener>
```

Note that `<source-class>` could better have been a `javax.faces.component.html.HtmlHead`, but this doesn't necessarily work across all JSF implementations. In, for example, Mojarra, `<h:head>` implicitly creates an instance of `UIOutput` instead of `HtmlHead`.

Once installed, this `DynamicResourceListener` will result in the following HTML output for exactly the last shown test Facelet with `style1.css`, `script1.js`, `script2.js`, etc. (also here, URLs are simplified for brevity).

```
<head>
    <title>Resource component relocation demo.</title>
    <script type="text/javascript" src="script1.js"></script>
    <script type="text/javascript" src="foo.js"></script>
    <link type="text/css" rel="stylesheet" href="foo.css" />
    <link type="text/css" rel="stylesheet" href="style1.css" />
    <script type="text/javascript" src="script2.js"></script>
    <link type="text/css" rel="stylesheet" href="style2.css" />
    <script type="text/javascript" src="script5.js"></script>
</head>
<body>
    <p>Paragraph 1</p>
    <script type="text/javascript" src="script4.js"></script>
    <p>Paragraph 2</p>
    <script type="text/javascript" src="script3.js"></script>
    <script type="text/javascript" src="script6.js"></script>
</body>
```

The resource rendering order in the document head is thus

6. `<h:outputScript>` from `<h:head>` without `target`.

7. Dynamic script added to head during `PostAddToView`.

8. Dynamic stylesheet added to head during `PostAddToView`.

9. `<h:outputStylesheet>` from `<h:head>`.

10. `<h:outputScript>` from `<h:head>` with `target="head"`.

11. `<h:outputStylesheet>` from `<h:body>`.

12. `<h:outputScript>` from `<h:body>` with `target="head"`.

You see, the ordering is quite predictable. It shouldn't have been necessary to override the renderer of `<h:head>`. Moreover, overriding the renderer of `<h:head>` from a JSF library risks the possibility that it becomes incompatible with any other JSF library which coincidentally also overrides the renderer of `<h:head>`. You'd really want to avoid that.

Another advantage of using resource components is that JSF will automatically push all resources associated with the document to the client, so that the client will be able to retrieve them sooner than the time needed to parse the HTML document and locate all `<link>`, `<script>`, and `<img>` elements. This is new since JSF 2.3. This only requires that the JSF 2.3 web application is deployed to a Servlet 4.0-compatible container (Payara 5, GlassFish 5, Tomcat 9, WildFly 12, etc.), and that HTTPS is being used instead of HTTP, and that the client supports HTTP/2 protocol.[19] This does not require additional configuration from the JSF side on.

# Pass-Through Elements

JSF also supports implicitly interpreting any arbitrary HTML element as a full-fledged JSF component. This feature was introduced in JSF 2.2 and is formally known as "pass-through elements." This is particularly useful when you want to use HTML5 elements such as `<main>`, `<article>`, `<section>`, `<aside>`, `<nav>`, `<header>`, `<footer>`, etc. and want to be able to reference them in `<f:ajax render>`. Previously, before JSF 2.2, those elements didn't have a JSF component equivalent and you're therefore forced to wrap them in `<h:panelGroup layout="block">` which only makes the HTML less semantic.

---

[19]`https://caniuse.com/#feat=http2.`

The pass-through element trigger is available by the `http://xmlns.jcp.org/jsf` namespace. All you need to do is to specify at least one attribute on this namespace. The default namespace prefix is just "`jsf`".

```
<!DOCTYPE html>
<html lang="en"
    xmlns="http://www.w3.org/1999/xhtml"
    xmlns:jsf="http://xmlns.jcp.org/jsf"
    xmlns:h="http://xmlns.jcp.org/jsf/html"
>
    <h:head>
        <title>Title</title>
    </h:head>
    <h:body>
        <header>
            ...
            <nav jsf:id="menu">
                ...
            </nav>
        </header>
        <main jsf:id="main">
            ...
        </main>
        <footer>
            ...
        </footer>
    </h:body>
</html>
```

Under the hood, in the JSF component tree, those HTML5 elements are turned into a UIPanel component and are treated in the JSF component tree exactly like `<h:panelGroup>`. This way you can cleanly keep using semantic HTML5 markup while still being able to reference them via `<f:ajax render>`. In other words, the following construct won't work:

```
<main id="main">
    ...
    <h:form id="form">
        ...
```

```
        <h:commandButton id="submit" ...>
            <f:ajax render=":main" />
        </h:commandButton>
    </h:form>
</main>
```

It fails because UIViewRoot#findComponent() doesn't return anything when passing "main". JSF can't find any component with the given ID. The <main> element is here basically interpreted as template text. But the following construct will work:

```
<main jsf:id="main">
    ...
    <h:form id="form">
        ...
        <h:commandButton id="submit" ...>
            <f:ajax render=":main" />
        </h:commandButton>
    </h:form>
</main>
```

UIViewRoot#findComponent() on "main" will then return a UIPanel instance representing the <main> element. JSF will then be able to render it into the Ajax response. The pass-through element feature also works on other HTML elements, only they don't necessarily turn into a UIPanel instance. Instead, they will be turned into a JSF component whose generated HTML output matches the very HTML element (see Table 6-1). The following construct is, under the hood, identical to the previous one:

```
<main jsf:id="main">
    ...
    <form jsf:id="form">
        ...
        <input type="submit" jsf:id="submit" ...>
            <f:ajax render=":main" />
        </input>
    </form>
</main>
```

***Table 6-1.*** *Passthrough Elements Recognized by JSF*

| Passthrough HTML element | Implied JSF component |
| --- | --- |
| <a jsf:action="…"> | <h:commandLink> |
| <a jsf:actionListener="…"> | <h:commandLink> |
| <a jsf:value="…"> | <h:outputLink> |
| <a jsf:outcome="…"> | <h:link> |
| <body jsf:id="…"> | <h:body> |
| <button jsf:id="…"> | <h:commandButton type="button"> |
| <button jsf:outcome="…"> | <h:button> |
| <form jsf:id="…"> | <h:form> |
| <head jsf:id="…"> | <h:head> |
| <img jsf:id="…"> | <h:graphicImage> |
| <input jsf:id="…" type="button"> | <h:commandButton type="button"> |
| <input jsf:id="…" type="checkbox"> | <h:selectBooleanCheckbox> |
| <input jsf:id="…" type="file"> | <h:inputFile> |
| <input jsf:id="…" type="hidden"> | <h:inputHidden> |
| <input jsf:id="…" type="password"> | <h:inputSecret> |
| <input jsf:id="…" type="reset"> | <h:commandButton type="reset"> |
| <input jsf:id="…" type="submit"> | <h:commandButton type="submit"> |
| <input jsf:id="…" type="*"> | <h:inputText> |
| <label jsf:id="…"> | <h:outputLabel> |
| <link jsf:id="…"> | <h:outputStylesheet> |
| <script jsf:id="…"> | <h:outputScript> |
| <select jsf:id="…"> | <h:selectOneListbox> |
| <select jsf:id="…" multiple="*"> | <h:selectManyListbox> |
| <* jsf:id="…"> | <h:panelGroup> |

Any attribute specified on such a pass-through element is implicitly mapped to the corresponding attribute of the JSF component. In the following example, the JSF component and pass-through element pairs are equivalent.

```
<h:graphicImage library="common" name="some.svg" />
<img jsf:library="common" name="some.svg" />

<h:inputText value="#{bean.name}" />
<input type="text" jsf:value="#{bean.name}" />

<h:inputText a:type="email" value="#{bean.email}" />
<input type="email" jsf:value="#{bean.email}" />

<h:link outcome="contact" value="Contact" />
<a jsf:outcome="contact">Contact</a>
```

Note that you don't necessarily need to register every single attribute of a pass-through element on the "jsf" namespace. Only one is sufficient to trigger the pass-through element feature, preferably the first one. This keeps the code concise.

# CHAPTER 7

# Facelets Templating

When JSF (JavaServer Faces) came out for first time in 2004, only JSP (Java Server Pages) had view technology. It was immediately clear that it was an ill-suited view technology for web development with JSF. The problem with JSP is that it writes to the HTTP response as soon as it encounters template text, while JSF would like to first create a component tree based on the view declaration in order to be able to perform the life cycle processing on it. For example, the following JSF 1.0/1.1 page using JSP view technology,

```
<h:commandLink action="...">
    <strong>strong link text</strong>
</h:commandLink>
```

would produce the following HTML output, with template text emitted by JSP before the generated HTML output of JSF components[1]:

```
<strong>strong link text</strong>
<a href="..." onclick="..."></a>
```

The "correct approach" would be to wrap template text in `<f:verbatim>` tags,

```
<h:commandLink action="...">
    <f:verbatim><strong>strong link text</strong><f:verbatim>
</h:commandLink>
```

which would produce the following HTML output:

```
<a href="..." onclick="...">
  <strong>strong link text</strong>
</a>
```

This has obviously received a lot of criticism, and the general recommendation now is that people should not be mixing JSF with HTML. Another problem with JSF 1.0/1.1 was that there was no component to represent an HTML `<div>`. That was around the

---

[1]`www.onjava.com/pub/a/onjava/2004/06/09/jsf.html`.

© Bauke Scholtz, Arjan Tijms 2018
B. Scholtz and A. Tijms, *The Definitive Guide to JSF in Java EE 8*, https://doi.org/10.1007/978-1-4842-3387-0_7

time "web 2.0" had just started, and people also started to discommend the use of HTML tables to lay out a web page. The prevailing view was that only divs should be used, which made people dislike JSF 1.0/1.1 even more.

The peculiar JSP behavior of causing a disorganized HTML output was worked around in JSF 1.2 which was released only two years later in 2006, and the missing component to represent an HTML `<div>` was solved by giving the `<h:panelGroup>` component a new `layout="block"` attribute so that it renders a `<div>` instead of `<span>`. So, already, since JSF 1.2, people can safely mix plain HTML with JSF components in a JSP page and continue using divs in both plain HTML and JSF ways. However, the recommended plan to avoid plain HTML while authoring JSF 1.0/1.1 pages turned into a persistent myth which is even today still alive among some people.

Another problem with JSP is that existing JSP taglibs such as JSTL (JSP Standard Tag Library) and existing JSP expressions in the form of ${...} didn't integrate at all into the JSF life cycle and therefore mixing existing JSP taglibs and JSP expressions with JSF components in a JSP page would result in confusing and unintuitive behavior. People couldn't use `<c:forEach>` to render a list of JSF components as those components wouldn't see the variable declared by `<c:forEach var>`. There was no dedicated JSF component to loop over a list other than `<h:dataTable>` and ultimately people are stuck with tables while creating lists in the JSF page.

Finally, JSP also offers very limited templating capabilities with actually only one "templating" tag, `<jsp:include>`; therefore, templating with JSP would require a fairly complicated approach of creating a bunch of custom tags for every definition of a reusable template section.[2] This contradicts the philosophy of JSF, to have reusable components to minimize code duplication. With JSP, you would end up duplicating JSF components themselves. Existing templating frameworks such as Tiles and Thymeleaf are either JSP centric or don't support JSF at all and thus cannot be used.

There was clearly a strong need for a new-JSF oriented view technology which should supplant JSP and solve all of its problems with the JSF life cycle. And then Facelets was introduced in 2006. It could be installed separately for JSF 1.1 and 1.2, and it shipped built-in with JSF 2.0. It became the default view technology for JSF and JSP was deprecated as view technology for JSF. New tags introduced in JSF 2.0, such as `<f:ajax>`, `<h:head>`, `<h:body>`, `<h:outputScript>`, and `<h:outputStylesheet>`, are only available for Facelets and not for JSP. JSF 2.0 also introduced a new interface to more easily plug a custom view declaration language (VDL) as alternative to JSP and even Facelets, the `ViewDeclarationLanguage` API. This way, one could create, for example, a pure Java-based VDL for JSF.[3]

---

[2]https://stackoverflow.com/q/1296235/157882.

[3]http://arjan-tijms.omnifaces.org/2011/09/authoring-jsf-pages-in-pure-java.html.

# XHTML

The Facelets VDL specifies that the views are defined in XML-based files which are compiled using a SAX parser and kept around in memory. This memory cache is, since JSF 2.1, configurable using a custom `FaceletCacheFactory`. When the JSF project stage is set to `Development`, the SAX-compiled representations of Facelets files are by default not cached. This allows easier development against an already running server by just editing the Facelets files from inside an IDE (integrated development environment) which supports hot-publishing the local changes to the target runtime.

The Facelets files themselves usually use the `.xhtml` extension and therefore starters often call them "XHTML" instead of "Facelets." This is okay when talking in the context of JSF, but the term "XHTML" has another side in the web development world. At its core, XHTML is a markup language for HTML pages which need to be compiled using an XML-based tool. In other words, developers basically create XML files with HTML markup mixed with web framework-specific XML tags, after which the web framework will parse them into an XML tree, generate some web framework-specific representation of the XML tree (which is in JSF the `UIViewRoot`), and ultimately generate the desired HTML output based on the framework's internal representation of the XML tree.

But around the time of Facelets' introduction in 2006, XHTML was being overhyped by another group of web developers who were basically disappointed by seeing the W3 validator invalidate their HTML4 documents—generally because of the desire to explicitly close all tags for consistency, including those which should actually not be closed as per HTML4 specification, such as `<link>`, `<meta>`, `<br>`, and `<hr>`—and sometimes because of the desire to specify custom tag attributes in order to have some JavaScript plug-ins to interact more cleanly with the HTML document, which is also disallowed by the HTML4 specification.

Even though basically every single web browser in the world leniently accepted that, including Jurassic IE6, those developers didn't want to see their carefully crafted HTML4 documents being invalidated by the W3 validator and changed their HTML doctype declaration to use the XHTML DTD, an extension to HTML which requires every tag to be closed and allows custom attributes to be specified on existing tags. However, this is essentially abuse of XHTML as they didn't at all actually use any XML tool to compile the document and generate the desired HTML output. It was merely to keep the W3 validator happy.

Coincidentally, also around that time, HTML5 was just started in draft. Essentially, developers could just strip out any DTD from the HTML doctype declaration in order to get an HTML document which allows XML-based syntax wherein all tags are always closed and custom elements and attributes are allowed and, importantly, validated correctly in the W3 validator. In other words, <!DOCTYPE html> was been sufficient for those developers, even in IE6. Unfortunately, it took ages before HTML5 was officially finished, so developers kept abusing the XHTML doctype before they could switch back to the HTML doctype. When talking about Facelets to those group of developers, don't call it "XHTML" but just "Facelets"; otherwise it will generate confusion.

# Template Compositions

Facelets provides tags for easily creating template compositions based on a single master template file. This should reduce code duplication for site-wide sections which are repeated across all web pages, such as header, navigation menu, and footer. The master template file should represent a full-blown web page layout with all site-wide sections and use <ui:insert> tags to represent places where the page-specific sections can be inserted. Following is a basic example of such a master template file, /WEB-INF/templates/layout.xhtml:

```
<!DOCTYPE html>
<html lang="en"
    xmlns="http://www.w3.org/1999/xhtml"
    xmlns:h="http://xmlns.jcp.org/jsf/html"
    xmlns:ui="http://xmlns.jcp.org/jsf/facelets"
>
    <h:head>
        <title>#{title}</title>
    </h:head>
    <h:body>
        <header>
            <ui:include src="/WEB-INF/includes/layout/header.xhtml" />
        </header>
        <main>
            <ui:insert name="content" />
        </main>
```

```
    <footer>
        <ui:include src="/WEB-INF/includes/layout/footer.xhtml" />
    </footer>
  </h:body>
</html>
```

Note that the master template file and include files are explicitly placed in the /WEB-INF folder. This is done in order to prevent direct access by users who are guessing the path in URL. Also note that the page title is declared as a simple EL (Expression Language) expression #{title} instead of <ui:insert>. It is not allowed to have any markup in the <title> element.

The xmlns attribute basically defines, via a URI (uniform resource identifier), which tags can be used in the declared XML namespace. The root XML namespace specifies the URI of the W3 XHTML standard http://www.w3.org/1999/xhtml which thus defines "any XHTML and HTML5+ tag," such as <html>, <title>, <header>, <main>, and <footer> in above example. The Facelets compiler is aware of this standard XML namespace and will pass through all elements as "general UI instructions." The "h" XML namespace specifies the JSF HTML taglib URI and the "ui" XML namespace specifies the JSF Facelets taglib URI, which are both present in the JSF implementation JAR file and registered to Facelets during the web application's startup. The Facelets compiler can this way find the associated tag handlers, components, and composite components, which in turn do the hard work of building the view, decoding the HTTP request, and encoding the HTTP response. Those URIs are thus not per definition live Internet addresses. You can even specify your own via a *.taglib.xml file. This will be expanded later in the section "Tag Files."

Following is what the include file /WEB-INF/includes/layout/header.xhtml looks like:

```
<ui:composition
    xmlns="http://www.w3.org/1999/xhtml"
    xmlns:h="http://xmlns.jcp.org/jsf/html"
    xmlns:ui="http://xmlns.jcp.org/jsf/facelets"
>
    <a href="#{request.contextPath}/">
        <h:graphicImage name="images/layout/logo.svg" />
    </a>
```

```
    <nav>
        <ul>
            <li><h:link outcome="/about" value="About" /></li>
            <li><h:link outcome="/help" value="Help" /></li>
            <li><h:link outcome="/contact" value="Contact" /></li>
        </ul>
    </nav>
</ui:composition>
```

Note the link around the logo. It points to #{request.contextPath}/. This basically prints the domain-relative URL to the application's root. #{request} is an implicit EL object referring the current HttpServletRequest instance. contextPath refers to one of its properties, implied by the getContextPath() method.

Following is what the include file /WEB-INF/includes/layout/footer.xhtml looks like:

```
<ui:composition
    xmlns="http://www.w3.org/1999/xhtml"
    xmlns:h="http://xmlns.jcp.org/jsf/html"
    xmlns:ui="http://xmlns.jcp.org/jsf/facelets"
>
    <nav>
        <ul>
            <li><h:link outcome="/terms-of-service"
                        value="Terms of Service" /></li>
            <li><h:link outcome="/privacy-policy"
                        value="Privacy Policy" /></li>
            <li><h:link outcome="/cookie-policy"
                        value="Cookie Policy" /></li>
        </ul>
    </nav>
    <small>© Example Company</small>
</ui:composition>
```

Finally, here's how the template client can look, e.g., /home.xhtml:

```
<ui:composition template="/WEB-INF/templates/layout.xhtml"
    xmlns="http://www.w3.org/1999/xhtml"
    xmlns:h="http://xmlns.jcp.org/jsf/html"
    xmlns:ui="http://xmlns.jcp.org/jsf/facelets"
>
    <ui:param name="title" value="Welcome!" />

    <ui:define name="content">
        <h1>Welcome to Example Company!</h1>
        <p>Lorem ipsum dolor sit amet.</p>
    </ui:define>
</ui:composition>
```

Note the template attribute of the <ui:composition>. This must represent the server-side path to the master template, preferably as an absolute path, thus starting with "/".

In a template client, <ui:param> lets you define a simple parameter specific for the master template. Basically, you can use any parameter name, as long as it is supported by the master template and doesn't clash with an existing managed bean name. In this specific case, the value for the EL variable #{title} is specified as "Welcome!". This will ultimately end up inside the <title> element of the master template.

And the <ui:define> lets you define a block of markup specific for the master template. It will ultimately end up in the place where the <ui:insert> with exactly the same name is declared in the master template. Figure 7-1 gives a clear overview of how this all fits together.

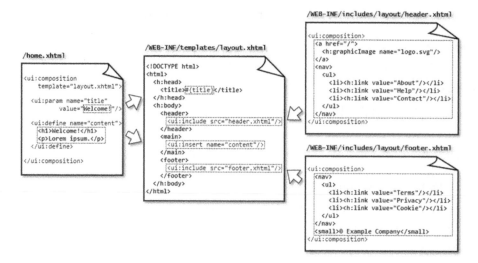

**Figure 7-1.** *The relationship between the master template* layout.xhtml, *include files* header.xhtml, *and* footer.xhtml, *and the template client* home.xhtml. *Note that template file paths and some tag attributes are omitted for brevity. Refer the previously shown code snippets for the actual coding.*

Finally, opening /home.xhtml should produce the final HTML output which you can inspect by right-clicking *View page source* in the average web browser.

# Single Page Application

A recent trend is the so-called Single Page Application (SPA). This concept is on its own not so new; in fact, it is older than JSF itself, but it was heavily popularized during "web 2.0" with JavaScript-based frameworks such as Angular. Basically, an SPA lets the web application behave like a desktop-oriented application by dynamically changing the main content with an Ajax request when navigating to a different page instead of loading the entire page via a GET request. Gmail is one such known example of an SPA.

Such an SPA is also achievable with JSF by simply using <ui:include> whose src attribute is dynamically updated by Ajax. Following is an example utilizing the same master template as shown in the previous section, /spa.xhtml:

```
<ui:composition template="/WEB-INF/templates/layout.xhtml"
    xmlns="http://www.w3.org/1999/xhtml"
    xmlns:jsf="http://xmlns.jcp.org/jsf"
    xmlns:f="http://xmlns.jcp.org/jsf/core"
```

```
    xmlns:h="http://xmlns.jcp.org/jsf/html"
    xmlns:ui="http://xmlns.jcp.org/jsf/facelets"
>

    <ui:param name="title" value="Single Page Application" />

    <ui:define name="content">
        <aside>
            <nav>
                <h:form>
                    <f:ajax render=":content">
                        <ul>
                            <li><h:commandLink value="page1"
                                action="#{spa.set('page1')}" /></li>
                            <li><h:commandLink value="page2"
                                action="#{spa.set('page2')}" /></li>
                            <li><h:commandLink value="page3"
                                action="#{spa.set('page3')}" /></li>
                        </ul>
                    </f:ajax>
                </h:form>
            </nav>
        </aside>
        <article jsf:id="content" data-page="#{spa.page}">
            <ui:include src="/WEB-INF/includes/spa/#{spa.page}.xhtml" />
        </article>
    </ui:define>
</ui:composition>
```

Do note that the <article> element is declared as a so-called pass-through element by explicitly specifying a JSF identifier via jsf:id="…". This feature was introduced in JSF 2.2. Under the hood, when declaring an HTML element which has no JSF component equivalent, such as <header>, <footer>, <main>, <article>, <section>, etc. as a pass-through element this way, it is turned into a UIPanel component and is treated in the JSF component tree exactly like <h:panelGroup>. This way you can cleanly keep using semantic HTML5 markup while still being able to reference it as if it were a JSF component and thus be able to Ajax-update it.

As you might have deciphered in the above /spa.xhtml example, there's a side navigation menu which sets the current page in the managed bean identified by #{spa} and Ajax-updates the component identified by id="content" which in turn contains a dynamic include. The above example excepts the following include files to be present in the /WEB-INF/includes/spa folder: page1.xhtml, page2.xhtml, and page3.xhtml. Each of them is a simple include file which looks as follows:

```
<ui:composition
    xmlns="http://www.w3.org/1999/xhtml"
    xmlns:h="http://xmlns.jcp.org/jsf/html"
    xmlns:ui="http://xmlns.jcp.org/jsf/facelets"
>
    <h1>First page</h1>
    <p>Lorem ipsum dolor sit amet.</p>
</ui:composition>
```

The backing bean associated with the #{spa} managed bean is fairly simple; it looks as follows:

```
@Named @ViewScoped
public class Spa implements Serializable {

    private String page;

    @PostConstruct
    public void init() {
        page = "page1";
    }

    public void set(String page) {
        this.page = page;
    }

    public String getPage() {
        return page;
    }
}
```

The default page is defined in @PostConstruct. Otherwise, the user might face an error page with the message "Invalid path : /WEB-INF/includes/spa/.xhtml".

Note that the backing bean is declared @ViewScoped. This is important in order to remember across postbacks which page is currently being opened. If it were @RequestScoped, and the user navigates to, e.g., page2 and submits a form therein, which creates a new HTTP request, then the @RequestScoped managed bean would be recreated again, with page1 as page value and thus not page2. This has the consequence that <ui:include> won't reference page2.xhtml when JSF is about to decode any input components in order to process the form submit during the postback request, and therefore JSF would fail to find the input components declared in page2.xhtml. A @ViewScoped bean lives as long as the user postbacks to the very same view, in this case /spa.xhtml, and therefore correctly remembers the currently selected page.

When playing around with this SPA example, you might have noticed one disadvantage: the pages are not bookmarkable. This is caused by the fact that the pages are not opened by an idempotent GET request. You can solve that by utilizing the HTML5 history.pushState API.[4] Basically, on completion of the Ajax request you should push the intended URL to the browser history, which will be reflected in the browser's address bar. And, you should modify the Spa backing bean to check if any specific page has been opened and then prepare the page variable accordingly.

Following is a kickoff example which just appends the ?page=xxx query string parameter. First adjust the <f:ajax> of the spa.xhtml to specify the onevent attribute as follows:

```
<f:ajax ... onevent="pageChangeListener">
```

And create the following JavaScript function:

```
function pageChangeListener(event) {
    if (event.status == "success") {
        var page = document.getElementById("content").dataset.page;
        var url = location.pathname + "?page=" + page;
        history.pushState(null, document.title, url);
    }
}
```

---

[4]https://developer.mozilla.org/en-US/docs/Web/API/History_API#Adding_and_
modifying_history_entries.

And, finally, adjust the Spa backing bean as follows:

```
@Inject @ManagedProperty("#{param.page}")
Private String page;

public void init() {
    if (page == null) {
        page = "page1";
    }
}
```

---

**Note**   The @ManagedProperty is currently available in two flavors: the deprecated one from the javax.faces.bean package and the JSF 2.3 introduced one from the javax.faces.annotation package.

---

You need the latter one. Also, note that you might want to validate the provided page parameter. Path probing by hackers is innocent, by the way, as JSF already doesn't allow traversing into the parent path as in /spa.xhtml?page=../../templates/layout.

## Template Decorations

In case you would like to have a reusable include file which is capable of inserting template definitions as if you would be using <ui:include> to reference an include file with one or more <ui:insert> sections, then you can use <ui:decorate>. Following is one such example, the /WEB-INF/decorations/contact.xhtml:

```
<ui:composition
    xmlns="http://www.w3.org/1999/xhtml"
    xmlns:ui="http://xmlns.jcp.org/jsf/facelets"
>
    <section class="contact">
        <header><ui:insert /></header>
        <nav>
            <ul>
                <li>⊘ <a href="tel:+31612345678"
                    title="Phone">+31 (0)6 1234 5678</a></li>
```

```
      <li>✉ <a href="mailto:info@example.com"
            title="Email">info@example.com</a></li>
        </ul>
      </nav>
    </section>
</ui:composition>
```

Here is how it can be used, you can put the `<ui:decorate>` anywhere in your template client, as a `<ui:include>`:

```
<ui:decorate template="/WEB-INF/decorations/contact.xhtml">
    <h2>Questions? Contact us!</h2>
</ui:decorate>
```

Note that the `contact.xhtml` has only one `<ui:insert>` and that it has no name. This will insert the entire `<ui:decorate>` tag body at the declared place of `<ui:insert>`. You can, of course, specify a name, but then you would need to explicitly specify `<ui:define>` with a name for that. That would be only useful if you have more than one insert sections.

You can, if necessary, use `<ui:param>` to pass parameters. This works the same way as with `<ui:composition template>`. The following example parameterizes the e-mail user name `/WEB-INF/decorations/contact.xhtml` with a default value of "info."

```
...
<li>✉ <a href="mailto: #{empty mailto ? 'info' : mailto}@example.com"
    title="Email">#{empty mailto ? 'info' : mailto}@example.com</a></li>
...
```

This can then be used as follows:

```
<ui:decorate template="/WEB-INF/decorations/contact.xhtml">
    <ui:param name="mailto" value="press" />
    <h3>Contact us</h3>
    <p>
        For press inquiries you can contact us by the below
        phone number and email address.
    </p>
</ui:decorate>
```

# Tag Files

As with `<ui:composition template>` and `<ui:decorate>`, you can also use `<ui:param>` in `<ui:include>`. However, watch out that you don't go overboard.

```
<ui:include src="/WEB-INF/includes/field.xhtml">
    <ui:param name="id" value="firstName" />
    <ui:param name="label" value="First Name" />
    <ui:param name="value" value="#{profile.user.firstName}" />
</ui:include>
```

Wherein the /WEB-INF/includes/field.xhtml looks something like the following:

```
<ui:composition
    xmlns="http://www.w3.org/1999/xhtml"
    xmlns:jsf="http://xmlns.jcp.org/jsf "
    xmlns:h="http://xmlns.jcp.org/jsf/html"
    xmlns:ui="http://xmlns.jcp.org/jsf/facelets"
    xmlns:a="http://xmlns.jcp.org/jsf/passthrough"
    xmlns:c="http://xmlns.jcp.org/jsp/jstl/core"
>
    <div class="field" jsf:rendered="#{rendered ne false}">
        <h:outputLabel id="#{id}_l" for="#{id}" value="#{label}" />
        <c:choose>
            <c:when test="#{type eq 'password'}">
                <h:inputSecret id="#{id}" label="#{label}"
                    value="#{value}">
                </h:inputSecret>
            </c:when>
            <c:when test="#{type eq 'textarea'}">
                <h:inputTextarea id="#{id}" label="#{label}"
                    value="#{value}">
                </h:inputTextarea>
            </c:when>
            <!-- More types can be added as c:when here -->
            <c:otherwise>
                <h:inputText id="#{id}" label="#{label}"
```

```
              value="#{value}" a:type="#{type}">
           </h:inputText>
        </c:otherwise>
      </c:choose>
      <h:messages id="#{id}_m" for="#{id}" styleClass="messages" />
   </div>
</ui:composition>
```

In such a case, you would prefer to have something more concise, like the following, instead:

```
<t:field id="firstName" label="First Name"
   value="#{profile.user.firstName}">
</t:field>
```

Having <ui:include> with two or more <ui:param> is a strong sign that the include file can better be registered as a tag file so that it can be used with less boilerplate code in the Facelet.

First move the include file into a different subfolder, /WEB-INF/tags/field.xhtml. This is not a technical requirement. It will work just fine wherever you put it, but we just want to organize the files clearly. Master template files go in /WEB-INF/templates, include files go there in /WEB-INF/includes, decorate files go in /WEB-INF/decorations, and tag files go in /WEB-INF/tags.

Then, create the following /WEB-INF/example.taglib.xml:

```
<?xml version="1.0" encoding="UTF-8"?>
<facelet-taglib
    xmlns="http://xmlns.jcp.org/xml/ns/javaee"
    xmlns:xsi="http://www.w3.org/2001/XMLSchema-instance"
    xsi:schemaLocation="http://xmlns.jcp.org/xml/ns/javaee
      http://xmlns.jcp.org/xml/ns/javaee/web-facelettaglibrary_2_3.xsd"
    version="2.3"
>
    <namespace>http://example.com/tags</namespace>
    <short-name>t</short-name>
```

```xml
    <tag>
        <description>Renders label + input + message field.</description>
        <tag-name>field</tag-name>
        <source>tags/field.xhtml</source>
        <attribute>
            <description>The type of the input component.</description>
            <name>type</name>
            <required>false</required>
            <type>java.lang.String</type>
        </attribute>
        <attribute>
            <description>The ID of the input component.</description>
            <name>id</name>
            <required>true</required>
            <type>java.lang.String</type>
        </attribute>
        <attribute>
            <description>The label of the input component.</description>
            <name>label</name>
            <required>true</required>
            <type>java.lang.String</type>
        </attribute>
        <attribute>
            <description>The value of the input component.</description>
            <name>value</name>
            <required>false</required>
            <type>java.lang.Object</type>
        </attribute>
        <attribute>
            <description>Whether the field is rendered.</description>
            <name>rendered</name>
            <required>false</required>
            <type>boolean</type>
        </attribute>
    </tag>
</facelet-taglib>
```

250

That's admittedly quite some boilerplate code. It is good to know that the `<attribute>` elements aren't mandatory for the technical functioning of the tag file. You could even omit them altogether. But then the IDE won't be able to load them into autosuggest boxes while attempting to autocomplete the custom tag. This is not really developer-friendly. So you'd better keep them in. The `<required>` property of the tag attribute, by the way, only results in a runtime error when the JSF project stage is set to `Development`. In other JSF project stages, it's ignored. And the average IDE will immediately prompt those required attributes during autocompleting the tag.

The file name, `example.taglib.xml`, is free to your choice. In order for JSF to automatically pick up a taglib file during the application's startup, there are only two requirements: it must have a `.taglib.xml` extension and it must be placed in `/WEB-INF` folder (or in case of a JAR file which ends up in `/WEB-INF/lib`, then in `/META-INF` folder of that JAR file). Unfortunately, placing the file in `/WEB-INF` doesn't always work quite well in some servers, such as GlassFish/Payara. In that case, you'd have to explicitly register it via the following context parameter in `web.xml` whose value represents the full path to the `*.taglib.xml` file from the web root on.

```
<context-param>
    <param-name>javax.faces.FACELETS_LIBRARIES</param-name>
    <param-value>/WEB-INF/example.taglib.xml</param-value>
</context-param>
```

In order to use any tag defined in the `*.taglib.xml`, you first have to declare exactly the `<namespace>` URI of the taglib in your Facelet, along with an arbitrary XML namespace prefix. For better maintainability of the code it's recommended to pick the taglib's preferred XML namespace prefix as specified in its `<short-name>`, which is "t" in case of our `example.taglib.xml`.

```
<ui:composition template="/WEB-INF/templates/layout.xhtml"
    xmlns="http://www.w3.org/1999/xhtml"
    xmlns:h="http://xmlns.jcp.org/jsf/html"
    xmlns:ui="http://xmlns.jcp.org/jsf/facelets"
    xmlns:t="http://example.com/tags"
>
    <ui:param name="title" value="Log In" />

    <ui:define name="content">
```

```
        <h:form>
            <fieldset>
                <header>
                    <h1>Log In</h1>
                </header>
                <t:field type="email" id="email" label="Email"
                    value="#{login.email}">
                </t:field>
                <t:field type="password" id="password" label="Password"
                    value="#{login.password}">
                </t:field>
                <footer>
                    <t:button id="submit" label="Log In"
                        action="#{login.submit()}">
                    </t:button>
                </footer>
            </fieldset>
        </h:form>
    </ui:define>
</ui:composition>
```

Do note that the type="email" of the e-mail field thus ends up in <c:otherwise> of the tag file implementation wherein it gets passed through the a:type="#{type}" attribute of <h:inputText>. This allows you to easily use HTML5 input fields, such as type="email", type="number", type="tel", etc. The type attribute being defined as a pass-through attribute a:type is mandatory, because the <h:inputText> by default ignores any custom type attribute and stubbornly renders type="text".

You might also have noticed another custom tag, <t:button>. Here's how it is implemented in /WEB-INF/tags/button.xhtml.

```
<ui:composition
    xmlns="http://www.w3.org/1999/xhtml"
    xmlns:jsf="http://xmlns.jcp.org/jsf"
    xmlns:f="http://xmlns.jcp.org/jsf/core"
    xmlns:h="http://xmlns.jcp.org/jsf/html"
    xmlns:ui="http://xmlns.jcp.org/jsf/facelets"
>
```

```
    <div class="button" jsf:rendered="#{rendered ne false}">
        <h:commandButton id="#{id}" value="#{label}">
            <f:actionListener binding="#{action}" />
            <f:ajax execute="@form" render="@form" />
        </h:commandButton>
        <h:messages id="#{id}_m" globalOnly="true" redisplay="false" />
    </div>
</ui:composition>
```

It's registered in example.taglib.xml nearly the same way as <t:field>, with one exception for the action attribute. Technically, you need to specify a <method-signature> instead of a (property) <type>:

```
<attribute>
    <description>
        Action method of the button.
        NOTE: must include method parenthesis.
    </description>
    <name>action</name>
    <required>true</required>
    <method-signature>void action()</method-signature>
</attribute>
```

You might have noticed that the actual tag implementation uses <f:actionListener binding="#{action}"> instead of action="#{action}". This is actually a necessary trick in order to get it to properly invoke the method. That is, the <method-signature> was initially intended for UI components, not for tag files. It's ignored in tag files. This may be worked on for JSF.next. For now, you can get away with the <f:actionListener binding> trick. This has only one additional requirement: you need to explicitly include the method parenthesis in the tag file client as in <t:button action="#{login.submit()}">.<t:button action="{login.submit}"> will otherwise fail with *javax.el.PropertyNotFoundException: The class 'com.example.project.view.Login' does not have the property 'submit'*.

In case you would like to customize tag files from the tag file client side on, e.g., by adding more specific input attributes, or nesting core tags, or by prepending or appending content to the label or message, then you can use <ui:define> and <ui:insert> the same way you're used to doing with master template files and decorate files. The following

example demonstrates how you can enhance the /WEB-INF/tags/field.xhtml on this
with a bunch of new <ui:insert> tags:

```
<ui:composition
    xmlns="http://www.w3.org/1999/xhtml"
    xmlns:jsf="http://xmlns.jcp.org/jsf "
    xmlns:h="http://xmlns.jcp.org/jsf/html"
    xmlns:ui="http://xmlns.jcp.org/jsf/facelets"
    xmlns:a="http://xmlns.jcp.org/jsf/passthrough"
    xmlns:c="http://xmlns.jcp.org/jsp/jstl/core"
>
    <div class="field" jsf:rendered="#{rendered ne false}">
        <ui:insert name="beforeLabel" />
        <ui:insert name="label">
            <h:outputLabel id="#{id}_l" for="#{id}" value="#{label}">
                <span><ui:insert name="insideLabel" /></span>
            </h:outputLabel>
        </ui:insert>
        <ui:insert name="beforeInput" />
        <ui:insert name="input">
            <c:choose>
                <c:when test="#{type eq 'password'}">
                    <h:inputSecret id="#{id}" label="#{label}"
                        value="#{value}">
                        <ui:insert />
                    </h:inputSecret>
                </c:when>
                <c:when test="#{type eq 'textarea'}">
                    <h:inputTextarea id="#{id}" label="#{label}"
                        value="#{value}">
                        <ui:insert />
                    </h:inputTextarea>
                </c:when>
                <!-- More types can be added as c:when here -->
                <c:otherwise>
                    <h:inputText id="#{id}" label="#{label}"
```

```
                    value="#{value}" a:type="#{type}">
                        <ui:insert />
                    </h:inputText>
                </c:otherwise>
            </c:choose>
        </ui:insert>
        <ui:insert name="beforeMessages" />
        <ui:insert name="messages">
            <h:messages id="#{id}_m" for="#{id}" styleClass="messages" />
        </ui:insert>
    </div>
</ui:composition>
```

Now, that's a lot of flexibility! In the tag file client you can use `<ui:define name="beforeLabel">` to define some content which should appear before the label of the field. And you can use `<ui:define name="label">` to override the label altogether. And you can use `<ui:define name="insideLabel">` to append some (HTML) content inside the label, and so forth. The following example demonstrates how `insideLabel` can be used to append a "Forgot password?" link to the label of the password field:

```
<t:field ...>
    <ui:define name="insideLabel">
        <h:link outcome="/reset-password" value="Forgot password?" />
    </ui:define>
</t:field>
```

Note that `<ui:insert name="insideLabel">` is wrapped in an HTML `<span>`. This allows you to more easily select "anything" that ends up in there via CSS, so that you can, for example, let it float to the right using just `.field label > span { float: right; }`.

Anything else in the tag file client which is not `<ui:define>` will end up inside the nameless `<ui:insert>` tag nested in the chosen input component. This allows you to easily nest any `<f:xxx>` core tag specifically for the input component:

```
<t:field ...>
    <f:attribute name="onkeypress" value="return event.key != 'Enter'" />
    <f:validateRegex pattern="[0-9]{4}" />
    <f:ajax render="otherField" />
</t:field>
```

This specific example prevents the form from submitting when the *Enter* key is pressed by returning false when the KeyBoardEvent.key equals "Enter", and registers a regex validator to accept only a value of four digits by matching against a regular expression pattern of "[0-9]{4}", and instructs JSF to update the component identified by "otherField" by Ajax when the value change event has occurred.

Coming back to the tag file implementation in /WEB-INF/tags/field.xhtml, you might have noticed that good old JSTL is being used there instead of JSF's own rendered attribute. This has advantages as JSTL has a different life cycle than JSF UI components. JSTL is executed when the JSF component tree is about to be built, during the view build time. JSF components are executed when HTML output is about to be generated, during the view render time. Moreover, if you were using JSF's own rendered attribute, then you would face "duplicate component ID" errors because of multiple components with the same ID physically ending up in the JSF component tree.

Might it happen that you are considering the use of plain Java code to dynamically create the component tree based on at least a view-scoped model, you should absolutely reconsider using JSTL instead. As JSTL itself is also XML-based and you can thus just put together everything in an XHTML file, you will end up with much better readable and maintainable code for a "dynamic" component.

# Composite Components

Sometimes, you would like to have a group of related input components to represent a single model value. A classic example is having three <h:selectOneMenu> drop-downs representing day, month, and year which are ultimately bound to a single java.time.LocalDate property in the backing bean. This is not trivial to implement with just an include file or a tag file. You would need some additional Java-based logic which makes sure that, e.g., the day drop-down doesn't show the values 29, 30, or 31 depending on the currently selected month, and that it converts the submitted values to a full-fledged LocalDate instance, and vice versa. But you can't and shouldn't put any Java code in any Facelet.

You'll perhaps think of just creating a dedicated backing bean for this case. But this is not sufficient either. It doesn't allow you to cleanly hook on the component's life cycle through the JSF phases: collecting the individual submitted values from multiple components, converting them into a single LocalDate instance, if necessary throwing a converter exception during the validations phase, and letting the JSF life cycle automatically skip the remaining phases. A backing bean's setter method or action method is far from the right place for that logic. It would be invoked too late anyway. And, it would feel strange to be able to reference and potentially manipulate the very same backing bean via an EL expression on an arbitrary place in the Facelet.

This is exactly where composite components come into the picture: composing a bunch of existing JSF components into virtually a single component tied to a single model value and ultimately using it exactly the same way as you would be using a plain `<h:inputText>`. Imagine a `<t:inputLocalTime>` composite component composed of two `<h:selectOneMenu>` components tied to a single `java.time.LocalTime` model value. Instead of a backing bean, you can use a full-fledged `UIComponent` instance as a so-called backing component.

First create a dedicated subfolder in `main/webapp/resources` folder (and thus not `main/java/resources!`), for example, `main/webapp/resources/components`. There you can put Facelets files representing composite components. The subfolder is then to be used in the XML namespace URI after `http://xmlns.jcp.org/jsf/composite` as shown next.

```
xmlns:t="http://xmlns.jcp.org/jsf/composite/components"
```

Note that the XML namespace prefix of "t" clashes with one which we already defined before for tag files. This is of course not the intent. You may choose a different XML namespace for composite components. It's, however, also possible to let them share the same custom XML namespace URI `http://example.com.tags`. This can be achieved by adding a `<composite-library-name>` to the `*.taglib.xml` which in turn must represent the name of the dedicated subfolder.

```
<composite-library-name>components</composite-library-name>
```

This way all composite components are also available by the same XML namespace as tag files.

```
<... xmlns:t="http://example.com/tags">
...
<t:inputLocalTime ... />
```

The file name of the Facelets file representing the composite component will become the tag name. So, in order to have a `<t:inputLocalTime>`, we need an `inputLocalTime.xhtml` file in the `main/webapp/resources/components` folder. Following is a kickoff example of what it can look like:

```
<ui:component
    xmlns="http://www.w3.org/1999/xhtml"
    xmlns:f="http://xmlns.jcp.org/jsf/core"
    xmlns:h="http://xmlns.jcp.org/jsf/html"
    xmlns:ui="http://xmlns.jcp.org/jsf/facelets"
    xmlns:cc="http://xmlns.jcp.org/jsf/composite"
>
    <cc:interface componentType="inputLocalTime">
        <cc:attribute name="value" type="java.time.LocalTime"
            shortDescription="Selected time. Defaults to 00:00.">
        </cc:attribute>
        <cc:attribute name="required" type="boolean"
            shortDescription="Required state. Defaults to false.">
        </cc:attribute>
    </cc:interface>
    <cc:implementation>
        <span id="#{cc.clientId}" class="inputLocalTime">
            <h:selectOneMenu id="hour" binding="#{cc.hour}"
                required="#{cc.attrs.required}">
                <f:selectItem itemValue="#{null}" />
                <f:selectItems value="#{cc.hours}" />
            </h:selectOneMenu>
            :
            <h:selectOneMenu id="minute" binding="#{cc.minute}"
                required="#{cc.attrs.required}">
                <f:selectItem itemValue="#{null}" />
                <f:selectItems value="#{cc.minutes}" />
            </h:selectOneMenu>
        </span>
    </cc:implementation>
</ui:component>
```

There are several things to notice here which makes a composite component different from a tag file. First, the composite component's body is always divided into two sections: an interface and an implementation.

The interface declares a `componentType` attribute which should reference the value of either the `@FacesComponent` annotation on a `UIComponent` subclass or the `<component-type>` entry of a `<component>` as declared in either `faces-config.xml` or `*taglib.xml`. When the `componentType` attribute is absent, it defaults to `UINamingContainer`. The interface also declares the supported attributes. To keep it simple, we restrict to only two: `value` and `required`. There are also implicitly inherited attributes from the `UIComponent` superclass, which we don't need to explicitly define as `<cc:attribute>`: `id`, `binding`, and `rendered`. That makes it a total of five attributes which you can use in the implementation.

The implementation defines the actual markup of the composite component. There you can find the two `<h:selectOneMenu>` drop-downs wrapped in a `<span>` element. There you can also find several occurrences of the special EL variable `#{cc}` which refers to the current `UIComponent` instance behind the composite component, which is thus one of the type as declared in the `componentType` attribute, or, if absent, a `UINamingContainer`. `#{cc.attrs}` is a shortcut to the component attribute map as available by `UIComponent#getAttributes()`. `#{cc.attrs.required}` as used in `<t:inputLocalTime>` thus refers to `<cc:attribute name="required">`.

`#{cc.clientId}` in the `<span>` element just prints the composite component's client ID as the `id` attribute of `<span>`. This is actually a trick in order to be able to reference the "whole" composite component using a client ID search expression from the template client on. Imagine the following case:

```
<h:inputText ...>
    <f:ajax render="time" />
</h:inputText>
<t:inputLocalTime id="time" ... />
```

This case wouldn't have worked without the `#{cc.clientId}` being rendered as an ID of any plain HTML element which wraps the entire body of `<cc:implementation>`, usually a `<span>` or `<div>`. The technical problem is, while the composite component itself is findable in the JSF component tree by the component ID search expression, the HTML representation of the composite component is by default not available by `document.getElementById(clientId)` in JavaScript. In other words, JSF Ajax wouldn't be able to update it. Explicitly adding a plain HTML element with the composite component's client ID thus solves that.

259

Finally, there are a bunch of #{cc} expressions which don't reference the attributes directly. Both of the <h:selectOneMenu> drop-downs are directly bound as properties of the so-called backing component, the concrete UIComponent instance behind the composite component. And, both <f:selectItems> options obtain their values directly from the backing component as well. Here's the backing component class, com.example. project.composite.InputLocalTime.

```
@FacesComponent("inputLocalTime")
public class InputLocalTime extends UIInput implements NamingContainer {

    private static final List<String> HOURS =
        IntStream.rangeClosed(0, 23).boxed()
            .map(InputLocalTime::pad).collect(Collectors.toList());
    private static final List<String> MINUTES =
        IntStream.rangeClosed(0, 59).boxed()
            .map(InputLocalTime::pad).collect(Collectors.toList());

    private UIInput hour;
    private UIInput minute;

    @Override
    public String getFamily() {
        return UINamingContainer.COMPONENT_FAMILY;
    }

    @Override
    public void encodeBegin(FacesContext context) throws IOException {
        LocalTime localTime = (LocalTime) getValue();

        if (localTime != null) {
            hour.setValue(pad(localTime.getHour()));
            minute.setValue(pad(localTime.getMinute()));
        }

        super.encodeBegin(context);
    }
```

```java
@Override
public Object getSubmittedValue() {
    String submittedHour = (String) hour.getSubmittedValue();
    String submittedMinute = (String) minute.getSubmittedValue();

    if (submittedHour == null || submittedMinute == null) {
        return null;
    }
    else if (submittedHour.isEmpty() || submittedMinute.isEmpty()) {
        return "";
    }
    else {
        return submittedHour + ":" + submittedMinute;
    }
}

@Override
protected Object getConvertedValue
    (FacesContext context, Object submittedValue)
{
    String submittedTime = (String) submittedValue;

    if (submittedTime == null || submittedTime.isEmpty()) {
        return null;
    }

    try {
        return LocalTime.parse(submittedTime,
            DateTimeFormatter.ISO_LOCAL_TIME);
    }
    catch (DateTimeParseException e) {
        throw new ConverterException(e);
    }
}

private static String pad(Integer value) {
    return String.format("%02d", value);
}
```

```
    public UIInput getHour() { return hour; }
    public void setHour(UIInput hour) { this.hour = hour; }
    public UIInput getMinute() { return minute; }
        public void setMinute(UIInput minute) { this.minute = minute; }
    public List<String> getHours() { return HOURS; }
    public List<String> getMinutes() { return MINUTES; }
}
```

Now, that was a bit of code. Not only will you see that the getters and setters are collapsed for brevity, but you'll also see that our composite extends UIInput and implements NamingContainer. Extending from UIInput gives us the benefit that we don't need to repeat most of the default encoding and decoding behavior of UIInput in our backing component, so we only need to override a few methods. Implementing NamingContainer is a technical requirement of <cc:interface>. This enables you to use multiple instances of the composite component in the same context without facing "duplicate component ID" errors. This requirement is also reflected by the overridden getFamily() method, which must as per the composite component's contract return the UINamingContainer.COMPONENT_FAMILY constant.

The actual UIInput components composing the composite component are declared as properties of the backing component. In this case they are both <h:selectOneMenu> drop-downs which are, via the binding attribute, tied to those properties. This enables us to easily set their values during encoding (read: processing the HTTP response), and to obtain the submitted values during decoding (read: processing the HTTP request). You can find the logic for that in the overridden encodeBegin() and getSubmittedValue() methods, respectively.

In the encodeBegin() method you thus have the opportunity to prepare the displayed values based on the model value, if any. The getValue() method is inherited from the UIInput superclass and is tied to the value attribute. You can break down the model value and set the desired values in the individual UIInput components of the composite component. The pad() helper method just pads the digit with a leading zero so that, e.g., the "1" gets displayed as "01". This helper method is also used during static initialization of the lists of available hours and minutes specifically for <f:selectItems>.

In the getSubmittedValue() method you should compose the submitted values of the individual UIInput components together to a single String. In the specific case of <t:inputLocalTime>, we compose a String following the ISO local time pattern HH:mm. In turn, the UIInput superclass passes this value through the getConvertedValue()

wherein we thus have the opportunity to convert the composed String to the concrete model value, which is in our case the LocalTime. Ultimately the UIInput superclass will make sure that this gets set in the backing bean during the update model values phase. Now you can use it as follows:

```
<ui:composition template="/WEB-INF/templates/layout.xhtml"
    xmlns="http://www.w3.org/1999/xhtml"
    xmlns:f="http://xmlns.jcp.org/jsf/core"
    xmlns:h="http://xmlns.jcp.org/jsf/html"
    xmlns:ui="http://xmlns.jcp.org/jsf/facelets"
    xmlns:cc="http://xmlns.jcp.org/jsf/composite/components"
>
    <ui:define name="content">
        <h:form>
            <h:outputLabel for="time:hour" value="Time" />
            <t:inputLocalTime id="time" value="#{bean.time}" />
            <h:commandButton value="Submit" action="#{bean.submit}">
                <f:ajax execute="@form" />
            </h:commandButton>
        </h:form>
    </ui:define>
</ui:composition>
```

where the backing bean represented by #{bean} looks as follows:

```
@Named @RequestScoped
public class Bean {

    private LocalTime time;

    public void submit() {
        System.out.println("Submitted local time: " + time);
    }

    public LocalTime getTime() {
        return time;
    }
```

```
    public void setTime(LocalTime time) {
        this.time = time;
    }
}
```

Might it happen that you need to nest <f:ajax> inside the composite component in order to run some Ajax during the change event of any of the individual drop-downs, then you can achieve that by adding <cc:clientBehavior> targeting both drop-downs as follows:

```
<cc:interface ...>
    ...
    <cc:clientBehavior name="change" default="true"
        targets="hour minute" event="change">
    </cc:clientBehavior>
</cc:interface>
```

The name attribute represents the event name which you should declare in template client in order to trigger it.

```
<t:inputLocalTime id="time" ...>
    <f:ajax event="change" execute="time" ... />
</t:inputLocalTime>
```

The default="true" indicates that this is the default event, which means that you could just omit it, as you could do with event="change" for existing input text and drop-down components, and with event="click" for existing check box and radio button components, and with event="action" for existing command components.

```
<t:inputLocalTime id="time" ...>
    <f:ajax execute="time" ... />
</t:inputLocalTime>
```

The targets attribute must define a space-separated collection of IDs of target UIInput components resembling the composite component on which you would like to trigger the Ajax event, and the event attribute must define the desired event name to be actually triggered on the target UIInput components. In other words, this does, under the hood, effectively the same as if the following is implemented in the composite component:

```
<h:selectOneMenu id="hour" ...>
    <f:ajax event="change" ... />
</h:selectOneMenu>
<h:selectOneMenu id="minute" ...>
    <f:ajax event="change" ... />
</h:selectOneMenu>
```

In this specific example, the event attribute coincidentally has just the same value as the name attribute. This is perhaps confusing at first, but it allows you to easily define a custom event name. For example, following is the code to use when you want to trigger an event solely on the change of the hour drop-down:

```
<cc:interface ...>
    ...
    <cc:clientBehavior name="hourChange"
        targets="hour" event="change">
    </cc:clientBehavior>
</cc:interface>
```

With this, the following Ajax listener will thus be fired only when the hour drop-down is changed and not when the minute drop-down is changed.

```
<t:inputLocalTime id="time" ...>
    <f:ajax event="hourChange" execute="time"
        listener="#{bean.hourChanged}">
    </f:ajax>
</t:inputLocalTime>
```

Note that execute="time" is consistently explicitly specified in the given examples. This is because the default of execute="@this" still does not, in the current JSF 2.3 version, work correctly within the context of the composite component implementation. JSF could have derived the target components from any <cc:clientBehavior default="true">, but it isn't specified as such yet.

All in all, it must be said that composite components have been overhyped after they were first introduced in JSF 2.0. People started using them to "composite" whole templates, includes, decorations, and even multiple tags, without using any backing component. That is, the zero-configuration nature as compared to tag files is very attractive. Everything is declared in the composite component file itself via `<cc:interface>`. And they can be directly used in the template client just by following a convention without the need to configure it in some XML file.

The caveat is that composite components are, due to their internal design, relatively expensive during building and restoring the view as compared to plain include files, decorate files, and tag files, especially when deeply nested. The best practice is therefore to use them only if you actually need a backing component via `<cc:interface componentType>`. For any other case, just use an include, a decorate, or a tag file instead. In the previous section you may already have learned that tag files can be quite powerful with help of JSTL.

## Recursive Composite Component

You can safely nest composite components in each other. However, when you nest the very same composite component recursively in itself, then it would fail with a stack overflow error when EL attempts to resolve the concrete composite component instance behind #{cc}.[5]

Imagine that you've got a recursive tree model which represents some sort of discussion thread, such as e-mail messages and all their replies, or blog comments and all their replies, whereby each reply can in turn have another set of replies. This can be represented as a single JPA entity as follows:

```
@Entity
public class Message {

    @Id @GeneratedValue(strategy=IDENTITY)
    private Long id;

    @Lob
    @Column(nullable = false)
    private @NotNull String text;
```

---

[5]http://balusc.omnifaces.org/2016/02/recursive-tree-of-composite-components.html.

```
@ManyToOne
private Message replyTo;

@OneToMany(mappedBy = "replyTo")
private List<Message> replies = Collections.emptyList();

// Add/generate remaining getters and setters.
}
```

Note that the replyTo property represents the parent message which the current message is a reply to, and that the replies property represents all replies to the current message. The tree structure can then be queried as follows in a MessageService:

```
public List<Message> tree() {
    return entityManager.createQuery(
        "SELECT DISTINCT m FROM Message m"
            + " LEFT JOIN FETCH m.replies r"
            + " ORDER BY m.id ASC", Message.class)
        .getResultList().stream()
        .filter(m -> m.getReplyTo() == null)
        .collect(toList());
}
```

Note that the filtering of the result list afterward is at first glance inefficient, but in reality every single message is retrieved only once and simply referenced in the replies property.

Now, you'd intuitively implement the <t:message> composite component as something like the following:

```
<cc:interface>
    <cc:attribute name="value" type="com.example.Message" />
</cc:interface>
<cc:implementation>
    #{cc.attrs.value.text}
    <c:if test="#{not empty cc.attrs.value.replies}">
        <ul>
            <c:forEach items="#{cc.attrs.value.replies}" var="reply">
                <li>
```

```
                    <t:message value="#{reply}" />
            </li>
        </c:forEach>
      </ul>
   </c:if>
</cc:implementation>
```

which is in turn used as follows:

```
<c:forEach items="#{messages.tree}" var="message">
    <t:message value="#{message}" />
</c:forEach>
```

You'll perhaps only wonder why `<c:forEach>` is being used instead of `<ui:repeat>`. The explanation is relatively simple: `<ui:repeat>` is ignored during view build time. In other words, `<t:message>` would include itself in an infinite loop. If you need to remember the why and how, head back to the section "JSTL Core Tags" in Chapter 3.

But even with the above implementation you would still run into an infinite loop. You know that #{cc} references the current instance of the composite component. Under the hood, when #{reply} is passed to the nested composite, then in reality a reference to #{cc.attrs.value.replies[index]} is being passed. This is, on its own, no problem. But when the nested composite in turn evaluates the #{cc} part from this alias, then it would reference itself instead of the parent composite. Hence, the infinite loop.

Theoretically, you could solve this by replacing #{cc} with #{cc.parent} which returns UIComponent#getParent().

```
<c:forEach items="#{cc.attrs.value.replies}" varStatus="loop">
    ...
    <t:message value="#{cc.parent.attrs.value.replies[loop.index]}" />
    ...
</c:forEach>
```

However, it still doesn't work. Under the hood, inside the nested composite, when the EL evaluator comes to #{cc.parent} and attempts to evaluate "attrs.value" on it, then the parent composite component would return yet another EL expression in form of #{cc.attrs.value} which ultimately gets evaluated. However, the #{cc} part still gets interpreted as "current composite component," which is inside the nested composite component and thus the nested composite itself.

We could only solve it to let the parent composite component not return yet another EL expression but instead the already-evaluated value. This can be achieved by overriding UIComponent#setValueExpression() in the backing component where you check whether the ValueExpression representing #{cc.attrs.value} is about to be set on the component and then immediately evaluate it and store the result as a local variable of the composite component. This shouldn't cause harm as it's supposed to be a read-only attribute.

```
@FacesComponent("messageComposite")
public class MessageComposite extends UINamingContainer {

    private Message message;

    @Override
    public void setValueExpression
        (String attributeName, ValueExpression expression)
    {
        if ("value".equals(attributeName)) {
            ELContext elContext = getFacesContext().getELContext();
            message = (Message) expression.getValue(elContext);
        }
        else {
            super.setValueExpression(attributeName, expression);
        }
    }

    public Message getMessage() {
        return message;
    }
}
```

With this backing component in place, and replacing "attrs.value" by "message", it finally works.

```
<cc:interface componentType="messageComposite">
    <cc:attribute name="value" type="com.example.Message" />
</cc:interface>
<cc:implementation>
```

```
#{cc.message.text}
<c:if test="#{not empty cc.message.replies}">
    <ul>
        <c:forEach items="#{cc.message.replies}" varStatus="loop">
            <li>
                <t:message
                    value="#{cc.parent.message.replies[loop.index]}">
                </t:message>
            </li>
        </c:forEach>
    </ul>
</c:if>
</cc:implementation>
```

# Implicit EL Objects

In Facelets files a bunch of implicit EL objects available. They are mainly shortcuts to important artifacts, scopes, maps, and components available in the current faces context. Table 7-1 provides an overview of them.

***Table 7-1.*** *Implicit EL Objects Available in EL Context of JSF*

| Implicit EL object | Resolves to | Returns | Since |
|---|---|---|---|
| #{facesContext} | FacesContext#getCurrentInstance() | FacesContext | 2.0 |
| #{externalContext} | FacesContext#getExternalContext() | ExternalContext | 2.3 |
| #{view} | FacesContext#getViewRoot() | UIViewRoot | 2.0 |
| #{component} | UIComponent#getCurrentComponent() | UIComponent | 2.0 |
| #{cc} | UIComponent#getCurrentComposite Component() | UIComponent | 2.0 |
| #{request} | ExternalContext#getRequest() | HttpServletRequest | 1.0 |
| #{session} | ExternalContext#getSession() | HttpSession | 1.0 |
| #{application} | ExternalContext#getContext() | ServletContext | 1.0 |

(*continued*)

***Table 7-1.*** (*continued*)

| Implicit EL object | Resolves to | Returns | Since |
|---|---|---|---|
| #{flash} | ExternalContext#getFlash() | Flash | 2.0 |
| #{requestScope} | ExternalContext#getRequestMap() | Map<String, Object> | 1.0 |
| #{viewScope} | UIViewRoot#getViewMap() | Map<String, Object> | 2.0 |
| #{flowScope} | FlowHandler#getCurrentFlowScope() | Map<Object, Object> | 2.2 |
| #{sessionScope} | ExternalContext#getSessionMap() | Map<String, Object> | 1.0 |
| #{applicationScope} | ExternalContext#getApplicationMap() | Map<String, Object> | 1.0 |
| #{initParam} | ExternalContext#getInitParameterMap() | Map<String, String> | 1.0 |
| #{param} | ExternalContext#getRequestParameterMap() | Map<String, String> | 1.0 |
| #{paramValues} | ExternalContext#getRequestParameter ValuesMap() | Map<String, String[]> | 1.0 |
| #{header} | ExternalContext#getRequestHeaderMap() | Map<String, String> | 1.0 |
| #{headerValues} | ExternalContext#getRequestHeader ValuesMap() | Map<String, String[]> | 1.0 |
| #{cookie} | ExternalContext#getRequestCookieMap() | Map<String, Cookie> | 1.0 |
| #{resource} | ResourceHandler#createResource() | Resource | 2.0 |

For the JSF artifacts and components, if the class in turn specifies a getter method somewhere, such as `HttpServletRequest#getContextPath()`, then you can of course access it in EL the usual way as in `#{request.contextPath}`.

For scoped maps, any property will be interpreted as the map key. If the property happens to contain period characters, then you can use the brace notation as in `#{map['key.with.periods']}` in order to access the map value. Note that `#{flash}` essentially extends from `Map<String, Object>`, so it could be treated as such. It should also be said that `#{flowScope}` indeed deviates from other scoped maps by accepting `Object` instead of `String` as a map key. This is most likely a historical mistake. The canonical approach to access scoped maps is to use a `String`-based key.

`#{cookie}` is mapped by the cookie name and the value actually returns a `javax. servlet.http.Cookie` which in turn has a `getValue()` property. So, in order to access the `JSESSIONID` cookie, you basically need `#{cookie.JSESSIONID.value}`. Of course, you can also just use `#{session.id}` instead.

#{resource} actually has its own EL resolver which interprets any property as a resource identifier in "library:name" format and then passes it to Resour ceHandler#createResource() and finally returns the URL of the resource via Resource#getRequestPath(). This is very useful in CSS resources in order to reference a JSF image resource as a CSS background image. The following example will actually render the URL of src/main/webapp/resources/images/background.svg.

```
body {
    background-image: url("#{resource['images/background.svg']}");
    background-size: cover;
}
```

Note that resolving EL expressions in CSS resources only works when the CSS resource itself is included via <h:outputStylesheet> instead of <link>. Also noted should be that JSF remembers by default only on the very first request of the CSS resource whether it contains EL expressions or not. If it didn't, then JSF won't recheck it on a later request, even not in the development stage. So if you notice that your first EL expression in an existing CSS resource doesn't seem to work, you'd better restart the web application. This feature of EL resolving in CSS resources is actually pretty useful. If SCSS (Sassy CSS) is a step too far for you, then you could use EL to parameterize some repeated CSS properties, such as colors.

```
.color-gray {
    color: #{applicationScope['gray']='#B8B8B8'};
}

...

.someSelector {
    border: 1px solid #{gray};
}
.otherSelector {
    color: #{gray};
}

...
```

No, this feature of EL resolving in CSS resources isn't available in JS resources. For that, you'd instead need to print a JS object in the global scope and let your JS resources intercept it if necessary. For example,

```
<h:outputScript>var config = #{configuration.script};</h:outputScript>
<h:outputScript name="scripts/some.js" />
```

whereby the `#{configuration.script}` just returns a JSON object as string from your managed bean. Or, you could let EL print it as a data attribute of an HTML element

```
<html lang="en" data-baseuri="#{request.contextPath}/">
    ...
</html>
```

which is in turn accessible in JS as follows:

```
var baseuri = document.documentElement.dataset.baseuri;
```

or if you're a jQuery fan:

```
var baseuri = $("html").data("baseuri");
```

That said, when creating managed beans on the Java side, or when declaring custom EL variables on the Facelets side, such as `<h:dataTable var="foo">`, `<ui:repeat var="foo">`, or `<c:set var="foo">`, you need to make absolutely sure that you don't explicitly or implicitly choose a managed bean name or EL variable name which clashes with one of the previously listed implicit EL objects, because implicit EL objects have higher precedence in EL resolving than user defined names. So, for example, the following construct wouldn't work as you might expect:

```
<ui:repeat value="#{bean.parameters}" var="param">
    #{param}<br />
</ui:repeat>
```

It would print literally "{}" for each iteration round, which is basically the default `Map#toString()` format of an empty `Map`. When you reopen the same page with a query string like `?foo=bar`, then it would print literally "{foo=bar}" for each iteration round. You'd better rename the `var="param"` to something else then.

# CHAPTER 8

# Backing Beans

The "backing bean" is a JSF-specific concept. It represents the sole JavaBean class which is ultimately used as a "managed bean" responsible for providing data, actions, and/or UI (User Interface) components in a JSF page.

## Model, View, or Controller?

JSF (JavaServer Faces) is a MVC (model-view-controller) framework. It's a widely used architectural design pattern for software applications which has its roots in desktop application development.[1]

In a JSF framework's point of view, the model is represented by the backing bean, the view is represented by the component tree, which in turn is usually defined in a Facelets file, and the controller is represented by the `FacesServlet` which is already provided by JSF. From a Java EE application server's point of view, however, the model is represented by the service layer which in turn is usually defined in EJB (Enterprise JavaBeans) classes and JPA (Java Persistence API) entities, the view is represented by all your JSF-based code, and the controller is the `FacesServlet`. In a JSF developer's point of view, the model is represented by the service layer, the view is represented by the Facelets file, and the controller is represented by the backing bean.

The backing bean class can thus be either the model, view, or controller, depending on your point of view, while the service layer is always the model, and the Facelets file is always the view, and the `FacesServlet` is always the controller. Note that in this context, the "JSF developer" is you, who develops a web application using the JSF framework for a Java EE application server.

---

[1]`https://en.wikipedia.org/wiki/Model%E2%80%93view%E2%80%93controller`.

© Bauke Scholtz, Arjan Tijms 2018
B. Scholtz and A. Tijms, *The Definitive Guide to JSF in Java EE 8*, https://doi.org/10.1007/978-1-4842-3387-0_8

Figure 8-1 illustrates the position of the backing bean in JSF's MVC paradigm. It's a Venn diagram where the intersection of the controller and the view is represented by the JSF component tree which could be bound to a backing bean via the component's `binding` attribute. The intersection of the view and the model is represented by property getters and setters of EL (Expression Language) value expressions which could be bound to a backing bean, usually via the component's `value` attribute. The intersection of the controller and the model is represented by action method invocations of EL method expressions which could be bound to a backing bean via the component's `action` attribute. Finally, the intersection of all intersections is represented by the backing bean itself.

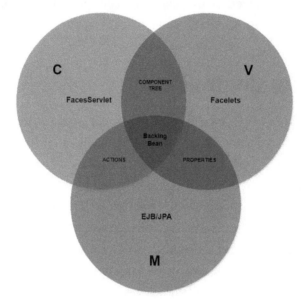

***Figure 8-1.*** *The position of the backing bean in JSF's MVC paradigm*

In this MVC paradigm the backing bean has thus a rather unique position. Note that the backing bean doesn't necessarily need to be represented by a single class. It can even be represented by multiple classes, each with its own managed bean scope, like the view can be represented by multiple Facelets files and the model can be represented by multiple EJB/JPA classes.

Coming back to the JSF developer's point of view, we can even get a step further with considering whether the backing bean is a model or a controller, depending on how you code the backing bean class. Following is one way:

```
@Named @RequestScoped @Stateful
public class ProductBacking {

    private String productName;
    private String productDescription;

    @Inject
    private ActiveUser activeUser;

    @PersistenceContext
    private EntityManager entityManager;

    public void save() {
        Product product = new Product();
        product.setName(productName);
        product.setDescription(productDescription);
        product.setCreatedBy(activeUser.get());
        entityManager.persist(product);
        FacesContext.getCurrentInstance().addMessage(null,
            new FacesMessage("Product created!"));
    }

    // Add/generate getters and setters for product name and description.
}
```

In this rather naïve way, the entity's properties are essentially duplicated in the backing bean class and the business logic is tightly coupled in the backing bean class. In other words, the backing bean class has incorrectly taken over the responsibilities of the real model. One would misinterpret such backing bean class as being the sole model. When we eliminate this duplication and unreusability, we find another way:

```
@Named @RequestScoped
public class ProductBacking {

    private Product product = new Product();
```

```
    @Inject
    private ProductService productService;

    public void save() {
        productService.create(product);
        FacesContext.getCurrentInstance().addMessage(null,
            new FacesMessage("Product created!"));
    }

    public Product getProduct() {
        return product;
    }
}
```

whereby the ProductService looks as follows:

```
@Stateless
public class ProductService {

    @PersistenceContext
    private EntityManager entityManager;

    @Inject
    private ActiveUser activeUser;

    public Long create(Product product) {
        product.setCreatedBy(activeUser.get());
        entityManager.persist(product);
        return product.getId();
    }
}
```

This is actually the correct way of authoring backing beans. When comparing it to the first way, you could argue that the backing bean has, in the JSF developer's point of view, become a controller for the EJB/JPA model. The backing bean being a controller is not wrong from the JSF developer's point of view, but this is not actually correct from the JSF framework's point of view where the FacesServlet is the real controller. The FacesServlet treats the backing bean as a model, because the FacesServlet doesn't have direct access to the real model, the service layer. You as the JSF developer can, of course, in your context treat the backing bean as a controller, because you can easily ignore all duties of the `FacesServlet` as you don't need to worry about its job while writing JSF code. All you need to worry about while writing JSF code is the view, the model, and the backing bean. The rest is done transparently by JSF.

# Managed Beans

The conceptual difference between a "backing bean" and a "managed bean" can be represented by the following lines of code executed under the hood of the bean management facility:

```
BackingBeanClass managedBeanInstance = new BackingBeanClass();
someContext.put("managedBeanName", managedBeanInstance, someScope);
```

In other words, the backing bean is the concrete class created by you, the JSF developer, and registered into some bean management facility, such as CDI. The bean management facility will automatically manage the bean's life cycle by performing construction, dependency injection, and destruction when necessary, without you having to do it manually. If you've ever developed with JSP/Servlets, this basically removes the need to manually instantiate beans and put them as an attribute of the `ServletContext`, `HttpSession`, or `ServletRequest`.[2] To register a backing bean class as a CDI managed bean for JSF views, simply put the `@javax.inject.Named` annotation[3] on the class signature.

```
@Named
public class BackingBeanClass {
    // ...
}
```

It will then immediately be available in EL context by `#{backingBeanClass}` and in all other managed beans via `@Inject`. The EL context is directly available in Facelets files. By default, the managed bean name is derived from the backing bean's class name by lowercasing the first character. This can optionally be overridden by specifying the value of the `@Named` annotation.

---

[2]https://stackoverflow.com/q/3106452/157882.
[3]https://javaee.github.io/javaee-spec/javadocs/javax/inject/Named.html.

```
@Named("managedBeanName")
public class BackingBeanClass {
    // ...
}
```

This is now in EL context available by #{managedBeanName}. Nothing has changed for the @Inject approach. Once a JSF backing bean becomes a managed bean, it will be automatically instantiated and initialized whenever it's accessed for the first time in the context associated with the bean's scope. It will be automatically destroyed when the life cycle associated with the bean's scope has ended. More about managed bean scopes in the next section.

Historically, JSF provided a native way to register backing bean classes as managed beans: first, in JSF 1.x via <managed-bean> entries in faces-config.xml, and since JSF 2.0 via @javax.faces.bean.ManagedBean annotation, which is, since JSF 2.3, officially deprecated in favor of CDI @Named. CDI was introduced for first time in Java EE 6, at the same time as JSF 2.0, with the aim of unifying the management of context-sensitive instances and injecting the currently available instances in each other. Unfortunately, the JSF 2.0 @ManagedBean was already set in stone long before CDI was finished, so those two ways of managing beans did exist in parallel for some time. The CDI bean management facility has several advantages on top of JSF bean management facility.

First, injecting one managed bean in another managed bean using CDI's @Inject doesn't require a getter/setter pair in the parent backing bean class, while JSF's @javax. faces.bean.ManagedProperty requires a getter/setter pair, which is considered poor practice as this exposes too much information to the outside, which is potentially confusing. Should we access the injected bean via #{bean} or #{parentBean.bean}?

Second, the injected CDI managed bean can be of a narrower scope than the parent managed bean. This is possible because CDI @Inject actually injects a proxy instance which in turn delegates to the currently available instance, while JSF @ManagedProperty "injects" the actual instance by invoking the setter method directly after the construction of the parent bean.

Third, CDI managed beans are accessible in all other Java EE artifacts which are not directly managed by JSF, such as web servlets, web filters, web listeners, socket end points, web service end points, enterprise beans, etc. This allows a very easy way of exchanging data across various layers within the same application, particularly within the same HTTP session.

Once again, the JSF bean management facility is officially deprecated since JSF 2.3. You should absolutely not use it any more in new JSF applications. It will still be there in the JSF API for backward compatibility, but chances are that the `javax.faces.bean` package will be removed altogether in a future JSF version. Existing JSF applications should be migrated to CDI as soon as possible. CDI is natively available in normal Java EE application servers and relatively easy to install in barebones servlet containers. For example, JBoss Weld, one of the CDI implementations, can already be installed in Tomcat by simply adding the single dependency `org.jboss.weld.servlet:weld-servlet-shaded` to the project[4] without any further effort.

# Scopes

The managed bean scope basically represents the lifetime of the managed bean. As hinted in the previous section, in plain JSP/Servlet perspective the scopes are represented by the object being put as an attribute of the `ServletContext`, `HttpSession`, or `ServletRequest`. Those objects will then become application scoped, session scoped, and request scoped, respectively. This is still how it works with CDI and all; it only adds an extra abstract layer over it so that you don't any more need to manually create and put the objects in a certain scope.

In standard JSF, the following CDI managed bean scopes are available for JSF backing beans, ordered from the longest living to the shortest living.

1. `@javax.enterprise.context.ApplicationScoped`

2. `@javax.enterprise.context.SessionScoped`

3. `@javax.enterprise.context.ConversationScoped`

4. `@javax.faces.flow.FlowScoped`

5. `@javax.faces.view.ViewScoped`

6. `@javax.enterprise.context.RequestScoped`

7. `@javax.enterprise.context.Dependent`

Note that the `javax.faces.bean` package also defines a set of scopes, but they are only applicable on the beans managed by JSF's `@ManagedBean`, not on beans managed by CDI. Moreover, the `javax.faces.bean` package is deprecated since JSF 2.3 in favor of CDI.

---

[4]`http://balusc.omnifaces.org/2013/10/how-to-install-cdi-in-tomcat.html`.

# @ApplicationScoped

An application-scoped managed bean instance is tied to the lifetime of the web application itself. It's under the hood represented as an attribute of the `ServletContext` which is created on the web application's deployment and destroyed on the web application's undeployment. Note that this is not equal to the server's startup and shutdown. Web applications can be deployed and undeployed on a running server.

In other words, there's only one instance of an application-scoped managed bean throughout the web application's lifetime which is shared across all requests and sessions. You could argue that it behaves like a singleton. However, it doesn't actually follow the singleton design pattern. It follows the "just create one" design pattern.[5] A real singleton doesn't have any public constructor but only a static method which returns a statically initialized lazy loaded instance. A real JavaBean, on the other hand, requires the presence of a default constructor.

By default, an application-scoped bean managed instance is created for the first time when the web application's code accesses it for the first time during the web application's lifetime. It's thus not, per definition, immediately created when the `ServletContext` instance is created. It is, however, guaranteed when the `ServletContext` instance is destroyed.

Application-scoped managed beans are useful for application-wide data which needs to be initialized only once in the application's lifetime, or needs to provide non-static getters which delegate to static variables, or needs to provide functions for usage in EL. The following example makes sure that application settings stored in the database are loaded only once and provided as a `Map` by `#{settings}` during the rest of the application's lifetime.

```
@ApplicationScoped
public class ApplicationSettingsProducer {

    private Map<String, String> settings;

    @Inject
    private ApplicationSettingsService applicationSettingsService;

    @PostConstruct
```

---

[5]http://butunclebob.com/ArticleS.UncleBob.SingletonVsJustCreateOne.

```
public void init() {
    settings = applicationSettingsService.getAll();
}

@Produces @Named
public Map<String, String> getSettings() {
    return settings;
}
}
```

Note that the @Named annotation is placed on the getter, which implies a managed bean name matching the property name: #{settings}. Also note that the getter in turn needs the @Produces annotation in order to be recognized as a managed bean producer. Following is another example which offers text formatting functions.

```
@Named @ApplicationScoped
public class Format {

    public String date(LocalDate localDate) {
        if (localDate != null) {
            return localDate.format(DateTimeFormatter.ISO_LOCAL_DATE);
        }
        else {
            return "n/a";
        }
    }

    public String currency(BigDecimal amount) {
        if (amount != null) {
            return NumberFormat.getCurrencyInstance(Locale.US)
                .format(amount);
        }
        else {
            return "n/a";
        }
    }
}
```

This could be useful in, for example, a data table to keep the Facelets code terse.

```
<h:dataTable value="#{cart.products}" var="product">
    <h:column>#{format.date(product.lastModified)}</h:column>
    <h:column>#{format.currency(product.discount)}</h:column>
</h:dataTable>
```

It's also useful in case you need a formatted value in an attribute which doesn't allow a nested `<h:outputText><f:convertXxx>`.

```
<h:commandLink ... title="Last visited #{format.date(user.lastVisited)}">
```

# @SessionScoped

A session-scoped managed bean instance is tied to the lifetime of the established HTTP session. It's under the hood represented as an attribute of the `HttpSession` which is created for every unique client on demand of the web application's code. When the web application's code directly or indirectly pokes the `HttpSession` for the first time via `HttpServletRequest#getSession()`, the servlet container will create a new `HttpSession` instance, generate a long and unique ID, and store it in server's memory. The servlet container will also set a session cookie on the HTTP response with "JSESSIONID" as the cookie name and the unique session ID as the cookie value. A "session cookie" is identified by the absence of the "maximum age" attribute.

As per the HTTP cookie specification, the client (the web browser) is required to send this cookie back in the header of the subsequent requests as long as the cookie is valid. In any decent web browser you can inspect the request and response headers in the "Network" section of the web developer's toolset which is accessible by pressing F12 in the web browser. The servlet container will check every incoming HTTP request for the presence of the cookie with the name "JSESSIONID" and use its value (the session ID) to get the associated `HttpSession` instance from server's memory.

On the server side, the `HttpSession` instance stays alive until it has not been accessed for more than the timeout value as specified in the `<session-timeout>` setting of `web.xml`, which defaults to 30 minutes on most if not all servlet containers. So, when the client doesn't visit the web application for longer than the time specified, the servlet container will destroy the `HttpSession` instance. Every subsequent HTTP request, even with the cookie specified, will not have access to the `HttpSession` instance anymore; the servlet container will create a new `HttpSession` instance and overwrite the cookie value with the new session ID.

On the client side, by default, all session cookies stay alive for as long as the browser instance is running. So, when the client shut downs the browser instance, all session cookies are destroyed on the client side. In a new browser instance, the session cookies from a previous browser session are not available any more, so the browser won't send any JSESSIONID cookie. The server will then interpret it as a brand-new session. The HttpSession instance associated with the previous browser session will silently expire on the server side.

By default, a session-scoped managed bean instance is created for the first time when the web application's code accesses it for the first time during the HTTP session's lifetime. It's thus not, per definition, immediately created when the HttpSession instance is created. It is, however, guaranteed to be destroyed when the HttpSession instance is destroyed. Session-scoped managed beans are effectively shared across all browser tabs within the same browser session.

Session-scoped managed beans are useful for keeping track of client-specific data, such as the entity representing the currently logged-in user, the selected language, and other user-related preferences. The following example calculates the current locale and provides a getter/setter for it so that it can be obtained in the view and modified by an UIInput component.

```
@Named @SessionScoped
public class ActiveLocale implements Serializable {

    private Locale current;

    @PostConstruct
    public void init() {
        FacesContext context = FacesContext.getCurrentInstance();
        current = context.getApplication()
            .getViewHandler().calculateLocale(context);
    }

    // Getter+setter.
}
```

A more elaborate example can be found in the section "Changing the Active Locale" in Chapter 14. Do note that session-scoped managed beans must implement Serializable because the HttpSession instance itself, where those beans are being stored, is subject to being written to disk in case of a server restart or even to being transferred over the network to a different server in case of a server cluster configuration with a distributable session.

Another classic example is a "shopping cart."

```
@Named @SessionScoped
public class Cart implements Serializable {

    private List<Product> products = new ArrayList<>();

    public void addProduct(Product product) {
        products.add(product);
    }

    // ...

}
```

# @ConversationScoped

A conversation-scoped managed bean is tied to the lifetime of the injected javax. enterprise.context.Conversation instance which offers begin() and end() methods which must be explicitly invoked by the web application's code in order to indicate the start and end of the conversation scope. The conversation scope is represented by a predefined HTTP request parameter with a default name of "cid" ("Conversation ID") whose value references represents the conversation ID. The conversation ID in turn references an isolated mapping in the current HTTP session where the conversation-scoped managed bean instances will be stored.

As long as the conversation scope has not started, the conversation-scoped managed bean will behave like a request-scoped managed bean. When the application code explicitly invokes Conversation#begin(), then the conversation scope will start and a custom javax.faces.application.ViewHandler provided by the CDI implementation will make sure that all its getXxxURL() methods such as getActionURL() and getBookmarkableURL() return a URL (uniform resource locator) with the conversation ID parameter included. In case of Weld, that's the ConversationAwareViewHandler.[6]

---

[6]https://github.com/weld/core/blob/master/modules/jsf/src/main/java/org/jboss/weld/ module/jsf/ ConversationAwareViewHandler.java.

All JSF `UIForm` and `UIOutcomeTarget` components derive their action and target URLs from those methods of the `ViewHandler`. The generated HTML output of those components will thus ultimately include the conversation ID in the target URL.

On an incoming HTTP request, when the conversation ID parameter is present in the request, and it is still valid, the CDI implementation will obtain the associated conversation scope from the HTTP session and make sure that all conversation-scoped managed beans are obtained from exactly this conversation scope identified by the conversation ID. This works on both GET and POST requests. Any form submit or any link/navigation to a URL with the conversation ID included will provide access to the very same conversation scope, as long as it's still valid. The conversation scope ends when the application code explicitly invokes `Conversation#end()`. When the end user reuses the "cid" request parameter later, or manipulates its value to one which isn't started in its own browser session, or when the underlying `HttpSession` instance is destroyed, then CDI will throw a `javax.enterprise.context.NonexistentConversationException`.

Conversation-scoped managed beans are particularly useful in order to be able to return to a particular stateful page within the same browser session after being redirected elsewhere. A classic example is a third-party web service which is included in an HTML `<iframe>` or opened in a new browser tab or even targeted in the action attribute of a plain HTML `<form>`, and can, via a specific request parameter, be configured to redirect back to your web application after completing the service. When you include the conversation ID in the redirect URL, then you will in the redirected page be able to resume with exactly the same conversation-scoped managed bean instance as it was before the redirect. This allows you the opportunity to finalize and unlock any pending transactions and, of course, end the conversation.

Given a checkout button which looks as follows,

```
<h:form>
    ...
    <ui:fragment rendered="#{empty payment.url}">
        ...
        <h:commandButton value="Checkout" action="#{payment.checkout}">
            <f:ajax render="@form" />
        </h:commandButton>
    </ui:fragment>
    <ui:fragment rendered="#{not empty payment.url}">
```

```
        <iframe src="#{payment.url}"></iframe>
    </ui:fragment>
</h:form>
```

here's what the associated conversation-scoped bean behind #{payment} looks like:

```
@Named @ConversationScoped
public class Payment implements Serializable {

    private Order order;
    private String url;

    @Inject
    private Cart cart;

    @Inject
    private OrderService orderService;

    @Inject
    private Conversation conversation;

    public void checkout() {
        conversation.begin();
        order = orderService.lockProductsAndPrepareOrder(cart);
        url = "http://third.party.com/pay?returnurl="
            + URLEncoder.encode("http://my.site.com/paid?cid="
            + conversation.getId(), "UTF-8");
    }

    public void confirm() {
        orderService.saveOrderAndCreateInvoice(order);
        conversation.end();
    }

    @PreDestroy
    public void destroy() {
        orderService.unlockProductsIfNecessary(order);
    }
```

```
public String getUrl() {
    return url;
}
}
```

Basically, the checkout button is only rendered when there's no payment URL set. Once the button is pressed, all products of the shopping cart are locked and the order is prepared. Also, depending on the third-party payment service, the URL referring it must be prepared whereby you include the return URL as some query parameter in the URL of the payment service. The return URL should in turn include the "cid" request parameter representing the conversation ID. In the redirected page which will actually be loaded in the `<iframe>`, you can just mark the conversation complete with `<f:viewAction>`.

```
<f:metadata>
    <f:viewAction action="#{payment.confirm}" />
</f:metadata>
```

Of course, the average third-party payment service should have a more elaborate Java or even JavaScript API instead of `<iframe>`; also, it should be possible to provide different return pages for each payment outcome such as payment failed and payment aborted. The above example is just to give the general idea.

# @FlowScoped

A flow-scoped managed bean is tied to the lifetime of a JSF flow. It uses the same principle as conversation scope, only the conversation is further narrowed down to a specific set of JSF views in an isolated subfolder. Once the end user clicks a JSF link or button component which navigates to a specific entry page of a JSF flow, then the flow scope will automatically start. The flow scope cannot be started when you open the entry page without navigating via a JSF component. That is, JSF will, with help of the ViewHandler, automatically append the predefined HTTP request parameter "jfwid" ("javax.faces Window ID") to the outcome URL whose value represents the JSF client window ID. The JSF client window ID in turn references an isolated mapping in the current HTTP session where the flow-scoped managed beans are stored.

Additionally, particularly when using a UIOutcomeTarget component instead of a UICommand component to navigate, the query string may be accompanied with "jffi" (javax.faces Flow ID) and "jftfdi" (javax.faces To Flow Document ID) request parameters. Those are actually only mandatory for starting a JSF flow using a GET request. Technically, for the rest of the JSF flow, "jfwid" is sufficient. As long as the "jfwid" parameter is present, and is still valid, then the JSF flow is idempotent and can be resumed using a GET request. When you open a new browser tab and navigate into the JSF flow, then actually a new flow scope will be started, independent of the JSF flow in other tab. Once a postback request within the JSF flow navigates to a page outside the JSF flow, then the flow scope will automatically end. When the end user reuses the "jfwid" request parameter later, or manipulates its value to one which isn't started in its own browser session, or enters the flow directly, or when the underlying HttpSession instance is destroyed, then CDI will throw a javax.enterprise.context. ContextNotActiveException.

The major difference between the flow scope and the conversation scope is thus that the pages within a JSF flow cannot be entered directly. They will automatically start when the end user navigates to the entry page of the JSF flow and they will automatically end when a postback navigates outside the JSF flow. Flow-scoped managed beans are useful in order to isolate a conversation to a specific set of JSF pages. A classic real-world example is a booking application which is spread over multiple forms in physically different pages.

There are various ways to define a JSF flow. One way is by convention, another way is by declarative configuration in the /[flowId]/[flowId]-flow.xml file, and yet another way is by programmatic configuration using javax.faces.flow.FlowBuilder API.[7] In this book we'll restrict ourselves to convention over configuration. First, create the following folder structure:

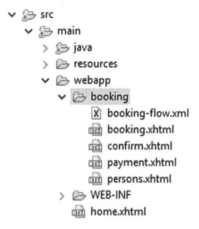

---

[7]https://javaee.github.io/javaee-spec/javadocs/javax/faces/flow/builder/ FlowBuilder.html.

The first convention is that the flow entry page must have exactly the same name as the subfolder it is sitting in. In this case, that's "booking". This is considered the Flow ID. The second convention is that there must be a `*-flow.xml` file in the subfolder whose name is prefixed with the Flow ID, i.e., `booking-flow.xml`. This XML configuration file can be kept empty for now. It's only useful when you want to fine-grain the JSF flow configuration, e.g., by specifying a different entry page. Without this file, the JSF flow scope won't be activated. One disadvantage of at least one activated JSF flow in the web application, however, is that the JSF client Window ID parameter "jfwid" will be appended to every single navigation URL, even when it doesn't target a JSF flow. This URL pollution may for some developers be the main reason to not use the JSF flow scope at all.

The navigation component in order to enter a JSF flow must be placed in a JSF page outside the flow subfolder. The navigation outcome must reference the subfolder name, which is the Flow ID. Here's an example in `/home.xhtml`.

```
<h:button value="Start booking" outcome="booking" />
```

Of course, this can be substituted with `<h:link>`. It's recommended to use GET just for this so that the booking page's URL reflects in the browser's address bar. Then, in all pages within the subfolder, you can reference a flow-scoped managed bean which will be shared across all these pages. You can navigate back and forth between these pages as well while retaining the flow-scoped managed bean instance. We recommend that you use Ajax with redirect for this. The Ajax submits will improve the user experience. The redirects will make sure that the individual pages are still bookmarkable.

`/booking/booking.xhtml`:

```
<h:form>
    <h:inputText value="#{booking.startDate}" />
    ...
    <h:commandButton value="Next" action="persons?faces-redirect=true">
        <f:ajax execute="@form" render="@form" />
    </h:commandButton>
</h:form>
```

`/booking/persons.xhtml`:

```
<h:form>
    <ui:repeat value="#{booking.persons}" var="person">
        <h:inputText value="#{person.name}" />
        ...
```

```
    </ui:repeat>
    ...
    <h:commandButton value="Back" action="booking?faces-redirect=true">
        <f:ajax execute="@form" render="@form" />
    </h:commandButton>
    <h:commandButton value="Next" action="confirm?faces-redirect=true">
        <f:ajax execute="@form" render="@form" />
    </h:commandButton>
</h:form>
```

/booking/confirm.xhtml:

```
<h:form>
    <h:outputText value="#{booking.startDate}" />
    ...
    <h:commandButton value="Back" action="persons?faces-redirect=true">
        <f:ajax execute="@form" render="@form" />
    </h:commandButton>
    <h:commandButton value="Next" action="payment?faces-redirect=true">
        <f:ajax execute="@form" render="@form" />
    </h:commandButton>
</h:form>
```

/booking/payment.xhtml:

```
<h:form>
    <h:selectOneMenu value="#{booking.paymentMethod}">
        ...
    </h:selectOneMenu
    ...
    <h:commandButton value="Back" action="confirm?faces-redirect=true">
        <f:ajax execute="@form" render="@form" />
    </h:commandButton>
    <h:commandButton value="Submit" actionListener="#{booking.submit()}"
        action="/home?faces-redirect=true">
        <f:ajax execute="@form" render="@form" />
    </h:commandButton>
</h:form>
```

And, finally, the flow-scoped bean behind #{booking}:

```
@Named @FlowScoped("booking")
public class Booking implements Serializable {

    private LocalDate startDate;
    private List<Person> persons;
    private PaymentMethod paymentMethod;
    // ...

    public void submit() {
        // ...
    }
}
```

You see, the most of navigation task is done by the action attribute of the command components.?faces-redirect=true is a special request parameter which is internally recognized by JSF as an instruction to perform a redirect after postback and of course strip off from the target URL before performing the actual redirect. Once the postback leaves the flow, the flow-scoped managed bean is destroyed and the previously presented page URLs are not reusable anymore.

## @ViewScoped

A view-scoped managed bean is tied to the lifetime of the JSF view state. The JSF view state is elaborated in the section "View State" in Chapter 3. In a nutshell, a view-scoped managed bean lives as long as the end user is performing postback requests on the very same JSF view and the invoked action methods keep returning null or void. Once the action method returns non-null, even if it's an empty string or represents the same view, then the view scope will end. View-scoped managed beans are not shared across browser tabs within the same browser session. Each one gets its own unique instance. Effectively, they are indirectly identified by the javax.faces.ViewState hidden input field in the generated HTML representation of a JSF form.

However, view-scoped managed beans are not stored in the JSF view state, not even when client-side state saving is enabled. They are actually stored in the HTTP session, regardless of the JSF state saving method. They are not immediately destroyed when the end user unloads the web page either by performing a GET request via a link or bookmark or editing the URL in browser's address bar, or by closing the browser tab. They will stick around in the HTTP session and only get destroyed when the HTTP session expires.

As an end user can in theory spawn an unlimited amount of browser tabs within the same session, and thus also as many JSF view states and view-scoped managed beans, there's a configurable maximum limit on the amount of JSF view states and view-scoped managed beans which will be stored in the HTTP session. Once this limit is reached, the least recently used JSF view state and view-scoped managed bean will be expired and destroyed. When the end user actually goes back to the tab that originally referenced the now expired JSF view state, and performs a postback request on it, JSF will throw a ViewExpiredException. The limit on the amount of JSF view states is dependent on the JSF implementation used. In Mojarra, this limit is configurable by the com.sun.faces. numberOfLogicalViews context parameter in web.xml whose default value is 15.[8]

```
<context-param>
    <param-name>com.sun.faces.numberOfLogicalViews</param-name>
    <param-value>25</param-value>
</context-param>
```

If your web application, however, invites being opened in many more browser tabs, such as a discussion forum or a Q&A site, then you'd better switch to client-side state saving. This way the JSF view states are no longer stored in the HTTP session and will therefore also never expire. However, the associated view-scoped managed beans are still stored in the HTTP session and expirable. When the end user actually goes back to the tab that originally referenced the now expired view scoped-managed bean, and performs a postback request on it, JSF will not throw a ViewExpiredException but instead will create a new one from scratch, thereby losing all the state changes to the original managed bean instance. The limit on the amount of view-scoped managed beans is also dependent on the JSF implementation used. In Mojarra, this limit is not yet configurable by a web.xml context parameter. It's only configurable by explicitly setting the session attribute with the name com.sun.faces.application. view.activeViewMapsSize whose default value is 25. This can be achieved with an application-scoped managed bean as follows, which observes the initialization of the session scope.

---

[8]https://stackoverflow.com/q/4105439/157882.

```
@ApplicationScoped
public class Config {

    public void sessionCreated
        (@Observes @Initialized(SessionScoped.class) HttpSession session)
    {
        session.setAttribute
            ("com.sun.faces.application.view.activeViewMapsSize", 15);
    }
}
```

This configuration actually decreases the default value to be equal to default maximum amount of JSF view states in session. This is fine when you're using server-side state saving and all your JSF views effectively reference only one view-scoped managed bean instance. However, in a decently developed and refactored JSF web application, the average JSF page usually references multiple view-scoped managed beans. If you have, for example, a maximum amount of three different view-scoped managed beans per JSF view, then you'd best set the limit to three times the value of com.sun.faces.numberOfLogicalViews. You only need to take into account the possible memory consumption. It will quickly go overboard when the view-scoped managed beans in turn hold, relatively, a lot of data.

View-scoped managed beans are very useful for retaining state across Ajax-based postbacks on the same JSF view, particularly if those postbacks result in changes in the value of the rendered attribute of any UIComponent, or the disabled or readonly attribute of an UIInput component, or the disabled attribute of any UICommand component within the same JSF view. That is, on a subsequent postback, JSF will, as part of a safeguard against a tampered request, recheck them before actually processing the component. If the managed bean holding the state was request scoped instead of view scoped, then those changes in the conditions would get lost in a subsequent postback and the postback wouldn't get processed as intuitively expected. In other words, view-scoped managed beans are particularly useful in dynamic forms.

One example is a drop-down which conditionally renders a free text field when the "other" option is chosen.

```
<f:metadata>
    <f:importConstants type="com.example.project.model.Title" />
</f:metadata>
```

```
...
<h:form>
    <h:selectOneMenu value="#{bean.customer.title}">
        <f:selectItems value="#{Title}" />
        <f:ajax render="other" />
    </h:selectOneMenu>
    <h:panelGroup id="other">
        <h:inputText rendered="#{bean.customer.title eq 'OTHER'}"
            value="#{bean.customer.titleOther}" required="true" />
    </h:panelGroup>
    ...
    <h:commandButton value="Save" action="#{bean.save}" />
</h:form>
```

This construct won't work when the managed bean is request scoped and is thus recreated on every request. When the drop-down changes, it creates a new instance of the request-scoped bean, sets the title there, and renders the free text field and finally the request-scoped bean instance gets destroyed. When the form submits, it creates a new instance of the request-scoped bean, thus without the customer title, and when JSF checks the rendered attribute during the apply request values phase (second phase) of the free text field and notices it's false, ultimately it won't process the free text field at all. It will only work when the managed bean is view scoped because the customer title set during the drop-down change is still available during the apply request values phase (second phase) of the form submit.

There is, however, a work-around. You could let the rendered attribute check the HTTP request parameter instead of the model value. As explained in Chapter 4, the HTTP request parameter name is specified by the component's client ID. You could bind the drop-down component to the view and then use its client ID to obtain the HTTP request parameter value.

```
<h:selectOneMenu binding="#{title}" value="#{bean.customer.title}">
    <f:selectItems value="#{Title}" />
    <f:ajax render="other" />
</h:selectOneMenu>
<h:panelGroup id="other">
```

```
<h:inputText rendered="#{param[title.clientId] eq 'OTHER'}"
    value="#{bean.customer.titleOther}" required="true" />
</h:panelGroup>
```

This way, when JSF checks the rendered attribute during the apply request values phase (second phase) of the form submit, it will notice it's true and continue processing the free text field, even when the managed bean is request scoped and thus #{bean.customer.title} is still null at that point. Note that the binding attribute doesn't reference a managed bean property. This is unnecessary as it wouldn't be used over there. All of this is also applicable on the readonly attribute of any UIInput component and the disabled attribute of any UIInput and UICommand component.

There may also be cases wherein a request-scoped managed bean will work just fine but imposes a risk of a corrupted state as compared to a view-scoped managed bean, certainly when relying on data coming from a shared database which could be mutated by other users. This affects primarily use cases whereby UIInput or UICommand components are nested in an iterating component such as <h:dataTable>, <ui:repeat> and <c:forEach> which iterates over a model coming from the database. This was explained previously in Chapter 6, but for the sake of refreshment, we will explain it once more. Imagine a table of products with a delete button in a column.

```
<f:form id="list">
    <h:dataTable id="products" value="#{products.list}" var="product">
        ...
        <h:column>
            <h:commandButton id="delete" value="Delete"
                action="#{products.delete(product)}">
                <f:ajax render="@namingcontainer" />
            </h:commandButton>
        </h:column>
    </h:dataTable>
</h:form>
```

With this backing bean:

```
@Named @ViewScoped
public class Products implements Serializable {

    private List<Product> list;
```

```
    @Inject
    private ProductService productService;

    @PostConstruct
    public void init() {
        list = productService.list();
    }

    public void delete(Product product) {
        productService.delete(product);
        list.remove(product);
    }

    public List<Product> getList() {
        return list;
    }
}
```

The submitted button is under the hood identified by the iteration index. When JSF is about to process the form submit, and a product has been added or removed or even reordered in the meanwhile, causing the iteration index to be changed, then the invoked action would possibly be performed against the wrong item currently at the initially known index. This is dangerous for the integrity of the model. In such a case the value of the iteration component must refer a view-scoped model.

Also here, there is a work-around. Instead of relying on the iteration index, you can also rely on the unique identifier of the iterated object which must be passed as an HTTP request parameter instead of as an EL method argument.

```
<f:form id="list">
    <h:dataTable id="products" value="#{products.list}" var="product">
        ...
        <h:column>
            <h:commandButton id="delete" value="Delete"
                action="#{products.delete}">
                <f:param name="id" value="#{product.id}" />
                <f:ajax render="@namingcontainer" />
            </h:commandButton>
```

```
        </h:column>
    </h:dataTable>
</h:form>
```

Whereby the backing bean is adjusted as follows:

```
@Named @RequestScoped
public class Products {

    private List<Product> list;

    @Inject @ManagedProperty("#{param.id}")
    private Long id;

    @Inject
    private ProductService productService;

    @PostConstruct
    public void init() {
        list = productService.list();
    }

    public void delete() {
        productService.delete(id);
        list.removeIf(product -> product.getId().equals(id));
    }

    public List<Product> getList() {
        return list;
    }

}
```

No, the action="#{products.delete(product.id)}" instead of using <f:param>
won't work. The technical reason is that <f:param> is executed immediately during the
render response phase of the form, long before the end user presses the delete button.
Thus, at the moment the end user presses the delete button, it's guaranteed to have the
correct value. The EL method argument, on the contrary, is only evaluated after the end
user has pressed the delete button. When the model has changed in the meanwhile, it
would thus evaluate to the wrong ID when the iteration index of the particular product
has changed.

As explained in the beginning of this section, the standard JSF view-scoped bean management facility has thus two major disadvantages: first, the instances don't immediately expire when the end user unloads the web page and stick around in the HTTP session; second, even with client-side state saving enabled they are stored in the HTTP session. Those problems are currently not yet solved in the standard JSF API.

For now, the JSF utility library OmniFaces offers an enhanced `@ViewScoped` annotation which solves those two disadvantages.[9] View-scoped managed beans annotated with `@org.omnifaces.cdi.ViewScoped` will actually get destroyed when the end user unloads the page. This is under the hood done with help of `Navigator. sendBeacon` API[10] in JavaScript, and a specialized `ViewHandler` implementation provided by OmniFaces which listens on those unload requests. There have been production applications making heavy use of view-scoped managed beans whereby the memory usage has reduced for up to 80% after switching from standard JSF `@ViewScoped` to OmniFaces `@ViewScoped`. This makes the destroy-on-unload feature a major candidate to be added to the future version of the standard JSF API.

In order to save the physical view-scoped managed bean in the JSF view state when client-side state saving is enabled, the `saveInViewState` attribute of the OmniFaces `@ ViewScoped` annotation must be set to `true`. You only need to keep in mind that those beans will never expire, not even when the page gets unloaded, or when the HTTP session expires. In fact, the entire bean has physically become part of the generated HTML output, in the `javax.faces.ViewState` hidden input field. There have been community requests to make JSF state management more flexible, such as toggling between client- and server-side state saving on a per-view (per `UIViewRoot`) or even per-form (per `UIForm`) basis, and being able to store view-scoped managed beans in the actual view state instead of in the HTTP session. This may also be reconsidered in a future version of the standard JSF API.

# @RequestScoped

A request-scoped managed bean is among others tied to the lifetime of the HTTP request, which is for JSF the most important case. Other cases include the lifetimes of a call to an EJB asynchronous method invocation (method annotated by `@Asynchronous`),

---

[9] http://showcase.omnifaces.org/cdi/ViewScoped.

[10] https://developer.mozilla.org/en-US/docs/Web/API/Navigator/sendBeacon.

an EJB timer timeout method, or when a message-driven bean (MDB) processes a message. Note that an Ajax request also counts as a single HTTP request.

When the client sends an HTTP request to the server, the servlet container will create HttpServletRequest and HttpServletResponse instances representing the HTTP request and response, and pass them through the authentication modules, filters, and servlets. They will be destroyed immediately after all authentication modules, filters, and servlets are finished processing the request and response. In other words, every HTTP request creates a new instance of a request-scoped managed bean which is available only during that request and not in other requests.

Request-scoped managed beans are useful for simple and static forms which don't have any dynamic Ajax-based updates, for which you would rather use a view-scoped managed bean. Think of a login form or a contact form.

```java
@Named @RequestScoped
public class Login {

    private String username;
    private String password;

    // ...
}
```

Sure, those forms can be tied to a view-scoped managed bean as well without problems, but that's a waste of memory space. Note that you should absolutely not make the JPA entity itself a managed bean. In other words, the following approach is factually wrong:

```java
@Named @RequestScoped
@Entity
public class Product {
    // ...
}
```

Not only does this violate the Law of Demeter,[11] but it also risks that JPA won't be able to persist it, because CDI actually wraps the managed bean in a proxy class and JPA would then not be able to obtain the entity information from it when you're about to

---

[11]https://en.wikipedia.org/wiki/Law_of_Demeter.

pass an injected instance to JPA. Hibernate would in such case throw "Unknown entity: com.example.Entity$Proxy$_$$_WeldClientProxy", which thus actually represents the CDI proxy class.

You might at this point wonder how exactly CDI actually works. First, it will during the web application's startup collect all classes that are annotated with a CDI-compatible scope annotation. Then, it will generate proxy classes for all of them. Ultimately instances of those proxy classes are being injected. Given an example bean class com.example.Bean, the generated CDI proxy class may look as follows:

```
public class Bean$Proxy$_$$_CDI extends Bean implements Serializable {

    public String getSomeProperty() {
        Bean actualInstance = CDI.resolveItSomehow();
        return actualInstance.getSomeProperty();
    }

    public void setSomeProperty(String someProperty) {
        Bean actualInstance = CDI.resolveItSomehow();
        actualInstance.setSomeProperty(someProperty);
    }
}
```

You see, it extends the bean class, makes it serializable, and uses an "impossible to clash" class name and lets all methods delegate to the actual instance obtained from the CDI context. You'll probably also immediately understand why the CDI bean management facility requires the bean classes to be public and have a public default constructor. You'll also see that when such a proxy class is created and injected, the underlying actual instance is not necessarily created. It's only automatically created when the fictive CDI.resolveItSomehow() method is invoked. Under the hood, it will obtain the context from a thread local variable, exactly how FacesContext#getCurrentInstance() works.

By the way, EJB also works with serializable proxies this way. That's why it could seemingly magically perform all the heavy lifting of starting or joining a transaction and use pooled instances. The legacy JSF @ManagedBean facility, however, did not use proxies at all. That's exactly why it was impossible to inject a JSF managed bean of a narrower scope in a JSF managed bean of a broader scope. With CDI bean management facility this is just possible.

Note that CDI has also a `@javax.enterprise.inject.Model` stereotype annotation which basically bundles both `@Named` and `@RequestScoped` into a single annotation. This is in no way different from a request-scoped managed bean. Unfortunately, it does not represent a non-proxy instance; otherwise it would be nice to put it on an `@Entity`. The `@Model` annotation exists just for convenience.

# @Dependent

A dependent-scoped managed bean is tied to the lifetime of the scope wherein it's being created for the first time. So, if you inject it into an `@ApplicationScoped`, then it will become application scoped too. And if you inject it into a `@ViewScoped`, it will become view scoped too. And so on. This is the default CDI scope.

This has, however, a caveat. When you forget to declare the CDI scope annotation on your backing bean, or import a scope with exactly the same name from the wrong package, e.g., `javax.faces.bean.RequestScoped` instead of `javax.enterprise.context.RequestScoped`, and you reference it directly in EL, as in `#{dependentScopedBean}`, instead of referencing it via another managed bean, as in `#{requestScopedBean.dependentScopedBean}`, then every EL evaluation will basically create a brand-new instance which exists only within that EL context. In other words, imagine a JSF form with two input fields and a submit button, each bound to a dependent-scoped managed bean, then you will effectively end up with three separate instances. One wherein the first input field is set, one wherein the second input field is set, and one wherein the action method is invoked. So, if you ever observe odd behavior of `null` submitted values in the action method even though the required validation has passed, the first thing to check is the actually used CDI managed bean scope.

The major technical difference with other scopes is that dependent-scoped managed beans are not proxied. In other words, what's being injected is the actual instance.

```
@Dependent
public class Entities {

    @Produces
    public Product getProduct() {
        return new Product();
    }
}
```

303

```
@Named @RequestScoped
public class Products {

    @Inject
    private Product product;

    @Inject
    Private ProductService productService;

    public void add() {
        productService.create(product);
    }

    public Product getProduct() {
        return product;
    }
}
```

Note that you still can't use `<h:inputText value="#{product.name}">`, because it would get its own instance. You still need to use #{products.product.name}. For exactly this reason, the producer isn't @Named. Also note that in case of a view-scoped managed bean, you'd need to force JSF to restart the view scope by returning a non-null outcome from action method; otherwise the injected `Product` instance would be reused for the next view.

# Which scope to choose?

Which scope to choose depends solely on the data (instance variables aka the state) the bean holds and represents. You should strive to put the state in the shortest possible acceptable scope. Start with a @RequestScoped bean. Once you notice that some state needs to be retained after a postback on the same view, split that state exactly into a new @ViewScoped bean which you, in turn, @Inject in the @RequestScoped bean. Once you notice that some state needs to be retained on another GET request within the same session, split that state exactly into a new @ConversationScoped bean which you in turn @Inject in the @RequestScoped bean. And so on.

Abusing an `@ApplicationScoped` bean for session-, conversation-, flow-, view-, or request-scoped data would make it to be shared among all users, so anyone else can see each other's data, which is just plain wrong. Abusing a `@SessionScoped` bean for conversation-, flow-, view-, or request-scoped data would make it to be shared among all browser tabs in the same session, so the end user may experience inconsistencies when interacting with every view after switching between tabs, which is bad for user experience. Abusing a `@RequestScoped` bean for view-, flow-, or conversation-scoped data would make view-, flow-, or conversation-scoped data be reinitialized to default on every single (Ajax) postback, causing possibly non-working forms. Abusing a `@ViewScoped`, `@FlowScoped`, or `@ConversationScoped` bean for request-, session-, or application-scoped data, and abusing a `@SessionScoped` bean for application-scoped data doesn't affect the end user, but it unnecessarily occupies server memory and is plain inefficient.

Note that the scope should rather not be chosen based on performance implications, unless you really have a low memory footprint and want to go completely stateless. You'd then need to exclusively use stateless forms with `@RequestScoped` beans and fiddle with request parameters to maintain any client's state. In other words, you would possibly need to reinvent whatever already is being done by the `javax.faces.ViewState` hidden input field.

# Where Is @FlashScoped?

At last, JSF also supports the flash scope. It is backed by a short living cookie which is associated with a data entry in the session scope. Before the redirect, a cookie will be set on the HTTP response with a value which is uniquely associated with the data entry in the session scope. After the redirect, the presence of the flash scope cookie will be checked and the data entry associated with the cookie will be removed from the session scope and be put in the request scope of the redirected request. Finally the cookie will be removed from the HTTP response. This way the redirected request has access to request-scoped data which was been prepared in the initial request.

This is actually not available as a managed bean scope by standard JSF API. In other words, there is no such thing as `@FlashScoped`. The flash scope is only available as a map via `ExternalContext#getFlash()` in managed beans and `#{flash}` in EL. Historically, the flash scope was primarily introduced in order to be able to show a faces message set in the action method in the redirected page. Imagine the use case of saving an edited product in a detail page and redirecting back to the master page.

```
public String save() {
    FacesContext context = FacesContext.getCurrentInstance();

    try {
        productService.update(product);
        context.addMessage(null, new FacesMessage("Product saved!"));
        return "/products?faces-redrect=true";
    }
    catch (Exception e) {
        context.addMessage(null, new FacesMessage(
            "Cannot save product. Error: " + e.getMessage()));
        return null;
    }
}
```

The faces message "Product saved!" wouldn't show up in the <h:messages globalOnly> of the redirected page because faces messages are inherently request scoped (actually, "faces context scoped"). Historically, during the JSF 1.x era, this problem was solved with a phase listener which copies after the render response phase all undisplayed faces messages into the HTTP session and re-adds after the restore view phase any of them back into the faces context. Since the introduction of the flash scope in JSF 2.0, this problem could be solved in an easier way by simply invoking Flash#setKeepMessages()[12].

```
productService.update(product);
context.addMessage(null, new FacesMessage("Product saved!"));
context.getExternalContext().getFlash().setKeepMessages(true);
return "/products?faces-redrect=true";
```

This way, the faces messages are before redirect automatically stored in the flash scope and restored after redirect.

The flash scope is not only useful for faces messages. It's also useful for passing entire objects while redirecting from one view to another view, without needing to pass some object identifier as a request parameter. Following is an example which prepares an entity for the next step without needing to save it in the database first:

---

[12]https://javaee.github.io/javaee-spec/javadocs/javax/faces/context/Flash.
html#setKeepMessages-boolean-.

```
@Named @RequestScoped // or @ViewScoped
public class Home {

    private Product product = new Product();

    public String prepareProduct() {
        FacesContext context = FacesContext.getCurrentInstance();
        context.getExternalContext().getFlash().put("product", product);
        return "/next?faces-redirect=true";
    }

    public Product getProduct() {
        return product;
    }
}
```

Whereby the bean of the next step looks as follows:

```
@Named @ViewScoped
public class Next implements Serializable {

    @Inject @ManagedProperty("#{flash.product}")
    private Product product;

    public void save() {
        // ...
    }

    public Product getProduct() {
        return product;
    }
}
```

And the /next.xhtml redirects back to /home.xhtml when the entity is absent in the flash scope.

```
<f:metadata>
    <f:viewAction action="/home" if="#{empty flash.product}" />
</f:metadata>
```

Note that this redirect will take place when you open /next.xhtml directly, or when you refresh the page in the web browser. In case you'd like to avoid that, you can instruct the flash scope to keep the entry value in the flash scope by prefixing the entry key with the predefined "keep" key on the #{flash} map.

```
@Named @RequestScoped
public class Next {

    @Inject @ManagedProperty("#{flash.keep.product}")
    private Product product;

    // ...
}
```

This way, the lifetime of the flash scope will expand until the end user closes the browser window, or when the application navigates to a different view, or when the underlying HTTP session expires. This way you can even make the managed bean request scoped instead of view scoped and not lose the entity while submitting a form in the /next.xhtml page or even refreshing the page. This is a relatively powerful feature of the flash scope.

# Managed bean initialization and destruction

Managed bean instances can be initialized based on injected dependencies in a @PostConstruct annotated method. Managed bean instances can hook on destroy event in a @PreDestroy annotated method.

```
@Named
public class Bean {

    @PostConstruct
    public void init() {
        // ...
    }

    @PreDestroy
    public void destroy() {
        // ...
    }
}
```

The method names are not predefined. The method names `init()` and `destroy()` are basically taken over from the `HttpServlet`. You can of course choose your own, such as `onload()` and `cleanup()`. It's useful to know that those annotations are inheritable. In other words, you could put those methods and annotations in an abstract base class.

In the postconstruct method you have the opportunity to perform initialization based on injected dependencies. They are not available in the constructor yet. The bean management facility can only inject the dependencies after having constructed the managed bean instance. It will then immediately invoke the `@PostConstruct` annotated method. In the pre-destroy method you have the opportunity to perform any necessary cleanup, such as closing resources, deleting files, etc.

# Injecting JSF vended types

Backing beans can obviously be injected as demonstrated many times over in the examples above. Next to injecting your own types, a variety of JSF vended types can be injected via CDI as well. These types largely correspond to the implicit EL objects we saw in Table 7-1 in Chapter 7. This is no coincidence. Internally implicit objects in JSF are implemented by so-called `Bean<T>` instances from CDI. These CDI `Bean<T>` instances are effectively the factory objects that know how to generate beans, with what type and optional qualifier and/or with what name.

When the name of an implicit object is used in expression language, the CDI EL resolver does a lookup for that object by name, which results in a call to a certain `Bean<T>` instance. When we're injecting, the type into which we inject, together with any explicit or implicit qualifiers, forms an alternative key that's being used for this lookup. Both types of keys will result in the exact same CDI `Bean<T>` instance being used.

It should be noted that compared to the implicit EL objects mentioned in Table 8-1 a few are missing for CDI-injectable JSF vended types, namely:

- `#{component}`
- `#{cc}`
- `#{request}`
- `#{session}`
- `#{application}`

Both #{component} and #{cc} resolve to UIComponent which is not injectable, since this would require a special proxy or custom scope that's narrow enough to resolve the "current" instance of those at the time the injected type is accessed. Since such scope is not available in JSF yet, and there was only a little time and few resources remaining to finish the JSF 2.3 spec, these had been excluded from CDI injection.

The #{request}, #{session}, and #{application}, respectively, representing HttpServletRequest, HttpSession, and ServletContext in a Servlet container have been omitted since these types are not owned by JSF and therefore JSF should not provide CDI injection capabilities for those. The fact that JSF does provide implicit EL objects for those is mostly historical. The only specification that should provide injection for those types is the Servlet API, which owns those types directly.

Table 8-1 shows the JSF vended types that are injectable via CDI.

***Table 8-1.***  *Injectable JSF Vended types, All Since 2.3*

| Injectable JSF type | Resolves to |
| --- | --- |
| javax.faces.context.FacesContext | FacesContext#getCurrentInstance() |
| javax.faces.context.ExternalContext | FacesContext#getExternalContext() |
| javax.faces.component.UIViewRoot | FacesContext#getViewRoot() |
| javax.faces.context.Flash | ExternalContext#getFlash() |
| @RequestMap Map<String, Object> | ExternalContext#getRequestMap() |
| @ViewMap Map<String, Object> | UIViewRoot#getViewMap() |
| @FlowMap Map<Object, Object> | FlowHandler#getCurrentFlowScope() |
| @SessionMap Map<String, Object> | ExternalContext#getSessionMap() |
| @ApplicationMap Map<String, Object> | ExternalContext#getApplicationMap() |
| @InitParameterMap Map<String, String> | ExternalContext#getInitParameterMap() |
| @RequestParameterMap Map<String, String> | ExternalContext#getRequestParameterMap() |
| @RequestParameterValuesMap Map<String, String[]> | ExternalContext#getRequestParameterValuesMap() |
| @HeaderMap Map<String, String> | ExternalContext#getRequestHeaderMap() |
| @HeaderValuesMap Map<String, String[]> | ExternalContext#getRequestHeaderValuesMap() |
| @RequestCookieMap Map<String, Cookie> | ExternalContext#getRequestCookieMap() |
| javax.faces.application.ResourceHandler | Application#getResourceHandler() |

As can be seen from Table 8-1, for objects for which there is only one instance and that instance is vended (owned) by JSF, no qualifier is needed. When it concerns more general types, such as the various maps, a qualifier is needed. All these qualifier annotations are available from the `javax.faces.annotation` package.[13]

A caveat is that all of the above types are request scoped, but the time during which they are valid is actually smaller, namely, from shortly after the moment the `service()` method of the `FacesServlet` is called until shortly before the moment that method is exited. Care should be taken not to inject and access these types outside that time. It's expected that a future revision of the JSF spec will address this problem.

The following shows an example of injecting two of the JSF vended types:

```
@Named @RequestScoped
public class Bean {

    @Inject
    private Flash flash;

    @Inject @RequestParameterMap
    private Map<String, String> requestParameterMap;

    public void someMethod() {
        if (requestParameterMap.containsKey("something")) {
            flash.put("aKey", "aValue");
        }
    }
}
```

# Eager Initialization

Managed beans are by default lazily initialized whenever they are, for the first time, referenced in an EL expression or as an injected dependency. Managed beans can be eagerly initialized on the start of any scope by an observer method which observes the initialization of the scope of interest. One example was previously given in the "@ViewScoped" section. The method pattern is as follows:

---

[13]https://javaee.github.io/javaee-spec/javadocs/javax/faces/annotation/package-summary.html.

```
public void startup(@Observes @Initialized(XxxScoped.class) S scope) {
    // ...
}
```

Where XxxScoped.class can be any CDI-compatible scope and the S represents the owner of the scope. For the following scopes that are thus:

- ApplicationScoped.class – javax.servlet.ServletContext

- SessionScoped.class – javax.servlet.http.HttpSession

- ConversationScoped.class – javax.servlet.ServletRequest

- FlowScoped.class – javax.faces.flow.Flow

- ViewScoped.class – javax.faces.component.UIViewRoot

- RequestScoped.class - javax.servlet.ServletRequest

Note that the containing bean must be of at least the same scope in order to have @Observes @Initialized take effect. Eager initialization has for an application-scoped managed bean the advantage that you can configure it as a "startup" bean without needing to reference it in some other bean in order to get it initialized.

```
@ApplicationScoped
public class Startup {

    public void contextInitialized
        (@Observes @Initialized(ApplicationScoped.class)
            ServletContext context)
    {
        // ...
    }
}
```

Eager initialization has for a request-scoped bean the advantage that you can if necessary invoke an asynchronous DB query long before the FacesServlet is invoked.

```
@Named @RequestScoped
public class EagerProducts {

    private Future<List<Product>> list;
```

```
    @Inject
    private ProductService productService;

    public void requestInitialized
        (@Observes @Initialized(RequestScoped.class)
            HttpServletRequest request)
    {
        if ("/products.xhtml".equals(request.getServletPath())) {
            list = productService.asyncList();
        }
    }

    public List<Product> getList() {
        try {
            return list.get();
        }
        catch (InterruptedException e) {
            Thread.currentThread().interrupt();
            throw new FacesException(e);
        }
        catch (ExecutionException e) {
            throw new FacesException(e);
        }
    }
}
```

Where the ProductService looks like this:

```
@Stateless
public class ProductService {

    @TransactionAttribute(SUPPORTS)
    public List<Product> list() {
        return entityManager
            .createQuery("FROM Product ORDER BY id DESC", Product.class)
            .getResultList();
    }
```

```
@Asynchronous
public Future<List<Product>> asyncList() {
    return new AsyncResult<>(list());
}
```
}

Note particularly the requestInitialized() method which observes the start of any request scope and thus needs to determine the actual path beforehand so that it doesn't unnecessarily hit the business service. In this specific example, that will only happen once the request hits /products.xhtml. That JSF page can in turn just reference the product list as usual.

```
<h:dataTable value="#{eagerProducts.list}" var="product">
    ...
</h:dataTable>
```

When opening this JSF page, the request scoped bean will be initialized before the FacesServlet is invoked and asynchronously fetch the List<Products> from the database. Depending on the server hardware used, the available server resources and all code running between the invocation of the first servlet filter and entering the JSF render response, this approach may give you a time space of 10ms ~ 500ms (or perhaps even more when there's some inefficient code in the pipeline) to fetch data from DB in a different thread parallel with the HTTP request, and thus a speed improvement equivalent to the time the DB needs to fetch the data (which thus doesn't need to be done in the same thread as the HTTP request).

# Layers

While implementing backing beans, it's very important to understand the importance of the separation of the JSF backing bean from the JPA entity and the EJB service. In other words, when developing backing beans, you should make sure that your backing beans are as slick as possible and that they delegate as much as possible model properties to JPA entities and business logic to EJB services. You should realize that JPA entities and EJB services should be fully reusable on a completely different front end than JSF, such as JAX-RS or even plain JSP/Servlet.

This thus also means that you should make sure that you don't directly or indirectly include a JSF-specific dependency in a JPA entity or an EJB service. For example, the following approach is factually wrong:

```
@Entity
public class Product {

    private String name;
    private String description;

    public static Product of(ProductBacking backingBean) {
        Product product = new Product();
        product.setName(backingBean.getName());
        product.setDescription(backingBean.getDescription());
        return product;
    }

    // ...
}
```

Here, the JPA entity is tightly coupled to a JSF backing bean. Not only are the entity properties reused in the backing bean, but also the entity has a dependency on the backing bean. It wouldn't be possible to extract the entity into a JAR module which is reusable across different JSF web applications.

And the following approach is also factually wrong:

```
@Stateless
public class ProductService {

    @Inject
    private EntityManager entityManager;

    public void create(Product product) {
        entityManager.persist(product);
        FacesContext.getCurrentInstance().addMessage(null,
            new FacesMessage("Product created!"));
    }
}
```

Here, the EJB pokes the faces context and sets a message there. This would fail with a `NullPointerException` when the EJB method is being invoked from, e.g., a JAX-RS service or a Servlet, because there's no instance of the faces context anywhere over there. This UI messaging task is not the responsibility of the back-end code but of the front-end code. In other words, adding a faces message should only happen in the JSF artifact, such as a backing bean.

The correct approach is as follows, as demonstrated previously in the section "Model, View, or Controller?":

```java
@Named @RequestScoped
public class ProductBacking {

    private Product product = new Product();

    @Inject
    private ProductService productService;

    public void save() {
        productService.create(product);
        FacesContext.getCurrentInstance().addMessage(null,
            new FacesMessage("Product created!"));
    }

    public Product getProduct() {
        return product;
    }
}
```

# Naming Conventions

There is no strict convention specified by JSF itself. I've seen the following conventions across various JSF projects:

- Foo

- FooBean

- FooBacking

- FooBackingBean

- FooManager

- FooManagedBean

- FooController

whereby Foo can in turn represent one of the following:

- JSF view ID,
  e.g., EditProduct for /edit/product.xhtml

- JSF view name,
  e.g., Products for /view/products.xhtml

- JPA entity name,
  e.g., Product for @Entity class Product

- JSF form ID,
  e.g., EditProduct for <h:form id="editProduct">

First and foremost, names ending with Bean like FooBean, FooBackingBean, and FooManagedBean must be avoided to all extent. The "bean" suffix is superfluous and too ambiguous as practically any class in Java can be marked as a JavaBean. You don't immediately use "ProductBean" for your JPA entity or "ProductServiceBean" or even "ProductServiceEnterpriseBean" for your EJB service, right? True, #{bean} or #{myBean} or even #{yourBean} to indicate a JSF or CDI managed bean is very often used across generic code examples in blogs, forums, Q&A sites, and even this book. But this is merely done for clarity and simplicity of the code snippets.

That leaves us with Foo, FooBacking, FooManager, and FooController. All are equally acceptable. Personally, I tend to use FooBacking for request-, view-, flow-, and conversation-scoped beans, and FooManager for session- and application-scoped beans. As to the naming convention of Foo part, that generally depends on whether the backing bean is tightly tied to a particular JSF view or a JSF form, or generally reusable across multiple JSF views or forms referring a particular entity.

In any case, this is a pretty subjective item which can hardly be answered objectively with "the One and Correct" answer. It really doesn't matter that much to me or anyone else what you make of it, as long as you're consistent with it throughout the entire project.

# CHAPTER 9

# Exception Handling

Sometimes things can unexpectedly go wrong. In Java, that usually manifests as an Exception being thrown. In Java EE, it's basically no different. The issue is how and when to properly handle them. By default, any uncaught exception during an HTTP request will end up in a default error page provided by the application server. Figure 9-1 shows what WildFly's default HTTP 500 error page looks like:

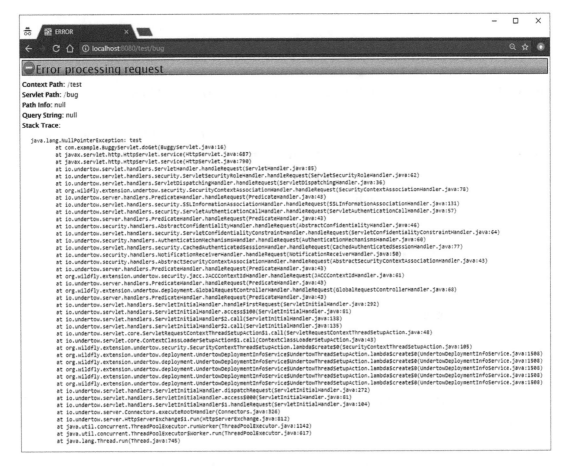

***Figure 9-1.*** *The default HTTP 500 error page of WildFly 11.0.0*

© Bauke Scholtz, Arjan Tijms 2018
B. Scholtz and A. Tijms, *The Definitive Guide to JSF in Java EE 8*, https://doi.org/10.1007/978-1-4842-3387-0_9

The JSF (JavaServer Faces) implementation being used may even provide its own default error page. Both Mojarra and MyFaces provide an internal default implementation based on the `javax.faces.context.ExceptionHandler` API,[1] which is only shown when the JSF project stage is set to `Development`. Figure 9-2 shows how that page looks for Mojarra.

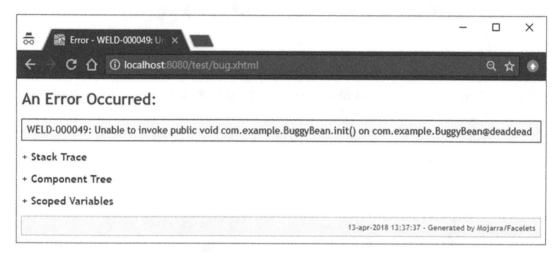

***Figure 9-2.*** *The default HTTP 500 error page of Mojarra 2.3.3 in development stage*

It not only includes the stack trace but also the textual representation of the JSF component tree and any scoped variables, which might be helpful in nailing down the root cause, although, in reality, the stack trace alone and re-executing the use case with a debugger is much more helpful than that.

# Custom Error Pages

While useful to the average web developer, those default error pages are, quite frankly, scary to the average end user. The "look 'n' feel" is completely off from the rest of the site and the text is like abracadabra to the average end user. Such an error page doesn't even provide escape points for the end user. The disgruntled end user cannot quickly find its way to the home or contact page. Fortunately for the end user, you can override those default error pages by including an error page in the web application and registering its location in an `<error-page>` entry in `web.xml`.

---

[1]`https://javaee.github.io/javaee-spec/javadocs/javax/faces/context/`
`ExceptionHandler.html`.

```
<error-page>
    <error-code>500</error-code>
    <location>/WEB-INF/errorpages/500.xhtml</location>
</error-page>
```

The custom error page is purposefully being placed in a /WEB-INF folder so that end users can't access or bookmark them directly. By default, the servlet container will set error page related attributes in the request scope whose keys are defined as javax. servlet.RequestDispatcher.ERROR_XXX constants.[2] This way you can, if necessary, include them in the custom error page. Following is an example:

```
<dl>
    <dt>Request URI</dt>
    <dd>#{requestScope['javax.servlet.error.request_uri']}</dd>
    <dt>Exception type</dt>
    <dd>#{requestScope['javax.servlet.error.exception']['class']}</dd>
    <dt>Exception message</dt>
    <dd>#{requestScope['javax.servlet.error.exception'].message}</dd>
    <dt>Stack trace</dt>
    <dd><pre>#{
        facesContext.externalContext.response.writer.flush()
    }#{
        requestScope['javax.servlet.error.exception'].printStackTrace
            (facesContext.externalContext.response.writer)
    }</pre></dd>
</dl>
```

Note the trick to print the stack trace. It's important that the response writer is flushed before printing the stack trace, and that there's no whitespace in template text outside the EL (Expression Language) expressions within the <pre> element, otherwise it would be appended to the stack trace.

---

[2]https://javaee.github.io/javaee-spec/javadocs/javax/servlet/RequestDispatcher.
html#ERROR_EXCEPTION.

Coming back to the scariness of such an error page, you'd better hide away all the error detail behind a condition that evaluates only true when the JSF project stage equals Development. First set an application-scoped shortcut variable in some master template:

```
<c:set var="DEV" scope="application"
    value="#{facesContext.application.projectStage eq 'Development'}">
</c:set>
```

Now you can conditionally display technical information in the error page when the JSF project stage equals Development.

```
<c:if test="#{DEV}">
    <h3>Error detail for developer</h3>
    <dl>
        ...
    </dl>
</c:if>
```

In any case, it's very important that the error page is entirely stateless. In other words, a decent error page may not contain any JSF forms, not even a logout form. Not only will you avoid the risk that the form submit fails because the initial exception was actually caused by a corrupted JSF state, but those forms will actually submit to the wrong URL (uniform resource locator), namely, the one of the error page itself. As the error page is hidden in the /WEB-INF folder, the form submit would only result in a 404 error. Instead of moving the error page outside the /WEB-INF folder, you could work around the logout case by using a plain HTML form which submits to a plain Servlet. The SecurityContext is also just injectable over there, as are session-scoped managed beans, if any.

# Ajax Exception Handling

By default, when an exception occurs during a JSF Ajax request, the end user would not get any form of feedback whether or not the action was successfully performed. In Mojarra, only when the JSF project stage is set to Development, the end user would see a bare JavaScript alert with only the exception type and message (see Figure 9-3).

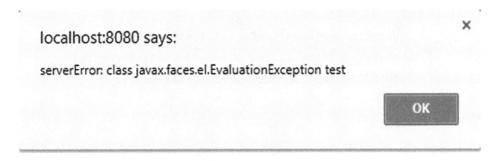

***Figure 9-3.*** *The JavaScript alert when an exception is thrown during an Ajax request in Mojarra 2.3.3 in Development stage*

This isn't terribly useful. And in the Production stage the end user wouldn't even get any feedback. The web application would fail silently, leaving the end user behind as if nothing had happened, which is just confusing and bad for user experience. It would make more sense if exceptions during JSF Ajax requests are handled the same way as exceptions during synchronous requests, which reuse exactly the same error page as the one declared as <error-page> in web.xml. In other words, the end user should be able to see the error page in full glory. This can be achieved by creating a custom ExceptionHandler implementation which basically instructs JSF to create a new UIViewRoot based on the error page and then build and render it. It's only quite a bit of code. At its simplest it can look as follows:

```
public class AjaxExceptionHandler extends ExceptionHandlerWrapper {

    public AjaxExceptionHandler(ExceptionHandler wrapped) {
        super(wrapped);
    }

    @Override
    public void handle() {
        handleAjaxException(FacesContext.getCurrentInstance());
        getWrapped().handle();
    }

    protected void handleAjaxException(FacesContext context) {
        Iterator<ExceptionQueuedEvent> unhandledExceptionQueuedEvents =
            getUnhandledExceptionQueuedEvents().iterator();
```

```
if (context == null
    || context.getExternalContext().isResponseCommitted()
    || !context.getPartialViewContext().isAjaxRequest()
    || !unhandledExceptionQueuedEvents.hasNext()
) {
    return;
}

Throwable exception = unhandledExceptionQueuedEvents
    .next().getContext().getException();

while (exception.getCause() != null
    && (exception instanceof FacesException
        || exception instanceof ELException)
) {
    exception = exception.getCause();
}

ExternalContext external = context.getExternalContext();
String uri = external.getRequestContextPath()
    + external.getRequestServletPath();
Map<String, Object> requestScope = external.getRequestMap();
requestScope.put(RequestDispatcher.ERROR_REQUEST_URI, uri);
requestScope.put(RequestDispatcher.ERROR_EXCEPTION, exception);

String viewId = "/WEB-INF/errorpages/500.xhtml";
Application application = context.getApplication();
ViewHandler viewHandler = application.getViewHandler();
UIViewRoot viewRoot = viewHandler.createView(context, viewId);
context.setViewRoot(viewRoot);

try {
    external.responseReset();
    ViewDeclarationLanguage viewDeclarationLanguage =
        viewHandler.getViewDeclarationLanguage(context, viewId);
    viewDeclarationLanguage.buildView(context, viewRoot);
    context.getPartialViewContext().setRenderAll(true);
    viewDeclarationLanguage.renderView(context, viewRoot);
```

```
            context.responseComplete();
        }
        catch (IOException e) {
            throw new FacesException(e);
        }
        finally {
            requestScope.remove(RequestDispatcher.ERROR_EXCEPTION);
        }

        unhandledExceptionQueuedEvents.remove();

        while (unhandledExceptionQueuedEvents.hasNext()) {
            unhandledExceptionQueuedEvents.next();
            unhandledExceptionQueuedEvents.remove();
        }
    }

    public static class Factory extends ExceptionHandlerFactory {

        public Factory(ExceptionHandlerFactory wrapped) {
            super(wrapped);
        }

        @Override
        public ExceptionHandler getExceptionHandler() {
            return new AjaxExceptionHandler
                (getWrapped().getExceptionHandler());
        }
    }
}
```

The handleAjaxException() will first check if there is a faces context, if the response isn't yet committed, if the request is an Ajax request, and if there's any unhandled exception event in the queue. If none of those conditions matches, it will return and let JSF continue as usual.

The HTTP response is considered committed when the response or a part thereof has physically already been sent to the client. This is a point of no return. You can't take the already sent bytes back. This may happen when the exception occurs halfway during the render response phase. The first half of the HTTP response may already have been sent to the client. Also the default exception handler of JSF and the server can't deal with it. Effectively, the client gets a half-baked HTML page. Best what you could do to avoid this is to make sure that you aren't performing business logic in getter methods of backing beans, which on its own is always a bad idea, and that backing beans are initialized as soon as possible. That could be achieved by executing exception-sensitive business logic in <f:viewAction> instead of @PostConstruct. Another option is to increase the HTTP response buffer size to match the size of the generated HTML response of the largest exception-sensitive page. Assuming that it's 100 kB, the following web.xml context parameter can be used.

```
<context-param>
    <param-name>javax.faces.FACELETS_BUFFER_SIZE</param-name>
    <param-value>102400</param-value> <!-- 100 kB. -->
</context-param>
```

The next step in handleAjaxException() is extracting the root cause of interest from the unhandled exception events queue. Any exception that occurs during the processing of the JSF life cycle will be wrapped in javax.faces.FacesException. Any exception that occurs during the evaluation of an EL expression will be wrapped in javax.el.ELException. Those are not our interest.

Next, the #{requestScope['javax.servlet.error.request_uri']} and #{requestScope['javax.servlet.error.exception']} variables will be set so that the error page can access them. Also the UIViewRoot instance representing the error page will be created with help of the ViewHandler and set in the JSF context. You could, if necessary, conditionally prepare the view ID of the error page based on the actual root cause of the exception. For example:

```
String viewId;

if (exception instanceof ViewExpiredException) {
    viewId = "/WEB-INF/errorpages/expired.xhtml";
}
else {
    viewId = "/WEB-INF/errorpages/500.xhtml";
}
```

Coming back to the handleAjaxException(), in the try block, the HTTP response buffer will be cleared, the UIViewRoot will be populated with components, the Ajax context will be instructed to render the entire view, the UIViewRoot will be rendered, the JSF context will be instructed that the response is already manually taken care of so that it won't perform any navigation, and finally the exception will be removed from the request scope. The removal of the exception in the finally block is not mandatory, but servlet containers exist which consider this a trigger to write an internal error page to the response, such as Tomcat.

Finally, the queue of unhandled exception events will be drained. This is also not mandatory but done on purpose so that it matches the default behavior of web.xml-configured error pages, and also to prevent any next ExceptionHandler in the chain from handling any remaining exception events.

In order to get it to run, you actually need to create a factory as well. As many other application-wide customizations in JSF, custom exception handlers can only be registered through a factory. It might look verbose, but that's just part of the design. In this specific case, it allows you to return a different exception handler implementation depending on some global configuration setting. You can find the Factory as a nested class in the bottom of the previously shown AjaxExceptionHandler class. It extends from javax.faces.context.ExceptionHandlerFactory[3] and can be registered in faces-config.xml as follows:

```
<factory>
    <exception-handler-factory>
        com.example.project.exceptionhandler.AjaxExceptionHandler$Factory
    </exception-handler-factory>
</factory>
```

By the way, it must be said that such an exception handler is also suitable on non-Ajax requests. You just have to remove the PartialViewContext#isAjaxRequest() check. You only need to keep in mind to manually set the HTTP response status code to 500 depending on whether or not it's an Ajax request. Do this after the ExternalContext#responseReset() line.

---

[3]https://javaee.github.io/javaee-spec/javadocs/javax/faces/context/ExceptionHandlerFactory.html.

```
if (!context.getPartialViewContext().isAjaxRequest()) {
    external.setResponseStatus
        (HttpServletResponse.SC_INTERNAL_SERVER_ERROR);
}
```

When you do so on an Ajax request, the JSF Ajax script won't process the Ajax response as you'd expect. Instead of displaying the error page, it will trigger the `onerror` handler.

# ViewExpiredException Handling

If you've worked with JSF before, then the chance is great that you've seen or heard about a `ViewExpiredException`. To the point, it will be thrown when the JSF view state associated with the postback cannot be found in the HTTP session any more—in other words, when the `javax.faces.STATE_SAVING_METHOD` context parameter is set to its default value of "`server`", and the end user submits a JSF form whose view state cannot be found any more on the server side. Note that when the context parameter is set to "`client`", you still need a "`jsf/ClientSideSecretKey`" environment entry in order to avoid expired views when the server restarts. This all is elaborated in the section "View State" in Chapter 3. Also, in the section "@ViewScoped" in Chapter 8, you can find how to configure the amount of views and managed beans JSF will save in the HTTP session.

There are several circumstances where a `ViewExpiredException` may unexpectedly occur. All of them are related to page navigation and the browser cache while the end user has recently logged out from the web application. Normally, the HTTP session is, during logout, invalidated as a security measure, and the end user is redirected to some landing page. When the previously visited web page is cacheable, and the end user presses the browser's back button after logout, then the end user may successfully get to see the previously visited web page from the browser cache. If it contains any JSF form, then its `javax.faces.ViewState` hidden input field will actually refer a view state which does not exist in the current session any more. When the end user submits such JSF form, then JSF will inevitably throw a `ViewExpiredException`.

Although this is an excellent security measure, the end user may get confused as the previously visited web page actually got successfully loaded in end user's experience. This is not good for user experience. You'd therefore best make sure that stateful JSF pages are not cacheable, so that the web browser is forced to actually hit the web server when the end user presses the back button and thus load a fresh new page with a view state which is actually valid in the current HTTP session. This can be achieved with a servlet filter which sets specific response headers which instruct the client not to cache the HTTP response. Following is an example of such a servlet filter:

```
@WebFilter(servletNames="facesServlet")
public class NoCacheFilter implements Filter {

    @Override
    public void doFilter
        (ServletRequest req, ServletResponse res, FilterChain chain)
            throws IOException, ServletException
    {
        HttpServletRequest request = (HttpServletRequest) req;
        HttpServletResponse response = (HttpServletResponse) res;
        String resourcePath = request.getContextPath()
            + ResourceHandler.RESOURCE_IDENTIFIER;

        if (!request.getRequestURI().startsWith(resourcePath)) {
            response.setHeader
                ("Cache-Control", "no-store, must-revalidate");
        }

        chain.doFilter(request, response);
    }
}
```

Basically, it hooks on all requests which are going to hit the FacesServlet, provided that it's configured on a servlet name of "facesServlet" in web.xml as follows:

```
<servlet>
    <servlet-name>facesServlet</servlet-name>
    <servlet-class>javax.faces.webapp.FacesServlet</servlet-class>
</servlet>
```

Alternatively, if you have divided your web application into a public area with only stateless JSF pages and a restricted area with only stateful JSF pages, then you could also map this filter on a specific URL pattern which matches only the stateful section, such as /admin/*.

```
@WebFilter("/admin/*")
```

The filter example checks first if the HTTP request doesn't represent a JSF resource request before setting the cache control header. Those requests are identified by the /javax.faces.resource path after the context path, which is available by the ResourceHandler#RESOURCE_IDENTIFIER constant. This is automatically used when you use a JSF resource component, such as <h:graphicImage>, <h:outputScript>, or <h:outputstyleSheet>. (See also the section "Resource Components" in Chapter 6.) You don't want to disable the browser cache on them as that would otherwise impact the page loading performance.

The cache control header being set is actually only recognized by HTTP 1.1-capable clients. HTTP 1.1 was introduced in 1997. In case you would like to cover HTTP 1.0 clients as well, which these days are generally only ancient proxies or poor users who can't get something better than Internet Explorer 6.0, then you'd best add two more response headers.

```
response.setHeader("Pragma", "no-cache"); // HTTP 1.0.
response.setDateHeader("Expires", 0); // Proxies.
```

Now, with this filter in place, the end user won't any more get to see any JSF page from the browser cache and thus can no longer get a ViewExpiredException on them. However, there are still cases where a ViewExpiredException is unavoidable. One such case is an end user who has several JSF pages open in different browser tabs and logs out in one of them and then performs an action in another tab without refreshing the page beforehand. For such a case, you'd really need a "Sorry, your session has timed out" error page. This can easily be configured as another error page in web.xml as follows:

```
<error-page>
    <exception-type>
        javax.faces.application.ViewExpiredException
    </exception-type>
    <location>/WEB-INF/errorpages/expired.xhtml</location>
</error-page>
```

Do not let it point to a public JSF page, such as a login page. In case you really need it to be a public JSF page, use a meta refresh header in the error page which redirects the end user further to a public JSF page.

```
<!DOCTYPE html>
<html lang="en">
    <head>
        <title>Session expired</title>
        <meta http-equiv="refresh"
            content="0;url=#{request.contextPath}/login.xhtml" />
    </head>
    <body>
        <h1>Sorry, your session has timed out</h1>
        <h3>You will be redirected to login page</h3>
        <p>
            <a href="#{request.contextPath}/login.xhtml">
                Click here if the redirect didn't work,
                or when you're impatient.
            </a>
        </p>
    </body>
</html>
```

Note that the "0" in the meta refresh content represents the amount of seconds before redirect. Thus, "0" means "redirect immediately." You can use, for example, "3" to let the browser wait 3 seconds before the redirect.

Keep in mind also to configure this location in any custom exception handler such as the AjaxExceptionHandler demonstrated in the previous section. You also need to make sure that your "general" error page is mapped on an error code of 500 instead of an exception type of, e.g., java.lang.Exception or java.lang.Throwable; otherwise all exceptions wrapped in ServletException would still end up in the general error page. JSF will wrap any exception in a ServletException when it's thrown during a synchronous (non-Ajax) postback instead of an asynchronous (Ajax) postback. The web.xml error page mechanism will only extract the root cause from the ServletException for a second pass through error pages by exception type when no matching error page by exception type is found.

A completely different alternative to avoid ViewExpiredException is to use stateless JSF views. This way nothing of the JSF view state will be saved and the JSF views will never expire but will just be rebuilt from scratch on every request. You can turn on stateless views by setting the transient attribute of <f:view> to true. This is elaborated in the section "Stateless Forms" in Chapter 4.

Regardless of the solution, make sure you do **not** use the Mojarra-specific `com.sun.faces.enableRestoreView11Compatibility` context parameter. This will basically turn on JSF 1.0/1.1 behavior with regard to expired views. It won't throw the `ViewExpiredException` any more, but neither does it actually restore the original view state at all. It basically recreates the view and all associated view scoped beans from scratch and hereby thus loses all of original state. As the application will behave in a confusing way ("Hey, where are my input values..??"), this is bad for user experience. Better use stateless JSF views instead so that you can manage the application in specific views only instead of for all views.

# IOException Handling

Some methods of the underlying `HttpServletRequest` and `HttpServletResponse` objects may throw an `IOException`. Usually, that only happens when the network connection unexpectedly breaks: for example, when the end user abruptly stops the HTTP request by pressing the Esc button in the web browser, or the end user abruptly navigates to a different web page while the current page is still loading, or even when the end user's computer or network cable catches fire. Those circumstances are really unavoidable. For you, as web application developer, it's best to let any `IOException` bubble up into the servlet container. In other words, there's absolutely no need to catch it as follows:

```
public void someAjaxListener() {
    try {
        FacesContext.getCurrentInstance()
            .getExternalContext().redirect(url);
    }
    catch (IOException e) {
        throw new UncheckedIOException(e);
    }
}
```

Instead, just let it go.

```
public void someAjaxListener() throws IOException {
    FacesContext.getCurrentInstance()
        .getExternalContext().redirect(url);
}
```

# EJBException Handling

Sometimes, invoking service methods may also cause an exception. Generally, those are on purpose, such as "entity not found," "unique constraint violation," "invalid user credentials", "entity is in meanwhile modified by another user," etc. By default, any non-application-specific RuntimeException, such as NullPointerException and even JPA's PersistenceException which is thrown from an EJB service method, is wrapped in an EJBException. This makes it clumsy to nail down the actual root cause in the JSF action method.

```
public void addProduct() {
    FacesMessage message;

    try {
        Long id = productService.create(product);
        message = new FacesMessage(FacesMessage.SEVERITY_INFO,
            "Product successfully saved", "ID is " + id);
    }
    catch (EJBException e) {
        if (e.getCause() instanceof ConstraintViolationException) {
            message = new FacesMessage(FacesMessage.SEVERITY_ERROR,
                "Duplicate product!", e.getMessage());
            context.validationFailed();

        }
        else {
            throw e;
        }
    }

    context.addMessage(null, message);
}
```

This is not the best practice. Not only would you need to determine the root cause of the EJB exception by inspecting Exception#getCause(), the web.xml error page mechanism would also not be able to show a specific error page for, for example, a

ConstraintViolationException, because it's wrapped in an EJBException. In order to
get EJB to throw it unwrapped, you need to create a custom exception superclass first
which you then annotate with @javax.ejb.ApplicationException.[4]

```
@ApplicationException(rollback=true)
public abstract class BusinessException extends RuntimeException {
    public BusinessException() {
        super();
    }
    public BusinessException(Exception cause) {
        super(cause);
    }
}
```

Note the rollback=true attribute on the annotation. This is very important in case you'd
like the EJB container to roll back any active transaction from where this exception is being
thrown. Following are some examples of subclasses of this custom business exception.

```
public abstract class QueryException extends BusinessException {}
public class EntityNotFoundException extends QueryException {}
public class DuplicateEntityException extends QueryException {}
public abstract class CredentialsException extends BusinessException {}
public class InvalidUsernameException extends CredentialsException {}
public class InvalidPasswordException extends CredentialsException {}
```

Note that you don't necessarily need to repeat the @ApplicationException over all
subclasses as it's already @Inherited. Following are some concrete use cases on which
those exceptions could be thrown:

```
public User getById(Long id) {
    try {
        return entityManager
            .createQuery("FROM User u WHERE u.id = :id", User.class)
            .setParameter("id", id)
            .getSingleResult();
    }
```

---

[4]https://javaee.github.io/javaee-spec/javadocs/javax/ejb/ApplicationException.html.

```java
        catch (NoResultException e) {
            throw new EntityNotFoundException(e);
        }
    }

    public Optional<User> findByEmail(String email) {
        try {
            return Optional.of(entityManager
                .createQuery("FROM User u"
                    + " WHERE u.email = :email", User.class)
                .setParameter("email", email)
                .getSingleResult());
        }
        catch (NoResultException e) {
            return Optional.empty();
        }
    }

    public User getByEmailAndPassword(String email, String password) {
        User user = findByEmail(email)
            .orElseThrow(InvalidUsernameException::new);
        Credentials credentials = user.getCredentials();
        byte[] passwordHash = digest(password, credentials.getSalt());

        if (!Arrays.equals(passwordHash, credentials.getPasswordHash())) {
            throw new InvalidPasswordException();
        }

        return user;
    }

    public Long create(User user) {
        if (findByEmail(user.getEmail()).isPresent()) {
            throw new DuplicateEntityException();
        }
        entityManager.persist(user);
        return user.getId();
    }
```

In the JSF backing bean action methods, you could then handle them accordingly.

```
public void signup() {
    FacesMessage message;

    try {
        userService.create(product);
        message = new FacesMessage("You are successfully signed up!");
    }
    catch (DuplicateEntityException e) {
        message = new FacesMessage(FacesMessage.SEVERITY_ERROR,
            "Sorry, username already taken!", e.getMessage());
        context.validationFailed();
    }

    context.addMessage(null, message);
}
```

In order to further reduce the boilerplate code, you could even let all business exceptions go and have a custom exception handler to handle them.

```
public class BusinessExceptionHandler extends ExceptionHandlerWrapper {

    public BusinessExceptionHandler(ExceptionHandler wrapped) {
        super(wrapped);
    }

    @Override
    public void handle() {
        handleBusinessException(FacesContext.getCurrentInstance());
        getWrapped().handle();
    }

    protected void handleBusinessException(FacesContext context) {
        Iterator<ExceptionQueuedEvent> unhandledExceptionQueuedEvents =
            getUnhandledExceptionQueuedEvents().iterator();

        if (context == null
            || !unhandledExceptionQueuedEvents.hasNext()
        ) {
            return;
        }
```

```
    Throwable exception = unhandledExceptionQueuedEvents
        .next().getContext().getException();

    while (exception.getCause() != null
        && (exception instanceof FacesException
            || exception instanceof ELException)
    ) {
        exception = exception.getCause();
    }

    if (!(exception instanceof BusinessException)) {
        return;
    }

    context.addMessage(null, new FacesMessage(
        FacesMessage.SEVERITY_FATAL,
        exception.toString(),
        exception.getMessage()));
    context.validationFailed();
    context.getPartialViewContext()
        .getRenderIds().add("globalMessages");

    unhandledExceptionQueuedEvents.remove();

    while (unhandledExceptionQueuedEvents.hasNext()) {
        unhandledExceptionQueuedEvents.next();
        unhandledExceptionQueuedEvents.remove();
    }
}

public static class Factory extends ExceptionHandlerFactory {

    public Factory(ExceptionHandlerFactory wrapped) {
        super(wrapped);
    }
```

```
    @Override
    public ExceptionHandler getExceptionHandler() {
        return new BusinessExceptionHandler
            (getWrapped().getExceptionHandler());
    }
  }

}
```

Yes, it's indeed similar to the `AjaxExceptionHandler` as shown in the earlier section "Ajax Exception Handler." However, the first difference is that it doesn't skip handling the exception when the response is already committed or when it's not an Ajax request. The second difference is the logic between extracting the root cause of the exception and draining the remaining unhandled exception events. This `BusinessExceptionHandler` will instead check if the root cause is an instance of `BusinessException` and if so, it will add a faces message and instruct JSF to explicitly update the component identified by "globalMessages", which should refer to a global messages component in your master template something like the following:

`<h:messages id="globalMessages" globalOnly="true" />`

Ultimately, all business exception-related faces messages will end up there. You might have noticed that the faces context is explicitly marked as "validation failed" via the `FacesContext#validationFailed()` call. This is generally useful in case any code in the Facelet template is relying on it. If you would like to run it together with the `AjaxExceptionHandler` for non-business exceptions, then you need to register it in the `faces-config.xml` *after* the `AjaxExceptionHandler`. Anything that is declared later in the `faces-config.xml` will effectively wrap the previously declared one. This also applies to custom exception handler factories. When the `BusinessExceptionHandler` confirms that the exception is not an instance of `BusinessException`, then it will leave the unhandled exception in the queue and return from the method and finally delegate to the `handle()` method of the wrapped `ExceptionHandler`, which shall be the `AjaxExceptionHandler`.

```
<factory>
    <exception-handler-factory>
        com.example.project.AjaxExceptionHandler$Factory
    </exception-handler-factory>
    <exception-handler-factory>
        com.example.project.BusinessExceptionHandler$Factory
    </exception-handler-factory>
</factory>
```

With the BusinessExceptionHandler in place, you could further reduce the backing bean action method as follows:

```
public void signup() {
    userService.create(product);
    context.addMessage(null,
        new FacesMessage("You are successfully signed up!");
}
```

# CHAPTER 10

# WebSocket Push

JSF 1.0 introduced HTML form-based POST action support. JSF 2.0 introduced AJAX-based POST support. JSF 2.0 introduced GET query string parameter mapping support. JSF 2.2 introduced GET-based action support. JSF 2.3 introduces WebSocket support.

JSF's WebSocket support is represented by the new `<f:websocket>` tag, the `PushContext` interface, and the `@Push` annotation. It is built on top of the JSR-356 WebSockets specification, introduced in Java EE 7. Therefore, it is technically possible to use it in a Java EE 7 environment as well. JSR-356 is even natively supported in Tomcat since 7.0.27 and in Jetty since 9.1.0.

In Mojarra, the `<f:websocket>` has an additional Java EE 7 dependency: JSON-P (JSR-353). In case you're targeting Tomcat or Jetty instead of a Java EE application server, you might need to install it separately. JSON-P is internally used to convert Java objects to a JSON string so that it can, without much hassle, be transferred to the client side and be provided as an argument of JavaScript listener function attached to `<f:websocket>`.

## Configuration

The JSR-356 WebSocket specification does not officially support programmatic initialization of the socket end point during runtime. So we cannot initialize it by simply declaring `<f:websocket>` in the view and wait until a JSF page referencing it is being opened for the first time. We really need to initialize it explicitly during deployment time. We could do that by default, but having an unused WebSocket end point open forever is not really nice if it's never used by the web application. So we cannot avoid having a context parameter to explicitly initialize it during deployment time.

```
<context-param>
    <param-name>javax.faces.ENABLE_WEBSOCKET_ENDPOINT</param-name>
    <param-value>true</param-value>
</context-param>
```

341

© Bauke Scholtz, Arjan Tijms 2018
B. Scholtz and A. Tijms, *The Definitive Guide to JSF in Java EE 8*, https://doi.org/10.1007/978-1-4842-3387-0_10

If you prefer programmatic initialization over declarative initialization, then you can always use ServletContext#setInitParameter() in a ServletContainerInitializer of your web fragment library as follows:

```
public class YourInitializer implements ServletContainerInitializer {

    @Override
    public void onStartup(Set<Class<?>> types, ServletContext context) {
        context.setInitParameter(
            PushContext.ENABLE_WEBSOCKET_ENDPOINT_PARAM_NAME, "true");
    }
}
```

Note that it is not possible to perform this task in a ServletContextListener as JSF will actually register the WebSocket end point in its own ServletContainerInitializer implementation which always runs before any ServletContextListener.

Once the WebSocket end point is enabled and successfully initialized during deployment, it will listen for WebSocket handshake requests on the URL (uniform resource locator) pattern /javax.faces.push/*. The first path element will represent the WebSocket channel name.

Coming back to "officially," some WebSocket implementations do, however, support programmatic initialization, such as the one provided by Undertow, which is in turn used in WildFly. Unfortunately, the spec doesn't say so, and there may be WebSocket implementations that simply do not support programmatic initialization, such as Tyrus as used in Payara.[1]

The WebSocket container will, by default, listen for handshake requests on the same port as the application server is listening for HTTP requests. You can optionally change the port with another web.xml context parameter,

```
<context-param>
    <param-name>javax.faces.WEBSOCKET_ENDPOINT_PORT</param-name>
    <param-value>8000</param-value>
</context-param>
```

---

[1]https://github.com/javaee/websocket-spec/issues/211.

or programmatically in a ServletContainerInitializer:

```
context.setInitParameter(
    PushContext.WEBSOCKET_ENDPOINT_PORT_PARAM_NAME, "8000");
```

# Usage

In your JSF page, just declare the <f:websocket> tag along with the required channel attribute representing the channel name and the optional onmessage attribute representing a reference to a JavaScript function.

```
<f:websocket channel="test" onmessage="logMessage" />

<script>
    function logMessage(message, channel, event) {
        console.log(message);
    }
</script>
```

The JavaScript function will be invoked with three arguments.

1.  message: the push message as JSON object.

2.  channel: the WebSocket channel name. This may be useful in case you intend to have a global listener, or want to manually control the close of the WebSocket.

3.  event: the original MessageEvent object. This may be useful in case you intend to inspect it in the JavaScript function.

On the WAR side, you can inject the PushContext via the @Push annotation in any web artifact that supports CDI injection. This can be a simple CDI managed bean, but it can also be a @WebServlet, @WebFilter or @WebListener.

```
import javax.inject.Named;
import javax.enterprise.context.RequestScoped;

import javax.inject.Inject;
import javax.faces.push.Push;
import javax.faces.push.PushContext;
```

```
@Named @RequestScoped
public class Bean {

    @Inject @Push
    private PushContext test;

    public void submit() {
        test.send("Hello World!");
    }
}
```

The PushContext variable name *test* must match the channel name declared in the JSF page. In case you cannot match the variable name with the channel name, you can always specify the channel name in the optional channel attribute of the @Push annotation.

```
@Inject @Push(channel="test")
private PushContext foo;
```

Once the submit() method of the bean shown before is invoked by some JSF command component, even in a different JSF page, the push message "Hello World!" will be sent to **all** opened sockets on the very same channel name, application wide.

## Scopes and Users

As you may have realized, <f:websocket> is thus, by default, application scoped. You can control the scope by the optional scope attribute. Allowed values are application, session, and view.

When set to session, the message will be sent to all opened sockets on the very same channel in the current session only.

```
<f:websocket channel="progress" scope="session" />
```

This is particularly useful for progress messages coming from long-running session-scoped background tasks initiated by the user itself. This way the user can just continue browsing the site without the need to wait for the result on the very same page.

Alternatively, you can also set the optional user attribute to a serializable value representing the unique user identifier, which can be a String representing the user login name or a Long representing the user ID. When this attribute is set, the scope of the socket will automatically default to session and it cannot be set to application.

```
<f:websocket channel="chat" user="#{loggedInUser.id}" />
```

This offers the opportunity to send a message to a specific user as follows:

```
private String message;
private User recipient;

@Inject @Push
private PushContext chat;

public void sendMessage() {
    Long recipientId = recipient.getId();
    chat.send(message, recipientId);
}
```

You can even send it to multiple users by providing a Set argument.

```
private String message;
private Set<User> recipients;

@Inject @Push
private PushContext chat;

public void sendMessage() {
    Set<Long> recipientIds = recipients.stream()
        .map(User::getId)
        .collect(Collectors.toSet());
    chat.send(message, recipientIds);
}
```

In other words, you can easily implement a chat box this way. Incidentally, real-time user targeted notifications at, for example, Stack Overflow and Facebook work this way.

When the `scope` is set to `view`, the message will be sent to the opened socket on the specified channel in the current view only. This won't affect any sockets on the same channel in all other views throughout the application.

```
<f:websocket channel="push" scope="view" />
```

This is also supported in combination with the `user` attribute.

```
<f:websocket channel="chat" user="#{user.id}" scope="view" />
```

This construct is somewhat unusual though and should only be used if the logged-in user represented by `user` attribute can have a shorter lifetime than the HTTP session. This is, however, in turn considered a poor security practice. The best security practice is, namely, that the HTTP session is invalidated during login and during logout. Invalidating the HTTP session during login prevents session fixation attacks and invalidating the session during logout prevents dirty user-specific data lingering around in HTTP session.

# Channel Design Hints

You can declare multiple push channels on different scopes with or without user target throughout the application. However, be aware that the same channel name can easily be reused across multiple views, even if it is view scoped. It's more efficient if you use as few different channel names as possible and tie the channel name to a specific push socket scope/user combination, not to a specific JSF view. In case you intend to have multiple view-scoped channels for different purposes, it is best to use only one view-scoped channel and have a global JavaScript listener which can distinguish its task based on the delivered message, for example, by sending the message in a server as follows,

```
Map<String, Object> message = new HashMap<>();
message.put("functionName", "someFunction");
message.put("functionData", functionData); // Can be Map or Bean.
someChannel.send(message);
```

which is then processed in the `onmessage` JavaScript listener function as follows:

```
function someSocketListener(message) {
    window[message.functionName](message.functionData);
}
```

346

```
function someFunction(data) {
    // ...
}

function otherFunction(data) {
    // ...
}

// ...
```

# One-Time Push

You can use the connected attribute to prevent the socket from automatically connecting during page load.

```
<f:websocket ... connected="false" />
```

This is particularly useful when you want to perform a one-time push of the result after invoking a view-scoped Ajax action method which might take a bit more time to complete, and you'd like the user to immediately continue using the very same page without being annoyed about a "slow web site" experience. This approach only requires a bit of additional work with the jsf.push JavaScript API (application programming interface).[2] It has three functions, but only two are of interest to us: jsf.push.open(...) and jsf.push.close(...). The third one, jsf.push.init(...), basically initializes the socket and that's up to the renderer of the <f:websocket> tag.

Right before invoking the Ajax action method, you'd need to explicitly open the socket by invoking the jsf.push.open(...) function with the socket client ID as argument. And right after the push message arrives, you'd need to explicitly close the socket by invoking the jsf.push.close(...) function with the socket client ID as argument. The following example demonstrates this approach:

```
<script>
    function startLongRunningProcess() {
        jsf.push.open("push");
        document.getElementById("status").innerHTML =
```

---

[2]https://javaserverfaces.github.io/docs/2.3/jsdocs/symbols/jsf.push.html.

```
                "Long running process has started ...";
    }
    function endLongRunningProcess(result) {
        jsf.push.close("push");
        document.getElementById("status").innerHTML = result;
    }
</script>
<h:form>
    <h:commandButton value="submit"
        onclick="startLongRunningProcess()"
        action="#{longRunningProcess.submit}">
        <f:ajax />
    </h:commandButton>
</h:form>
<div id="status" />
<f:websocket id="push" channel="push" scope="view"
    connected="false" onmessage="endLongRunningProcess">
</f:websocket>
```

It must be said that it's a poor practice to put JavaScript code right in the HTML source as shown above. It's, of course, for demonstration purposes only. For better maintenance, performance, and tooling support, you should, in real-world code, put JavaScript code in a JS file and include it via `<h:outputScript>`. And then I'm not talking about the lack of jQuery magic for demonstration purposes.

In the example, opening the socket is performed during the `onclick` of the command button. The `onmessage` listener function in turn closes the socket. Of course, you can also keep the socket open all the time without fiddling with JavaScript, but it may be a waste of resources if the socket isn't used for purposes other than presenting the result of a view-scoped Ajax action method. Here is what the associated backing bean looks like.

```
@Named @RequestScoped
public class LongRunningProcess {

    @Inject
    private LongRunningProcessService service;

    @Inject @Push
    private PushContext push;
```

```
    public void submit() {
        service.asyncSubmit(result -> push.send(result));
    }
}
```

And here is what the service class looks like.

```
@Stateless
public class LongRunningProcessService {

    @Asynchronous
    public void asyncSubmit(Consumer<String> callback) {
        String result = someLongRunningProcess();
        callback.accept(result);
    }

}
```

Note the EJB @Asynchronous annotation. This is very important in this construct. It will ensure that the EJB (Enterprise Java Bean) method is executed in a separate thread. This allows the backing bean method to return immediately without waiting for the EJB method to complete.

## Stateful UI Updates

As you may have noticed, the onmessage JavaScript listener function is generally only useful for small stateless tasks, such as displaying a feedback message or adding a new item to some stateless list using JavaScript. It isn't terribly useful when you want to update a stateful UI (user interface) represented by another JSF component. Think of replacing a trivial loading image with a whole JSF table.

For that you'd better nest <f:ajax> listening on a specific push message. Via its render attribute you have the opportunity to automatically update an arbitrary JSF component in an incoming push message. Following is an example which initially shows a loading image and then the table when it's ready to load:

```
<h:form>
    <f:websocket channel="push" scope="view">
        <f:ajax event="loaded" render=":results" />
    </f:websocket>
```

```
</h:form>
<h:panelGroup id="results" layout="block">
    <h:graphicImage name="images/loading.gif"
        rendered="#{empty longRunningSearch.results}">
    </h:graphicImage>
    <h:dataTable value="#{longRunningSearch.results}" var="result"
        rendered="#{not empty longRunningSearch.results}">
        <h:column>#{result.id}</h:column>
        <h:column>#{result.name}</h:column>
        <h:column>#{result.value}</h:column>
    </h:dataTable>
</h:panelGroup>
```

Note that <f:websocket> is placed in <h:form>. This is mandatory when it has
<f:ajax> nested. Normally this is not required. Here is what the backing bean looks like.

```
@Named @ViewScoped
public class LongRunningSearch implements Serializable {

    private List<Result> results;

    @Inject
    private LongRunningSearchService service;

    @Inject @Push
    private PushContext push;

    @PostConstruct
    public void init() {
        service.asyncLoadResults(results -> {
            this.results = results;
            push.send("loaded");
        });
    }

    public List<Result> getResults() {
        return results;
    }
}
```

Note that the push message "loaded" matches exactly the <f:ajax event> value. You can use any value you want and you can nest as many <f:ajax> tags as you need. It's important that the managed bean is @ViewScoped as the Ajax call is basically performed in a different request within the same view. Finally the service class looks as follows:

```
@Stateless
public class LongRunningSearchService {

    @Asynchronous
    public void asyncLoadResults(Consumer<List<Result>> callback) {
        List<Result> results = someLongRunningProcess();
        callback.accept(results);
    }
}
```

The someLongRunningProcess() method represents your implementation of some long-running process (e.g., calling a third-party web service API).

## Site-Wide Push Notifications

For this, you can use an application-scoped socket. Such a socket is particularly useful for application-wide feedback messages triggered by the web application itself on a particular event which may be interest to all application users. Think of site-wide statistics, real-time lists, stock updates, etc. The following example shows the case of a real-time top 10 list:

```
<h:dataTable id="top10" value="#{bean.top10}" var="item">
    <h:column>#{item.ranking}</h:column>
    <h:column>#{item.name}</h:column>
    <h:column>#{item.score}</h:column>
</h:dataTable>
<h:form>
    <f:websocket channel="top10Observer">
        <f:ajax event="updated" render=":top10" />
    </f:websocket>
</h:form>
```

Here is what the service class looks like, with a little help from CDI events.

```
@Stateless
public class ItemService {

    @Inject
    private EntityManager entityManager;

    @Inject
    private BeanManager beanManager;

    public void update(Item item) {
        List<Item> previousTop10 = getTop10();
        entityManager.merge(item);
        List<Item> currentTop10 = getTop10();

        if (!currentTop10.equals(previousTop10)) {
            beanManager.fireEvent(new Top10UpdatedEvent());
        }
    }

    pulic List<Item> getTop10() {
        return entityManager
            .createNamedQuery("Item.top10", Item.class)
            .getResultList();
    }
}
```

Note that the Top10UpdatedEvent is, in this specific example, basically just an empty class like public class Top10UpdatedEvent {}. Also note that we're not injecting the PushContext here. This is otherwise considered tight coupling of layers. All JSF-related code belongs in the front end, not in the back end. This way the back-end service classes are better reusable across all kinds of front-end frameworks other than JSF, such as JAX-RS or even plain vanilla JSP/Servlet. In other words, you should ensure that none of your back-end classes directly or indirectly use any front-end-specific classes such as those from javax.faces.*, javax.ws.*, and javax.servlet.* packages.

Any event fired with the BeanManager#fireEvent() method can be observed using CDI @Observes annotation. This works across all layers. In other words, even when it's fired in the back end, you can observe it in the front end. The only requirement is that the backing bean must be @ApplicationScoped. That is, there's not necessarily any means of an HTTP request, HTTP session, or JSF view anywhere at that moment.

```java
@Named @ApplicationScoped
public class Bean {

    private List<Item> top10;

    @Inject
    private ItemService service;

    @Inject @Push
    private PushContext top10Observer;

    @PostConstruct
    public void load() {
        top10 = service.getTop10();
    }

    public void onTop10Updated(@Observes Top10UpdatedEvent event) {
        load();
        top10Observer.send("updated");
    }

    public List<Item> getTop10() {
        return top10;
    }
}
```

# Keeping Track of Active Sockets

In order to keep track of active sockets, you can in an application-scoped bean observe @WebsocketEvent.Opened and @WebsocketEvent.Closed events. The following example assumes that you have <f:websocket channel="chat" user="..."> and that you intend to collect "active chat users":

```java
@ApplicationScoped
public class WebsocketEventObserver {

    private Map<Serializable, AtomicInteger> users;
```

```java
@PostConstruct
public void init() {
    users = new ConcurrentHashMap<>();
}

public void onopen(@Observes @Opened WebsocketEvent event) {
    if ("chat".equals(event.getChannel())) {
        getCounter(event.getUser()).incrementAndGet();
    }
}

public void onclose(@Observes @Closed WebsocketEvent event) {
    if ("chat".equals(event.getChannel())) {
        getCounter(event.getUser()).decrementAndGet();
    }
}

private AtomicInteger getCounter(Serializable user) {
    return users.computeIfAbsent(user, k -> new AtomicInteger());
}

public Set<Serializable> getActiveUsers() {
    return users.entrySet().stream()
        .filter(entry -> entry.getValue().intValue() > 0)
        .map(entry -> entry.getKey())
        .collect(Collectors.toSet());
}
}
```

You can use the above getActiveUsers() method to obtain a set of "active chat users." Do note that a single user can open the same web page multiple times within the same session (e.g., multiple browser tabs) and that's exactly why a counter is used instead simply adding and removing users from a Set.

# Detecting Session and View Expiration

The `<f:websocket>` tag will by default keep the connection open forever, as long as the document is open—as long as there's no `connected="false"` being set, or `jsf.push.close(clientId)` being invoked, of course. When the first connection attempt fails, it will immediately report an error. You can optionally use the `onclose` attribute to reference a JavaScript function which acts as a close listener.

```
<f:websocket ... onclose="logClose" />
```

```
<script>
    function logClose(code, channel, event) {
        if (code == -1) {
            // WebSocket API not supported by client. E.g. IE9.
        }
        else if (code == 1000) {
            // Normal close as result of expired view or session.
        }
        else {
            // Abnormal close as result of a client or server error.
        }
    }
</script>
```

The JavaScript function will be invoked with three arguments.

1.  code: the close reason code as integer. If this is -1, then the WebSocket JavaScript API is simply not supported[3] by the client. If this is 1000, then a normal closure has occurred as consequence of an expired view or session in the server side.

2.  channel: the WebSocket channel name. This may be useful in case you intend to have a global listener.

3.  event: the original `CloseEvent` object. This may be useful in case you intend to inspect it in the JavaScript function.

---

[3]http://caniuse.com/#feat=websockets.

When the first connection attempt succeeds but it later gets disconnected for some reason (e.g., because the server is restarting), then it will by default keep trying to reconnect. In the case of Mojarra, it will keep retrying up to 25 times, with an interval which is incremented 500ms each time, and it will eventually report an error.

As you might have noticed in the aforementioned `onclose` listener function example, you could just check if the close code of a `<f:websocket>` equals 1000 in order to perform some client-side action via JavaScript (e.g., displaying a warning message and/or redirecting to some "Session expired" page).

```
<f:websocket channel="push" scope="session" onclose="closeListener" />
<script>
    function closeListener(code) {
        if (code == 1000) {
            window.location = jsf.contextPath + "/expired.xhtml";
        }
    }
</script>
```

This works for both view- and session-scoped sockets. Application-scoped sockets, however, remain open forever as long as the document is still open on client side, even when the underlying view or session has expired.

# Breaking Down Mojarra's f:websocket Implementation

The `<f:websocket>` API specifies the following classes and methods:

- `javax.faces.push.Push`, a CDI qualifier to for `@Inject`. With help of this qualifier the socket channel name can be specified.

- `javax.faces.push.PushContext`, an interface with three `send()` methods: `send(String message)`, `send(String message, S user)`, and `send(String message, Collection<S> users)`. All those methods accept the push message as `Object` and will for JavaScript convert it to a JSON string. All those methods return `Future<Void>` for each message. If it returns null, then the target socket isn't open at all. If it doesn't throw `ExecutionException` on `Future#get()` method call, then the message was successfully delivered.

- `javax.faces.component.UIWebsocket`, a component which implements `ClientBehaviorHolder` in order to support nested `<f:ajax>`. Historically, the prototype tag used a `TagHandler` instead of `UIComponent`. It was later decided to let the tag support `<f:ajax>` as that would make complex and stateful UI updates much easier. However, it isn't possible to let a `TagHandler` implement `ClientBehaviorHolder` and benefit all of built-in Ajax magic, hence the conversion to `UIComponent`.

- `ViewHandler#getWebsocketURL()` method which takes a channel name and returns the absolute WebSocket URL in form of `ws://host:port/context/javax.faces.push/channel` with help of `ExternalContext#encodeWebsocketURL()`.

- `ExternalContext#encodeWebsocketURL()` method which basically takes a relative WebSocket URI in form of `/context/javax.faces.push/channel` and returns the absolute WebSocket URL.

The actual implementation is fairly extensive. It's directly based on OmniFaces `<o:socket>`[4] with, here and there, a few adjustments such as using a component's client ID instead of a channel name in JavaScript API functions.

- `com.sun.faces.renderkit.html_basic.WebsocketRenderer`, a faces renderer class which registers during encoding the socket channel, scope and user in `WebsocketChannelManager` and retrieves the WebSocket URL from it. Then it auto-includes the `jsf.js` script containing the necessary `javax.push.*` functions, and renders the `jsf.push.init(...)` inline script function call with among others the WebSocket URL as an argument. This function should in turn in JavaScript create a `new WebSocket(url)`. The `WebsocketRenderer` will also subscribe the `WebsocketFacesListener` to the current view.

- `com.sun.faces.push.WebsocketChannelManager`, a session-scoped CDI managed bean which keeps track of all so far registered `<f:websocket>` channels, scopes, and users and ensures that each socket gets its own unique channel identifier. It will register every channel identifier in `WebsocketSessionManager` and those of user-targeted sockets in `WebsocketUserManager`.

---

[4]`http://showcase.omnifaces.org/push/socket`.

- `com.sun.faces.push.WebsocketFacesListener`, a system event listener which listens on `PreRenderViewEvent` and renders if necessary the `jsf.push.open(...)` or `jsf.push.close(...)` inline script function calls depending on whether the connected attribute represents a dynamic EL expression which got changed during an Ajax request.

- `com.sun.faces.push.WebsocketEndpoint`, a class which implements JSR-356 `javax.websocket.Endpoint` and listens on the URI template `/javax.faces.push/{channel}`. When a new `WebSocket(url)` is created and opened on client-side JavaScript, then a new `javax.websocket.Session` is created on server-side Java and the `WebsocketEndpoint` will add this `Session` to `WebsocketSessionManager`. Equivalently, when a socket is closed, then the `WebsocketEndpoint` will remove it from `WebsocketSessionManager`.

- `com.sun.faces.push.WebsocketSessionManager`, an application-scoped CDI managed bean which collects all so far opened socket sessions and validates that their unique WebSocket URL has been registered by `WebsocketChannelManager`.

- `com.sun.faces.push.WebsocketUserManager`, an application-scoped CDI managed bean which collects the channel identifiers of all so far opened user-targeted sockets.

- `com.sun.faces.push.WebsocketPushContext`, the concrete implementation of the `PushContext` interface. It will send the push message via `WebsocketSessionManager` and if necessary obtain the user-targeted channels via `WebsocketUserManager`.

- `com.sun.faces.push.WebsocketPushContextProducer`, the CDI producer which creates the `WebsocketPushContext` instance based on channel name as obtained from `@Push` qualifier, the `WebsocketSessionManager` and `WebsocketUserManager`.

# CHAPTER 11

# Custom Components

In Chapter 7 you should have learned that Facelet templates as in `<ui:composition>`, `<ui:include>`, and `<ui:decorate>` are useful when you want to split main page layout fragments into reusable templates, such as header, menu, main content, and footer. And that Facelet tag files such as `<t:field>` are useful when you want to have a reusable group of components in order to minimize code duplication. And that composite components such as `<t:inputLocalTime>` are useful when you want to create a custom component with a single responsibility based on existing components and, if necessary, a bunch of HTML.

However, there may be cases in which no single component exists for the purpose you had in mind, even not when composed of existing components and a bunch of HTML. Or, perhaps the component does exist, but its renderer is not doing things you had in mind. At this point, you would need to create a custom component or a custom renderer.

JSF (JavaServer Faces) has since the beginning offered a high degree of abstraction around the `UIComponent` API (application programming interface). You can customize components by creating a brand-new custom `UIComponent`, or by extending an existing component from the standard HTML component set, or by plugging a custom `Renderer` for an existing component.

## Component Type, Family, and Renderer Type

Each `UIComponent` instance has "component type," "component family," and "renderer type" associated with it. The component type basically represents the unique component identifier associated with the component tag. It can be registered into JSF via either the `@FacesComponent` annotation or the `<component>` entry in `faces-config.xml`. The following example demonstrates the usage of the annotation on a minimal component class:

```
@FacesComponent(SomeComponent.COMPONENT_TYPE)
public class SomeComponent extends UIComponentBase {

    public static final String COMPONENT_TYPE = "project.SomeComponent";
```

359

© Bauke Scholtz, Arjan Tijms 2018
B. Scholtz and A. Tijms, *The Definitive Guide to JSF in Java EE 8*, https://doi.org/10.1007/978-1-4842-3387-0_11

```java
public static final String COMPONENT_FAMILY = "project.SomeFamily";

public SomeComponent() {
    setRendererType(SomeRenderer.RENDERER_TYPE);
}

@Override
public String getFamily() {
    return COMPONENT_FAMILY;
}
}
```

And the following example demonstrates the usage with the entry in `faces-config.xml`:

```xml
<component>
    <component-type>project.SomeComponent</component-type>
    <component-class>
        com.example.project.component.SomeComponent
    </component-class>
</component>
```

Note that when you register a Java EE artifact via both the annotation and the XML ways using the same identifier, then the XML declaration will always get precedence over the annotation declaration. The same holds true for all JSF annotations.

The public constants `COMPONENT_TYPE` and `COMPONENT_FAMILY` in the component class are not mandatory, but they follow the same convention as the standard JSF component set does and therefore give more consistency in developing with JSF. The public constant `COMPONENT_TYPE` allows the developer to programmatically create the component without needing to hard-code the component type.

```java
UIComponent component = FacesContext.getCurrentInstance()
    .getApplication().createComponent(SomeComponent.COMPONENT_TYPE);
```

Note that programmatically creating `UIComponent` instances this way is generally not the normal practice in an average JSF web application. Instead, you normally define the components in the view and leave the job of creating `UIComponent` instances up to JSF or any pluggable component library. In the case of Facelets view technology, the component tags can be registered into JSF via either `@FacesComponent(createTag=true)` or a `<tag>` entry in a `*.taglib.xml` file along with the component type as follows:

```
<tag>
    <tag-name>someComponent</tag-name>
    <component>
        <component-type>project.SomeComponent</component-type>
    </component>
</tag>
```

As said, the standard JSF component set has the component type also defined in the concrete UIComponent classes behind the component tags. Those UIComponent classes are all located in the javax.faces.component.html package. The UIComponent class name can be derived from the component tag name by prefixing it with "Html". So is the component tag <h:outputText> backed by the HtmlOutputText component. JSF can, via either the @FacesComponent annotation or the <component> entry in faces-config.xml, figure out which component class exactly is associated with the component tag, so JSF knows that, for the <h:outputText> tag, it should create a concrete HtmlOutputText instance.

Once JSF has the concrete UIComponent instance at hand, it can figure out the component family as well as the renderer type by invoking the methods UIComponent#getFamily() and UIComponent#getRendererType(), respectively. This information is mandatory in order to create a concrete Renderer instance for the given UIComponent instance, as you can see in the following snippet:

```
Renderer renderer = FacesContext.getCurrentInstance().getRenderKit()
    .getRenderer(component.getFamily(), component.getRendererType());
```

The component family is basically a "hard-coded" constant which can be shared across multiple component types. It's "hard-coded" in such way that there's no setter for it. This is needed in order to get the concrete Renderer instances as they are not registered into JSF by component type but rather by component family. This allows the developer of the pluggable render kit to register the renderer type just once instead of multiple times for each known standard component type and unknown custom component type. Normally, the component family and renderer type are registered into JSF via either the @FacesRenderer annotation or the <renderer> entry in faces-config.xml. The following example demonstrates the usage with the annotation on a minimal renderer class.

```
@FacesRenderer(
    componentFamily=SomeComponent.COMPONENT_FAMILY,
    rendererType=SomeRenderer.RENDERER_TYPE)
public class SomeRenderer extends Renderer {
    public static final String RENDERER_TYPE = "project.SomeRenderer";
}
```

And the following example demonstrates the usage with the entry in `faces-config.xml`:

```
<render-kit>
    <renderer>
        <component-family>project.SomeFamily</component-family>
        <renderer-type>project.SomeRenderer</renderer-type>
        <renderer-class>
            com.example.project.renderer.SomeRenderer
        </renderer-class>
    </renderer>
</render-kit>
```

The renderer type is by default defined in the constructor of the concrete component class, as you might already have noticed in the code snippet of the `SomeComponent` class as shown previously. In case it's needed, the component subclass developer or even yourself as component end user can always override the default renderer instance of a component with the desired renderer instance. This can be done in various ways, all via XML. The first way is via the `<tag>` entry associated with the component tag in the `*.taglib.xml` file.

```
<tag>
    <tag-name>someComponent</tag-name>
    <component>
        <component-type>project.SomeComponent</component-type>
        <renderer-type>custom.OtherRenderer</renderer-type>
    </component>
</tag>
```

This affects application-wide and targets only the specific component tag. The second way is via a new <renderer> entry in faces-config.xml which targets exactly the desired component family and its default renderer type.

```
<render-kit>
    <renderer>
        <component-family>project.SomeFamily</component-family>
        <renderer-type>project.SomeRenderer</renderer-type>
        <renderer-class>
            com.example.custom.renderers.OtherRenderer
        </renderer-class>
    </renderer>
</render-kit>
```

This affects application-wide and targets *every* component tag associated with the given component family currently associated with the given renderer type. The third way is via the rendererType attribute of the component tag.

```
<x:someComponent ... rendererType="custom.OtherRenderer" />
```

This affects only the declared component tag and not others. Table 11-1 provides an overview of all component types, families, and renderer types of the standard JSF component set.

*Table 11-1. Component class, component type, component family and renderer type of standard JSF HTML component set*

| Component tag | Component class | Component type | Component family | Renderer type |
|---|---|---|---|---|
| \<h:body\> | HtmlBody | javax.faces.OutputBody | javax.faces.Output | javax.faces.Body |
| \<h:button\> | HtmlOutcomeTargetButton | javax.faces.HtmlOutcomeTargetButton | javax.faces.OutcomeTarget | javax.faces.Button |
| \<h:column\> | HtmlColumn | javax.faces.HtmlColumn | javax.faces.Column | null |
| \<h:commandButton\> | HtmlCommandButton | javax.faces.HtmlCommandButton | javax.faces.Command | javax.faces.Button |
| \<h:commandLink\> | HtmlCommandLink | javax.faces.HtmlCommandLink | javax.faces.Command | javax.faces.Link |
| \<h:commandScript\> | HtmlCommandScript | javax.faces.HtmlCommandScript | javax.faces.Command | javax.faces.Script |
| \<h:dataTable\> | HtmlDataTable | javax.faces.HtmlDataTable | javax.faces.Data | javax.faces.Table |
| \<h:doctype\> | HtmlDoctype | javax.faces.OutputDoctype | javax.faces.Output | javax.faces.Doctype |
| \<h:form\> | HtmlForm | javax.faces.HtmlForm | javax.faces.Form | javax.faces.Form |
| \<h:graphicImage\> | HtmlGraphicImage | javax.faces.HtmlGraphicImage | javax.faces.Graphic | javax.faces.Image |
| \<h:head\> | HtmlHead | javax.faces.OutputHead | javax.faces.Output | javax.faces.Head |
| \<h:inputFile\> | HtmlInputFile | javax.faces.HtmlInputFile | javax.faces.Input | javax.faces.File |
| \<h:inputHidden\> | HtmlInputHidden | javax.faces.HtmlInputHidden | javax.faces.Input | javax.faces.Hidden |
| \<h:inputSecret\> | HtmlInputSecret | javax.faces.HtmlInputSecret | javax.faces.Input | javax.faces.Secret |

| Component tag | Component class | Component type | Component family | Renderer type |
|---|---|---|---|---|
| <h:inputText> | HtmlInputText | javax.faces.HtmlInputText | javax.faces.Input | javax.faces.Text |
| <h:inputTextarea> | HtmlInputTextarea | javax.faces.HtmlInputTextarea | javax.faces.Input | javax.faces.Textarea |
| <h:link> | HtmlOutcomeTargetLink | javax.faces.HtmlOutcomeTargetLink | javax.faces.OutcomeTarget | javax.faces.Link |
| <h:message> | HtmlMessage | javax.faces.HtmlMessage | javax.faces.Message | javax.faces.Message |
| <h:messages> | HtmlMessages | javax.faces.HtmlMessages | javax.faces.Messages | javax.faces.Messages |
| <h:outputFormat> | HtmlOutputFormat | javax.faces.HtmlOutputFormat | javax.faces.Output | javax.faces.Format |
| <h:outputLabel> | HtmlOutputLabel | javax.faces.HtmlOutputLabel | javax.faces.Output | javax.faces.Label |
| <h:outputText> | HtmlOutputText | javax.faces.HtmlOutputText | javax.faces.Output | javax.faces.Text |
| <h:outputScript> | UIOutput | javax.faces.Output | javax.faces.Output | javax.faces.Script |
| <h:outputStylesheet> | UIOutput | javax.faces.Output | javax.faces.Output | javax.faces.resource.Stylesheet |
| <h:panelGrid> | HtmlPanelGrid | javax.faces.HtmlPanelGrid | javax.faces.Panel | javax.faces.Grid |
| <h:panelGroup> | HtmlPanelGroup | javax.faces.HtmlPanelGroup | javax.faces.Panel | javax.faces.Group |
| <h:selectBooleanCheckbox> | HtmlSelectBooleanCheckbox | javax.faces.HtmlSelectBooleanCheckbox | javax.faces.SelectBoolean | javax.faces.Checkbox |

*(continued)*

365

*Table 11-1. (continued)*

| Component tag | Component class | Component type | Component family | Renderer type |
|---|---|---|---|---|
| \<h:selectManyCheckbox> | HtmlSelectManyCheckbox | javax.faces. HtmlSelectManyCheckbox | javax.faces. SelectMany | javax.faces. Checkbox |
| \<h:selectManyListbox> | HtmlSelectManyListbox | javax.faces. HtmlSelectManyListbox | javax.faces. SelectMany | javax.faces.Listbox |
| \<h:selectManyMenu> | HtmlSelectManyMenu | javax.faces. HtmlSelectManyMenu | javax.faces. SelectMany | javax.faces.Menu |
| \<h:selectOneListbox> | HtmlSelectOneListbox | javax.faces. HtmlSelectOneListbox | javax.faces. SelectOne | javax.faces.Listbox |
| \<h:selectOneMenu> | HtmlSelectOneMenu | javax.faces.HtmlSelectOneMenu | javax.faces. SelectOne | javax.faces.Menu |
| \<h:selectOneRadio> | HtmlSelectOneRadio | javax.faces.HtmlSelectOneRadio | javax.faces. SelectOne | javax.faces.Radio |

If you carefully inspect the table, you'll see a certain pattern in the component family and renderer type, particularly with input, select, and command components. You'll notice that a renderer type can be shared across multiple components, even of a different family.

You'll also notice that there's one HTML component without a renderer type, `<h:column>`. This is a special component which cannot be used stand-alone but can only be used when nested in a specific parent component. From the standard JSF component set, that's so far only `<h:dataTable>`. Its renderer recognizes children of the type `UIColumn` and can act on them accordingly.

# Creating New Component and Renderer

If you paid closer attention to Table 3-1 in Chapter 3, you might have noticed that JSF doesn't provide any component to render a dynamic `<ul>` or `<ol>` or even `<dl>` element based on a provided array or collection value. It only supports that for the `<table>` element. True, the same could be achieved with Facelets `<ui:repeat>` and a bit of custom HTML code, but we'll take this as an opportunity to create a new custom component which renders an `<ul>` or `<ol>`.

The first step is to check which `UIComponent` subclass is suitable for the task we have in mind, so that we can reduce the custom code logic to a minimum. In the `javax.faces.component` package you can find a bunch of `UIXxx` component subclasses. If you want to create a new form component, extend from `UIForm`. If you want to create a new input component, extend from `UIInput`. If you want to create a new output component, extend from `UIOutput`. If you want to create a new data iterator component, extend from `UIData`. There is rarely any need to extend from `UIComponent` directly. We'd like to be able to iterate over a collection in order to generate `<li>` elements inside the `<ul>`, so we'll pick `UIData`. It has a lot of iteration and state saving logic already implemented. Following is the custom component class `com.example.project.component.DataList`:

```
@FacesComponent(createTag=true)
public class DataList extends UIData {

    public DataList() {
        setRendererType(DataListRenderer.RENDERER_TYPE);
    }
}
```

Is that really all? Yes, the `UIData` superclass already hsd everything we need and all the HTML producing code just goes into the `DataListRenderer` which will be shown shortly. You'll notice that the `@FacesComponent` annotation declares a `createTag=true` attribute. This basically instructs JSF that it should automatically create a component tag the predefined XML namespace `http://xmlns.jcp.org/jsf/component`. In other words, the above tag is available in the Facelets file as follows:

```
< ... xmlns:my="http://xmlns.jcp.org/jsf/component">
    ...
    <my:dataList ...>
        ...
    </my:dataList>
```

The XML namespace prefix "my" is of course your choice. Generally, you'd like to pick some sort of abbreviation of your company name here. You can also override the predefined XML namespace with the `namespace` attribute.

```
@FacesComponent(createTag=true, namespace="http://example.com/ui")
```

This will then be available as follows:

```
< ... xmlns:ex="http://example.com/ui">
    ...
    <ex:dataList ...>
        ...
    </ex:dataList>
```

This namespace is unfortunately not unifiable with the `<namespace>` of a custom `*.taglib.xml` file. If you use the same namespace for both, then JSF will prefer the `*.taglib.xml` one over the `@FacesComponent` one and hence be unable to find the custom component tag. That is, in practically anything Java EE related, any XML-based registration of a thing has higher precedence than Java annotation-based registration of the very same thing.

You'd basically need to explicitly register the custom component over there in the `*.taglib.xml` file as well. Here's how the `/WEB-INF/example.taglib.xml` as created in the section "Tag Files" in Chapter 7 could be extended with the registration of the custom component, which is essentially the same as what the `@FacesComponent` is doing for you.

```xml
<?xml version="1.0" encoding="UTF-8"?>
<facelet-taglib
    xmlns="http://xmlns.jcp.org/xml/ns/javaee"
    xmlns:xsi="http://www.w3.org/2001/XMLSchema-instance"
    xsi:schemaLocation="http://xmlns.jcp.org/xml/ns/javaee
      http://xmlns.jcp.org/xml/ns/javaee/web-facelettaglibrary_2_3.xsd"
    version="2.3"
>

    <namespace>http://example.com/tags</namespace>
    <short-name>t</short-name>

    <!-- Other tags here -->

    <tag>
        <description>Renders a HTML list.</description>
        <tag-name>dataList</tag-name>
        <component>
            <component-type>dataList</component-type>
        </component>
    </tag>
</facelet-taglib>
```

This way the custom component is available in the same namespace as the other tags.

```
< ... xmlns:t="http://example.com/tags">
    ...
    <t:dataList ...>
        ...
    </t:dataList>
```

Now, you can essentially remove all attributes of the @FacesComponent so that it becomes just @FacesComponent. Yes, as you have seen in the example.taglib.xml, the component type defaults to the class name with the first character lowercased. You can always override it by explicitly specifying it as the value of the @FacesComponent annotation. Generally, you'd like to prefix it with the name of the company. It's a good practice to define it as a public constant so that others could, if necessary, look it up in the Javadoc and/or use it for Application#createComponent().

```
@FacesComponent(DataList.COMPONENT_TYPE)
public class DataList extends UIData {

    public static final String COMPONENT_TYPE = "example.DataList";

    public DataList() {
        setRendererType(DataListRenderer.RENDERER_TYPE);
    }
}
```

Now adjust the component type in the example.taglib.xml accordingly.

```
<component>
    <component-type>example.DataList</component-type>
</component>
```

The *.taglib.xml also gives you room to register the attributes via <attribute> entries, although that may end up in some verbose code. You should already have seen that in the section "Tag files" in Chapter 7. Unfortunately, the current JSF version doesn't offer an annotation to declaratively declare an "official" component attribute. There's no such thing as @FacesAttribute private Iterable value. Yet. This may come in a JSF.next. The non-official way, without any <attribute>, also works just fine. You can declare any attribute you want on the component tag in the view.

```
<t:dataList foo="bar" bar="foo" />
```

That's just the freedom of XML. Whether the actual component or renderer implementation actually does something with it is another story. You could even declare a custom attribute on an existing component and just plug an extended Renderer in order to process that attribute. More later in the section "Extending Existing Renderer." Talking about renderers, our <t:dataList> still needs its renderer as registered in its constructor. Here's what the com.example.project.renderer.DataListRenderer looks like.

```
@FacesRenderer(
    componentFamily=UIData.COMPONENT_FAMILY,
    rendererType=DataListRenderer.RENDERER_TYPE)
public class DataListRenderer extends Renderer {

    public static final String RENDERER_TYPE = "example.List";
```

```java
@Override
public void encodeBegin
    (FacesContext context, UIComponent component)
        throws IOException
{
    ResponseWriter writer = context.getResponseWriter();
    UIData data = (UIData) component;

    if (data.getRowCount() > 0) {
        writer.startElement("ul", component);
    }
}

@Override
public void encodeChildren
    (FacesContext context, UIComponent component)
        throws IOException
{
    ResponseWriter writer = context.getResponseWriter();
    UIData data = (UIData) component;

    for (int i = 0; i < data.getRowCount(); i++) {
        data.setRowIndex(i);
        writer.startElement("li", component);

        if (component.getChildCount() > 0) {
            for (UIComponent child : component.getChildren()) {
                child.encodeAll(context);
            }
        }

        writer.endElement("li");
    }

    data.setRowIndex(-1);
}

@Override
public void encodeEnd
```

```
        (FacesContext context, UIComponent component)
            throws IOException
    {
        ResponseWriter writer = context.getResponseWriter();
        UIData data = (UIData) component;

        if (data.getRowCount() > 0) {
            writer.endElement("ul");
        }
    }
}
```

In hindsight, it's relatively simple. We're delegating as much as possible of the hard work to the JSF-provided UIData superclass. In the encodeBegin() you start the <ul> element when the data model is not empty. This is to be checked by examining the result of UIData#getRowCount(). Its Javadoc[1] basically says:

*Return the number of rows in the underlying data model. If the number of available rows is unknown, return -1.*

The term "rows" is indeed strongly related to tables. This is also what this superclass is originally designed for: <h:dataTable>. The term "item" would have been more general, but it is what it is.

Then, in the encodeChildren() method, we set the current row index via the UIData#setRowIndex() method, start the <li> element, encode all children as is via UIComponent#encodeAll() on each of them, and finally end the <li> element. Once the loop is done, we explicitly make it clear to the UIData superclass by invoking UIData#setRowIndex() with a value of -1. Its Javadoc[2] says:

*If the new rowIndex value is -1: If the var property is not null, remove the corresponding request scope attribute (if any). Reset the state information for all descendant components.*

---

[1]https://javaee.github.io/javaee-spec/javadocs/javax/faces/component/UIData.html#getRowCount--.

[2]https://javaee.github.io/javaee-spec/javadocs/javax/faces/component/UIData.html#setRowIndex-int-.

It thus clears out any state related to the iteration. This is very important;z otherwise it might cause side effects further down in the component tree or even cause a corrupted view state when it by itself needs to traverse the data model. Finally, in the encodeEnd() method, it will end the <ul> element based on same conditions as in encodeBegin().

The UIData#setRowIndex() call in the encodeChildren() method will under the hood extract the data model from the value attribute and wrap it in a suitable implementation of the javax.faces.model.DataModel abstract class.[3] So far, as per the Javadoc of UIData#getValue(),[4] the following types of the object behind the value attribute are supported, in this scanning order:

1.  java.util.List (since 1.0)

2.  Arrays (since 1.0)

3.  java.sql.ResultSet (since 1.0)

4.  javax.servlet.jsp.jstl.sql.Result (since 1.0)

5.  java.util.Collection (since 2.2)

6.  java.lang.Iterable (since 2.3)

7.  java.util.Map (since 2.3)

8.  Types for which a suitable DataModel has been registered via @FacesDataModel (since 2.3)

9.  All other types will be adapted using the ScalarDataModel class, which will treat the object as a single row of data (since 1.0)

You would indeed not expect to see anyone passing around a plain java.sql. ResultSet in a modern Java EE application, let alone see JSP pages with JSTL <sql:xxx> tags. But this all is for backward compatibility. Remember, JSF was introduced in 2004. Backward compatibility was one of its strongest keys in surviving up to today. They're certainly candidates to be removed, but not now.

And, there's indeed an overlap between some types; List and Collection could easily be covered by Iterable as they both implement this interface. But this has a performance reason. For a List, the items are accessed directly by index by the

---

[3]https://javaee.github.io/javaee-spec/javadocs/javax/faces/model/DataModel.html.
[4]https://javaee.github.io/javaee-spec/javadocs/javax/faces/component/UIData. html#getValue--.

ListDataModel; for a Collection, the items are extracted first via Collection#toArray() and then accessed by index by the CollectionDataModel; and for an Iterable, the items are simply iterated and collected into a new List first by the IterableDataModel. It may make a difference.

You'll also see that JSF 2.3 has not only added two new data models but even introduces a new annotation to register a custom one. Previously, you'd need to manually wrap the custom collection in the custom data model every time before passing to a UIData component. The DataModel abstract class has the disadvantage of not being Serializable itself which more or less forces you to make a @ViewScoped bean holding such a data model to have a lazy loading getter on a transient data model property as follows:

```
private YourCollection yourCollection;
private transient YourDataModel dataModel;

public DataModel getDataModel() {
    if (dataModel == null) {
        dataModel = new YourDataModel(yourCollection);
    }
    return dataModel;
}
```

Ideally, the UIData should by itself recognize YourCollection type and automatically wrap it in a YourDataModel. The new @FacesDataModel annotation does exactly that.

```
@FacesDataModel(forClass=YourCollection.class)
public class YourDataModel<E> extends DataModel<E> {}
```

Coming back to the custom renderer, there's one method left unexplained: the getRendersChildren(). It's been overridden to explicitly return true. You'll probably ask yourself, why was it initially false? Why not just let it be the default behavior of encodeChildren() and rely on any overridden encodeChildren() method whether it wants to invoke encodeAll() on the children? This was actually an historic oversight in the specification. Originally, the encodeAll() method didn't exist. It was only added in JSF 1.2 and it basically made the getRendersChildren() obsolete. But for backward compatibility this complexity was introduced.

In a nutshell, always let getRendersChildren() return true if you have overridden the encodeChildren() method. Otherwise the children won't be encoded at all.

Last but not least, you'll probably also wonder why we don't "simply" override the encodeBegin(), encodeChildren(), (and getRendersChildren()), and encodeEnd() of the DataList component but instead create a "whole" renderer implementation. The main reason is: simplicity and extensibility. Those methods are on UIComponent specified to do more than only rendering. They also check if the UIComponent#isRendered() returns true. encodeBegin() also fires PreRenderComponentEvent and pushes the current component into the EL (Expression Language) scope as #{component}. encodeEnd() pops #{component} out of the EL scope. And they also check if there's a renderer attached and, if so, delegate to it. That's all specified in their Javadoc. You'd need to manually take care of them yourself when you override those methods. That's unnecessarily repeated work. And, when someone in the future wants to adjust the rendering of the component, they won't be able to plug a custom renderer if your component doesn't check for it.

# Extending Existing Component

Imagine that there's an existing component whose behavior you'd like to adjust, usually by adding one or more new custom attributes. If those attributes are purely output-only, then you could just make use of the pass-through attributes feature which was introduced in JSF 2.2. Previously, any custom attribute which wasn't officially supported by the component was simply ignored during view render time. For example, when you'd like to add the missing accept attribute[5] to the existing <h:inputFile> component,[6] simply adding the attribute as follows won't work.

```
<h:inputFile id="photo" value="#{editProfile.photo}" accept="image/*" />
```

With the pass-through attributes feature you could explicitly instruct JSF to render the custom attribute anyway. This can be done in two ways. The first way is registering it via the http://xmlns.jcp.org/jsf/passthrough XML namespace.

```
< ... xmlns:h="http://xmlns.jcp.org/jsf/html"
    xmlns:a="http://xmlns.jcp.org/jsf/passthrough">
```

---

[5]https://developer.mozilla.org/en-US/docs/Web/HTML/Element/input/file.
[6]https://javaserverfaces.github.io/docs/2.3/vdldocs/facelets/h/inputFile.html.

```
...
<h:form enctype="multipart/form-data">
    <h:inputFile ... a:accept="image/*" />
</h:form>
```

Another way is declaring it via the `<f:passThroughAttribute>` tag.

```
< ... xmlns:f="http://xmlns.jcp.org/jsf/core"
    xmlns:h="http://xmlns.jcp.org/jsf/html">
    ...
    <h:form enctype="multipart/form-data">
        <h:inputFile ...>
            <f:passThroughAttribute name="accept" value="image/*" />
        </h:inputFile>
    </h:form>
```

It'll just work fine on the client side either way. On the browsers supporting this attribute, the file browse dialog will only show the files matching the comma separated IANA (Internet Assigned Numbers Authority) media types[7] specified in the `accept` attribute. However, this won't work in browsers not supporting this attribute,[8] nor will it validate anything on the server side. Even if the browser supports it, any malicious-minded end user can easily manipulate the retrieved HTML document and remove the `accept` attribute and hence be able to upload a different file type.

For exactly that server-side work, you'd like to extend the `<h:inputFile>` component to perform validation based on the `accept` attribute. The first step is looking at which `UIComponent` class exactly is represented by `<h:inputFile>`. As you can see in Table 11-1, that's `javax.faces.component.html.HtmlInputFile`. Let's start by extending it and adding the new `accept` attribute.

```
@FacesComponent(createTag=true)
public class InputFile extends HtmlInputFile {

    @Override
    public void encodeBegin(FacesContext context) throws IOException {
        String accept = getAccept();
```

---

[7]www.iana.org/assignments/media-types/media-types.xhtml.
[8]https://caniuse.com/#feat=input-file-accept.

```
        if (accept != null) {
            getPassThroughAttributes().put("accept", accept);
        }
        super.encodeBegin(context);
    }

    public String getAccept() {
        return (String) getStateHelper().eval("accept");
    }

    public void setAccept(String accept) {
        getStateHelper().put("accept", accept);
    }
}
```

Note that there's no property for the accept attribute. Any public component attribute must be represented by a getter/setter pair which delegates further to UIComponent#getStateHelper(). Basically, you must delegate all view-scoped component attributes to the StateHelper. This will in turn take care that the right deltas end up in the JSF view state. This is of course optional, but not doing so will make the component instance not programmatically manipulatable. Any changes performed during a previous HTTP request would get lost during the subsequent HTTP postback request for the very simple reason that the UIComponent instance is recreated from scratch.

Also note that the new accept attribute is simply added as a pass-through attribute in the encodeBegin() method before delegating to the superclass method where the actual rendering job takes place. This removes the need to create a whole custom renderer for the particular purpose of rendering a new attribute. Let's test it now.

```
< ... xmlns:h="http://xmlns.jcp.org/jsf/html"
    xmlns:my="http://xmlns.jcp.org/jsf/component">
    ...
    <h:form enctype="multipart/form-data">
        <my:inputFile id="photo" value="#{editProfile.photo}"
            accept="image/*" required="true">
            <f:ajax listener="#{editProfile.upload}" render="photo_m" />
        </my:inputFile>
        <h:message id="photo_m" for="photo" />
    </h:form>
```

For the sake of completeness, here's what the backing bean looks like.

```
@Named @RequestScoped
public class EditProfile {

    private Part photo;

    public void upload() {
        String fileName = photo.getSubmittedFileName();
        String fileType = photo.getContentType();
        long fileSize = photo.getSize();

        System.out.println("File name: " + fileName);
        System.out.println("File type: " + fileType);
        System.out.println("File size: " + fileSize);
    }

    // Add/generate getter and setter.
}
```

Now we have basically created the UIComponent equivalent of <h:inputFile> with a pass-through accept attribute. The next step is implementing server-side validation of whether the media type of the uploaded file matches the specified accept attribute. For this, we'd like to override UIInput#validateValue() in our InputFile class as below. This runs during the process validations phase (third phase).

```
@Override
protected void validateValue(FacesContext context, Object newValue) {
    String accept = getAccept();

    if (accept != null && newValue instanceof Part) {
        Part part = (Part) newValue;
        String contentType = context.getExternalContext()
            .getMimeType(part.getSubmittedFileName());
        String acceptPattern = accept.trim()
            .replace("*", ".*").replaceAll("\\s*,\\s*", "|");

        if (contentType == null || !contentType.matches(acceptPattern)) {
            String message = "Unacceptable file type";
            context.addMessage(getClientId(context), new FacesMessage(
```

```
                FacesMessage.SEVERITY_ERROR, message, null));
            setValid(false);
        }
    }

    if (isValid()) {
        super.validateValue(context, newValue);
    }
}
```

As you see, it will basically check if the accept attribute is specified and if there's a submitted file, and if so then convert the accept attribute to a regular expression pattern and match the content type of the submitted file against it. The accept attribute represents a comma separated string of IANA media types wherein the asterisk is used as a wildcard and the comma is used as a disjunction operator. An example accept value of "image/*,application/pdf" is this way converted to a regular expression of "image/.*|application/pdf". If it doesn't match, then it will add a faces message associated with the component to the faces context and mark the component as invalid by calling UIInput#setValid() with false. In the end, if the component is valid, it will continue the validation call to the superclass.

Further there's another thing to mention: the content type is not obtained from Part#getContentType() but from ExternalContext#getMimeType() based on the submitted file name. This is just to cover the corner case that the client doesn't send a content type along, or even sends one which is not understood by the server. ExternalContext#getMimeType() basically obtains the list of known content types from <mime-mapping> entries in web.xml. The server itself has some default values and you can override or extend them in the web application's own web.xml.

Now the file's content type attribute is filtered on the client side and validated on the server side. All good and well, but this of course only validates the file's content type based on the file name and not the file's actual content. Imagine that one creates a ZIP file and simply renames the file extension to become an image file, or even an executable file with malware. It would still pass through the file type validation on both the client and server side. Frankly, this responsibility is not up to the component itself, but to you, the JSF developer. The correct solution would be to create a custom validator and attach it to the component. Here's what such an image file validator can look like, with a little help from the Java2D API which is capable of parsing image files. If it throws an exception or returns null, then it's very definitely not an image file.

```java
@FacesValidator("project.ImageFileValidator")
public class ImageFileValidator implements Validator<Part> {

    @Override
    public void validate
        (FacesContext context, UIComponent component, Part value)
            throws ValidatorException
    {
        if (value == null) {
            return; // Let @NotNull or required="true" handle.
        }

        try {
            ImageIO.read(value.getInputStream()).toString();
        }
        catch (Exception e) {
            String message = "Not an image file";
            throw new ValidatorException(new FacesMessage(message), e);
        }
    }
}
```

In order to get it to run, declare it as validator attribute of the component tag.

```
<my:inputFile ... validator="project.ImageFileValidator" />
```

It works beautifully. Now, when validation passes as well, the backing bean action method is invoked wherein you can save the uploaded file to the desired location. This could be implemented as follows:

```java
public void upload() {
    Path folder = Paths.get("/path/to/uploads");
    String fileName = Paths.get(photo.getSubmittedFileName())
        .getFileName().toString();
    int indexOfLastDot = fileName.lastIndexOf('.');
    String name = fileName.substring(0, indexOfLastDot);
    String extension = fileName.substring(indexOfLastDot);
    FacesMessage message = new FacesMessage();
```

```
try (InputStream contents = photo.getInputStream()) {
    Path file = Files.createTempFile(folder, name + "-", extension);
    Files.copy(contents, file, StandardCopyOption.REPLACE_EXISTING);
    message.setSummary("Uploaded file successfully saved.");
}
catch (IOException e) {
    message.setSummary("Could not save uploaded file, try again.");
    message.setSeverity(FacesMessage.SEVERITY_ERROR);
    e.printStackTrace();
}

FacesContext.getCurrentInstance().addMessage(null, message);
}
```

You might wonder why it seems to save the uploaded file as a temporary file. This is actually not true. We're just utilizing the Files#createTempFile() facility in order to guarantee the uniqueness of the file name of the saved file. It will automatically include a unique random string between the file name and the file extension. Otherwise, when multiple people upload different files with coincidentally the same name, they may overwrite each other and we'd lose information.

# Extending Existing Renderer

Imagine that there's an existing renderer which has logic bugs or shortcomings and you'd like to quickly patch it by extending it instead of rewriting from scratch. Unfortunately, it sounds far easier than it actually is. That is, standard renderer implementations are not part of the standard JSF API, contrary to standard HTML component implementations which are available in the javax.faces.component.html package. The actual standard HTML renderer implementations are provided by the JSF implementation itself. Mojarra has them in the com.sun.faces.renderkit.html_basic package and MyFaces has them in the org.apache.myfaces.renderkit.html package.

Another problem with those standard HTML renderers is relatively poor abstraction of the code. Basically all those standard HTML renderers don't have abstracted-out pieces of code which solely emit HTML markup in such way that it's fully separated from the logic. In other words, when you need to fix some logic, you'd almost always also have to write or copy/paste all the code responsible for emitting HTML.

A common real-world example is the desire to let <h:message> or <h:messages> render the faces message unescaped, so that you can embed some HTML code in a faces message, more than often to provide a link to the desired target page (e.g., "Unknown user, perhaps you want to <a href="login">Log in</a>?"). The standard <h:message> component doesn't support such facility and the HTML-escaping is controlled by its renderer which in turn is thus JSF implementation dependent. This JSF built-in HTML escaping is found over all place and is a very important guard against possible XSS attack holes when you're about to embed user-controlled data in the web page. There are a handful of components which have an explicit attribute to turn off this HTML-escaping, such as <h:outputText> with its escape attribute, <f:selectItem> with its itemEscaped attribute, and <f:selectItems> with its itemLabelEscaped attributes. Such an attribute is, however, absent in <h:message> and <h:messages>. See also JSF spec issue 634.[9] Perhaps it will be added in JSF.next, but for now you can't go around a third-party component library or extending the existing standard HTML renderer.

We'll take that as an example to extend an existing standard HTML renderer for <h:message>. The first step is looking at which renderer exactly is currently used by the <h:message> component. In Table 11-1 you will see that this component is backed by the HtmlMessage class. The currently used renderer implementation is programmatically as follows:

```
String componentFamily = HtmlMessage.COMPONENT_FAMILY;
String rendererType = new HtmlMessage().getRendererType();
Renderer renderer = FacesContext.getCurrentInstance().getRenderKit()
    .getRenderer(componentFamily, rendererType);
System.out.println(renderer.getClass());
```

In case you're using Mojarra as JSF implementation, it'll print as follows:

```
class com.sun.faces.renderkit.html_basic.MessageRenderer
```

That's thus exactly the renderer class we'd like to extend. Mojarra is open source and its source code is currently available at https://github.com/javaserverfaces/mojarra. Once you've gotten the MessageRenderer source code at hands, the next step is to figure out where exactly the summary and detail of the FacesMessage is being rendered and how exactly we can override it with a minimum of code. We can see in the source code that it takes place in the encodeEnd() method which, in the current Mojarra

---

[9]https://github.com/javaee/javaserverfaces-spec/issues/634.

2.3.3 version, is already 182 lines of code. It's using `ResponseWriter#writeText()`[10] to render the summary and detail. We'd like to replace this by `ResponseWriter#write()` so that it doesn't perform any escaping.

We can of course extend the class, copy/paste all the 182 lines of the `encodeEnd()` method, and adjust the `writeText()` calls for the `summary` as well as `detail` variables as follows:

```
Object escape = component.getAttributes().get("escape");

if (escape == null || Boolean.parseBoolean(escape.toString())) {
    writer.writeText(summary, component, null);
}
else {
    writer.write(summary);
}
```

However, this is not terribly elegant. What if we were to capture all `writeText()` calls during the `encodeEnd()` method and transparently delegate to `write()`? That would look much better. You can achieve this by wrapping the `ResponseWriter`, setting it on the faces context, and passing it through the superclass. Almost any public JSF API artifact has an equivalent `XxxWrapper` class as well in the API. You can find them all in the "All known implementing classes" section of the `javax.faces.FacesWrapper` Javadoc.[11] All those wrapper classes make JSF very easily customizable and extensible. All of them have a constructor taking the to-be-wrapped class and you basically just need to pick one or more of the methods you'd like to decorate.

All in all, here's how we could extend the `MessageRenderer` to delegate all `writeText()` calls during the `encodeEnd()` method to `write()`.

```
public class EscapableMessageRenderer extends MessageRenderer {

    @Override
    public void encodeEnd
        (FacesContext context, UIComponent component)
            throws IOException
```

---

[10]https://javaee.github.io/javaee-spec/javadocs/javax/faces/context/ResponseWriter.html#writeText-java.lang.Object-javax.faces.component.UIComponent-java.lang.String-.

[11]https://javaee.github.io/javaee-spec/javadocs/javax/faces/FacesWrapper.html.

```
    {
        ResponseWriter writer = context.getResponseWriter();

        try {
            context.setResponseWriter(new ResponseWriterWrapper(writer) {
                @Override
                public void writeText
                    (Object text, UIComponent component, String property)
                        throws IOException
                {
                    String string = text.toString();
                    Object escape = component.getAttributes()
                        .get("escape");
                    if (escape == null
                        || Boolean.parseBoolean(escape.toString()))
                    {
                        super.writeText(string, component, property);
                    }
                    else {
                        super.write(string);
                    }
                }
            });

            super.encodeEnd(context, component);
        }
        finally {
            context.setResponseWriter(writer);
        }
    }
}
```

Do note that it's very important to restore the original response writer in the `finally` of the `try` block wherein the wrapped response writer is being used. In order to get it to run, register it as follows in `faces-config.xml` on the component family and renderer type as associated with the `<h:message>` component:

```
<render-kit>
    <renderer>
        <component-family>javax.faces.Message</component-family>
        <renderer-type>javax.faces.Message</renderer-type>
        <renderer-class>
            com.example.project.renderer.EscapableMessageRenderer
        </renderer-class>
    </renderer>
</render-kit>
```

No, you cannot use the `@FacesRenderer` annotation for this. This won't work when extending an existing renderer. The original renderers are by themselves already registered on the very same component family and renderer type, somewhere in an XML file. And you know, an XML-based configuration always gets higher precedence over an annotation-based configuration when both are discovered.

Now you can just set the `escape` attribute of the existing `<h:message>` component to `false` in order to get the extended renderer to do its job.

```
<h:message ... escape="false" />
```

Beware that you don't embed user-controlled input in any faces message which gets displayed in there, or you'll open up a potential XSS attack hole.

## Custom Tag Handlers

In Chapter 3, you learned about the difference between the view build time and the view render time, and that tag handlers such as JSTL run while building the JSF component tree while JSF components run while processing the HTTP request and response through the JSF life cycle. Not only can JSF components be customized but also tag handlers. This is particularly useful when you want to control the building of the JSF component tree instead of processing the HTTP request and response.

<f:viewParam> is useful on master-detail pages. From the master page, you can link to the detail page with the entity ID as the parameter. In the detail page, you can load the entity by ID via <f:viewParam>. It goes as follows:

```
<f:metadata>
    <f:viewParam name="id" value="#{editItem.item}"
        converter="project.ItemConverter" converterMessage="Unknown item"
        required="true" requiredMessage="Bad request">
    </f:viewParam>
</f:metadata>
```

When conversion or validation fails, a faces message will be added to the faces context of the current page. However, more often you'd just like to directly redirect the user back to the master page. This is relatively trivial to implement with <f:event> on PostValidateEvent. No, <f:viewAction> won't work as that wouldn't be invoked in first place when there's a conversion or validation error.

```
<f:metadata>
    ...
    <f:event type="postValidate" listener="#{editItem.onload()}" />
</f:metadata>
```

Wherein the onload() method looks as follows:

```
public void onload() throws IOException {
    FacesContext context = FacesContext.getCurrentInstance();
    if (context.isValidationFailed()) {
        ExternalContext ec = context.getExternalContext();
        ec.redirect(ec.getRequestContextPath() + "/items.xhtml");
    }
}
```

Okay, that works, but this will end up in boilerplate code when you have more of such pages. Ideally, you'd like to be able to declaratively register an event listener on <f:viewParam> itself in a self-documenting way like below so that you can keep the backing bean code free of manual request-response processing clutter.

```
<f:metadata>
    <f:viewParam ...>
        <t:viewParamValidationFailed redirect="/items.xhtml" />
    </f:viewParam>
</f:metadata>
```

This can be achieved with a tag handler which basically registers a new system event listener on the `UIViewParameter` component represented by the `<f:viewParam>` tag. The tag handler class must extend from `javax.faces.view.facelets.TagHandler`.

```java
public class ViewParamValidationFailed extends TagHandler
    implements ComponentSystemEventListener
{
    private String redirect;

    public ViewParamValidationFailed(TagConfig config) {
        super(config);
        redirect = getRequiredAttribute("redirect").getValue();
    }

    @Override
    public void apply(FaceletContext context, UIComponent parent)
        throws IOException
    {
        if (parent instanceof UIViewParameter
            && !context.getFacesContext().isPostback())
        {
            parent.subscribeToEvent(PostValidateEvent.class, this);
        }
    }

    @Override
    public void processEvent(ComponentSystemEvent event)
        throws AbortProcessingException
    {
        UIComponent parent = event.getComponent();
        parent.unsubscribeFromEvent(PostValidateEvent.class, this);
        FacesContext context = event.getFacesContext();
```

```
    if (context.isValidationFailed()) {
        try {
            ExternalContext ec = context.getExternalContext();
            ec.redirect(ec.getRequestContextPath() + redirect);
        }
        catch (IOException e) {
            throw new AbortProcessingException(e);
        }
    }
}
```

Indeed, this also implements `javax.faces.event.ComponentSystemEventListener`. This is not strictly required for a tag handler; it's just done for code convenience in this specific example. The overridden `apply()` method is for `TagHandler` and the overridden `processEvent()` method is for `ComponentSystemEventListener`. In the `apply()` method we have the opportunity to programmatically manipulate the parent component, before it's being added to the component tree.

We can programmatically achieve the same behavior as `<f:event>` by calling `UICo mponent#subscribeToEvent()`, passing the component system event type and listener instance of interest. The listener instance of interest happens to be just the current tag handler instance. When the component system event of interest has been published by the application, then the `processEvent()` method of the listener instance will be invoked.

The first thing we do in `processEvent()` is to unsubscribe the listener instance. This is done on purpose because component system event listeners are considered stateful and therefore are inherently saved in the JSF view state. An easy way to observe this is to reconfigure JSF to save the view state on the client side by explicitly setting the `javax.faces.STATE_SAVING_METHOD` context parameter to `client` in `web.xml` and inspecting the size of the `javax.faces.ViewState` hidden input field in the generated HTML output of any JSF form. Every time you add `<f:event>`, or don't unsubscribe `ComponentSystemEventListener` after it has done its job, the size of the JSF view state grows with the serialized form of the listener instance. In this specific use case of a listener which should only run during a non-postback, that's just unnecessary; hence the explicit unsubscribe.

Now, in order to get it to run, register it in /WEB-INF/example.taglib.xml as follows:

```
<tag>
    <tag-name>viewParamValidationFailed</tag-name>
    <handler-class>
        com.example.project.taghandler.ViewParamValidationFailed
    </handler-class>
</tag>
```

# Packaging in a Distributable JAR

In case you have developed a bunch of reusable components, renderers, tag handlers, tag files, composite components, and what not, and you'd like to package it in a JAR file for inclusion in /WEB-INF/lib of a web application, then you need to create a so-called web fragment project. Basically all JSF-oriented components and utility libraries such as OmniFaces, PrimeFaces, OptimusFaces, BootsFaces, ButterFaces, and DeltaSpike are built like this. In Maven perspective, it's merely a JAR project. The key is to put files which you normally put in the src/main/webapp folder of a Maven WAR project in the src/main/resources/META-INF/resources/[libraryName] folder of the Maven JAR project. There is one main exception, all deployment descriptor files which you normally put in src/main/webapp/WEB-INF, such as web.xml, faces-config.xml, *.taglib.xml, and beans.xml go directly in the src/main/resources/META-INF folder. Another exception is that the web.xml file is to be replaced by web-fragment.xml.

The [libraryName] subfolder in the resources folder represents the "library name" which is generally the URL-friendly form of the project name. For example, "omnifaces", "primefaces", "optimusfaces", "bsf", "butterfaces", etc. Exactly this library name is then usable in the library attribute of resource components such as <h:outputScript>, <h:outputStylesheet>, and <h:graphicImage>. Below is what such a Maven JAR project looks like in Eclipse when organized to conform to the "web fragment" rules. Note particularly the structure of the src/main/resources folder. Of course, any Java classes can go inside the src/main/java folder in the usual way.

```
∨ 🗂 common
   > 🗁 src/main/java
   ∨ 🗁 src/main/resources
      ∨ 🗁 META-INF
         ∨ 🗁 resources
            ∨ 🗁 common
               ∨ 🗁 components
                     someComposite.xhtml
               ∨ 🗁 images
                     some.svg
               ∨ 🗁 includes
                     some.xhtml
               ∨ 🗁 scripts
                     some.js
               ∨ 🗁 styles
                     some.css
               ∨ 🗁 tags
                     someTag.xhtml
               ∨ 🗁 templates
                     some.xhtml
         X beans.xml
         X common.taglib.xml
         X faces-config.xml
         X web-fragment.xml
   > 🗁 src/test/java
   > 🗁 src/test/resources
   > 📚 JRE System Library [JavaSE-1.8]
   > 🗁 src
   > 🗁 target
     M pom.xml
```

Whereby the common.taglib.xml looks like the following, with the composite library name set to a path relative to src/main/resources/META-INF/resources and the tag file source set to a path relative to the location of the *.taglib.xml file itself.

```
<?xml version="1.0" encoding="UTF-8"?>
<facelet-taglib
    xmlns="http://xmlns.jcp.org/xml/ns/javaee"
    xmlns:xsi="http://www.w3.org/2001/XMLSchema-instance"
    xsi:schemaLocation="http://xmlns.jcp.org/xml/ns/javaee
        http://xmlns.jcp.org/xml/ns/javaee/web-facelettaglibrary_2_3.xsd"
    version="2.3"
>
```

```
<namespace>http://example.com/common</namespace>
<short-name>common</short-name>
<composite-library-name>common/components</composite-library-name>

<tag>
    <tag-name>someTag</tag-name>
    <source>resources/common/tags/someTag.xhtml</source>
</tag>
</facelet-taglib>
```

And whereby the web-fragment.xml looks as follows, nearly identical to web.xml, only with a different root element, <web-fragment> instead of <web-app>.

```
<?xml version="1.0" encoding="UTF-8"?>
<web-fragment
    xmlns="http://xmlns.jcp.org/xml/ns/javaee"
    xmlns:xsi="http://www.w3.org/2001/XMLSchema-instance"
    xsi:schemaLocation="http://xmlns.jcp.org/xml/ns/javaee
        http://xmlns.jcp.org/xml/ns/javaee/web-fragment_4_0.xsd"
    version="4.0"
>
    <name>common</name>
</web-fragment>
```

Once such a web fragment project is built as a JAR file and included in /WEB-INF/lib of the main web application project, then the resources of the JAR are available in the Facelets files of the main web application project via the library name "common" as follows:

```
<ui:composition template="/common/templates/some.xhtml"
    xmlns="http://www.w3.org/1999/xhtml"
    xmlns:h="http://xmlns.jcp.org/jsf/html"
    xmlns:ui="http://xmlns.jcp.org/jsf/facelets"
    xmlns:common="http://example.com/common"
>
    <ui:define name="content">
        <common:someComposite />
        <h:graphicImage library="common" name="js/some.svg" />
        <ui:include src="/common/includes/some.xhtml" />
        <h:outputScript library="common" name="scripts/some.js" />
```

```
        <h:outputStylesheet library="common" name="styles/some.css" />
        <common:someTag />
    </ui:define>
</ui:composition>
```

# Resource Dependencies

There may be cases whereby your custom component or renderer depends on a specific JavaScript or Stylesheet resource, for which you would like to avoid the end user having to manually include it via <h:outputScript> or <h:outputStylesheet>. In such cases, you may find the @javax.faces.application.ResourceDependency annotation[12] useful. Imagine that you would like to automatically include common:scripts/some.js and common:styles/some.css along with a particular custom component; then you can do so as follows:

```
@ResourceDependency(library="common", name="some.css", target="head")
@ResourceDependency(library="common", name="some.js", target="head")
public class SomeCustomComponent extends UIComponent {
    // ...
}
```

You can of course also include JSF's own javax.faces:jsf.js when necessary, i.e., when your custom component happens to rely on, for example, the jsf.ajax.request() or other functions provided by the standard JSF JavaScript API. javax.faces:jsf.js can be included as follows, with the script library and name available as constants of ResourceHandler.

```
@ResourceDependency(
    library=ResourceHandler.JSF_SCRIPT_LIBRARY_NAME,
    name=ResourceHandler.JSF_SCRIPT_RESOURCE_NAME,
    target="head")
public class SomeCustomComponent extends UIComponent {
    // ...
}
```

---

[12]https://javaee.github.io/javaee-spec/javadocs/javax/faces/application/ResourceDependency.html.

# CHAPTER 12

# Search Expressions

As stated in the sections "Ajax Life Cycle" in Chapter 3 and "Ajaxifying Components" in Chapter 4, the execute and render attributes of `<f:ajax>` tag take a space-separated collection of so-called component search expressions.

The search expressions have always been part of JSF (JavaServer Faces) since the beginning as this is used in the `for` attribute of `<h:outputLabel>`, `<h:message>`, and `<h:messages>`, but they have only become essential knowledge for the JSF developer since the introduction of `<f:ajax>` in JSF 2.0. Namely, labels and messages are in almost any case already within the very same naming container parent as the target input component, so simply specifying the ID of the target input component in the `for` attribute already suffices, but this is not necessarily true for the execute and render attributes of `<f:ajax>` as the target component may sit in a different naming container context or even in a physically different Facelets file.

To overcome these difficulties, JSF 2.0 introduced a few more abstract search expressions: `"@this"`, `"@form"`, `"@all"`, and `"@none"`. Something like `"@form"` is particularly easy to use, as it just means target whatever the current form is. If that current form is defined two parent templates up from the page where it's referenced, this really makes referencing it much easier.

Although they made things much easier, these keywords were quite limited. Not only are there just four of them, but they're also not extensible and the default JSF component set only uses them internally in the `<f:ajax>` tag. Using them in other components, even in JSF's own `<h:outputLabel>`, `<h:message>`, and `<h:messages>`, as well as using them programmatically, was left out. Therefore, in JSF 2.3 a "Component Search Expression Framework" was at the last moment introduced that greatly expands upon those four keywords. It was largely based on a proven API (application programming interface) of PrimeFaces.[1]

---

[1] https://www.primefaces.org/search-expression-framework/.

© Bauke Scholtz, Arjan Tijms 2018
B. Scholtz and A. Tijms, *The Definitive Guide to JSF in Java EE 8*, https://doi.org/10.1007/978-1-4842-3387-0_12

# Relative Local IDs

This is the simplest form of a component search expression. The most common use cases are found in the for attribute of <h:outputLabel>, <h:message>, and <h:messages> components. It simply references the sole ID of the target UIInput component.

```
<h:outputLabel for="email" value="Email address" />
<h:inputText id="email" value="#{login.email}" required="true" />
<h:message for="email" />
```

This only prerequires that the target component is also sitting within the very same naming container parent. A naming container parent is a component that implements the NamingContainer interface.[2] In standard JSF, only <h:form>, <h:dataTable>, <ui:repeat>, and <f:subview> are an instance of NamingContainer. All composite components are also an instance of NamingContainer, but tag files are not.

In case you need to reference a specific UIInput component within a naming container from <h:outputLabel> on, then you need to append the so-called naming container separator character to the ID of the naming container component and then the ID of the target UIInput component. The default naming container separator character is a colon ":". The currently configured separator character is programmatically available by UINamingContainer#getSeparatorCharacter().[3]

```
char separatorCharacter = UINamingContainer
    .getSeparatorCharacter(FacesContext.getCurrentInstance);
```

This is configurable via the javax.faces.SEPARATOR_CHAR context parameter in web.xml.

```
<context-param>
    <param-name>javax.faces.SEPARATOR_CHAR</param-name>
    <param-value>-</param-value>
</context-param>
```

---

[2]https://javaee.github.io/javaee-spec/javadocs/javax/faces/component/
NamingContainer.html.

[3]https://javaee.github.io/javaee-spec/javadocs/javax/faces/component/
UINamingContainer.html#getSeparatorChar-javax.faces.context.FacesContext-.

---

**Caution**    Changing this to something else like a hyphen "-" or even an
underscore "_" is **not** recommended.[4]

---

In the long term, it is confusing and brittle as those characters are also allowed in
the ID attribute itself. JSF does not validate the component ID against the currently
configured naming container separator character and thus it may easily slip through and
cause trouble while referencing such a component in a search expression.

Coming back to referencing a specific `UIInput` component within a naming
container from `<h:outputLabel>` on, in the example composite component
`<t:inputLocalTime>` as demonstrated in the section "Composite Components"
in Chapter 7, the hour drop-down component has an ID of "hour". Thus, for
`<h:outputLabel>`, when using the default naming container separator character, the
relative local ID of the hour dropdown inside the composite component is "time:hour".

```
<h:outputLabel id="l_time" for="time:hour" value="Time" />
<t:inputLocalTime id="time" value="#{schedule.time}" required="true" />
<h:message id="m_time" for="time" />
```

Note that this is not necessary for `<h:message>` as faces messages are under the hood
already added to the faces context with the client ID of the composite component itself.

Using relative local IDs also works within the context of `<h:column>` of
`<h:dataTable>`. It's then interpreted in the context of the currently iterated row, even
when the target component is sitting in another column. The following example
demonstrates that:

```
<h:dataTable id="users" value="#{admin.users}" var="user">
    ...
    <h:column>
        <f:facet name="header">Country</f:facet>
        <h:selectOneMenu id="country" value="#{user.address.country}">
            <f:selectItems value="#{data.countries}" />
            <f:ajax render="city" />
        </h:selectOneMenu>
    </h:column>
```

---

[4]https://stackoverflow.com/q/10726653/157882.

```
    <h:column>
        <f:facet name="header">City</f:facet>
        <h:selectOneMenu id="city" value="#{user.address.city}">
            <f:selectItems value="#{user.address.country.cities}" />
        </h:selectOneMenu>
    </h:column>
    ...
</h:dataTable>
```

Under the hood, relative local IDs are resolved using the algorithm as described in the UIComponent#findComponent() API.[5] This means that you can also resolve them programmatically. You only need to ensure that the findComponent() method is invoked on the correct base component, not on, for example, UIViewRoot.

# Absolute Hierarchical IDs

In case the target component is not within the same naming container parent as the current component, then you need an absolute hierarchical ID instead of a local relative ID. The key difference is that an absolute hierarchical ID starts with the naming container separator character. It will then search for the target component from the UIViewRoot on. Such construct is often used in the render attribute of <f:ajax> when it needs to reference a component that is not located inside the same form.

```
<h:form id="search">
    ...
    <h:commandButton id="submit" ...>
        <f:ajax execute="@form" render=":results" />
    </h:commandButton>
</h:form>
<h:panelGroup id="results" layout="block">
    ...
</h:panelGroup>
```

---

[5]https://javaee.github.io/javaee-spec/javadocs/javax/faces/component/UIComponent.
html#findComponent-java.lang.String-.

A less common use case where an absolute hierarchical ID is needed is when you need to reference a component that is in turn nested in another naming container—for example, when you want to update <h:message> associated with a composite component during a <cc:clientBehavior> event inside the composite component.

```
<h:form id="form">
    <h:outputLabel id="l_time" for="time:hour" value="Time" />
    <t:inputLocalTime id="time" value="#{schedule.time}" required="true">
        <f:ajax render=":form:m_time" />
    <h:message id="m_time" for="time" />
</h:form>
```

You could argue that this is a bug or an oversight in the JSF specification. This is very true and should be worked on for a next version of JSF. Another yet less common use case is when you need to update a specific iteration round of an iteration component, such as <h:dataTable> and <ui:repeat>.

```
<h:form id="form">
    <h:dataTable id="table" value="#{bean.items}" var="item">
        <h:column>
            <h:panelGroup id="column1" layout="block">
                ...
            </h:panelGroup>
        </h:column>
        <h:column>
            <h:panelGroup id="column2" layout="block">
                ...
            </h:panelGroup>
        </h:column>
    </h:dataTable>
    <h:commandButton value="Update second row">
        <f:ajax render=":form:table:1:column1
                        :form:table:1:column2">
        </f:ajax>
    </h:commandButton>
</h:form>
```

Note that the iteration index is zero-based as with normal Java collections and arrays. Also note that you basically need to wrap the cell's content in another component in order to properly reference the cell's content, and that you need to explicitly specify every column in order to update the entire row, as demonstrated above. Updating the entire column is also possible, but less convenient because you basically need to specify the search expression for every single row. Fortunately, the render attribute can take an EL (Expression Language) expression and the EL stream API can be used to concatenate a bunch of strings in the :form:table:[i]:column format depending on the amount of items in the table.

```
<h:commandButton value="Update second column">
    <f:ajax render="#{bean.items.stream()
        .map(i -> ' :form:list:' += bean.items.indexOf(i) += ':column2')
        .reduce((l, r) -> (l += r)).get()}">
    </f:ajax>
</h:commandButton>
```

Admittedly, this is not the most elegant approach. You'd better delegate to a custom function in an application-scoped bean. It could look something like the following:

```
<h:commandButton value="Update second column">
    <f:ajax
        render="#{ajax.columnIds(bean.items, ':form:table::column2')}"
    </f:ajax>
</h:commandButton>
```

Whereby the #{ajax} application-scoped bean looks something like the following:

```
@Named @ApplicationScoped
public class Ajax {

    public String columnIds(List<?> list, String idTemplate) {
        return IntStream.range(0, list.size()).boxed()
            .map(i -> idTemplate.replace("::", ":" + i + ":"))
            .collect(Collectors.joining(" "));
    }
}
```

That's already something better, but still boilerplate-ish. If necessary, you can also programmatically add Ajax render IDs from a backing bean on. You can use the `PartialViewContext#getRenderIds()`[6] for this. The returned collection is, namely, mutable and only consulted during the render response phase (sixth phase). You also need to specify an absolute hierarchical ID here, but with only one important difference: it cannot start with the naming container separator character. In other words, ":form:table:0:column2" isn't going to work; you need to specify "form:table:0:column2" instead. It's always resolved relative to `UIViewRoot`.

```
FacesContext context = FacesContext.getCurrentInstance();
PartialViewContext ajaxContext = context.getPartialViewContext();
ajaxContext.getRenderIds().add("form:table:0:column2");
```

As a tip, in case you're having a hard time figuring out the absolute hierarchical ID and/or memorizing which components exactly are naming containers, then you can always look in the generated HTML output. Open the JSF page in your favorite web browser, do a *View Page Source*, locate the HTML element representation of the JSF component of interest, take the value of its ID attribute, and finally prefix it with the naming container separator character.

Also, in case you encounter an autogenerated ID prefixed with `j_id`, then you absolutely need to give the associated JSF component a fixed ID; otherwise its value would be off when the component's position in the component tree is subject to be changed because of, for example, a conditionally included component somewhere before the position of the component of interest. (See also the section "Text-Based Input Components" in Chapter 4.)

Like relative local IDs, absolute hierarchical IDs can be programmatically resolved using the algorithm as described in the `UIComponent#findComponent()` API.[7] The following example demonstrates how to get hold of the `UIData` component representing `<h:form id="form"><h:dataTable id="table">`.

```
UIViewRoot root = FacesContext.getCurrentInstance().getViewRoot();
UIData table = (UIData) root.findComponent("form:table");
```

---

[6]https://javaee.github.io/javaee-spec/javadocs/javax/faces/context/
PartialViewContext.html#getRenderIds--.

[7]https://javaee.github.io/javaee-spec/javadocs/javax/faces/component/UIComponent.
html#findComponent-java.lang.String-.

# Standard Search Keywords

JSF provides a set of more abstract search expressions, known as "search keywords." They all start with the "@" character. They can be used to substitute a fixed component ID in the search expression. Table 12-1 provides an overview of them.

***Table 12-1.*** *Standard Search Keywords Provided by JSF*

| Keyword | Resolves to | Since |
|---|---|---|
| @this | UIComponent#getCurrentComponent() | 2.0 |
| @form | UIComponent#getNamingContainer() until an UIForm is encountered | 2.0 |
| @all | Everything | 2.0 |
| @none | Nothing | 2.0 |
| @parent | UIComponent#getParent() | 2.3 |
| @child(index) | UIComponent#getChildren() at given index | 2.3 |
| @next | UIComponent#getParent() and then UIComponent#getChildren() at next index | 2.3 |
| @previous | UIComponent#getParent() and then UIComponent#getChildren() at previous index | 2.3 |
| @namingcontainer | UIComponent#getNamingContainer() | 2.3 |
| @composite | UIComponent#getCompositeComponentParent() | 2.3 |
| @id(id) | UIComponent#findComponent() with given ID. | 2.3 |
| @root | FacesContext#getViewRoot() | 2.3 |

In a standard JSF component set, all search keywords, including custom ones, can be used in the following component attributes:

- `<f:ajax execute>`—Specifies components which must be processed during the apply request values, process validations, update model values, and invoke application phases (second, third, fourth, and fifth phases) of the Ajax postback request. Defaults to `@this`.

- `<f:ajax render>`—Specifies components which must be processed during the render response phase (sixth phase) of the Ajax postback request. Defaults to @none.

- `<h:outputLabel for>`—Specifies the target component of the generated HTML `<label>` element. Defaults to @none.

- `<h:message for>`—Specifies the target component for which the first faces message must be rendered. Defaults to @none.

- `<h:messages for>`—Specifies the target component for which all faces messages must be rendered. Defaults to @none.

Note that using search keywords is, for the `for` attribute of `<h:outputLabel>`, `<h:message>`, and `<h:messages>`, has only been possible since JSF 2.3. In older versions, only relative and absolute IDs were supported.

The most commonly used search keyword is undoubtedly @form. You have basically no other choice when using `<f:ajax>` in a `UICommand` component which is supposed to process the entire form.

```
<h:form>
    ...
    <h:commandButton value="Submit" ...>
        <f:ajax execute="@form" />
    </h:commandButton>
</h:form>
```

Also new since JSF 2.3 is that search keywords can be chained with regular component IDs. Following is an example which expands on the example given before in the section "Absolute Hierarchical IDs."

```
<h:form>
    <h:outputLabel id="l_time" for="time:hour" value="Time" />
    <t:inputLocalTime id="time" value="#{schedule.time}" required="true">
        <f:ajax render="@form:m_time" />
    <h:message id="m_time" for="time" />
</h:form>
```

And following is an example that updates the entire table when a row is deleted.

```
<h:form>
    <h:dataTable value="#{products.list}" var="product">
        ...
        <h:column>
            <h:commandButton id="delete" value="Delete"
                action="#{products.delete(product)}">
                <f:ajax render="@namingcontainer" />
            </h:commandButton>
        </h:column>
    </h:dataTable>
</h:form>
```

Note particularly that it thus references the closest component implementing the NamingContainer interface, which, in this context, is <h:dataTable> and thus not <h:form>.

As to programmatic resolution, search expressions with keywords cannot be programmatically resolved using UIComponent#findComponent(). For that, you need SearchExpressionHandler#resolveComponent() or resolveComponents()[8] instead. SearchExpressionHandler is in turn available by Application#getSearchExpressionH andler(). You also need to create SearchExpressionContext[9] beforehand which wraps the component to start searching from.

```
FacesContext context = FacesContext.getCurrentInstance();
UIComponent base = context.getViewRoot(); // Can be any component.
String expression = "@namingcontainer";

SearchExpressionContext searchContext = SearchExpressionContext
    .createSearchExpressionContext(context, base);
SearchExpressionHandler searchHandler = context.getApplication()
    .getSearchExpressionHandler();
handler.resolveComponent(searchContext, expression, (ctx, found) -> {
    System.out.println(found);
});
```

---

[8]https://javaee.github.io/javaee-spec/javadocs/javax/faces/component/search/
SearchExpressionHandler.html#resolveComponent-javax.faces.component.search.
SearchExpressionContext-java.lang.String-javax.faces.component.ContextCallback-.
[9]https://javaee.github.io/javaee-spec/javadocs/javax/faces/component/search/
SearchExpressionContext.html.

Frankly, it's quite verbose, but it's JSF API's own. Fortunately, utility libraries such as OmniFaces exist.

# Custom Search Keywords

The Component Search Expression Framework introduced in JSF 2.3 also comes with an API which allows us to create custom search keywords. Imagine that you have a form with multiple <h:message> components, and that you'd like to re-render them all when submitting the form. Then you'd be tempted also to use @form in the render attribute of <f:ajax>.

```
<h:form>
    <h:outputLabel for="input1" ... />
    <h:inputText id="input1" ... />
    <h:message for="input1" />

    <h:outputLabel for="input2" ... />
    <h:inputText id="input2" ... />
    <h:message for="input2" />

    <h:outputLabel for="input3" ... />
    <h:inputText id="input3" ... />
    <h:message for="input3" />

    <h:commandButton value="Submit" ...>
        <f:ajax execute="@form" render="@form" />
    </h:commandButton>
</h:form>
```

But this is not terribly efficient. In fact, it also unnecessarily re-renders all label and input components and any other static content inside the very same form which doesn't at all change during the Ajax postback request. This is a waste of resources. Ideally, we should have a search keyword like "@messages" which basically references all message components within the same form.

```
<h:form>
    <h:outputLabel for="input1" ... />
    <h:inputText id="input1" ... />
    <h:message id="m_input1" for="input1" />
```

403

```
    <h:outputLabel for="input2" ... />
    <h:inputText id="input2" ... />
    <h:message id="m_input2" for="input2" />

    <h:outputLabel for="input3" ... />
    <h:inputText id="input3" ... />
    <h:message id="m_input3" for="input3" />

    <h:commandButton value="Submit" ...>
        <f:ajax execute="@form" render="@messages" />
    </h:commandButton>
</h:form>
```

Note that each <h:message> component has an explicit ID set, because without an explicit ID, they will by default render nothing to the HTML output, and then the JSF Ajax API JavaScript wouldn't be able to find them in order to update its content based on the Ajax response.

In order to get JSF to recognize the new search keyword @messages, first extend the javax.faces.component.search.SearchKeywordResolver[10] as follows:

```
public class MessagesKeywordResolver extends SearchKeywordResolver {

    @Override
    public boolean isResolverForKeyword
        (SearchExpressionContext context, String keyword)
    {
        return "messages".equals(keyword);
    }

    @Override
    public void resolve
        (SearchKeywordContext context, UIComponent base, String keyword)
    {
        UIComponent form = base.getNamingContainer();
```

---

[10]https://javaee.github.io/javaee-spec/javadocs/javax/faces/component/search/
  SearchKeywordResolver.html.

```
        while (!(form instanceof UIForm) && form != null) {
            form = form.getNamingContainer();
        }

        if (form != null) {
            Set<String> messageClientIds = new HashSet<>();
            VisitContext visitContext = VisitContext.createVisitContext
                (context.getSearchExpressionContext().getFacesContext());

            form.visitTree(visitContext, (visit, child) -> {
                if (child instanceof UIMessage) {
                    messageClientIds.add(child.getClientId());
                }
                return VisitResult.ACCEPT;
            });

            if (!messageClientIds.isEmpty()) {
                context.invokeContextCallback(new UIMessage() {
                    @Override
                    public String getClientId(FacesContext context) {
                        return String.join(" ", messageClientIds);
                    }
                });
            }
        }

        context.setKeywordResolved(true);
    }
}
```

It should be noted that this approach is already slightly hacky. Namely, the intent of the SearchKeywordResolver is to resolve a keyword to exactly one component whose client ID will then be used to substitute the keyword. This component will then be passed to SearchKeywordContext#invokeContextCallback(). In the above approach, we instead collect the client IDs of all UIMessage components found within the parent UIForm and then supply a fake UIMessage component to invokeContextCallback() who will in turn call the getClientId() of the fake UIMessage component which actually returns the desired collection of client IDs.

It should also be noted that `UIComponent#visitTree()`[11] is being used instead of recursing over `UIComponent#getChildren()` in order to collect the client IDs of any `UIMessage` component. Namely, when plain iterating over children, you may sooner or later come across an iterator component such as `<h:dataTable>` or `<ui:repeat>`, and if it happens to have only one `UIMessage` component nested, then you'll effectively end up with only one client ID, namely, the one without the iteration index. `UIComponent#visitTree()` doesn't do that; any iterator component in the path will actually iterate over its model value and visually give back multiple `UIMessage` components, each with the correct client ID with the iteration index included.

In the end, `SearchKeywordContext#setKeywordResolved()` must be called with `true` in order to inform the search context that the keyword has successfully been resolved, even if it actually resolved to nothing. It doesn't actually do any harm if you forgot this, but if you don't mark the search keyword resolved this way, then the search context will continue consulting all other search keyword resolvers, which might end up being less efficient.

Finally, in order to get the new `MessagesKeywordResolver` to run, register it in `faces-config.xml` as follows:

```
<application>
    <search-keyword-resolver>
        com.example.project.MessagesKeywordResolver
    </search-keyword-resolver>
</application>
```

Or, programmatically in a @WebListener as follows:

```
@WebListener
public class ApplicationConfig implements ServletContextListener {

    @Override
    public void contextInitialized(ServletContextEvent event) {
        FacesContext.getCurrentInstance().getApplication()
            .addSearchKeywordResolver(new MessagesKeywordResolver());
    }
}
```

---

[11]https://javaee.github.io/javaee-spec/javadocs/javax/faces/component/UIComponent.html#visitTree-javax.faces.component.visit.VisitContext-javax.faces.component.visit.VisitCallback-.

Note that the `FacesContext` must be available at this point and hence a `ServletContainerInitializer` won't necessarily work, and that the `FacesServlet` may not have serviced a request yet and hence registration in some managed bean won't necessarily work.

# CHAPTER 13

# Security

Security for web applications is a broad field and includes a number of topics such as protecting access to resources, shielding against injection attacks of various kinds, and preventing users from being tricked into doing malicious actions on behalf of an attacker.

JSF (JavaServer Faces) supports these topics in various ways, either by providing native solutions or by integrating with the Java EE platform's facilities. For access to resources, which includes both authentication (the caller proving its identity) and authorization (the system determining to which resources the caller has access) JSF (JavaServer Faces) integrates with the Java EE Security machinery, which in turn is defined by, among others, the Servlet spec and the Java EE Security spec.

Java EE Security (JSR 375) is supported by both the Web- and Full profile in Java EE 8. Additionally, the reference implementation Soteria works on Java EE 7 servers, and because it's built on JASPIC (Java EE authentication SPI) (JSR 196), it also works on Servlet containers that support JASPIC (such as Tomcat since 8.5 and Jetty since 7.0).

## Java EE Security Overview and History

In Java EE, security is not specified in a single specification but is in fact spread over multiple specifications that integrate with each other in various ways. While this allows for different aspects of security to be evolved at their own pace, and practically speaking even allows some to be replaced by non-spec implementations, it does muddy the waters of what spec is responsible for what.

In this introductory section we'll start off with providing a somewhat broad overview of what some of the pieces are and how they fit together. We'll focus on the web aspects of security. Security is also present in things like EJB (Enterprise JavaBeans) and JCA (Java Connector Architecture) connectors, but these are outside the scope of this book.

© Bauke Scholtz, Arjan Tijms 2018
B. Scholtz and A. Tijms, *The Definitive Guide to JSF in Java EE 8*, https://doi.org/10.1007/978-1-4842-3387-0_13

Historically, security in Java EE is mostly based on the security model introduced by the Servlet spec. That is, a model where the core elements are an "authentication mechanism" (FORM, BASIC, ...), a set of security constraints in web.xml where a specific pattern (the URL pattern) is combined with a collection of roles (including the empty collection), and a few ways to programmatically test the caller's details, such as HttpServletRequest.isUserInRole.

While effective, many details were left out in the early days. The Servlet spec did ask for implementations (Servlet containers) to be extendible with respect to the authentication mechanisms but did not specify how exactly this should be done. Likewise, the Servlet spec implicitly requires an "identity store" (File, Database, LDAP, ...) that holds the caller details such as credentials, name, and roles but left all details about how to configure these to the Servlet container.

The Servlet spec did not define any way to access the security constraints defined in web.xml in a programmatic way, or to programmatically influence their execution (e.g., to make certain constraints time based). Furthermore, the very early versions of the Servlet spec did not specify the constraint resolution in the strictest way, which allowed for some small differences in interpretation between various Servlet containers.

The first additional spec to address these concerns was JACC (JSR 115), which, simply stated, deals with authorization concerns. JACC specifies how the web.xml security constraints should be represented in code, namely, as a collection of *Permission* instances. JACC also specifies how these can be accessed (queried) by code, and finally allows for custom authorization modules that can replace or augment the logic that the container executes to determine its access decision. A perhaps somewhat difficult thing to understand about JACC is that it's not so much something that can be implemented on its own and then added to a Servlet container (as we can do with JSF), but it standardizes and more concisely specifies what all Servlet containers internally are already doing.

The second additional spec to address the above-mentioned concerns was JASPIC (JSR 196), which deals with authentication concerns. JASPIC specifies at what moments the Servlet container should call the authentication mechanism and defines an explicit interface type for these authentication mechanisms, so custom authentication mechanisms can use this interface instead of the Servlet container's proprietary one and thus be portable. JASPIC says a few things about the identity store, but too little to be really usable in practice. Like JACC, JASPIC isn't something that can be implemented independently, but it standardizes something that all Servlet containers are already doing.

Both JACC and JASPIC define low-level SPIs (server provider interfaces) that are mainly intended to be implemented and used by vendors to provide extension products. They are quite bare and fairly abstract. As such they are not (rich) APIs (application programming interfaces) that are targeted at application developers. Here is where the Java EE Security API (JSR 375) comes in. Java EE Security offers a higher-level and easier-to-register (just implement the interface) and easier-to-use (CDI based) version of the JASPIC authentication module. The Java EE Security API also fully defines the identity store artifact, but perhaps most important it provides a number of concrete implementations of all of these, among which is a FORM-based authentication mechanism optimized for use with JSF and several identity stores such as a JDBC (Java Database Connectivify) store and an LDAP (Lightweight Directory Access Protocol) store.

The RI (reference implementation) of the Java EE Security API is called Soteria. This implementation is of course provided by the Java EE 8 RI GlassFish and its derivative Payara. Soteria, like Mojarra and MyFaces, has been designed to run independently on basically every Servlet container provided that it adheres to the JASPIC specs (which both Tomcat and Jetty do as mentioned in the chapter's introduction). Its dependencies (at the time of writing, for Soteria 1.0) are CDI 1.2 and Expression Language 3.0. These two dependencies are provided by all Java EE 7 implementations. Servlet containers typically provide EL (Expression Language) support while CDI can be added separately, for instance, using the RI Weld. For a few *optional* features Soteria takes advantage of Servlet containers that adhere to the JACC spec.

# Protect Access to Resources

In JSF the main resources to protect are views, which are accessed via URL patterns. It's therefore these URL patterns we need to define security constraints. These constraints are primarily defined in web.xml. In fact, as of Java EE 8, web.xml is pretty much the only viable place to define security constraints for JSF views.

Java EE has three kinds of security constraints:

- Excluded
- Unchecked
- By role

# Excluded

"**Excluded,**" aka "deny all," means that no external caller will be granted access to the resources covered by this constraint. One might ask what the purpose of such a constraint is. If the resources can never be accessed, why are those resources there in the first place?

The answer is twofold. For one, a single application may be configured for different purposes. An excluded security constraint is an easy way then to quickly disable a number of resources that are not applicable to a certain configuration of the application. A more important use case is to be able to make a distinction between external use and internal use of a resource. The key insight here is that security constraints are only applied to external requests for that resource, i.e., to a caller requesting `https://example.com/resources/template.xhtml`, but **not** to internal requests such as includes, forwards, and any of the methods to load a resource from the classpath or file system.

This is specifically important for JSF because of a somewhat unfortunate design choice regarding composite components. Composite components are components that are implemented via a Facelet instead of a Java class. By convention, they have to be placed in a directory inside a directory named `/resources` that resides in the web root. For instance, `/resources/bar/foo.xhtml`. This will make a composite component "foo" available in the namespace `http://xmlns.jcp.org/jsf/composite/bar`.

Components are of course not views and the caller should not be able to request those directly. Unfortunately, `/resources` is not in any way a special directory to Java EE. JSF assigns a special meaning to it by convention, but to the Servlet container it's a directory like any other. This specifically means there's no protection applied to it and any caller can directly request resources from it. In other words, this directory is "unchecked," aka "world readable." Even with an `*.xhtml` mapping, this not only allows the user to guess which components we have but lets the user attempt to execute those as well. Clearly this is not what we want. There are two solutions for this:

- Configure another directory to be the JSF resources directory

- Add the mentioned security constraint to `web.xml`

Via the `javax.faces.WEBAPP_RESOURCES_DIRECTORY` context parameter another directory can be configured to be the JSF resources directory instead of `/resources`. For example,

```
<context-param>
    <param-name>javax.faces.WEBAPP_RESOURCES_DIRECTORY</param-name>
    <param-value>WEB-INF/resources</param-value>
</context-param>
```

Note that the path is relative to the web root and must not begin with a "/."

While this is a good default for our own applications, it still doesn't totally protect us. Namely, third-party jars can still provide their resources via /resources and aren't affected by that context parameter. For that reason, the aforementioned "Excluded" constraint is needed. It looks as follows:

```
<security-constraint>
    <web-resource-collection>
        <web-resource-name>The /resources folder</web-resource-name>
        <url-pattern>/resources/*</url-pattern>
    </web-resource-collection>
</security-constraint>
```

As can be seen, defining an *excluded* constraint boils down to defining the URL pattern that we wish to constrain, without defining any specific constraints.

## Unchecked

"**Unchecked**," aka "permit all," "public," and "world readable," means that all callers, independent of whether or not they are authenticated, have access to the resources covered by the "constraint." Internally an explicit constraint may exist for this, but in web.xml this "constraint" is defined simply by not defining any constraint at all for a URL pattern. In other words, every URL that's not covered explicitly by any other pattern is "unchecked."

## By Role

"**By role**" means a so-called role is associated with a URL pattern, and the authenticated caller must have that role in order to access the resource. A role itself is frequently seen as a concept with strict semantics, but it's essentially little more than just an opaque string that needs to match from the set of such strings associated with an authenticated caller, and the set of strings associated with a URL pattern. The content of that string is completely up to the application, meaning it could be a "type of caller," like "admin", "user", etc., but also something fine-grained as "may_add_item", or even tokens such as "AYUDE-OPWR-BM1OP".

The following gives an example:

```
<security-constraint>
    <web-resource-collection>
        <web-resource-name>User pages</web-resource-name>
        <url-pattern>/user/*</url-pattern>
    </web-resource-collection>
    <auth-constraint>
        <role-name>VIEW_USER_PAGES</role-name>
    </auth-constraint>
</security-constraint>

<security-constraint>
    <web-resource-collection>
        <web-resource-name>Admin pages</web-resource-name>
        <url-pattern>/admin/*</url-pattern>
    </web-resource-collection>
    <auth-constraint>
        <role-name>VIEW_ADMIN_PAGES</role-name>
    </auth-constraint>
</security-constraint>

<security-role>
    <role-name>VIEW_USER_PAGES</role-name>
</security-role>
<security-role>
    <role-name>VIEW_ADMIN_PAGES</role-name>
</security-role>
```

In the above fragment we define two security constraints—one for the /user/* pattern, for which the caller needs to have the role "VIEW_USER_PAGES", and one for the /admin/* pattern, for which the caller needs the role "VIEW_ADMIN_PAGES". With the above constraints in place, a caller accessing, say, /user/account.xhtml has to be authenticated and has to have the mentioned role.

An auth-constraint can contain multiple roles, for which OR semantics are applied. This means the authenticated caller only needs to have one of the roles in that constraint in order to be granted access. Constraints can additionally be restricted to a specific HTTP method (such as GET or POST). This does come with a caveat, since by default all methods that are not specified will be unchecked (public). This can be countered by using the top-level <deny-uncovered-http-methods/> tag. The following gives an example of this:

```
<deny-uncovered-http-methods />

<security-constraint>
    <web-resource-collection>
        <web-resource-name>User pages</web-resource-name>
        <url-pattern>/user/*</url-pattern>
        <http-method>GET</http-method>
        <http-method>POST</http-method>
    </web-resource-collection>
    <auth-constraint>
        <role-name>VIEW_USER_PAGES</role-name>
    </auth-constraint>
</security-constraint>
```

# Setting the Authentication Mechanism

After the security constraints have been defined, we need to set how the caller will authenticate. The artifact that handles the interaction with the caller (i.e., asks the caller for credentials in a certain way) is called an "authentication mechanism." Java EE provides a number of these out of the box. The Servlet spec provides four, namely, FORM, BASIC, DIGEST, and CERT, while Java EE Security provides FORM and BASIC as well (with the difference that these correspond to CDI beans), but also a variant of FORM called "Custom FORM".

FORM and Custom FORM are both suitable for interactive web applications, such as the ones we would build primarily with JSF. Contrary to, say, BASIC, the FORM authentication mechanisms call back into the application and let it render the form that asks the caller for credentials, hence, the name of these mechanisms.

The difference between the two is mainly in how the mechanism requires the application to continue the so-called authentication dialog after it has rendered the form. In FORM this is done by letting the caller post the filled-out form to the virtual URL j_security_check, while in Custom FORM this is done programmatically via a call to the injected SecurityContext. This small difference makes all the difference for JSF though. In JSF, a form view by default submits to the same URL it was requested from, so posting back to a single mechanism mandated URL is not at all natural. In addition to that, in JSF we often need to have server-side code running after a postback; just think about converters and validators and the ability to emit a faces message. We can't really do any of this if we have to post back to the virtual non-faces j_security_check URL, but it's quite doable when we can continue the authentication dialog programmatically from the backing bean's action method.

We'll first show you how to configure a web application to use the Custom FORM authentication mechanism. Later on, we'll explain how to actually use JSF to fulfill the requirements this mechanism imposes on the application.

All of the authentication mechanisms provided by Java EE Security are installed and configured via its own AuthenticationMechanismDefinition annotation. This annotation tells the container which type of authentication mechanism to install, and with which configuration. The annotation can be placed on pretty much every class on the classpath. Logically it fits in quite well with the @FacesConfig annotation. The following shows an example:

```
@CustomFormAuthenticationMechanismDefinition(
    loginToContinue = @LoginToContinue(
        loginPage = "/login.xhtml",
        errorPage = ""
    )
)
@FacesConfig @ApplicationScoped
public class ApplicationConfig {
    // ...
}
```

A perhaps somewhat unfortunate requirement here is that the errorPage attribute has to be specified and set to the empty string. This is needed since the *@LoginToContinue* element has a default value for an actual error page. In JSF we rarely use an explicit error page to display errors but instead redisplay the original page with the error messages rendered on it via faces messages.

Do note that the current version of Java EE Security only allows one authentication mechanism to be active at the same time. Technically what happens when the container encounters the @CustomFormAuthenticationMechanismDefinition annotation is that it adds an enabled CDI bean to the system of type HttpAuthenticationMechanism. This is important to know, since its being a regular CDI bean means we can inject it, decorate it, intercept it, and basically do everything with it that we can normally do with CDI beans.

The loginToContinue attribute is used to configure the view that the container forwards to whenever the caller tries to access a protected view. This is called "container initiated authentication"; the container starts the authentication dialog as opposed to the application.

Note that the default is to *forward* to the login page, meaning that if the caller tries to access https://example.com/foo.xhtml, and /foo.xhtml is protected, the caller will still see /foo.xhtml in the address bar and not /login.xhtml. However, the postback is to /login.xhtml, so after entering credentials the caller would get to see this in the address bar. Alternatively we can configure the loginToContinue attribute to use a redirect instead.

```
@CustomFormAuthenticationMechanismDefinition(
    loginToContinue = @LoginToContinue(
        loginPage = "/login.xhtml",
        useForwardToLogin = false,
        errorPage = ""
    )
)
@FacesConfig @ApplicationScoped
public class ApplicationConfig {
    // ...
}
```

# Setting the Identity Store

After having declared the security constraints and setting the mechanism that we'd like to use to authenticate, there's one final piece of the puzzle remaining: setting the artifact that contains the caller's data, such as credentials, name, and roles. In Java EE Security this artifact is called an identity store.

Java EE provides two of these out of the box; one to connect to a database and one to connect to LDAP (Lightweight Directory Access Protocol). The Java EE Security RI (Soteria) additionally ships with an embedded identity store. Most application servers provide additional ones of their own, which are often configured outside the application (e.g., via an admin console, CLI, or XML configuration file that's stored inside the server).

Setting and configuring the Java EE Security-provided identity stores and the one provided by the RI happens in a similar fashion as the authentication mechanisms: via an `IdentityStoreAnnotation`. Just like the authentication mechanism version, this will cause the container to add an enabled CDI bean to the system, this time one implementing the `IdentityStore` interface.

The following shows an example together with our earlier definition of the authentication mechanism:

```java
@CustomFormAuthenticationMechanismDefinition(
    loginToContinue = @LoginToContinue(
        loginPage = "/login.xhtml",
        useForwardToLogin = false,
        errorPage = ""
    )
)
@EmbeddedIdentityStoreDefinition({
    @Credentials(
        callerName = "admin@example.com",
        password = "secret1",
        groups = { "VIEW_USER_PAGES", "VIEW_ADMIN_PAGES" }
    ),
    @Credentials(
        callerName = "user@example.com",
        password = "secret2",
        groups = { "VIEW_USER_PAGES" })
    )
})
@FacesConfig @ApplicationScoped
public class ApplicationConfig {
    // ...
}
```

The above causes an embedded (in-memory) store to be created, with two callers (users), the first one being in the groups "VIEW_USER_PAGES" and "VIEW_ADMIN_PAGES" and the second one only in the group "VIEW_USER_PAGES". The authentication mechanism will use this identity store to validate that the credentials (caller name and password) match and, if they do, to get the correct groups from the identity store.

The observant reader may notice that the terminology has changed. Before we were talking about "roles," while all of a sudden this has changed to "groups." Is this a mistake? Well, not really. Groups and roles are subtly different. Both are just opaque strings to the container, but groups can be *optionally* mapped to roles. We won't elaborate on this process further here, but suffice it to say that by default, Java EE mandates a so-called 1:1 group-to-role mapping, which simply means groups and roles are the same.

To better understand identity stores we'll give two more examples here. For the first example we'll look at one of the identity stores that's provided by the Java EE Security API—the database identity store. This store is activated and configured using the @ DatabaseIdentityStoreDefinition annotation. The three most important attributes to configure are the data source (which represents the SQL data base), the SQL query to obtain the (hashed!) password given a caller name, and the SQL query to identify which groups a caller is in given the caller name. The following gives an example:

```
@CustomFormAuthenticationMechanismDefinition(
    loginToContinue = @LoginToContinue(
        loginPage = "/login.xhtml",
        errorPage = ""
    )
)
@DatabaseIdentityStoreDefinition(
    dataSourceLookup = "java:app/MyDataSource",
    callerQuery = "SELECT password FROM caller WHERE name = ?",
    groupsQuery = "SELECT name FROM groups WHERE caller_name = ?"
)
@DataSourceDefinition(
    name = "java:app/MyDataSource",
    className = "org.h2.jdbcx.JdbcDataSource",
    url="jdbc:h2:~/test;DB_CLOSE_ON_EXIT=FALSE"
)
```

```
@FacesConfig @ApplicationScoped
public class ApplicationConfig {
    // ...
}
```

In this example, a data source is defined for the H2 database using the org.h2.jdbcx. JdbcDataSource driver. Naturally this can be done in a similar way for any other database that has a JDBC driver. Alternatively, the data source can be defined externally to the application. The caller query that we used is "select password from caller where name = ?", which means we assume a table with at least two columns—one holding the caller name, and the other the hashed password. Such table could be created by, for example, the following SQL statement:

```
CREATE TABLE caller(
    name VARCHAR(32) PRIMARY KEY,
    password VARCHAR(255)
)
```

The query that we used for the groups is "select name from groups where caller_name = ?", which assumes a table with at least two columns—the caller name, and the group name, with one row for each group the caller is in. Such a table could be created by, for example, the following SQL statement:

```
CREATE TABLE caller_groups(
    caller_name VARCHAR(32),
    name VARCHAR(32)
)
```

When populating the caller table, it must be noted that a default hash algorithm is assumed for the password column, namely, PBKDF2WithHmacSHA256. This algorithm can (should) be customized by setting the number of iterations, the key size, and the salt size.

Instead of using an identity store that's provided by the Java EE Security API we also have the option of providing our own custom one. A common use case for that is using the application's own services to load the application-specific user data.

The following shows an example of such an identity store:

```
@ApplicationScoped
public class UserServiceIdentityStore implements IdentityStore {

    @Inject
    private UserService userService;

    @Override
    public CredentialValidationResult validate(Credential credential) {
        UsernamePasswordCredential login =
            (UserNamePasswordCredential) credential;
        String email = login.getCaller();
        String password = login.getPasswordAsString();

        Optional<User> optionalUser =
            userService.findByEmailAndPassword(email, password);

        if (optionalUser.isPresent()) {
            User user = optionalUser.get();
            return new CredentialValidationResult(
                user.getEmail(),
                user.getRolesAsStrings()
            );
        }
        else {
            return CredentialValidationResult.INVALID_RESULT;
        }
    }
}
```

There is no specific registration needed; the above given class simply needs to be present in the application (be on its classpath). With such custom identity store present the ApplicationConfig class therefore doesn't need any config for the identity store.

```
@CustomFormAuthenticationMechanismDefinition(
    loginToContinue = @LoginToContinue(
        loginPage = "/login.xhtml",
        errorPage = ""
    )
)
@FacesConfig @ApplicationScoped
public class ApplicationConfig {
    // ...
}
```

The `UserServiceIdentityStore` as given above delegates most of the work to a `UserService`, which would be responsible for handling `User` entities in the application. Fully discussing such service is outside the scope of this book, but we can imagine it could use, for example, JPA to persist and load `User` entities. Our custom identity store uses the service to try to find a `User` based on the user name and the password that's being passed in via the credentials. If a `User` instance is returned, it means the name referred to an existing user, and the password was the correct one. In that case the identity store in turn returns `CredentialValidationResult` which does two things: it indicates that authentication was successful, and it provides the container with the data that will eventually be used to set the authenticated identity for the current request. If the service couldn't find the user, then either the name or the password was wrong. In that case the store returns `INVALID_RESULT` to indicate that authentication was not successful.

## Providing Our Custom JSF Code

In the sections above, we first defined our security constraints (which views are protected), then we set up the authentication mechanism (how do our callers interact with our application in order to authenticate), and finally we set up the identity store (where the caller data resides).

It's now time to plug our own custom code into the authentication process. This primarily happens by providing the view that the authentication mechanism directs to when it needs to collect the caller's credentials (e-mail and password in this case).

The login page can be kept relative simple—a standard form page, with two inputs bound to our backing bean, and a button to submit.

```
<!DOCTYPE html>
<html lang="en"
    xmlns="http://www.w3.org/1999/xhtml"
    xmlns:h="http://xmlns.jcp.org/jsf/html"
>
    <h:head>
        <title>Log In</title>
    </h:head>
    <h:body>
        <h1>Log In</h1>
        <h:form>
            <h:outputLabel for="email" value="Email" />
            <h:inputText id="email" value="#{login.email}" />
            <br />
            <h:outputLabel for="password" value="Password" />
            <h:inputSecret id="password" value="#{login.password}" />
            <br />
            <h:commandButton value="Login" action="#{login.submit}" />
            <h:messages />
        </h:form>
    </h:body>
</html>
```

The page above is a totally normal JSF view. This specifically means that contrary to classical HTML `<form method="post" action="j_security_check">` of FORM authentication the authentication mechanism does not monitor the postback URL in any way and therefore there aren't any constraints being placed on the input elements that collect the credentials.

Instead, the JSF backing bean has to collect these credentials and then programmatically pass these along and signal the authentication mechanism to continue the dialog. Before passing the credentials along, JSF is free to do its own validation and engage in its own dialog with the caller without the authentication mechanism having to be involved with this. Note that the command button explicitly doesn't use Ajax to submit. You can do so, but then the average web browser won't suggest the end user to remember the login credentials on its behalf.

The following shows a full example of the backing bean handling the login call. We'll discuss the parts individually below.

```java
@Named @RequestScoped
public class Login {

    @NotNull
    @Email
    private String email;

    @NotNull
    @Size(min = 8, message = "Password must be at least 8 characters")
    private String password;

    @Inject
    private SecurityContext securityContext;

    @Inject
    private ExternalContext externalContext;

    @Inject
    private FacesContext facesContext;

    public void submit() {
        switch (continueAuthentication()) {
            case SEND_CONTINUE:
                facesContext.responseComplete();
                break;

            case SEND_FAILURE:
                facesContext.addMessage(null, new FacesMessage(
                    FacesMessage.SEVERITY_ERROR, "Login failed", null));
                break;

            case SUCCESS:
                facesContext.addMessage(null, new FacesMessage(
                    FacesMessage.SEVERITY_INFO, "Login succeed", null));
                break;
```

```
            case NOT_DONE:
                // Doesn't happen here
        }
    }

    private AuthenticationStatus continueAuthentication() {
        return securityContext.authenticate(
            (HttpServletRequest) externalContext.getRequest(),
            (HttpServletResponse) externalContext.getResponse(),
            AuthenticationParameters.withParams().credential(
                new UsernamePasswordCredential(email, password))
        );
    }

    public String getEmail() {
        return email;
    }

    public void setEmail(String email) {
        this.email = email;
    }

    public String getPassword() {
        return password;
    }

    public void setPassword(String password) {
        this.password = password;
    }
}
```

We start the backing bean with two instance variables corresponding with the credentials we collect.

```
@NotNull
@Email
private String email;
```

```
@NotNull
@Size(min = 8, message = "Password must be at least 8 characters")
private String password;
```

This clearly shows the advantage over the FORM authentication mechanism in that we can easily pre-validate the user's input using bean validation. Because of JSF's built-in integration with bean validation a standard faces message will be made available for rendering should the input not pass validation.

Next, we defined injecting the contextual objects it needs. These are

```
@Inject
private SecurityContext securityContext;
```

```
@Inject
private ExternalContext externalContext;
```

```
@Inject
private FacesContext facesContext;
```

The observant reader will recognize ExternalContext and FacesContext as being two well-known native JSF classes, with the SecurityContext being the odd one out. This class is from Java EE Security and we'll use that here to communicate with the authentication mechanism.

Continuing the dialog happens in the continueAuthentication() method as follows:

```
private AuthenticationStatus continueAuthentication() {
    return securityContext.authenticate(
        (HttpServletRequest) externalContext.getRequest(),
        (HttpServletResponse) externalContext.getResponse(),
        AuthenticationParameters.withParams().credential(
            new UsernamePasswordCredential(email, password))
    );
}
```

The call to SecurityContext#authenticate() will trigger the authentication mechanism again. Since that mechanism will be a state where it waits for credentials to be passed, it will indeed look for the credentials we pass in, and use those to continue. As we'll later see, we can also request that any potentially existing state is discarded and a new dialog is started. Note that we have to cast the request and response objects to

HttpServletRequest and HttpServletResponse. Unfortunately, this is needed since ExternalContext abstracts over Servlet and Portlet requests and only returns Object for those two.

The SecurityContext#authenticate() method returns a status that indicates in broad lines what the authentication mechanism did. The action method of our JSF backing bean has to handle the following:

```
switch (continueAuthentication()) {
    case SEND_CONTINUE:
        facesContext.responseComplete();
        break;

    case SEND_FAILURE:
        facesContext.addMessage(null, new FacesMessage(
            FacesMessage.SEVERITY_ERROR, "Login failed", null));
        break;

    case SUCCESS:
        facesContext.addMessage(null, new FacesMessage(
            FacesMessage.SEVERITY_INFO, "Login succeed", null));
        break;

    case NOT_DONE:
        // Doesn't happen here
}
```

As can be seen, there are four possible outcomes.

The first one is SEND_CONTINUE, which basically means "authentication in progress." The authentication mechanism returned that status when it took over the dialog again (e.g., by rendering its own response or, more likely, by redirecting the caller to a new location). A JSF backing bean should make sure the JSF life cycle is ended by calling FacesContext#responseComplete() and furthermore refrain from interacting with the response itself in any way.

The second one is SEND_FAILURE, which basically means "authentication failed." This status is returned when the authentication mechanism wasn't able to validate the credentials that were provided. In most cases this is when the caller provided the wrong credentials. A JSF backing bean can respond to this by setting a faces message and re-display the login form.

The third status is SUCCESS, which means "authentication succeeded." This is returned when the authentication mechanism successfully validated the credentials provided. It's only after this status is returned that HttpServletRequest#getUserPrincipal(), Securi tyContext#getCallerPrincipal(), etc., return non-null values to indicate the current caller is authenticated. A JSF backing bean can respond to this in various ways (e.g., by setting a faces message and continuing to render the view, or issuing a redirect of itself).

The fourth and final status is NOT_DONE, which is returned when the authentication mechanism chooses to not authenticate at all. This happens, for instance, when the authentication mechanism is pre-emptively called but authentication appeared not to be necessary. Typically, a JSF backing bean would not need to take any special action here.

# Caller-Initiated Authentication

The previous code discussed the situation where an unauthenticated caller tries to access a protected resource (URL/page) and the authentication dialog is automatically started. Since this authentication dialog is started by the container, we call this "container-initiated authentication."

Another case is where a caller explicitly starts the authentication dialog (e.g., by clicking on a "login" button). Because the caller starts this dialog we call it "caller-initiated authentication."

In case of caller-initiated authentication, the core authentication mechanism is effectively directly invoked and the platform-provided login-to-continue functionality is skipped. This means that if an authentication mechanism depends on login-to-continue to redirect to a login page and after authentication to redirect back to the protected resource, neither of these two actions will happen when the application programmatically triggers authentication.

The CustomFormAuthenticationMechanism that we defined earlier via an annotation is indeed a mechanism that uses the platform's login-to-continue service, so we'll start the authentication dialog by directing to the same login view we used before. To indicate this is a new login, an extra request parameter is provided. The view from which we start looks as follows:

```
<!DOCTYPE html>
<html lang="en"
    xmlns="http://www.w3.org/1999/xhtml"
    xmlns:f="http://xmlns.jcp.org/jsf/core"
```

```
    xmlns:h="http://xmlns.jcp.org/jsf/html"
    xmlns:c="http://xmlns.jcp.org/jsp/jstl/core"
>
    <h:head>
        <title>Welcome</title>
    <h:head>
    <h:body>
        <c:if test="#{not empty request.userPrincipal}">
            <p>Logged-in as #{request.userPrincipal}</p>
        </c:if>
        <c:if test="#{empty request.userPrincipal}">
            <h:form>
                <h:button value="Login" outcome="/login">
                    <f:param name="new" value="true" />
                </h:button>
            </h:form>
        </c:if>
    </h:body>
</html>
```

In the backing bean we'll inject two additional objects: an instance to obtain and store the mentioned request parameter and a reference to the Flash, which we'll use later.

```
@Inject
private Flash flash;

@Inject @ManagedProperty("#{param.new}")
private boolean isNew;
```

The managed bean's scope needs to be changed to @ViewScoped, so we can retain the value of the isNew instance variable after the login form's postback.

An important addition is to the SecurityContext#authenticate() method where we'll now provide an extra parameter: newAuthentication. The authentication mechanism does not strictly need this though, and it's just smart enough to distinguish between an initial new authentication and continuing an authentication dialog that's in progress. However, things get more difficult when a caller is in the midst

429

of an authentication dialog and then navigates away, only to explicitly click a login button later. If the state associated with said dialog hasn't expired at that point, the authentication mechanism doesn't know a new authentication is required and will likely continue the aborted but still valid dialog.

To prevent this, we can force a new authentication by setting newAuthentication to true. This will discard all existing states. The modified continueAuthentication() method looks as follows:

```
private AuthenticationStatus continueAuthentication() {
    return securityContext.authenticate(
        (HttpServletRequest) externalContext.getRequest(),
        (HttpServletResponse) externalContext.getResponse(),
        AuthenticationParameters.withParams()
            .newAuthentication(isNew).credential(
                new UsernamePasswordCredential(email, password))
    );
}
```

Note that this version can be used for the case where we continue the dialog as well as to start a new one. When we continue the dialog, isNew will simply be false, which also happens to be the default when the parameter is not specified at all.

When using the CustomFormAuthenticationMechanism we know there will not be any redirects or other writes to the response after we provide the credentials in caller-initiated authentication, so that gives us a convenient location to handle the redirect to a landing page after the caller authenticates: the SUCCESS case.

```
case SUCCESS:
    flash.setKeepMessages(true);
    facesContext.addMessage(null, new FacesMessage(
        FacesMessage.SEVERITY_INFO, "Login succeed", null));
    externalContext.redirect(
        externalContext.getRequestContextPath() + "/index.xhtml");
    break;
```

We're redirecting the caller here to the index.xhtml landing page. Note that this is also the view where the caller initiated the authentication dialog, but that's just a coincidence in this example. In general, the view or even URL where we redirect the caller to is completely free for the application developer to choose. Typically, a landing page of some sort is chosen, which could be the index of the application or a dashboard corresponding to the main role the caller is in. As we mentioned above, when SUCCESS is returned the caller is fully authenticated. This means we can query the caller's roles and use these in our decision where to redirect to.

Outlook: a future version of Java EE Security may introduce a hybrid option where caller-initiated authentication can still start with the same redirect as container-initiated authentication and allows for the redirect-back URL to be provided by the application.

# Remember Me

Once a caller has been authenticated for a JSF (web) application, we naturally don't want to ask the caller to re-authenticate with every request. To prevent this, the result of a successful authentication is typically coupled in some way to the caller's HTTP session. In fact, the CustomFormAuthenticationMechanism internally uses the Java EE Security's provided "auto-apply-session" service to do just this. This service stores the data associated with said successful authentication (at least the caller name plus any groups the caller is in). Although implementation ultimately depends on where this data exactly lives and with what lifetime, in practice it's typically in a special section of the server's memory associated with the HTTP session. This section is special in the way that it's typically session scoped, but the data is not accessible via HttpSession#getAttribute().

In order to not exhaust the server's memory, an HTTP session expires after a certain amount of time. Typical expiration times are between 10 minutes and an hour. If the caller accesses the application after this time, authentication is required to be performed again.

Often though even re-authenticating after a period of inactivity as long as an hour is undesirable. But extending the HTTP session to a longer period is undoable for the aforementioned reasons of server resource exhaustion.

Here's where "Remember Me" (remember-me) comes in. Remember-me is a somewhat playful term for a process where the caller's credentials are exchanged for a token, and where this token is typically stored in a cookie that's distinct from the HTTP session cookie and has a longer time to live.

A remember-me token effectively functions as a new credential for the caller, without exposing the caller's original password. A remember-me token can basically be vended multiple times, for instance, once per device or IP (Internet protocol) that the caller uses to connect to the application. Care must be taken that while the token does not expose the caller's original credentials, it still functions as the key to a caller's account and therefore should be treated with the same precautions as one would apply to any other type of credential. Specifically, cookies containing the remember-me token should be sent over HTTPS/SSL only, and applications should not store the actual token verbatim but a strong hash of it.

As the primary reason for having remember-me is to not exhaust server memory and to be long-lived, the remember-me token is almost always stored in stable storage (e.g., a database). As such, a lookup from such storage is costlier than a lookup from the server's memory, and this could seriously affect performance when required to be done for every request, especially when many Ajax requests are being done all the time.

For this reason, remember-me is almost always used in combination with some kind of cache. The modular nature of the services that the `CustomFormAuthenticationMechanism` uses makes it possible for remember-me to be inserted between the auto-apply-session service mentioned above and the actual authentication mechanism. That way we effectively get a kind of memory hierarchy; the authentication data is first attempted to be found in the HTTP session storage, if it's not there the remember-me service is attempted, and if that one doesn't contain the data then finally the authentication mechanism is tried.

To make use of remember-me, two things have to be done.

1. Activating the remember-me service for the installed authentication mechanism

2. Providing a special identity store that's capable of vending and validating the remember-me token

# Activating Remember-Me Service

The remember-me service in Java EE Security is represented by an Interceptor. Via the interceptor binding annotation @RememberMe [the remember-me service] is easily applied to our own custom authentication mechanism, one for which we have the source code. Unfortunately, it isn't as easy when these have to be applied to a bean for which we don't have the source code and in fact for which we don't even know the exact implementation type.

As the CustomFormAuthenticationMechanism that we've been using for the examples above is indeed of the latter type, there's a bit more work to do. Essentially, we need to obtain a reference of the actual CustomFormAuthenticationMechanism implementation that the container makes available and then use the CDI 2.0 InterceptionFactory to programmatically add the @RememberMe annotation. The result is then to be returned from an alternative producer method.

This is demonstrated in the following code via the new method produceAuthenticationMechanism() in the ApplicationConfig bean which we showed before:

```
@CustomFormAuthenticationMechanismDefinition(
    loginToContinue = @LoginToContinue(
        loginPage = "/login.xhtml",
        useForwardToLogin = false,
        errorPage = ""
    )
)
@FacesConfig @ApplicationScoped
@Alternative @Priority(500)
public class ApplicationConfig {

    @Produces
    public HttpAuthenticationMechanism produceAuthenticationMechanism(
        InterceptionFactory<HttpAuthenticationMechanismWrapper>
        interceptionFactory, BeanManager beanManager
    ) {
        @RememberMe
        class RememberMeClass {};
        interceptionFactory.configure().add(
```

```
            RememberMeClass.class.getAnnotation(RememberMe.class));
        return interceptionFactory.createInterceptedInstance(
            new HttpAuthenticationMechanismWrapper(
                (HttpAuthenticationMechanism) beanManager
                .getReference(beanManager
                .resolve(beanManager
                .getBeans((HttpAuthenticationMechanism.class).stream()
                .filter(b -> b.getBeanClass() != ApplicationConfig.class)
                .collect(Collectors.toSet())),
                    HttpAuthenticationMechanism.class,
                    beanManager.createCreationalContext(null))));
    }
}
```

The ApplicationConfig bean is annotated with the @Alternative and @Priority
annotations. @Alternative is used here to indicate that the producer is not just any
regular producer but one that should be called instead of any existing producer or bean.
That is, the bean we are producing here is an alternative for the bean with the same
type that would otherwise be selected by CDI for injection. @Priority is used to enable
(activate) our alternative producer. Without this annotation the producer is present but
not enabled, meaning that CDI won't call it. Another way of enabling an alternative is
using beans.xml. The number 500 here is used to select between various alternatives
if multiple alternatives are enabled. In that case the one with the highest number is
selected.

The code shown above uses the somewhat well-known CDI pattern
BeanManager#getBeans()/resolve()/getReference() to obtain the
CustomFormAuthenticationMechanism that the container makes available. This pattern
is more verbose than the simpler CDI.current().select(...) variant, but it allows
us to filter out the Bean<T> that represents the producer method. Getting a reference
from that Bean<T> from within the producer method would invoke that same producer
method again, and thus would cause a recursive series of calls eventually leading to a
stack overflow. It goes without saying this is unwanted, hence the reason we filter that
particular Bean<T> out.

The bean instance that is returned from the BeanManager#getReference() is almost certainly a proxy; CustomFormAuthenticationMechanism is specified to be application scoped, and it implicitly makes use of an interceptor. Due to the technical difficulty of proxying an existing proxy (think of generated proxies often being final and proxy caches being used) CDI 2.0 imposes a limitation on what types of objects it can create an intercepted instance from. To work around this limitation, we have little choice but to insert an extra manually created "pass-through wrapper" HttpAuthenticationMechanismWrapper instance as shown in the code above. The code of this wrapper is as follows:

```
public class HttpAuthenticationMechanismWrapper
    implements HttpAuthenticationMechanism
{

    private HttpAuthenticationMechanism wrapped;

    public HttpAuthenticationMechanismWrapper() {
        //
    }

    public HttpAuthenticationMechanismWrapper
        (HttpAuthenticationMechanism httpAuthenticationMechanism)
    {
        this.wrapped = httpAuthenticationMechanism;
    }

    public HttpAuthenticationMechanism getWrapped() {
        return wrapped;
    }

    @Override
    public AuthenticationStatus validateRequest(
        HttpServletRequest request,
        HttpServletResponse response,
        HttpMessageContext context) throws AuthenticationException
    {
        return getWrapped().validateRequest(request, response, context);
    }
```

```
@Override
public AuthenticationStatus secureResponse(
    HttpServletRequest request,
    HttpServletResponse response,
    HttpMessageContext context) throws AuthenticationException
{
    return getWrapped().secureResponse(request, response, context);
}
@Override
public void cleanSubject(
    HttpServletRequest request,
    HttpServletResponse response,
    HttpMessageContext context)
{
    getWrapped().cleanSubject(request, response, context);
}
}
```

Outlook: it's expected that a convenience method for the above task will be added to a future version of Java EE Security, thereby greatly simplifying this task.

# Logging Out

Regardless of which method to login has been used, at some point the caller may wish to explicitly log out. A normal login (authentication) in Java EE is always primarily valid per request only, but various authentication mechanisms or the services they're using (such as @AutoApplySession and @RememberMe) may keep the state beyond a single request and automatically re-authenticate the caller at every next request.

This state may be kept at various places: in cookies, in the HTTP session, in client storage, etc. In order to log out we have to make sure all this state is cleared. In JSF we can do this simply by calling the HttpServletRequest#logout() method. This will immediately remove the authenticated identity from the current request and call the cleanSubject() method of the authentication mechanism, which in turn will remove any session data, cookies, etc., that it used.

The following gives an example:

```
@Named @RequestScoped
public class Logout {

    @Inject
    private HttpServletRequest request;

    public void submit() throws ServletException {
        request.logout();
        request.getSession().invalidate();
    }
}
```

Note that for a full logout it's typically good practice to invalidate the session as well. The call to HttpServletRequest#logout() should only remove the session state used by the authentication mechanism (if any), while after a full logout we often don't want any other session state lingering around either. Depending on the application design it's typical to redirect the caller to the home page of the application after a logout as well.

# Custom Principals

The default principal that we can obtain from the security context contains very little other than just the name or, more exactly, the caller principal name (also known as the user principal name). This is typically a unique name and often, but not necessarily, the name the caller used to authenticate with.

In practice, a web application almost always needs more information than just this name, and a richer application-specific model object representing the user is often desired. The lifetime of this model object does need to be very tightly coupled to that of the principal. For example, if the caller is logged out mid-request, the associated model object must disappear right away, and if the caller is logged in again right after (possibly still in the same request) a new model object must become available.

There are various patterns to realize this, some of them including Servlet filters and others containing CDI producers. The pattern we're going to show here, though, involves a custom principal.

A custom principal means that a specific `Principal` type is returned from the identity store, instead of just providing a `String` and letting the container decide the type. This specific `Principal` type can then either *contain* our model object (aggregation) or *be* the model object (inheritance). We'll give an example of the aggregation approach here.

First consider the following custom `Principal`:

```
public class UserPrincipal extends CallerPrincipal {

    private final User user;

    public UserPrincipal(User user) {
        super(user.getEmail());
        this.user = user;
    }

    public User getUser() {
        return user;
    }
}
```

This principal extends from `javax.security.enterprise.CallerPrincipal` which is the Java EE Security API-specific caller principal representation.

With this `Principal` implementation we can now adjust the identity store that we presented earlier to return our custom principal instead.

```
@ApplicationScoped
public class UserServiceIdentityStore implements IdentityStore {

    @Inject
    private UserService userService;

    @Override
    public CredentialValidationResult validate(Credential credential) {
        UsernamePasswordCredential login =
            (UserNamePasswordCredential) credential;
        String email = login.getCaller();
        String password = login.getPasswordAsString();
```

```
    Optional<User> optionalUser =
        userService.findByEmailAndPassword(email, password);

    if (optionalUser.isPresent()) {
        User user = optionalUser.get();
        return new CredentialValidationResult(
            new UserPrincipal(user), // Principal instead of String.
            user.getRolesAsStrings()
        );
    }
    else {
        return CredentialValidationResult.INVALID_RESULT;
    }
    }
}
```

Subsequently, we can access our model object again from an injected security context.

```
@Inject
private SecurityContext securityContext;
[...]
Optional<User> OptionalUser =
        securityContext.getPrincipalsByType(UserPrincipal.class)
                                .stream()
                                .map(e -> e.getUser())
                                .findAny();
```

# Conditionally Rendering Based on Access

In web applications one often wants to render parts of a view differently based on whether a caller is authenticated or not, and if so based on what roles this caller is in.

JSF component tags don't really need special attributes for this, as the existing implicit objects combined with expression language are powerful enough to do most of the checks needed for this.

One of the most common checks is determining whether the user is authenticated. This was briefly shown in the index.xhtml view above:

```
<c:if test="#{not empty request.userPrincipal}">
    <p>Logged-in as #{request.userPrincipal}</p>
</c:if>
```

You can, of course, also use the rendered attribute of any JSF component here.

```
<ui:fragment rendered="#{not empty request.userPrincipal}">
    <p>Logged-in as #{request.userPrincipal}</p>
</ui:fragment>
```

However, as you learned in the section "JSTL Core Tags" in Chapter 3, this will only end up in a slightly more verbose component tree. Moreover, the rendered attribute checks will be done throughout the JSF life cycle over and over while JSTL tags are executed only once during view build time.

Note that we're using the implicit object #{request} here instead of the more general SecurityContext. This is because in Java EE 8 there's no implicit EL object available corresponding to this SecurityContext. In Java EE Security, as well as in the Servlet API (from which the request, which is of type HttpServletRequest originates) it's defined that a null return from getUserPrincipal() means the user is not authenticated. A better alignment between Java EE Security and Expression Language is planned for a future version of Java EE.

Another common check as mentioned is to test for the caller being in a specific role. Here too we can use the implicit object #{request}, as shown in the following:

```
<c:if test="#{request.isUserInRole('foo')}">
    <!-- foo specific things here -->
</c:if>
```

It's good to remember that as explained in the beginning of this chapter, the role "foo" doesn't have to be something that we would call a role in our normal usage of the word. That its, it doesn't have to be something like "admin", or "manager". In fact, for such very local usage as in a fragment on a view it's often preferred to use a finer-grained name (e.g., "CAN_UPDATE_SALARY"). A common technique is to map fine-grained roles to more coarse-grained roles, such as, indeed, "ADMIN". Via this technique a user is given these more coarse-grained roles, and the data store that stores the authentication data then only contains these coarse-grained roles as well. When an identity store such as we saw above retrieves this authentication data for a certain caller and sees "ADMIN" it would return a collection of roles to which "ADMIN" is mapped (e.g., {"CAN_UPDATE_SALARY", "CAN_ADJUST_MARGINS", ...}).

A special role that we can test for is the "**" role which is an alternative for the #{not empty request.userPrincipal} check. This role is implicitly assigned to any authenticated caller, but with the caveat that the application has not declared this in any way. If it has done so, "**" loses its special meaning and is just another opaque string for which the security system explicitly tests. Using the "**" check, the first fragment that we showed in this section looks as follows:

```
<c:if test="#{request.isUserInRole('**')}">
    <p>Logged-in as #{request.userPrincipal}</p>
</c:if>
```

In the standard Java EE programmatic APIs there are no methods available to test whether the caller is in any of two or more roles, or in all of two or more roles. If this is required, utility methods such as shown in the following code can be used:

```
public static boolean isInAnyRole(HttpServletRequest request, String...
roles) {
    for (String roles : roles) {
        if (request.isUserInRole(role)) {
            return true;
        }
    }
    return false;
}
public static boolean isInAllRoles(HttpServletRequest request, String...
roles) {
    for (String roles : roles) {
        if (!request.isUserInRole(role)) {
            return false;
        }
    }
    return true;
}
```

Sometimes it's necessary not only to render content on a view differently, depending on what roles a caller is in, but also to take into account what other views (web resources) a caller is allowed to access. This comes into play, for instance, when rendering navigation menus (omitting the entries for views a caller does not have access to), or rendering links or buttons that navigate to views to which the caller does not have access in a special way (e.g., in red or with a lock icon next to it).

A traditional way to implement this is to test for the roles that the programmer knows give access to the given view. While this may seem to work well, it's often brittle in practice as it lets the code work under the assumption of a specific role/view relationship without any strong guarantees that this relationship actually holds.

A more stable way to test whether a caller has access to a given view is quite simply to test directly for exactly that; does the caller have access to this view (web resource). The SecurityContext has a method that can be used for almost exactly this: SecurityContext#hasAccessToWebResource(). Since the SecurityContext is not a named bean or implicit object, we have to create a small helper bean in order to use this in EL. This is shown as follows:

```
@Named @ApplicationScoped
public class Security {

    @Inject
    private SecurityContext securityContext;

    public boolean hasAccessToWebResource(String resource) {
        return securityContext.hasAccessToWebResource(resource, "GET");
    }
}
```

There are two things to be aware of here.

First, the hasAccessToWebResource() method takes a web resource pattern, which is the same pattern as used for the url-pattern in the web.xml fragment we looked at earlier. This is close to, but not exactly the same as, the JSF view. The JSF view is often specified in a mapping independent way (e.g., /foo instead of /faces/foo or /foo.xhtml). The web resource pattern, however, has to be the URL itself, with the mapping included.

Second, hasAccessToWebResource() requires us to specify the HTTP method for which we test the access. This is required since in Java EE Security constraints actually apply per URL and per HTTP method. For instance, a caller can have access to POST to /foo.xhtml but not to GET /foo.xhtml. As we're going to use our utility method for navigation tests, GET is typically the right HTTP method to use, but we should be aware that sometimes we may need to test for another HTTP method.

With the helper bean in place, we can now easily check for access to a target resource on a view and alter the rendering based on that. To demonstrate this, we'll first define three new web resource constraints in web.xml.

```
<security-constraint>
    <web-resource-collection>
        <web-resource-name>Bar</web-resource-name>
        <url-pattern>/bar.xhtml</url-pattern>
    </web-resource-collection>
    <auth-constraint>
        <role-name>bar</role-name>
    </auth-constraint>
</security-constraint>
<security-constraint>
    <web-resource-collection>
        <web-resource-name>Foo</web-resource-name>
        <url-pattern>/foo.xhtml</url-pattern>
    </web-resource-collection>
    <auth-constraint>
        <role-name>foo</role-name>
    </auth-constraint>
</security-constraint>
<security-constraint>
    <web-resource-collection>
        <web-resource-name>Baz</web-resource-name>
        <url-pattern>/baz.xhtml</url-pattern>
    </web-resource-collection>
    <auth-constraint>
        <role-name>baz</role-name>
    </auth-constraint>
</security-constraint>
```

After these constraints have been defined we can render links to them with access checks on the enabled attribute.

```
<h:link value="Go to Bar" outcome="/bar"
    disabled="#{not security.hasAccessToWebResource('/bar.xhtml')}" />
<h:link value="Go to Foo" outcome="/foo"
    disabled="#{not security.hasAccessToWebResource('/foo.xhtml')}" />
<h:link value="Go to Baz" outcome="/baz"
    disabled="#{not security.hasAccessToWebResource('/baz.xhtml')}" />
```

Authenticating with a caller having, for instance, the roles "bar" and "foo", but not "baz", will result in the link to /baz being rendered as disabled.

# Cross-Site Request Forgery Protection

Cross-site request forgery (CSRF) is an attack that lets users without their consent or even knowledge do a request to a site where they may possibly be logged in. Such request then has some side effect that in some particular way may be beneficial to the attacker.

For instance, suppose your bank has a URL of the form `https:/example.com/tr ansferAmount=4000&targetAccount=7836` which means "transfer 4000 euros from my account to the account with ID 7836." In this statement the "my account" is being determined via the logged-in session (typically a cookie) that you have with your bank. Now an attacker might not be able to capture your session cookie, but that's not necessary in this example if only your browser can be tricked into sending the `https:/ example.com/transferAmount=4000&targetAccount=7836` request from any other web site that you visit while you're logged in to your bank in another tab or window, with the `targetAccount` parameter set to an ID of an account that the attacker controls. Note that in practice a GET request and request parameters would not likely be used, but POST and POST parameters would be used instead. However, for both the same basic vulnerability holds.

If we want to protect our application against receiving such malicious requests, then one of the ways to do so is including "something" (i.e., a token) in the request that is

1. Specific to a certain caller.

2. Expires after some time.

3. Can't be easily guessed.

As it happens JSF already has something that fulfills all these three requirements, and that's the `javax.faces.ViewState` hidden parameter that one finds within JSF forms.

---

**Caution**  There's a caveat though, and that's that this parameter only fully fulfills those requirements when using postbacks, state saving on server is used, and the view in question is not stateless. Only in that case is the value of `javax.faces.ViewState` effectively a token. Since this is the default, JSF is relatively safe out of the box here, but this protection is compromised as soon as we deviate from these defaults, for instance, by using stateless views. See also the section "Stateless Forms" in Chapter 4.

---

Next to this implicit CSRF protection, JSF also has explicit CSRF protection. This explicit CSRF protection adds a token for all cases, and additionally adds checks for the "`referer`" and "`origin`" HTTP headers. Note that HTTP headers should normally not be trusted for incoming requests, as they can be very easily spoofed. However, for this particular attack we're not trying to defend against just any random HTTP request but specifically against requests sent from a trusted browser. The header checks are also in addition to the token check, and the token check must always pass first.

Defining which views should be protected by a CSRF token and the additional header checks happens in a way that's somewhat similar to how we defined roles for views—a collection of URL patterns in a deployment descriptor. This time the deployment descriptor is `faces-config.xml` instead of `web.xml` though. The following gives an example for these entries in `faces-config.xml`:

```
<protected-views>
    <url-pattern>/bar.xhtml</url-pattern>
    <url-pattern>/foo.xhtml</url-pattern>
    <url-pattern>/baz.xhtml</url-pattern>
</protected-views>
```

Note that the `url-pattern` here is the exact same pattern that is used in `web.xml`. One thing to be aware of here is that despite `faces-config.xml` being a JSF-specific deployment descriptor, the `url-pattern` here is again for the full URL relative to the application root which means it has to include all mappings used such as `/faces/` and `.xhtml`.

Adding a `faces-config.xml` with the above shown `protected-views` fragment to the example application code we've been working on in this chapter will render the link on `index.xhtml` to, for example, `/bar.xhtml` in the following way:

`/bar.xhtml?javax.faces.Token=gdMoNbfOycv2v80gr`

As can be seen, the `javax.faces.Token` request parameter has been added by JSF. The token is tied to the user's HTTP session, so if the HTTP session expires, the token also expires. The token is cryptographically strong, meaning that it fulfills all three requirements for a CSRF protection token as stated above.

If the token is tampered (e.g., we use `xxMoNbfOycv2v80gr` instead of `gdMoNbfOycv2v80gr`), or is missing altogether (i.e., we request `/bar.xhtml`) JSF will throw a `javax.faces.application.ProtectedViewException`. In case the link originated from a stateless page, JSF applications can handle this exception by notifying the user and allowing to re-render the original page again. In the example above that would mean re-rendering `index.xhtml`. The genuine user would get a new CSRF protection token then, while an attacker will not get the expected side effect from the original request.

As mentioned, there's a `referer` and `origin` header check as well. For this check, JSF checks whether the `referer` header, if available, is set to a URL that originates from the same application. To demonstrate this, consider a second JSF application with only an empty `faces-config.xml` and the following view:

```
<!DOCTYPE html>
<html lang="en"
    xmlns="http://www.w3.org/1999/xhtml"
    xmlns:h="http://xmlns.jcp.org/jsf/html"
>
    <h:head />
    <h:body>
        <h:outputLink value="http://localhost:8080/project/bar.xhtml?javax.
        faces.Token=gdMhNbfOycv2v80gr">
            test
        </h:outputLink>
    </h:body>
</html>
```

Assuming our first application with the CSRF-protected bar.xhtml is deployed to
http://localhost:8080/project, clicking the output link from this second application
will cause the javax.faces.application.ProtectedViewException to be thrown again
in the first application. Note that the referer is an optional check that's only done
when the referer header is actually present, as is the case with the link in the second
application.

If we enter http://localhost:8080/project/bar.xhtml?javax.faces.
Token=gdMhNbfOycv2v80gr directly into the address bar of a browser, or request it
directly via a command-line utility such as wget or curl, there won't be a referer and
the request will be accepted.

In practice, a GET request has less value of being protected against CSRF attacks
since these actually *should* be idempotent (should not have side effects and should
only display data). Instead of shielding GET requests with CSRF protection tokens, it's
probably a far better idea to refactor an application to not have non-idempotent GET
requests.

For postbacks the CSRF protection token works in much the same way though.
To demonstrate, consider changing the /bar.xhtml view into the following:

```
<!DOCTYPE html>
<html lang="en"
    xmlns="http://www.w3.org/1999/xhtml"
    xmlns:h="http://xmlns.jcp.org/jsf/html"
>
    <h:head />
    <h:body>
        <h:form>
            <h:commandButton value="Test" action="#{bar.submit}" />
        </h:form>
    </h:body>
</html>
```

Rendering this page will result in the form target URL having the CSRF protection
token applied to it in the same way as we saw for the GET requests—for example,

```
<form method="post"
    action="/project/bar.xhtml?javax.faces.Token=gdMhNbfOycv2v80gr" ...>
```

This is thus another difference with the implicit `javax.faces.ViewState` token, which is always a POST parameter.

# Web Parameter Tampering Protection

Web parameter tampering is an attack against an application where an attacker modifies parameter values that are sent (back) to the server hosting the application. If the application doesn't validate those values correctly, an attacker could gain more benefits than entitled to, or may get the opportunity to carry out additional attacks.

For example, suppose a web application renders a list of roles that can be assigned to another user, say "user," "manager," and "sales." An attacker could attempt to modify the data posted back and change the selection of "user" into "admin." If the server blindly accepts the input and "admin" is an existing value, this allows the attacker to give another user the "admin" role, even when the attacker is not privileged to do that.

JSF has an implicit protection against a subset of this attack; namely, against values being posted back from a selection (specifically, from `UISelectOne`- and `UISelectMany`-based components). This works by JSF either restoring the view from `javax.faces.ViewState` after a postback (when full state saving is used) or re-creating it (when partial state saving is used). Only values that were also rendered are accepted. The usual caveat applies though, and that's that with partial state saving, the data bound to the component needs to be identical before and after the postback. This, however, can easily be accomplished by using the view scope.

To demonstrate, consider the following view:

```
<!DOCTYPE html>
<html lang="en"
    xmlns="http://www.w3.org/1999/xhtml"
    xmlns:h="http://xmlns.jcp.org/jsf/html"
    xmlns:f="http://xmlns.jcp.org/jsf/core"
>
    <h:head />
    <h:body>
        <h:form>
            <h:selectOneMenu value="#{bean.selected}">
```

```
            <f:selectItems value="#{bean.available}" />
        </h:selectOneMenu>
        <h:commandButton value="Select" />
    </h:form>
    <p>Chosen value: #{bean.selected}</p>
  </h:body>
</html>
```

And the following backing bean:

```
@Named @RequestScoped
public class Bean {

    private List<String> available = Arrays.asList("foo", "bar", "kaz");
    private String selected;

    public List<String> getAvailable() {
        return available;
    }

    public String getSelected() {
        return selected;
    }
    public void setSelected (String selected) {
        this.selected = selected;
    }
}
```

Choosing, for example, "bar" and clicking "select" will render "Chosen value: bar," as expected. Changing the value being sent can be done in various ways, for instance via an intercepting proxy like Burp Proxy or by editing the live source via the developer tools from a browser such as Chrome.

Selecting the "foo" entry after the change as shown in Figure 13-1 and clicking the select button again will cause the "foox" value to be sent to the application. This value will be rejected by JSF and as a result "Chosen value:" will be rendered, indicating that our tampered value indeed has not been accepted.

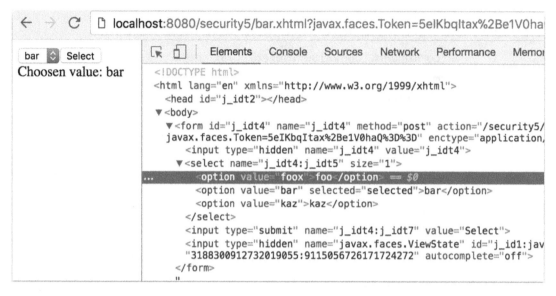

*Figure 13-1.* *Tampering the selected value in HTML source code*

# Cross-Site Scripting Protection

Cross-site scripting or XSS is an attack that has a couple of variations, but practically it boils down to a web application rendering data that it got from (other) users directly as part of the markup sent to the client. If this data itself contains scripting code (typically JavaScript), the browser may execute it blindly, allowing the attacker to read, for example, cookie data and to send that over to a server controlled by the attacker.

JSF provides protection against this type of attack by having contextual output escaping enabled for many common contexts. The most common context is writing out HTML, where all JSF's output writers by default XML escape their output.

To demonstrate, consider the following backing bean:

```java
@Named @RequestScoped
public class Bean {

    private String value = "<script>alert('hi')</script>";

    public String getValue() {
        return value;
    }
}
```

The value instance variable contains a script that we don't want the browser to execute. In this example it's hard-coded, but in practice it could come from stored data in, for example, a database.

Now we'll render this value using two simple default constructs of JSF: a direct expression language expression on a Facelet and the <h:outputText> component.

```
<!DOCTYPE html>
<html lang="en"
    xmlns="http://www.w3.org/1999/xhtml"
    xmlns:h="http://xmlns.jcp.org/jsf/html"
    xmlns:f="http://xmlns.jcp.org/jsf/core"
>
    <h:head />
    <h:body>
        <p>#{bean.value}</p>
        <p><h:outputText value="#{bean.value}" /></p>
    </h:body>
</html>
```

When requesting this view and looking at the HTML source, we'll see that both times the value has been rendered as "<script>alert('hi')</script>" (i.e., in an escaped form that the browser won't execute).

In case we explicitly don't want this escaping to be done, the escape attribute of <h:outputText> can be set to false. For example,

```
<h:outputText value="#{bean.value}" escape="false" />
```

Requesting the view again with the above component on it will cause a JavaScript alert to appear to be saying "hi." Had this been malicious code being input by an attacker, the security of the client's system would have been compromised. The escape attribute should therefore only be used with the utmost care.

Output for usage in URLs is escaped as well, but there it's escaped differently, since it's a different context. To demonstrate, consider adding the following component to the view:

```
<h:link outcome="/foo">
    Go to foo
    <f:param name="param" value="#{bean.value}" />
</h:link>
```

451

After requesting this view, we'll see the link has been rendered as

```
<a href="/project/foo.xhtml?param=%3Cscript%3Ealert%28%27hi%27%29%3C%2F
script%3E">
    Go to foo
</a>
```

What has happened here is that our original value has been escaped for usage as a URL parameter using URL encoding, which as can be seen is different from XML escaping, hence the term "contextual output escaping."

Related to XSS protection, sensitive cookies that the application uses should be set to `HttpOnly`, meaning they'll be sent to the server with each request but can't be read by scripts on the client. For the session ID cookie this can be done in `web.xml` as follows:

```
<session-config>
    <cookie-config>
        <http-only>true</http-only>
        <secure>true</secure>
    </cookie-config>
</session-config>
```

Note that the cookie is set to "secure" as well here. This is not related to XSS, but sets that the cookie is to be sent only when HTTPS/SSL is used. This protects the cookie from being eavesdropped (e.g., on a shared WiFi network). Since development often happens over HTTP using localhost, such a setting may be problematic for development purposes. If this is the case, then alternatively the cookie can be set to secure or not using `ServletContext#getSessionCookieConfig()` in a `ServletContextListener`

```
@WebListener
public class ApplicationConfig implements ServletContextListener {

    @Override
    public void contextInitialized(ServletContextEvent event) {
        if (...) {
            event.getServletContext()
```

```
        .getSessionCookieConfig()
        .setSecure(false);
    }
  }
}
```

where "..." is an application-specific check to see if it's running in "dev mode." You could even use JSF's own `Application#getProjectStage()` for this.

# Source Exposure Protection

Source exposure in the context of server-side web applications refers to the unwanted disclosure of parts of the web application's source. This is a security risk, not only because of the exposure of the source itself (which may be a trade secret) but also because it may give an attacker insight on which to base follow-up attacks (the source may contain references to other systems, beans, or even comments with passwords, although those kinds of comments should of course not be there to begin with).

Due to a number of somewhat perhaps unfortunate design choices in the past, JSF has some specific vulnerabilities here, which mostly concern how URL mapping is done but also concern the location of resource files. To understand this vulnerability we first explain how JSF mapping and the `FacesServlet` work.

The main entry into every JSF application is the `FacesServlet`. This is a Servlet provided by the JSF framework that acts as a so-called front controller through which all JSF requests are routed.

A request to a JSF view such as `foo.jsf` will thus first need to go through this Servlet, which will then in some way locate the definition of the tree of components that represent the view `foo.jsf`. We'll call this actual definition the "physical resource." Out of the box, JSF supports two types of physical resources: Facelets and JSP files with the extension `.xhtml`, `.view.xml`, and `.jsp`. Note that JSP files are largely deprecated.

In order for the `FacesServlet` to be able to handle all these requests it has to be mapped to one or more URL patterns that capture them. To be able to do this, JSF supports prefix, suffix, and exact mapping.

If no explicit mapping in web.xml is specified and a recognized JSF artifact is found in the application (such as an empty faces-config,xml or the @FacesConfig annotation) then the FacesServlet is automatically mapped. Since JSF 2.1 and Servlet 3.0 this automatic mapping is to the following patterns:

- /faces/* (prefix mapping)

- *.jsf (suffix mapping)

- *.faces (suffix mapping)

Since JSF 2.3 this also includes:

- *.xhtml (suffix mapping)

Especially older (existing) JSF applications still explicitly map the FacesServlet in web.xml, which then looks for example as follows:

```
<servlet>
    <servlet-name>facesServlet</servlet-name>
    <servlet-class>javax.faces.webapp.FacesServlet</servlet-class>
</servlet>
<servlet-mapping>
    <servlet-name>facesServlet</servlet-name>
    <url-pattern>/faces/*</url-pattern>
    <url-pattern>*.jsf</url-pattern>
</servlet-mapping>
```

In suffix mapping and when using Facelets, the FacesServlet will first try to locate the physical resource with the same path and name as the requested resource, but with the suffix replaced by .xhtml. For example, a request for /path/foo.jsf will result in a lookup for the file /path/foo.xhtml.

With prefix mapping, the FacesServlet will try to locate the physical resource with the same name and path as the requested resource, but minus the prefix path. For example, a request for /faces/path/foo.xhtml will result in a lookup for the file /path/foo.xhtml.

This, however, may introduce a security issue that will result in exposure of the Facelet source code. Namely, the lookup for /path/foo.xhtml is done in the web root of the WAR in which the FacesServlet resides. Unless otherwise (implicitly) mapped, every file in the web root is directly accessible for download. In this case, if /path/foo.xhtml is directly requested instead of /path/foo.jsf or /faces/path/foo.xhtml this request will not go through the FacesServlet and returns the bare Facelets source code of that page instead of the rendered markup.

There are two ways to prevent this exposure of source code.

1.  Map the FacesServlet directly to *.xhtml

2.  Add a security constraint to web.xml

Mapping the FacesServlet directly to *.xhtml may be the most natural solution. With this mapping, the requested resource is identical to the physical resource. If /path/foo.xhtml is requested, then the FacesServlet will try to locate /path/foo.xhtml. Via this mapping, there is no second path to reach the Facelets source and hence no risk of exposing it.

Side note: being able to use *.xhtml mapping was a new feature in JSF 2.0. Doing this in JSF 1.x resulted in an infinite loop.

To map the FacesServlet to *.xhtml, the easiest way is to rely on the default mapping of JSF 2.3 as explained above. If this is not possible for some reason, add the mapping to the FacesServlet mapping in web.xml as shown in the following code:

```
<servlet-mapping>
    <servlet-name>facesServlet</servlet-name>
    <url-pattern>/faces/*</url-pattern>
    <url-pattern>*.jsf</url-pattern>
    <url-pattern>*.xhtml</url-pattern>
</servlet-mapping>
```

As an alternative, a security constraint can be defined that prevents access to *.xhtml resources. There is rarely a good reason to prefer this over the simpler *.xhtml to *.xhtml mapping, but for completeness, this can be done as follows:

```
<security-constraint>
    <display-name>No access to Facelets source</display-name>
    <web-resource-collection>
        <web-resource-name>XHTML</web-resource-name>
```

```
        <url-pattern>*.xhtml</url-pattern>
    </web-resource-collection>
    <auth-constraint />
</security-constraint>
```

A special case of exposing Facelets source code happens with composite components. Composite components are components that are implemented via a Facelet instead of a Java class. By convention, they have to be placed in a directory inside a directory named `/resources` that resides in the web root—for instance, `/resources/bar/foo.xhtml`. This will make a component "foo" available in the namespace "`http://xmlns.jcp.org/jsf/composite/bar`".

Components are of course not views and the user should not be able to request those directly. Unfortunately, `/resources` is not in any way a special directory to Java EE. JSF assigns a special meaning to it by convention, but to the Servlet container it's a directory like any other. This specifically means there's no protection applied to this and any user can directly request resources from it. In other words, this directory is "world readable." Even with an `*.xhtml` mapping, this not only allows the user to guess which components we have but lets the user attempt to execute those as well. Clearly this is not what we want.

There are again two solutions for this:

1. Configure another directory to be the JSF resources directory

2. Add a security constraint to `web.xml`

In JSF 2.2 a method was introduced to address this security vulnerability. Namely, via the `javax.faces.WEBAPP_RESOURCES_DIRECTORY` context parameter another directory can be configured to be the JSF resources directory instead of `/resources`. For example,

```
<context-param>
    <param-name>javax.faces.WEBAPP_RESOURCES_DIRECTORY</param-name>
    <param-value>WEB-INF/resources</param-value>
</context-param>
```

Note that the path is relative to the web root and may not begin with a "/".

Alternatively, or for JSF 2.0/2.1, a security constraint can be configured in web.xml again that prohibits caller access to /resources. This can be done in a similar way as protecting for *.xhtml access.

```
<security-constraint>
    <web-resource-collection>
        <web-resource-name>resources</web-resource-name>
        <description>The resources directory</description>
        <url-pattern>/resources/*</url-pattern>
    </web-resource-collection>
    <auth-constraint />
</security-constraint>
```

# CHAPTER 14

# Localization

JSF has always had decent internationalization support. Since JSF 1.0 you can supply
`java.util.ResourceBundle`-based bundle files in different locales, which in turn
get dynamically included as text in the web page at the declared places. Also, all JSF
converters and validators have their own set of localized default messages which you
can easily customize via a message bundle or, since JSF 1.2, via new `requiredMessage`,
`converterMessage`, and `validatorMessage` attributes. JSF 2.0 adds, via the new
`javax.faces.application.ResourceHandler`, API (application programing interface)
support for localizable assets such as stylesheets, scripts, and images.

The act of internationalization, "I18N," is distinct from the act of localization, "L10N."
The internationalization part is basically already done by JSF (JavaServer Faces) itself
as being a MVC (model-view-controller) framework. All you need to do is to take care
of the localization part. Basically, you need to specify the "active locale" in the view,
supply the desired resource bundle files, if necessary translated with help of a third-party
translation service, and declare references to the bundle file in your JSF page.

In this chapter you will learn how to prepare a JSF web application for different
languages and how to develop it in order to make localization easier for yourself as to
maintenance.

## Hello World, Olá mundo, नमस्ते दुनिया

To start off, create a bunch of new bundle files in `main/java/resources` folder of
the project. The `main/java/resources` folder of a Maven WAR project is intended
for non-class files which are supposed to end up in the `/WEB-INF/classes` folder of
the final build. The bundle files can be in `java.util.Properties` format, with the
`.properties` extension.

© Bauke Scholtz, Arjan Tijms 2018
B. Scholtz and A. Tijms, *The Definitive Guide to JSF in Java EE 8*, https://doi.org/10.1007/978-1-4842-3387-0_14

The filename of those files must have a common prefix (e.g., "text"), followed by an underscore and the two-letter ISO 639-1-Alpha-2[1] language code (e.g., "en" for English, "pt" for Portuguese, and "hi" for Hindi). It can optionally be followed by another underscore and the two-letter ISO 3166-1-Alpha-2[2] country code (e.g., "GB" for Great Britain, "US" for United States, "BR" for Brazil, "PT" for Portugal).

```
main/java/resources/com/example/project/i18n/text.properties
title = Localization example
heading = Hello World
paragraph = Welcome to my website!
main/java/resources/com/example/project/i18n/text_pt_BR.properties
title = Exemplo de localização
heading = Olá mundo
paragraph = Bem-vindo ao meu site!
main/java/resources/com/example/project/i18n/text_hi.properties
title = स्थानीयकरण उदाहरण
heading = नमस्ते दुनिया
paragraph = मेरी वेबसाइट पर स्वागत है!
```

Do note that all those bundle files have common keys "title", "heading", and "paragraph", which are usually in English. It's basically the lingua franca of the Internet and web developers. It's considered the best practice to keep the source code entirely in English, particularly if it is open source.

Also note that the English bundle file doesn't have the "en" language code in the filename as in text_en.properties but is just text.properties. Basically, it has become the fallback bundle file which is supposed to contain every single bundle key used in the entire web application. This way, when a bundle file with a specific language code doesn't contain the desired bundle entry, then the value will be looked up from the fallback bundle file. This is useful for situations wherein you'd like to gradually upgrade the bundle files, or when you have certain sections in the web application which don't necessarily need to be localized, such as back-end admin pages.

---

[1]https://en.wikipedia.org/wiki/List_of_ISO_639-1_codes.
[2]https://en.wikipedia.org/wiki/ISO_3166-1_alpha-2.

# Configuration

In order to familiarize the JSF application with those bundle files and the desired locales, we need to edit its `faces-config.xml` file to add the following entries to the `<application>` element:

```
<application>
    <locale-config>
        <default-locale>en</default-locale>
        <supported-locale>pt_BR</supported-locale>
        <supported-locale>hi</supported-locale>
    </locale-config>
    <resource-bundle>
        <base-name>com.example.project.i18n.text</base-name>
        <var>text</var>
    </resource-bundle>
</application>
```

The `<base-name>` must specify the fully qualified name (FQN) following the same convention as for Java classes and that it doesn't include the file extension. The `<var>` basically declares the EL (Expression Language) variable name of the bundle file. This will make the currently loaded resource bundle available as a `Map`-like object in EL via `#{text}`. To avoid conflicts, you only need to make sure that this name isn't already possessed by any managed bean or any implicit EL objects.

# Referencing Bundle in JSF Page

It's relatively simple, just treat `#{text}` as a `Map` with the bundle keys as map keys.

```
<!DOCTYPE html>
<html lang="#{view.locale.toLanguageTag()}"
    xmlns="http://www.w3.org/1999/xhtml"
    xmlns:h="http://xmlns.jcp.org/jsf/html">
    <h:head>
        <title>#{text['title']}</title>
    </h:head>
```

```
<h:body>
    <h1>#{text['heading']}</h1>
    <p>#{text['paragraph']}</p>
</h:body>
</html>
```

JSF will already automatically determine the closest matching active locale based on the HTTP Accept-Language header[3] and set it as locale property of UIViewRoot. The Accept-Language header is configurable in browser's settings. In, for example, Chrome, you can configure it via chrome://settings/languages. If you play around with it, for example, by switching between English, Portuguese, and Hindi as the top-ranked language setting in browser and refresh the JSF page, then you'll notice that it changes the text to conform the browser-specified language setting. If you check the browser's developer tools—usually accessible by pressing F12—and inspect the HTTP request headers in the network monitor, then you'll also notice that the Accept-Language header changes accordingly.

You might have noticed that the lang attribute of the <html> tag references #{view. locale.toLanguageTag()}. Basically, this will print the IETF BCP 47 language tag[4] of the locale property of the current UIViewRoot, which is in turn available as an implicit EL object #{view}. The locale property is an instance of java.util.Locale which has actually no getter method for the language tag such as getLanguageTag(), but only a toLanguageTag() method, hence the direct method reference in EL instead of the expected property reference.

The lang attribute of the <html> tag is not mandatory for the functioning of JSF localization feature. Moreover, JSF treats it as template text and does nothing special with it. You can safely leave out it. It is, however, important for search engines. This way a search engine like Google will be informed which language the page's copy is in. This is not only important in order to end up correctly in localized search results, but also important in case you serve the very same page in different languages. This would otherwise by the average search engine algorithm be penalized as "duplicate content," which is thus bad for SEO (search engine optimization) ranking.

---

[3]https://www.w3.org/Protocols/rfc2616/rfc2616-sec14.html#sec14.4.
[4]https://en.wikipedia.org/wiki/IETF_language_tag.

You'll also have noticed that the bundle keys are specified in the so-called brace notation #{text['...']}. The string between single quotes basically represents the bundle key. In this specific case you could also have used #{text.title}, #{text.heading}, and #{text.paragraph} instead. This is, however, not the common practice. Using the brace notation not only gives a generally clear meaning to what the EL variable represents (a resource bundle), but it also allows you to use dots in the bundle key name such as #{text['meta.description']}. The EL expression #{text.meta.description} has, namely, an entirely different meaning: "get the description property of the nested meta property of the text object," which is incorrect.

# Changing the Active Locale

You can also change the active locale on the server side. This is best to be done in a single place in a site-wide master template which contains the <f:view> tag. The active locale can be set in the locale attribute of the <f:view> which can accept either a static string representing the language tag or a concrete java.util.Locale instance. The locale attribute accepts an EL expression and can be changed programmatically via a managed bean. This offers you the opportunity to let the user change it via the web page without fiddling around in the browser's language settings. You could present the available language options to the user in a JSF page and let each selection change the active locale. This can be achieved with the following JSF page:

```
<!DOCTYPE html>
<html lang="#{activeLocale.languageTag}"
    xmlns="http://www.w3.org/1999/xhtml"
    xmlns:f="http://xmlns.jcp.org/jsf/core"
    xmlns:h="http://xmlns.jcp.org/jsf/html">
    <f:view locale="#{activeLocale.current}">
        <h:head>
            <title>#{text['title']}</title>
        </h:head>
        <h:body>
            <h1>#{text['heading']}</h1>
            <p>#{text['paragraph']}</p>
```

```
            <h:form>
                <h:selectOneMenu value="#{activeLocale.languageTag}">
                    <f:selectItems
                        value="#{activeLocale.available}" var="l"
                        itemValue="#{l.toLanguageTag()}"
                        itemLabel="#{l.getDisplayLanguage(l)}">
                    </f:selectItems>
                    <f:ajax listener="#{activeLocale.reload()}" />
                </h:selectOneMenu>
            </h:form>
        </h:body>
    </f:view>
</html>
```

It is slightly adjusted from the previous example; there is now <f:view> around
<h:head> and <h:body>. The locale attribute of <f:view> references the currently active
locale via the #{activeLocale} managed bean, which is as follows:

```
@Named @SessionScoped
public class ActiveLocale implements Serializable {

    private Locale current;
    private List<Locale> available;

    @Inject
    private FacesContext context;

    @PostConstruct
    public void init() {
        Application app = context.getApplication();
        current = app.getViewHandler().calculateLocale(context);
        available = new ArrayList<>();
        available.add(app.getDefaultLocale());
        app.getSupportedLocales().forEachRemaining(available::add);
    }
```

```
public void reload() {
    context.getPartialViewContext().getEvalScripts()
        .add("location.replace(location)");
}

public Locale getCurrent() {
    return current;
}

public String getLanguageTag() {
    return current.toLanguageTag();
}

public void setLanguageTag(String languageTag) {
    current = Locale.forLanguageTag(languageTag);
}

public List<Locale> getAvailable() {
    return available;
}
```

}

To reiterate, @Inject FacesContext works only if you have placed @FacesConfig on an arbitrary CDI bean somewhere in the web application. Otherwise you have to replace it by inline FacesContext.getCurrentInstance() calls. There's only one caveat with those inline calls: you need to make absolutely sure that you don't assign it as a field in, for example, @PostConstruct, because the actual instance is subject to being changed across method calls on the very same bean instance. Injecting as a field via CDI takes transparently care of this, and is therefore safe, but manually assigning is not.

In @PostConstruct, ViewHandler#calculateLocale() is used to calculate the current locale based on Accept-Language header and the default and supported locales as configured in faces-config.xml. This follows exactly the same JSF-internal behavior as if when there's no <f:view locale> defined. Finally, the available locales are collected based on the configured default and supported locales.

The available locales are, via <f:selectItems> of <h:selectOneMenu>, presented to the user as drop-down options (see Figure 14-1). The nested <f:ajax> makes sure that the selected option is set in the managed bean as soon as the user changes the option.

**Figure 14-1.** *Changing the active locale*

The #{activeLocale.languageTag} property delegates internally to the current java.util.Locale instance. This is basically done for convenience so that we don't necessarily need to add a converter for #{activeLocale.current} in case we want to use it in <h:selectOneMenu>.

<f:ajax listener> basically performs a full page reload with the help of a piece of JavaScript which is executed on completion of the Ajax request. This is done by adding a script to the PartialViewContext#getEvalScripts() method, which is new since JSF 2.3. Any added script will end up ordered in the <eval> section of the JSF Ajax response, which in turn gets executed after JSF Ajax engine has updated the HTML DOM (Document Object Model) tree.

The script itself, location.replace(location), basically instructs JavaScript to reload the current document without keeping the previous document in history. This means that the back button won't redisplay the same page. You can also use location.reload(true) instead, but this won't work nicely if a synchronous (non-Ajax) POST request has been fired on the same document beforehand. It would be re-executed and cause a double submit. And, it unnecessarily remembers the previous page in the history. This may end up in confusing behavior, because the back button would then seem to have no effect as it would redisplay exactly the same page as the active locale is stored in the session, not in the request.

Alternatively, instead of invoking `<f:ajax listener>`, you can in this specific use case also use just `<f:ajax render="@all">` without any listener. It has at least one disadvantage: the document's title won't be updated. In any case, using `@all` is generally considered a bad practice. There's only one legitimate real-world use case for it: displaying a full error page on an Ajax request.

As a completely different alternative, you could make the active locale request scoped instead of session scoped by including the language tag in the URL as in `http://example.com/en/page.xhtml`, `http://example.com/pt/page.xhtml`, `http://example.com/hi/page.xhtml`. This way you can change the active locale by simply following a link. This only involves a servlet filter which extracts the `java.util.Locale` instance from the URL and forwards it to the desired JSF page, and a custom view handler which includes the language tag in the generated URL of any `<h:form>`, `<h:link>`, and `<h:button>` component. You can find a kickoff example in the Java EE Kickoff Application.[5]

# Organizing Bundle Keys

When the web application grows, you may notice that bundle files start to become unmaintainable. The key is to organize the bundle keys following a very strict convention. Reusable site-wide entries, usually those used as input labels, button labels, link labels, table header labels, etc., should be keyed using a general prefix (e.g., "`label.save=Save`"). Page-specific entries should be keyed using a page-specific prefix (e.g., "`foldername_pagename.title=Some Page Title`"). Following is an elaborate example of a localized Facelets template, `/WEB-INF/templates/page.xhtml`:

```
<!DOCTYPE html>
<html lang="#{activeLocale.language}"
    xmlns="http://www.w3.org/1999/xhtml"
    xmlns:f="http://xmlns.jcp.org/jsf/core"
    xmlns:h="http://xmlns.jcp.org/jsf/html"
    xmlns:ui="http://xmlns.jcp.org/jsf/facelets"
    xmlns:c="http://xmlns.jcp.org/jsp/jstl/core"
    xmlns:fn="http://xmlns.jcp.org/jsp/jstl/functions"
>
```

---

[5]`https://github.com/javaeekickoff/java-ee-kickoff-app.`

```
<c:set var="page" value="page#{fn:replace(
    fn:split(view.viewId, '.')[0], '/', '_')}" scope="view" />
<f:view locale="#{activeLocale.current}">
    <h:head>
        <title>#{text[page += '.title']}</title>
        <meta name="description"
            content="#{text[page += '.meta.description']}" />
    </h:head>
    <h:body id="#{page}">
        <header>
            <nav>
                <h:link outcome="/home"
                    value="#{text['label.home']}" />
                <h:link outcome="/login"
                    value="#{text['label.login']}" />
                <h:link outcome="/signup"
                    value="#{text['label.signup']}" />
            </nav>
            <h:form>
                <h:selectOneMenu
                        value="#{activeLocale.languageTag}">
                    <f:selectItems
                        value="#{activeLocale.available}" var="l"
                        itemValue="#{l.toLanguageTag()}"
                        itemLabel="#{l.getDisplayLanguage(l)}">
                    </f:selectItems>
                    <f:ajax listener="#{activeLocale.reload()}" />
                </h:selectOneMenu>
            </h:form>
        </header>
        <main>
            <h1>#{text[page += '.title']}</h1>
            <ui:insert name="content" />
        </main>
```

```
            <footer>
                © #{text['page_home.title']}
            </footer>
        </h:body>
    </f:view>
</html>
```

The JSTL `<c:set>` basically converts the `UIViewRoot#getViewId()` to a string which is suitable as a page-specific prefix. The JSF view ID basically represents the absolute server-side path to the physical file representing the JSF page (e.g., "`/user/account.xhtml`"). This needs to be manipulated to a format suitable as a resource bundle key. The `fn:split()` call extracts the part "`/user/account`" from it and the `fn:replace()` call converts the forward slash to underscore so that it becomes "`_user_account`". Finally, `<c:set>` stores it as "`page_user_account`" in the view scope under the name "`page`" so that it's available as #{page} elsewhere in the same view.

You'll notice that #{page} is in turn being used as, among others, the ID of `<h:body>`. This makes it easier to select a specific page from a general CSS (Cascading Style Sheets) file just in case that's needed. #{page} is also being used in several resource bundle references, such as `#{text[page += '.title']}` which ultimately references in case of "`/home.xhtml`" the key "`page_home.title`". With such a template you can have the following page-specific resource bundle entries:

```
page_home.title = My Website
page_home.meta.description = A Hello World JSF application.

page_login.title = Log In
page_login.meta.description = Log in to My Website.

page_signup.title = Sign Up
page_signup.meta.description = Sign up to My Website.
```

Following is an example of a template client which utilizes the previously shown template `/WEB-INF/templates/page.xhtml`, the `/login.xhtml`:

```
<ui:composition template="/WEB-INF/templates/page.xhtml"
    xmlns="http://www.w3.org/1999/xhtml"
    xmlns:f="http://xmlns.jcp.org/jsf/core"
```

```
    xmlns:h="http://xmlns.jcp.org/jsf/html"
    xmlns:ui="http://xmlns.jcp.org/jsf/facelets"
>

    <ui:define name="content">
        <h:form id="login">
            <fieldset>
                <h:outputLabel for="email"
                    value="#{text['label.email']}" />
                <h:inputText id="email" required="true"
                    value="#{login.email}" />
                <h:message for="email" styleClass="message" />

                <h:outputLabel for="password"
                    value="#{text['label.password']}" />
                <h:inputSecret id="password" required="true"
                    value="#{login.password}" />
                <h:message for="password" styleClass="message" />

                <h:commandButton id="submit" action="#{login.submit}"
                    value="#{text['label.login']}" />
                <h:message for="login" styleClass="message" />
            </fieldset>
        </h:form>
    </ui:define>
</ui:composition>
```

Following is what the associated resource bundle entries look like:

```
label.email = Email
label.password = Password
label.login = Log In
```

Note: in case you find that the page looks crippled, simply add a CSS file with the following rule to start with:

```
nav a, fieldset label, fieldset input {
    display: block;
}
```

# Localizing Conversion/Validation Messages

In case you have prepared a simple backing bean class `Login` with two string properties `email` and `password` and a method `submit()`, and submit the above shown login page without filling out the e-mail input field, then you'll face a validation error in the following format:

```
login:email: Validation Error: Value is required.
```

When you switch the language to Portuguese and resubmit the empty form, then you'll see that it's also localized. However, when you switch the language further to Hindi, then you'll notice that there's no standard Hindi message bundle in the standard JSF implementation. You'd need to provide your own. There are several ways to achieve this.

First, JSF input and select components support three attributes to override the default message: `requiredMessage`, `validatorMessage`, and `converterMessage`. The following example shows how to override the default required message:

```
<h:inputText ... requiredMessage="#{text['message.required']}" />
```

This is arguably the easiest approach. The major caveat is that you have to copy/paste it everywhere in case you haven't wrapped it in a reusable tag file like `<my:inputText>`. This is not DRY.[6]

Another way is to supply a custom message bundle which overrides all predefined bundle keys specific for JSF conversion/validation messages and register it as `<message-bundle>` in `faces-config.xml`. You can find the predefined bundle keys in chapter 2.5.2.4 "Localized Application Messages" of the JSF specification.[7] The bundle key of the default required message "Validation Error: Value is Required" is thus `javax.faces.component.UIInput.REQUIRED`. We can adjust it in new message bundle files as follows:

```
main/java/resources/com/example/project/i18n/messages.properties
javax.faces.component.UIInput.REQUIRED = {0} is required.
main/java/resources/com/example/project/i18n/messages_pt_BR.properties
javax.faces.component.UIInput.REQUIRED = {0} é obrigatório.
main/java/resources/com/example/project/i18n/messages_hi.properties
javax.faces.component.UIInput.REQUIRED = {0} आवश्यक है.
```

---

[6]https://en.wikipedia.org/wiki/Don%27t_repeat_yourself.
[7]http://download.oracle.com/otn-pub/jcp/jsf-2_3-final-eval-spec/JSF_2.3.pdf.

471

Finally, configure it in the `<application>` element of the `faces-config.xml` file:

```
<application>
    ...
    <message-bundle>com.example.project.i18n.messages</message-bundle>
</application>
```

You'll perhaps have noticed the {0} placeholders in the messages. They represent the labels of the associated input and select components. The labels default to the component's client ID, which is basically the ID of the JSF-generated HTML element as you can find in the browser's page source. You can override it by explicitly setting the `label` attribute of the component.

```
<h:inputText id="email" ... label="#{text['label.email']}" />
<h:inputSecret id="password" ... label="#{text['label.password']}" />
```

Note that putting the message bundle in a different file than the resource bundle is not strictly necessary. You can also just put the message bundle entries in `text.properties` files and adjust the `<message-bundle>` entry to point to the same FQN as `<resource-bundle>`.

# Obtaining Localized Message in a Custom Converter/Validator

The value of the `<message-bundle>` entry can be obtained programmatically via `Applicat ion#getMessageBundle()`. You can in turn use it to obtain the actual bundle via the `java.util.ResourceBundle` API, along with `UIViewRoot#getLocale()`. This allows you to obtain a localized message in a custom converter and validator. Following is an example of such a validator, which checks if the specified e-mail address is already in use:

```
@FacesValidator(value = "duplicateEmailValidator", managed = true)
public class DuplicateEmailValidator implements Validator<String> {

    @Inject
    private UserService userService;
```

```
    @Override
    public void validate
        (FacesContext context, UIComponent component, String value)
            throws ValidatorException
    {
        if (value == null) {
            return;
        }

        Optional<User> user = userService.findByEmail(value);

        if (user.isPresent()) {
            throw new ValidatorException(new FacesMessage(getMessage(
                context, "message.duplicateEmailValidator")));
        }
    }

    public static String getMessage(FacesContext context, String key) {
        return ResourceBundle.getBundle(
            context.getApplication().getMessageBundle(),
            context.getViewRoot().getLocale()).getString(key);
    }
}
```

You might have noticed the new managed attribute of the @FacesValidator annotation. This will basically turn on CDI support on the validator instance and hence allow you to inject a business service into a validator. The same attribute is also available for @FacesConverter.

The shown validator example assumes that the following entry is present in the resource bundle files as identified by <message-bundle>:

```
message.duplicateEmailValidator = Email is already in use.
```

# Localizing Enums

The cleanest approach to localize enums is to simply use their own identity as a bundle key. This keeps the enum class free of potential UI-specific clutter such as hard-coded bundle keys. Generally, the combination of the enum's simple name and the enum value should suffice to represent a site-wide unique identifier (UI). Given the following com. example.project.model.Group enum representing a user group:

```
public enum Group {
    USER,
    MANAGER,
    ADMINISTRATOR,
    DEVELOPER;
}
```

and the following resource bundle entries in text.properties:

```
Group.USER = User
Group.MANAGER = Manager
Group.ADMINISTRATOR = Administrator
Group.DEVELOPER = Developer
```

you can easily localize them as follows:

```
<f:metadata>
    <f:importConstants type="com.example.project.model.Group" />
</f:metadata>
...
<h:selectManyCheckbox value="#{editUserBacking.user.groups}">
    <f:selectItems value="#{Group.values()}" var="group"
        itemLabel="#{text['Group.' += group]}" />
</h:selectManyCheckbox>
```

Note that the <f:importConstants> is new since JSF 2.3. It is required to be placed inside <f:metadata>. Its type attribute must represent the fully qualified name of the enum or any class or interface which contains public constants in flavor of public static final fields. <f:importConstants> will automatically import them into the EL scope as a Map<String, Object> wherein the map key represents the name of the constant as string and the map value represents the actual value of the constant.

With #{Group.values()} you can thus obtain a collection of all constant values and each value is then localized in itemLabel. Also note that itemValue is omitted as it defaults to the value of the var attribute which is already sufficient.

# Parameterized Resource Bundle Values

You can also parameterize your resource bundle entries using the {0} placeholders of the java.text.MessageFormat API.[8] They can on the JSF side only be substituted with <h:outputFormat> whereby the parameters are provided as <f:param> children, in the same order as the placeholders. Given the following entry:

```
page_products.table.header = There {0, choice, 0#are no products
                                           | 1#is one product
                                           | 1<are {0} products}.
```

it can be substituted using <h:outputFormat> as follows:

```
<h:outputFormat value="#{text['page_products.table.header']}">
    <f:param value="#{bean.products.size()}" />
</h:outputFormat>
```

# Database-Based ResourceBundle

JSF also supports specifying a custom ResourceBundle implementation as <base-name>. This allows you to programmatically fill and supply the desired bundles, for example, from multiple bundle files, or even from a database. In this example we'll replace the default properties file-based resource bundle by one which loads the entries from a database. This takes us a step further as to organizing the resource bundle keys. This way, you can even edit them via a web-based interface. Following is what the JPA entity looks like:

```
@Entity
@Table(uniqueConstraints = {
    @UniqueConstraint(columnNames = { "locale", "key" })
})
```

---

[8]https://docs.oracle.com/javase/8/docs/api/java/text/MessageFormat.html.

```java
public class Translation {

    @Id @GeneratedValue(strategy = GenerationType.IDENTITY)
    private Long id;

    @Column(length = 5, nullable = false)
    private @NotNull Locale locale;

    @Column(length = 255, nullable = false)
    private @NotNull String key;

    @Lob @Column(nullable = false)
    private @NotNull String value;

    // Add/generate getters and setters here.
}
```

Note that the JPA (Java Persistence API) annotations provide sufficient hints as to what the DDL (Data Definition Language) of the table should look like. When having the property javax.persistence.schema-generation.database.action set to create or drop-and-create in persistence.xml, then it will automatically generate the proper DDL. For sake of completeness, here it is in HSQL/pgSQL flavor.

```sql
CREATE TABLE Translation (
    id BIGINT GENERATED BY DEFAULT AS IDENTITY PRIMARY KEY,
    locale VARCHAR(5) NOT NULL,
    key VARCHAR(255) NOT NULL,
    value CLOB NOT NULL
);

ALTER TABLE Translation
    ADD CONSTRAINT UK_Translation_locale_key
    UNIQUE (locale, key);
```

And here's what the EJB (Enterprise JavaBeans) service looks like.

```java
@Stateless
public class TranslationService {

    @PersistenceContext
    private EntityManager entityManager;
```

```
@TransactionAttribute(value = REQUIRES_NEW)
@SuppressWarnings("unchecked")
public Object[][] getContent
    (Locale locale, Locale fallback)
{
    List<Object[]> resultList = entityManager.createQuery(
        "SELECT t1.key, COALESCE(t2.value, t1.value)"
            + " FROM Translation t1"
            + " LEFT OUTER JOIN Translation t2"
                + " ON t2.key = t1.key"
                + " AND t2.locale = :locale"
            + " WHERE t1.locale = :fallback")
        .setParameter("locale", locale)
        .setParameter("fallback", fallback)
        .getResultList();
    return resultList.toArray(new Object[resultList.size()][]);
}
}
```

For JPA we only need an additional converter which converts between
java.util.Locale in the model and VARCHAR in the database, which is represented
by java.lang.String. You can use the JPA 2.0 AttributeConverter for this. It's much
like a JSF converter but for JPA entities. It's relatively simple; there's no additional
configuration necessary. See the following:

```
public class LocaleConverter
    implements AttributeConverter<Locale, String>
{
    @Override
    public String convertToDatabaseColumn(Locale locale) {
        return locale.toLanguageTag();
    }

    @Override
    public Locale convertToEntityAttribute(String languageTag) {
        return Locale.forLanguageTag(languageTag);
    }
}
```

Now we have the custom ResourceBundle; it's called DatabaseResourceBundle. Put it in the package com.example.project.i18n.

```
public class DatabaseResourceBundle extends ResourceBundle {

    private static final Control CONTROL = new DatabaseControl();

    @Override
    public Object handleGetObject(String key) {
        return getCurrentInstance().getObject(key);
    }

    @Override
    public Enumeration<String> getKeys() {
        return getCurrentInstance().getKeys();
    }

    private ResourceBundle getCurrentInstance() {
        FacesContext context = FacesContext.getCurrentInstance();
        String key = CONTROL.getClass().getName();
        return (ResourceBundle) context.getAttributes()
            .computeIfAbsent(key, k -> ResourceBundle.getBundle(key,
                context.getViewRoot().getLocale(),
                Thread.currentThread().getContextClassLoader(),
                CONTROL));
    }

    private static class DatabaseControl extends Control {
        @Override
        public ResourceBundle newBundle
            (String baseName, Locale locale, String format,
                ClassLoader loader, boolean reload)
            throws IllegalAccessException, InstantiationException,
                IOException
        {
            FacesContext context = FacesContext.getCurrentInstance();
            final Object[][] contents = CDI.current()
                .select(TranslationService.class).get()
                .getContent(
```

```
                locale,
                context.getApplication().getDefaultLocale());
        return new ListResourceBundle() {
            @Override
            protected Object[][] getContents() {
                return contents;
            }
        };
    }
}
}
```

Finally, adjust the `<resource-bundle><base-name>` entry in `faces-config.xml` to specify the fully qualified name of the custom `ResourceBundle` as follows:

`<base-name>com.example.project.i18n.DatabaseResourceBundle</base-name>`

The actual implementation of this `ResourceBundle` is frankly somewhat hacky, only and only because of the following limitations:

1.  JSF doesn't allow defining a custom `ResourceBundle.Control` via `faces-config.xml`.

2.  Providing a custom `ResourceBundle.Control` via SPI (Serial Peripheral Interface) as `java.util.spi.ResourceBundleControlProvider` doesn't work from WAR on.

3.  Create multiple separate `DatabaseResourceBundle` subclasses for each single locale registered in `faces-config.xml`, such as `DatabaseResourceBundle_en`, `DatabaseResourceBundle_pt_BR`, and `DataBaseResourceBundle_hi`, in order to satisfy the default `ResourceBundle.Control` behavior is not maintenance friendly in long term.

An additional advantage of this approach is that it allows you to programmatically clear out any database bundles in the cache by simply calling `ResourceBundle#clearCache()`. Namely, the JSF implementation may in turn cache it in its `Application` implementation, causing the `ResourceBundle#clearCache()` to seem to have no effect at all. Mojarra is known to do that.[9]

---

[9]https://stackoverflow.com/q/4325164/157882.

# HTML in ResourceBundle

This is a bad practice. It adds a maintenance burden. For large sections of content you'd better pick a more lightweight markup language than HTML, such as Markdown.[10] This is not only safer as to XSS (cross-site scripting) risks but also easier for the user to edit via a text area in some Content Management System (CMS) screens. This is best to implement in combination with a database-based resource bundle. You could add an extra boolean flag to the `Translation` model indicating whether the value should be parsed as Markdown.

```
@Column(nullable = false)
private boolean markdown;
```

Then, inside `TranslationService#getContents()`, select it as the third column.

```
"SELECT t1.key, COALESCE(t2.value, t1.value), t1.markdown"
```

And, finally, in the `DatabaseControl#newBundle()` method, after retrieving the contents, you could postprocess them based on the boolean. You could use any Java-based Markdown library for this, such as CommonMark.[11]

```
static final Parser PARSER = Parser.builder().build();
static final HtmlRenderer RENDERER = HtmlRenderer.builder().build();
...
for (Object[] translation : contents) {
    if ((boolean) translation[2]) {
        translation[1] = RENDERER.render(PARSER.parse(translation[1]));
    }
}
```

---

[10]https://en.wikipedia.org/wiki/Markdown.
[11]https://github.com/atlassian/commonmark-java.

# Extensions

If there is one single element or virtue of JSF (JavaServer Faces) to which we can attribute its lasting for so long, it's probably its ability to be extended in a large variety of ways. From the onset JSF made it possibly to have most of its core elements replaced, decorated, or augmented.

This gave rise to a large number of extension libraries and projects. In the very early days these were A4J (Ajax4JSF), Tomahawk, RichFaces, the stand-alone Facelets project, PrettyFaces, and many, many more. A4J was merged into RichFaces, and RichFaces itself was eventually sunset in 2016. Facelets was incorporated into JSF itself, while PrettyFaces became part of the Rewrite framework. These days well-known and active extension libraries are PrimeFaces, OmniFaces, and BootsFaces, among others. While individual libraries have come and gone, the main constant is the extensibility of JSF from its first days until the present.

It's sometimes said that all those libraries address defects or omissions in JSF, but this is not entirely accurate. In fact, JSF was explicitly designed to make such extensions possible and therefore to allow, even stimulate, such extension libraries to appear. For instance, a contemporary peer technology of JSF, EJB (Enterprise JavaBeans), had few to no extension points and, thus, despite its many shortcomings, we never saw much of an ecosystem flourish around it.

## Extension Types

There are a couple of different ways by which to use the various extension points in JSF. A major distinction is between the "classical" approach and the "CDI-centric approach."

In the latter approach there's very little to nothing that JSF has to explicitly support extensibillity, as CDI has a number of mechanisms built in to support extending or replacing CDI artifacts. This is the planned future for JSF (making most if not everything a CDI artifact), but for the moment JSF 2.3 is in an early transitional phase and only a few artifacts are vended via CDI. Table 8-1 in Chapter 8 showed these artifacts.

© Bauke Scholtz, Arjan Tijms 2018
B. Scholtz and A. Tijms, *The Definitive Guide to JSF in Java EE 8*, https://doi.org/10.1007/978-1-4842-3387-0_15

# Extending CDI Artifacts

One of the ways CDI augments or replaces a type fully is to provide an alternative producer. We already saw this technique being used in Chapter 13, albeit for a slightly different use case.

The easiest way is if you need to fully replace the type. If augmenting is needed, some code is necessary to obtain the previous type, which with the current version of CDI (2.0) is slightly verbose.

The following shows an example where we replace the request parameter map with a new map that has all the values of the original map, plus an additional value that we add ourselves:

```
@Dependent @Alternative @Priority(APPLICATION)
public class RequestParameterMapProducer {

    @Produces @RequestScoped @RequestParameterMap
    public Map<String, String> producer(BeanManager beanManager) {
        Map<String, String> previousMap = getPreviousMap(beanManager);
        Map<String, String> newMap = new HashMap<>(previousMap);
        newMap.put("test", "myTestValue");
        return newMap;
    }
}
```

The getPreviousMap() method is, as mentioned, somewhat verbose. It's defined as follows:

```
private Map<String, String> getPreviousMap(BeanManager beanManager) {
    class RequestParameterMapAnnotationLiteral
        extends AnnotationLiteral<RequestParameterMap>
        implements RequestParameterMap
    {
        private static final long serialVersionUID = 1L;
    }
```

```
    Type MAP_TYPE = new ParameterizedType() {
        @Override
        public Type getRawType() {
            return Map.class;
        }
        @Override
        public Type[] getActualTypeArguments() {
            return new Type[] {String.class, String.class};
        }
        @Override
        public Type getOwnerType() {
            return null;
        }
    };

    return (Map<String, String>) beanManager
        .getReference(beanManager
        .resolve(beanManager
        .getBeans(MAP_TYPE, new RequestParameterMapAnnotationLiteral())
        .stream()
        .filter(bean -> bean
            .getBeanClass() != RequestParameterMapProducer.class)
        .collect(Collectors.toSet())),
            MAP_TYPE,
            beanManager.createCreationalContext(null));
    }
}
```

It's expected that the task of obtaining this "previous" or "original" type will be made easier in a future revision of any of the specs involved. For instance, a future version of JSF will likely introduce ready-to-use annotation literals for its (CDI) annotations, such as the RequestParameterMapAnnotationLiteral shown here.

In order to test that this alternative producer works, consider the following backing bean:

```java
@Named @RequestScoped
public class TestBean {

    @Inject @RequestParameterMap
    private Map<String, String> requestParameterMap;

    public String getTest() {
        return requestParameterMap.get("test");
    }

    public String getFoo() {
        return requestParameterMap.get("foo");
    }
}
```

And the following Facelet:

```html
<!DOCTYPE html>
<html lang="en"
    xmlns="http://www.w3.org/1999/xhtml"
    xmlns:h="http://xmlns.jcp.org/jsf/html"
>
    <h:head/>
    <h:body>
        <p>Test: #{testBean.test}</p>
        <p>Foo: #{testBean.foo}</p>
    </h:body>
</html>
```

Deploying an application containing these artifacts with a request parameter of, say, "foo=bar", will reveal that the new map indeed contains the original request parameters as well as the value that we added ourselves.

# Extending Classical Artifacts

The classical approach to augment or fully replace a type in JSF is by installing a factory for that type. The basic way such a factory works is in broad lines identical to the CDI approach demonstrated above; the factory returns an implementation of the requested type and obtains a reference to the "previous" or "original" type.

Being classical in Java EE typically means XML, and indeed the classical factory involves XML. Specifically, registering a factory entails using the `<factory>` element in `faces-config.xml` and a specific element per type for which a factory is to be provided. As of JSF 2.3 the following factories are supported:

- `<application-factory>`
- `<exception-handler-factory>`
- `<external-context-factory>`
- `<faces-context-factory>`
- `<facelet-cache-factory>`
- `<partial-view-context-factory>`
- `<lifecycle-factory>`
- `<view-declaration-language-factory>`
- `<tag-handler-delegate-factory>`
- `<render-kit-factory>`
- `<visit-context-factory>`
- `<flash-factory>`
- `<flow-handler-factory>`
- `<client-window-factory>`
- `<search-expression-context-factory>`

Next to these, there are another number of artifacts that can be replaced/augmented in a somewhat similar but still different way; here there's no factory returning the type, but an implementation of the type is specified directly. This variant is specified using the `<application>` element in `faces-config.xml`. As of JSF 2.3 the following types can be replaced/augmented directly:

- `<navigation-handler>`

- `<view-handler>`

- `<resource-handler>`

- `<search-expression-handler>`

- `<flow-handler>`

- `<state-manager>`

- `<action-listener>`

Note that all of these are singletons. From the JSF runtime point of view there's only one of each, but multiple implementations each adding something are supported by means of wrapping, which therefore forms a chain (implementation A wrapping implementation B, wrapping implementation C, etc.).

The above specific elements used for each type immediately highlight an issue with the classical approach; JSF *has* to provide explicit support for each specific type to be replaced/augmented in this way. By contrast, the CDI approach allows us to pretty much replace/augment any type without requiring any special support from JSF other than that JSF uses CDI for that artifact.

On the bright side, the factory implementation is currently somewhat simpler compared to the CDI version, as the "previous" or "original" type is simply being passed to it in its constructor instead of having to be looked up using verbose code.

As an example, we'll show how to augment the external context factory. For this we start with the mentioned registration in `faces-config.xml`.

```
<factory>
    <external-context-factory>
        com.example.project.ExternalContextProducer
    </external-context-factory>
</factory>
```

The implementation then looks as follows:

```java
public class ExternalContextProducer extends ExternalContextFactory {
    public ExternalContextProducer(ExternalContextFactory wrapped) {
        super(wrapped);
    }

    @Override
    public ExternalContext getExternalContext
        (Object context, Object request, Object response)
    {
        ExternalContext previousExternalContext =
            getWrapped().getExternalContext(context, request, response);
        ExternalContext newExternalContext =
            new ExternalContextWrapper(previousExternalContext) {
                @Override
                public String getAuthType() {
                    return "OurOwnAuthType";
                }
            };
        return newExternalContext;
    }
}
```

There are a few things to observe here. First of all, every factory of this kind has to inherit from a pre-described parent factory, which in this case is ExternalContextFactory. Second, there's an implicit contract that must be followed, and that's implementing the constructor exactly as shown in the example. That is, add a public constructor with a single parameter the exact same type as the superclass, and pass this parameter on to the super constructor. This instance is then available in other methods using the getWrapped() method.

Testing that this indeed works is relatively easy. We use a similar backing bean as with the CDI version:

```java
@Named @RequestScoped
public class TestBean {

    @Inject
    private ExternalContext externalContext;
```

```
    public String getAuth() {
        return externalContext.getAuthType();
    }
}
```

And the following Facelet:

```
<!DOCTYPE html>
<html lang="en"
    xmlns="http://www.w3.org/1999/xhtml"
    xmlns:h="http://xmlns.jcp.org/jsf/html"
>
    <h:head />
    <h:body>
        <p>Test: #{testBean.auth}</p>
    </h:body>
</html>
```

As the external context is also a type that's injectable via CDI, the observant reader may wonder what happens when both a CDI alternative producer and a classic factory are provided for that type. The answer is that this is strictly speaking not specified (thus undefined behavior), yet in practice it's strongly implied that the classic factory is used as the source to ultimately get the external context from. This means that an alternative producer for ExternalContext will only affect the direct injection of ExternalContext, and not any situation when this type is obtained in any other way, for instance, by calling FacesContext#getExternalContext(). This is something users should clearly be aware of. The expectation is, though, that a future revision of the spec will make a CDI producer the initial source.

# Plug-ins

A different type of extending that JSF offers next to the alternative producers and factories is what's essentially a plug-in. Here, no core JSF type is replaced or augmented, but an additional functionality is added to some part of the runtime. Most of these additions, therefore, have to declare in some way what it is they are exactly adding, which is different from the factories which just provided an implementation of type X or Y.

Plug-ins are added as elements of the `<application>` element in `faces-config.xml`, just as some of the factory-like types mentioned above. The following are supported:

- `<el-resolver>`

- `<property-resolver>` (deprecated)

- `<variable-resolver>` (deprecated)

- `<search-keyword-resolver>`

We already saw an example of the Search Keyword Resolver in the section "Custom Search Keywords" in Chapter 12. Characteristic for that one being a plug-in was the method `isResolverForKeyWord()`, by which the plug-in could indicate for which keyword, or keyword pattern, it would operate.

We'll take a look at one other example here, namely, the EL resolver. The property resolver and variable resolver are both deprecated and have been replaced by the EL resolver. The EL resolver itself is not a JSF-specific type but originates from the Expression Language (EL) spec. This spec does, however, have important parts of its origins in JSF.

The EL resolver allows us to interpret the so-called base and property of an expression in a custom way. Considering the expression `#{foo.bar.kaz}`, then "`foo`" is the base and "`bar`" is the property when resolving "`bar`", while "`bar`" is the base and "`kaz`" is the property when resolving "`kaz`". Perhaps somewhat surprising at first is that when "`foo`" is being resolved, the base is `null` and "`foo`" is the property.

In practice, adding a custom EL resolver is not often needed, and we can often get by with simply defining a named CDI bean that does what we require. Custom EL resolvers could come into play when JSF is integrated in a completely different environment though, one where we'd like expressions to resolve to a completely different (managed) bean system. Even so, a CDI-to-other-beans-bridge might be a better option even there, but it's perhaps good to know a custom EL resolver is one other tool we have in our arsenal.

Anyway, to demonstrate what an EL resolver can do we'll show an example where the base of an EL expression is interpreted as a pattern, something we can't do directly with a named CDI bean.

The following shows an example EL resolver:

```java
public class CustomELResolver extends ELResolver {

    protected boolean isResolverFor(Object base, Object property) {
        return base == null
            && property instanceof String
            && ((String) property).startsWith("dev");
    }

    @Override
    public Object getValue
        (ELContext context, Object base, Object property)
    {
        if (isResolverFor(base, property)) {
            context.setPropertyResolved(true);
            return property.toString().substring(3);
        }
        return null;
    }

    @Override
    public Class<?> getType
        (ELContext context, Object base, Object property)
    {
        if (isResolverFor(base, property)) {
            context.setPropertyResolved(true);
            return String.class;
        }
        return null;
    }

    @Override
    public Class<?> getCommonPropertyType
        (ELContext context, Object base)
    {
        return base == null ? getType(context, base, null) : null;
    }
```

```
    @Override
    public boolean isReadOnly
        (ELContext context, Object base, Object property)
    {
        return true;
    }

    @Override
    public void setValue
        (ELContext context, Object base, Object property, Object value)
    {
        // NOOP;
    }

    @Override
    public Iterator<FeatureDescriptor> getFeatureDescriptors
        (ELContext context, Object base)
    {
        return null;
    }
}
```

If we now use the following Facelet

```
<!DOCTYPE html>
<html lang="en"
    xmlns="http://www.w3.org/1999/xhtml"
    xmlns:h="http://xmlns.jcp.org/jsf/html"
>
    <h:head />
    <h:body>
        <p>Test: #{devThisIsDev}</p>
    </h:body>
</html>
```

we'll see "Test: ThisIsDev" being printed when requesting it. What's happening here is that the custom EL resolver handles every name that starts with "dev."

# Dynamic Extensions

The previous examples were mostly about registering the extensions that we needed statically, e.g., by registering a factory or the type directly in `faces-config.xml`. Factories give us an opportunity for some dynamic behavior. That is, at the point the factory is called we can decide what new type (if any) to return.

For even more dynamic behavior it's frequently required to be able to dynamically add the factories, or in CDI to dynamically add the producers. CDI has an elaborate SPI (server provider interface) for this (simply called "CDI Extensions") which are, however, somewhat outside the scope of this book.

For classic factories and actually everything that's in `faces-config.xml`, there's a somewhat low-level method to add these dynamically: the Application Configuration Populator, which we'll discuss next.

## Application Configuration Populator

The Application Configuration Populator is a mechanism to programmatically provide an additional `faces-config.xml` file, albeit by using the XML DOM (Document Object Model) API (application programming interface). This DOM API can be slightly obscure to use, and the power of the Application Configuration Populator is limited by its ability to only configure. There's no SPI in JSF to directly modify other `faces-config.xml` at this level.

The mechanism works by implementing the abstract class `javax.faces.application.ApplicationConfigurationPopulator` and putting the fully qualified class name of this in a `META-INF/services/javax.faces.application.ApplicationConfigurationPopulator` file of a JAR library.

To demonstrate this, we'll create another version of the `ExternalContextProducer` that we demonstrated earlier, this time using the mentioned `ApplicationConfigurationPopulator`. For this we take the same code, remove the `faces-config.xml` file, and add the `META-INF/services` entry as well as the following Java class:

```
public class ConfigurationProvider
    extends ApplicationConfigurationPopulator
{
    @Override
    public void populateApplicationConfiguration(Document document) {
```

```
    String ns = document.getDocumentElement().getNamespaceURI();
    Element factory = document.createElementNS(ns, "factory");
    Element externalContextFactory =
        document.createElementNS(ns, "external-context-factory");
    externalContextFactory.appendChild(
        document.createTextNode(
            ExternalContextProducer.class.getName()));
    factory.appendChild(externalContextFactory);
    document.getDocumentElement().appendChild(factory);
    }
}
```

A caveat is that since this uses the java.util.ServiceLoader under the hood, it really only works when ConfigurationProvider and ExternalContextProducer are packaged together in an actual JAR library placed in the /WEB-INF/lib of the WAR, instead of just being put directly in the WAR.

## The Application Main Class

Above we discussed the Application Configuration Populator, which as we saw is actually a faces-config.xml provider of sorts. This means it works with fully qualified class names and elements that are still text in nature.

JSF features a variety of somewhat more traditional programmatic APIs as well, with perhaps the most well-known of them being the javax.faces.application. Application main class, which is among others a holder for the same singletons that we mentioned previously in the section "Extending Classical Artifacts." For completeness we'll repeat this list here.

- javax.faces.application.NavigationHandler

- javax.faces.application.ViewHandler

- javax.faces.application.ResourceHandler

- javax.faces.component.search.SearchExpressionHandler

- javax.faces.flow.FlowHandler

- javax.faces.application.StateManager

- javax.faces.event.ActionListener

All of these have corresponding setters on the `Application` class. For instance, the following shows the Javadoc and method declaration for `ActionListener`:

```
/**
 * <p>
 * Set the default {@link ActionListener} to be registered for all
 * {@link javax.faces.component.ActionSource} components.
 * </p>
 *
 * @param listener The new default {@link ActionListener}
 *
 * @throws NullPointerException
 *                 if <code>listener</code> is <code>null</code>
 */
public abstract void setActionListener(ActionListener listener);
```

Likewise, the `Application` class also has "add" methods for the plug-in types we mentioned in the section "Plug-ins."

- `javax.el.ELResolver`

- `javax.faces.el.PropertyResolver` (deprecated)

- `javax.faces.el.VariableResolver` (deprecated)

- `javax.faces.component.serarch.SearchKeywordResolver`

A difficulty with using the `Application` class to set these singletons is, first of all, that it's timing sensitive. This means we can only set such classes from a certain point, which is obviously not before the point that the `Application` itself is available, and for some singletons not until the first request is serviced. This first request is a somewhat difficult point to track.

Specifically, the resource handler, view handler, flow handler, and state handler, uhhh, state *manager*, can't be set anymore after the first request, while the EL resolver and search keyword resolver can't be added either after said first request.

To demonstrate this we'll add the custom EL resolver again that we demonstrated above, but in a more dynamic way now. To do this, we remove the EL resolver from our faces-config.xml file and add a system listener instead. Our faces-config.xml file then looks as follows:

```
<application>
    <system-event-listener>
        <system-event-listener-class>
            com.example.project.ELResolverInstaller
        </system-event-listener-class>
        <system-event-class>
            javax.faces.event.PostConstructApplicationEvent
        </system-event-class>
    </system-event-listener>
</application>
```

Indeed, this doesn't get rid of the XML and, in fact, it's even more XML, but reducing or getting rid of XML is not the main point here, which is the ability to register the EL resolver in a more dynamic way.

The system event listener that we just registered here looks as follows:

```
public class ELResolverInstaller implements SystemEventListener {

    @Override
    public boolean isListenerForSource(Object source) {
        return source instanceof Application;
    }

    @Override
    public void processEvent(SystemEvent event) {
        Application application = (Application) event.getSource();
        application.addELResolver(new CustomELResolver());
    }
}
```

What we have here is a system event listener that listens to the PostConstructApplicationEvent. This is generally a good moment to add plug-ins like the EL resolver. The Application instance is guaranteed to be available at this point, and request processing hasn't started yet, so we're surely in time before the first request has been handled.

# Local Extension and Wrapping

In some cases, we don't want to override, say, a view handler globally, but only for a local invocation of, typically, a method in a component. JSF gathers for this by passing on the FacesContext, which components to use as the main entry point from which to get pretty much all other things. Components are for JSF 2.3 not CDI artifacts or otherwise injectable, so the CDI approach for the moment doesn't hold for them.

Local extension can then be done by wrapping the faces context and passing that wrapped context to the next layer. Note that the Servlet spec uses the same pattern where the HttpServletRequest and HttpServletResponse can be wrapped by a filter and passed on to the next filter, which can wrap it again and pass it to its next filter, etc.

To illustrate this, suppose that for a certain component we'd like to augment the action URL generation used by, among others, form components in such a way that "?foo=bar" is added to this URL. If we do this by globally overriding the view handler all components and other code using the view handler would get to see this URL, while here we'd only want this for this very specific component.

To achieve just this, we use wrapping here as illustrated in the following component:

```
@FacesComponent(createTag = true)
public class CustomForm extends HtmlForm {

    @Override
    public void encodeBegin(FacesContext context) throws IOException {
        super.encodeBegin(new ActionURLDecorator(context));
    }
}
```

Implementing the wrapper without support from JSF would be a somewhat tedious task, to say the least, as the path from FacesContext to ViewHandler is a few calls deep and the classes involved have a large amount of methods. Luckily JSF greatly eases this task by providing wrappers for most of its important artifacts, with an easy-to-use constructor.

The pattern used here is that the top-level class (ActionURLDecorator from the example above) inherits from FacesContextWrapper and pushes the original faces context to its superclass. Then the path of intermediate objects is implemented by overriding the initial method in the chain (getApplication() here), and returning a wrapper for the return type of that method, with the super version of it passed into its constructor. This wrapper then does the same thing for the next method in the chain, until the final method is reached for which custom behavior is required.

The following gives an example of this:

```java
public class ActionURLDecorator extends FacesContextWrapper {

    public ActionURLDecorator(FacesContext context) {
        super(context);
    }

    @Override
    public Application getApplication() {
        return new ApplicationWrapper(super.getApplication()) {
            @Override
            public ViewHandler getViewHandler() {
                return new ViewHandlerWrapper(super.getViewHandler()) {
                    @Override
                    public String getActionURL
                        (FacesContext context, String viewId)
                    {
                        String url = super.getActionURL(context, viewId);
                        return url + "?foo=bar";
                    }
                };
            }
        };
    }
}
```

With these two classes present in the JSF application, now consider the following Facelet that makes use of our custom form component:

```
<!DOCTYPE html>
<html lang="en"
    xmlns="http://www.w3.org/1999/xhtml"
    xmlns:h="http://xmlns.jcp.org/jsf/html"
    xmlns:test="http://xmlns.jcp.org/jsf/component"
>
    <h:head />
    <h:body>
        <test:customForm action="index">
            <h:commandButton action="index" value="Go Index" />
        </test:customForm>
    </h:body>
</html>
```

Remember that no XML registration is needed for the custom component when it's annotated with @FacesComponent(createTag=true), and that its XML namespace defaults to http://xmlns.jcp.org/jsf/component and its component tag name to the simple class name. (See also Chapter 11.)

If we request the view corresponding to this Facelet and press the button, we'd indeed see "?foo=bar" appearing after the URL, meaning that our local extension of the view handler via a chain of wrappers has worked correctly.

# Introspection

An important aspect of being able to extend a framework correctly is not only to be able to utilize extension points but also to be able to introspect the framework and query it for what artifacts or resources it has available.

One of the places where JSF provides support for introspection is its ability to reveal which view resources are present in the system. Remember that in JSF, views like, for example, Facelets are abstracted behind the view handler, which in turn manages one or more view declaration language (VDL) instances. A VDL, also called a templating engine, has the ability to read its views via the resource handler. As we've seen in this chapter, all these things can be augmented or even fully replaced.

This specifically means that views can come from anywhere (e.g., from the filesystem (most typical)) but can also be generated in memory, be loaded from a database or fetched over the network, and much more. Also, the simple physical file to logically view name mapping such as that used by Facelets doesn't have to hold for other view declaration languages at all.

Together this means that without an explicit introspection mechanism where the view handler, VDL, and resource handler can be asked which views/resources they have available, we would not be able to reliably obtain a full list of views.

Such list of views is needed, for example, when we want to utilize so-called extensionless URLs, which are URLs without any extension such as `.xhtml` or `.jsf`, and without any extra path mapping present such as `/faces/*`. Lacking any hint inside the URL itself, the Servlet container on top of which JSF works has to have some other way of knowing that a certain request has to be routed to the faces servlet.

A particularly elegant way to do this is by utilizing Servlet's "exact mapping" feature, which is a variant of URL mapping where an exact name instead of a pattern is mapped to a given servlet, which in this case would be the faces servlet. Since the Servlet spec has an API for dynamically adding Servlet mappings, and JSF has an API to dynamical introspect which views are available, we pretty much only have to combine these two to implement extensionless URLs.

The following shows an example of how to do this:

```java
@WebListener
public class ExtensionLessURLs implements ServletContextListener {
    @Override
    public void contextInitialized(ServletContextEvent event) {
        FacesContext facesContext = FacesContext.getCurrentInstance();
        event.getServletContext()
            .getServletRegistrations()
            .values()
            .stream()
            .filter(servlet -> servlet
                .getClassName().equals(FacesServlet.class.getName()))
            .findAny()
            .ifPresent(facesServlet -> facesContext
                .getApplication()
                .getViewHandler()
```

```
        .getViews(facesContext, "/",
            ViewVisitOption.RETURN_AS_MINIMAL_IMPLICIT_OUTCOME)
        .forEach(view -> facesServlet.addMapping(view)));
    }
}
```

What happens here is that we first try to find the faces servlet, which incidentally is another example of introspection, this time in the Servlet spec. If found, we ask the view handler for all views. As mentioned above, this will internally introspect all the available view declaration instances, which in turn may introspect the resource handler. The "RETURN_AS_MINIMAL_IMPLICIT_OUTCOME" parameter is used to make sure all views are returned in their minimal form without any file extensions or other markers appended. This is the same form that can be returned from, for example, action methods or used with the action attribute of command components.

Having obtained the stream of views in the right format, we directly add each of them as exact mapping to the faces servlet that we found earlier.

For example, suppose we have a Facelet view in the web root in a folder /foo named bar.xhtml. Then getViews() will return a stream with the string "/foo/bar". When the faces servlet is mapped to this "/foo/bar", and assuming the JSF application is deployed to the context path /test on domain localhost port 8080, we can request http://localhost:8080/test/foo/bar to see the rendered response of that Facelet.

Note that even though it's relatively simple to achieve extensionless URLs in JSF this way, it's still somewhat tedious to have to do this for every application. It's expected that a next revision of JSF will support this via a single setting.

# Index

## A

Action listener method, 123, 125–126

ADF Faces, 4

Ajax
    action, 138
    apply request values phase, 140
    behavior listener methods, 140
    ClientBehaviorHolder, 136–137
    execute and render attributes, 139
    <f:ajax> tag, 138
    @form keyword, 140
    <h:form>, 137–138
    implementing class, 136
    invoke application phase, 140
    javax.faces.ViewState, 142
    JSF life cycle, 139
    life cycle, 69–70
    message component, 141
    navigation in, 143
    on[event] attributes, 139
    render response phase, 141
    supporting event types, 139
    valueChange, 138

Ajax exception handling, 338
    Ajax request, 328
    application-wide customizations, 327
    business logic, 326
    ExceptionHandler, 323–325

handleAjaxException(), 325–326
    HTTP response, 326
    JavaScript alert, 322
    Production stage, 323
    UIViewRoot instance, 326
    unhandled exception events, 327

Alexander Smirnov's Telamon
        framework, 5

Application programming interface (API),
        191, 359, 393, 411

Application servers, 13

Authentication mechanism
    AuthenticationMechanismDefinition
        annotation, 416
    caller-initiated authentication (*see*
        Caller-initiated authentication)
    Custom FORM, 415–416
    @CustomFormAuthentication
        MechanismDefinition
        annotation, 417
    @FacesConfig annotation, 416
    FORM, 415
    custom JSF code
        action method, 427
        backing bean, 424–426
        continueAuthentication()
            method, 426
        login page, 422–423
    loginToContinue attribute, 417

501

© Bauke Scholtz, Arjan Tijms 2018
B. Scholtz and A. Tijms, *The Definitive Guide to JSF in Java EE 8*, https://doi.org/10.1007/978-1-4842-3387-0

# L

# M